The Passionate Mind

The
Passionate Mind

❧

*Bringing Up an
Intelligent and Creative
Child*

Michael Schulman

THE FREE PRESS
A Division of Macmillan, Inc.
NEW YORK

Collier Macmillan Canada
TORONTO

Maxwell Macmillan International
NEW YORK   OXFORD   SINGAPORE   SYDNEY

Copyright © 1991 by Michael Schulman

All rights reserved. No part of this book may be reproduced
or transmitted in any form or by any means, electronic or
mechanical, including photocopying, recording, or by any
information storage and retrieval system, without permission
in writing from the Publisher.

The Free Press
A Division of Macmillan, Inc.
866 Third Avenue, New York, N.Y. 10022

Collier Macmillan Canada, Inc.
1200 Eglinton Avenue East
Suite 200
Don Mills, Ontario M3C 3N1

Printed in the United States of America

Poetry of Edgar A. Guest reprinted from *The
Collected Verse of Edgar A. Guest* © 1934
by Contemporary Books, Inc.

Library of Congress Cataloging-in-Publication Data

Schulman, Michael
    The passionate mind: bringing up an intelligent and creative
child/Michael Schulman.
        p.   cm.
    Includes bibliographical references and index.
    ISBN 0-02-928111-3
    1. Human information processing in children.   2. Creative ability
in children.   3. Child rearing.   I. Title.
BF723.I63S34   1991
649'.68—dc20   91-9526
                                                            CIP

To Eva, who taught me,
And Julia, who taught us both

Contents

Preface

This book offers a new framework for understanding intelligence and creativity, facts about intelligence and creativity established by a great deal of research, and detailed suggestions for promoting children's intelligence and creativity. It is intended for parents, educators, psychologists, and other professionals and students concerned with children's development.

Parents will find strategies and procedures for nurturing their children's curiosity, problem-solving ability, and creativity throughout childhood. But they will find more than a manual here. They will, I hope, gain an appreciation of their child as an avid seeker of information, and a deep enough understanding of the development of intelligence and creativity to enable them to tailor the program to their child's individual personality and learning style—fitting the program to the child, rather than the other way around.

Parents *will not* find here a set of exotic training activities for children (no flash card for infants). But they will read many dialogues and descriptions of parent/child interactions in everyday "learning" situations, based on interviews with parents like themselves. They should find these useful as models and guides as they seek to foster their children's development in natural ways. By the time parents finish this book, they should feel knowledgeable about, and comfortable in, their role as their child's first teacher.

Educators will see that the emphasis here is on what children *can* do, rather than what they cannot do, as stressed in much current educational theory. By the time they finish this book they will, I hope, become more sensitive to children's great passion for learning and their resilience in the face of challenge. In short, they should feel more free to *teach* and more confident in their search for creative teaching methods.

They should also recognize that the major developmental stage theories that have influenced educational practice have been called into serious question by a great deal of research. These theories were rarely based on studies of children in learning situations and paid little attention to what wise and imaginative teachers can accomplish.

Psychologists, researchers, and students will find here conceptions of intelligence and creativity that diverge in many ways from other current ones. Problem-solving tasks and skills are organized around what I call the "functions of intelligence." These are the fundamental types of information sought by children and adults, including *What's out there?* (What are the phenomena in my world and how are they organized?), *What leads to what?* (What are the temporal relationships between those phenomena?), *What makes things happen?* (Which temporal relationships are causal relationships?), and *What's controllable?* (What can *I* cause?).

Within this framework, problem-solving or *mastery* skills are grouped and analyzed in a new way—in terms of the goals they are directed toward; these include the solution of diagnostic, inventive, inductive, tactical, imaginative, and mathematical (or symbolic) reasoning problems. Successful problem solving in each of these areas yields increased control over the environment, and I describe techniques for enhancing each type of skill. The chapter on creativity focuses on the "catalytic" techniques and conscious motives of creative achievers and deemphasizes the mystical elements that most writers on the subject have stressed.

While the emphasis in the book is on the first six or seven years of childhood, the period when parents are still their child's primary teachers, there are also sections that pertain to older youngsters, particularly the chapters on problem solving and creativity. The book is organized in terms of the basic concepts and operations that children need to master rather than in terms of age or developmental level. For instance, both the 1-year-old and the 5-year-old need "lessons" in causality—yet obviously in very different ways. Each section provides suggestions and illustrations that are appropriate to children of different ages. In addition, although the book is not addressed solely to parents, in the "how to" sections, for the sake of simplicity, the reader is addressed directly, as if he or she were a parent.

Chapter 1 provides an overview of the "functions of intelligence" framework, depicting children as active information seekers and describing the four basic categories of information they seek. Chapter 2 covers common issues that parents encounter in their role as their child's teacher and guide, such as how to gauge intelligence in a young child, how to stimulate it without "pushing" or stifling a child's natural curiosity, and how to select schools and coordinate with teachers. Chapter 3 provides a brief critical survey of some influential explanations of intelligence. Chapters 4, 5, 6, and 7 present the "functions of intelligence" framework in detail, describing supporting research and specific steps for stimulating children's development in each domain.

Chapter 8 covers how and when to introduce children to reading, writing, and arithmetic. Chapter 9 partitions the universe of problems-to-be-solved into six basic types and offers procedures for fostering a child's ability to solve each type. The issues of giftedness and IQ are addressed in chapter 10, and creativity—what it is and how to encourage it—is dealt with in chapter 11.

One note of thanks—to Bambi Everson, an insightful, creative, and loving teacher of children, for sharing her insights with me.

1

❧

Your Child, The Problem Solver

The Functions of Intelligence

Intelligence as the term is used in this book refers to problem-solving ability. While some theoreticians offer more elaborate definitions, in practice whenever psychologists set out to measure intelligence, they do so by constructing a set of problems and then testing how well children or adults solve them. Those who score higher are said to have higher intelligence—at least for the kinds of problem-solving skills sampled by the test. The high scorers are those who solve problems that others of the same age cannot solve or who master new problems more quickly.

To be sure, problem-solving ability depends on many component skills and capacities. You cannot solve word problems if you do not understand all the words or recall the important information given, or if you cannot form and process the appropriate images (as in, "Two cars left Chicago at noon traveling in opposite directions . . ."). So vocabulary, memory, and imaging ability all contribute to intelligence (and are usually evaluated in intelligence tests). But we generally do not call someone intelligent for any or all of these components in isolation, independent of their contribution to problem solving. A poor problem solver who has a large vocabulary or a good memory is not ordinarily regarded as intelligent (recall the extraordinary memory of the idiot savant in the movie *Rain Man*).

Research shows that ordinary people use very much the same kinds of criteria for judging intelligence as psychologists (one study found a high correlation of .82 between the descriptions of psychologists and "laymen"). When describing someone as intelligent, they too underscored the person's exceptional ability to solve problems of one sort or another.[1] In general, when we, professional or layman, say that someone is intelligent, we are essentially predicting that he or she will be successful in problem solving, usually because we are aware that the person has been successful before.

Creativity too refers to successful problem solving, but when we call a solution creative we are also saying that we consider the problem solving unique in some way. It may be unique because the problems were hitherto unsolved (Einstein's theory of relativity explained observations that earlier theories could not explain, such as peculiarities in the orbit of the planet Mercury); or because the person came up with new and/or better ways of solving old problems (push-button dialing is faster and more flexible than rotary); or because he or she defined a new problem (abstract painters redefined what a painting could be about: form could be explored without content). Creativity is not only important in science and art. One can be creative in virtually any activity; one can be a creative accountant or a creative athlete (some of us remember when the "jump shot" was an innovation in basketball). In any problem area, the creative person shows us new possibilities.

The Functions of Intelligence: An Overview of the Framework

Virtually all the recent research on children's intelligence shows them to be far more capable than previously suspected. Of great significance are the findings that show them not to be mere passive receivers of stimulation, but active, impassioned, seekers of information about their world.

What kind of information does a child seek? From birth onward the child is faced with problem-solving tasks and seeks information to solve them. Now, there are an endless number of specific problems that one must solve during one's life—from how to get one's parents to show up more quickly with the milk bottle, to how best to invest one's money, to how to determine the temperature of the early universe. Clearly the content of problem-solving tasks changes continuously as infants grow into children and adults. Yet there is an underlying pattern that remains surprisingly consistent from task to task and age to age. All the many problem-solving tasks fall into four basic categories. That is, infants, like the rest of us, have four basic problem-solving tasks, and their nervous systems are wired so that they are ready and eager to solve them. The four basic problems to be solved are:

1. **What's out there?** The first task an infant must master is to distinguish and recognize coherent patterns or "things" in her world, including faces, voices, milk, nipples, diapers, rattles, etc. These things are located in the three-dimensional space surrounding and including the child. Their

spatial existence is part of their identity. They appear, move through, and disappear in particular places. Mommy is not an abstract entity, but is over there, and then moves there, and approaches me over here. Mommy is not just a thing, she is also an event.

The key processes in learning what's out there are recognizing similarities and patterns (those things are "dogs"), and discriminating differences (those are collies; those are poodles). As we will see, research shows that this process of sorting the world into meaningful units starts with the child's earliest experiences. Indeed, some researchers report evidence that children can discriminate and learn connections between stimuli even in the womb.[2]

In truth, it would be more accurate to refer to this first problem type as *What's there?* because one of the things all children must learn about is themselves; they must learn to discern and label their bodily sensations, emotional states, and other private experiences. None of these are "out" there; they exist within the space of the child's body. Most of the time I will stick with the expression "What's out there?" since it seems to better convey the active nature of the child's information seeking.

The search for what's out there may continue throughout life. A scientist asks, Is there life on other planets? A physician takes a throat culture to determine whether a virus or bacterium has taken up residence. A senator about to vote on a women's rights bill ponders, What is the true nature of men and women? A retiree decides that it's time to see the world. All of them are searching for more information about what's out there.

2. *What leads to what?* The infant needs to recognize that some experiences regularly follow other experiences, that there are temporal patterns that connect events—and they start learning this almost immediately. For example, if a newborn is regularly picked up and carried to the kitchen for a bottle whenever she cries for milk, by the time she is 2 weeks old she is likely to start calming down as soon as the kitchen is approached, moments before she actually gets her milk. She has associated the walk to the kitchen with receiving milk. Parents can test this by reversing direction just before they enter the kitchen with her. She will start to cry again.

As infants grow into children they continue to discover temporal patterns on their own (Mommy always puts that thing to her ear and says "Hello" after it rings). They will also learn about temporal patterns from others (as when grandfather tells her that such and such a sky means it will rain tomorrow). They will discover that some events occur in a certain order because that's the only way they make sense (such as going to the checkout counter as the *last* step in a supermarket trip), and that some sequences are arbitrary (such as having salad before the main course, rather than after it as they do in France).

Parents are sometimes surprised at how aware their children are of what leads to what. Here is a father's report of a child of 2 years, 3 months who has learned what leads to what:

> We were having a pleasant day. As I was changing her on the changing table, I sighed. She had not been looking directly at me and asked if I was angry. I often sigh when I'm angry and she had apparently learned the connection. I explained that I wasn't angry at all, that I had sighed just to take a deep breath because I was a little tired. I complimented her on her perceptiveness.

The infant's early awareness of *before-after* sequences will ultimately develop into a mature understanding of the continuity and connection between past, present, and future. The infant can only discover temporal connections between events that are seconds apart; as an adult he or she will be able to find such connections between events that span billions of years, understanding, for example, that radiation reaching the earth today started heading our way at the dawn of the universe. As we will see, the way parents pattern and schedule experiences for their young children will have an effect on their ability to discern that events occur in a regular and meaningful order.

3. *What makes things happen?* In certain cases, an event is recognized as doing more than merely preceding another event. The first event appears to make the second one happen. It is perceived as causing it. There is evidence that children begin to recognize causal relationships during their earliest months, and discovering what makes things happen often remains an important concern for the rest of their lives.

Children quickly realize that different kinds of things have different kinds of causes, and that these fall into three main categories: The causes of physical events (such as a doll falling over) are different from the causes of emotions and other psychological states (such as desires), which, in turn, are different from the causes of actions (such as tossing a ball or pursuing a law degree).

In learning causal relationships, children during their earliest weeks appear to perceive a distinction between people and physical objects as both causes and effects. People initiate events; they *do* things, they pursue ends. Physical objects do none of these. From the child's perspective, they simply move when they get bumped into or fall when they aren't supported. People too may move when they get bumped into, but they have other reactions that physical objects don't have. People react with emotions: they smile and frown and make other expressive faces, and their voices change in corresponding ways—and we now know that children attend to and differentiate these emotional changes during their earliest weeks.

And they soon learn that with physical objects, the stronger the force affecting them, the more they move, but people's emotional reactions are not a simple product of the physical forces impinging on the person. A soft-spoken threat may produce a stronger reaction than a loud "Hello, how are you?"

4. *What's controllable?* Another way of phrasing this question is, What can *I* make happen? Infants need to learn what *they* can do to reshape the world to their own liking: "When I cry, those big faces appear. When I make these sounds, those faces smile. When those faces smile, something feels nice inside me." The effort to control the physical and social world starts at birth and continues for the rest of one's life.

After a while, gaining control over outcomes requires mastering a number of reasoning techniques, which I group into six types: diagnostic, inventive, inductive, tactical, imaginative, and mathematical or symbolic. As children grow toward adulthood, the kinds of problems they'll face will depend increasingly on their school courses and the professions they enter. If they become physicians or computer repair people they had better be good at diagnostic reasoning. If they become police officers or business administrators, they had better be good at tactical reasoning.

As they grow, it will not take them long to discover that making things happen as they intend requires more than mastery of the things *out there*. It will also take increasing quantities of *self*-control, learning what to say to oneself in order to push on when problems seem intractable or frustration mounts. This can involve anything from calming oneself before an exam, to switching thoughts away from aching muscles during a race, to keeping oneself from laughing at the punch line as one tells a joke.

It may be seen that these four basic categories of problems to be solved are related to each other in a hierarchical fashion. *What's out there?* is the most inclusive, covering any and all phenomena and the spatial relationships between them. *What leads to what?* is concerned only with that portion of events that are related temporally, where one event follows another in an orderly and regular pattern. In turn, *What makes things happen?* covers only that portion of the temporally ordered events that are also connected causally, where the first event appears to make the second one occur. Finally, *What's controllable?* narrows the focus to just those causal connections in which one can be the causal agent oneself.

The function of intelligence is to solve these four types of problem, and as the infant grows into a child and then into an adult, the same four basic problems need to be solved over and over again. The categories are exactly the same for newborn babe and Nobel laureate. Scientists, for instance, are continually asking *What's out there?* Are there quarks? Are there black holes? Sometimes they discover totally new entities (the gene, viruses), and sometimes they uncover new patterns that give them a clearer understanding of what they already knew was there (as when the Scottish physicist James Clerk Maxwell realized that electricity and magnetism—two familiar phenomena—were really two aspects of a single phenomenon, electromagnetism).

Scientists also seek information on *what leads to what*. Meteorologists try to predict storms by charting the sequence of preceding weather patterns. Biologists look for developmental patterns within and across species. Archaeologists search for temporal patterns in the fossil record. Geologists seek to date strata in rock formations.

The child's search for *what makes things happen* is the forerunner of the scientist's search for causality. The child learns what makes things happen mostly through direct observation. The scientist has additional devices such as research instruments (telescopes, microscopes), experimental methodologies, and mathematical procedures, but the quest remains the same—to identify what prior events are sufficient and necessary to make something happen.

Similarly, the child's attempts to gain control over his small environment, to learn *what's controllable*, finds its exact parallel in the scientist's attempts to apply scientific principles for practical ends such as curing disease, increasing crop yields, and controlling the weather.

The artist also is concerned with *what's out there?* When we say that a painter or writer strives to reveal the "truth" about a subject, it is another way of saying that the artist is trying to define and convey *what's out there*. Eighteenth-century painters tried to capture nature in all her sensuous detail. A century later the impressionists said that this was not how things really look and depicted events from naturalistic viewing angles, using swabs and dots of color and light to better capture "reality." A while later the cubists came along and said, "No! To paint the truth about objects one must capture their many and ever-changing perspectives." Soon the surrealists said that this too wasn't sufficient. The way we see, they maintained, depends on our inner, psychological reality; to be "real" painting must render that reality too.

Even abstract, nonrepresentational artists address the same concern. In a recent interview, Frank Stella, the prominent abstract painter, talked about great abstract painting as confronting the viewer with "reality"—not with a single, literal version of it, but with the essence of reality. Not an object moving, but movement itself. The sculptor Brancusi expressed a similar vision: "They are fools who call my work abstract. What they think to be abstract is the most realistic, because what is real is not the outer form, but the idea, the essence of things."[3] When artists strive to capture the truth of one individual's way of moving or the very essence of movement, they are seeking an answer to the question, What's out there?

When writers explore the content and causes of human feelings they are concerned with questions of what's out there and what makes things happen; their goal, as Shakespeare expressed it, "to hold . . . the mirror up to nature." We honor writers who do this successfully, who reveal to us deep truths about the human condition. Artists are also concerned with What's controllable?—with increasing their control over their media and their impact on audiences. Van Gogh worked feverishly and deliberately for a decade, searching for a way to capture with paint on a static canvas the movement and dynamics of a windswept landscape. The poet T. S. Eliot referred to his long struggle "to learn to use words" as "a raid on the inarticulate with shabby equipment always deteriorating in the general mess of imprecision of feeling."[4]

The everyday life of the ordinary child or adult is also focused on solving these same four basic problems. They are universal—as significant for the stock market analyst reading the *Wall Street Journal* as the horse player reading the *Daily Racing Form*.

When a young child can tell an apple from a pear, she has mastered a problem in *What's out there?* When she knows the sequence of events entailed in a trip to the supermarket (select the food, line up at the checkout, unpack the cart, pay the bill), she has mastered a problem in *What leads to what?* When she knows that water will douse a lit match, she has mastered a problem in *What makes things happen?* And when she can use her arithmetic skills to come home from the store with the correct change, she has mastered a problem in *What's controllable?* She will face these same four problem-types for the rest of her life, whether she becomes a nanny, a nurse, or a nuclear physicist.

When a child appears to embrace the question, What's out there? we call her attentive and alert. When she is sensitive to the temporal regularities that partition the stream of events around her, we call her observant or perceptive. When she is determined to find out what makes things happen, we call her curious or inquisitive. And when her efforts gain her increasing control over her world, we call her capable and persevering. And we take all of these characteristics as indications of her intelligence.

Some prominent child development theorists—Piaget in particular—underestimated children's abilities and regarded their mode of thinking as fundamentally different from that of adults. As we shall see, a wealth of research during recent decades supports an opposite view. Children are

much brighter than Piaget believed. Indeed, parents who observe their
children day in and day out are constantly awestruck by the incredible
intelligence, creativity, and curiosity shown by even the average child.
What attentive parents have always suspected, child development researchers
are now, finally, corroborating.

The word "problem" in problem solving can sound so burdensome,
leading us to think of problem solving as something we humans do reluctantly
when confronted with unpleasant obstacles. On the contrary, humans seek
out problems to be solved. Solving problems is one of our great joys. We
even organize our recreational activities around problems. We do crossword
puzzles, play chess, charades, and trivia games, seek steeper mountains
to climb and deeper waters in which to snorkel—and we study manuals
to better meet the challenges. No longer content to follow recipes, we
take creative cooking courses. No longer happy as "couch potatoes," we
join survival groups in the wilderness. We enroll by the thousands in *not-
for-credit* courses in colleges everywhere in search of new problems to be
solved and new problem-solving skills. We are a problem-seeking species.
When we feel unchallenged in our jobs, we seek new ones (or bemoan
our timidity for failing to do so). When we finish a hard day at work, we
repair old radios in the cellar and star gaze through telescopes in the backyard.
Monotony is our foe, not problems.

Indeed, we go everywhere we can in search of problems and solutions.
We've sent rockets out beyond the solar system and gone diving miles
beneath the sea to see what's there. We've peered inside genes and blown
atoms apart to get a look at their insides. We've even probed into our
own brains, which as far as we know are the most complicated structures
in the universe. We are problem junkies.

So, intelligence refers to successful problem solving, and the myriad
problem types can be divided into four basic categories. The next question
is, How can we help a child become a better problem solver? In other
words, How can we make him more intelligent? That is what this book is
about. The focus is intellectual achievement in its broadest and richest
sense, encompassing problem-solving ability, curiosity, concentration,
aesthetic sensitivity, imagination, and creativity. Isolated elements such
as concept learning, reading, computation, and test-taking skills are dealt
with as part of a general program to support and stimulate a child's natural
passion for discovering and mastering his or her world. The goal is to
bring up a child who loves learning and is good at it—a child who wonders
and marvels and yearns to know more.

First, though, we start at the very beginning and address some issues
that most concerned parents will face.

2

∞

A Mind Is Born

A child is born. Her parents' first concern is, Is she physically normal and healthy? Is her breathing clear and easy? Does she have ten fingers that bend and grasp, two eyes that see, and ears that hear? If these and other body parts and functions check out normally, they will breathe a sigh of relief and very soon start to wonder, Is she an intelligent baby? Their interest in her physical health and intelligence will likely last throughout, and well beyond, her childhood years. And if they are like most parents they will want to do all they can to see that their child's body and mind live up to their fullest potential—and they will want to start right away.

But can a newborn be intelligent? If so, how can we tell? What are the indications of infant intelligence? And are there ways that parents can foster it? Philosophers and psychologists have debated the existence and nature of infant intelligence for centuries but, unfortunately, their debates were rarely informed by much careful observation of babies. So it is only during the last few decades that we have discovered that newborns start life with all five senses functioning and surprisingly acute, and that they find some things pleasing (such as sweet tastes) and other things displeasing (such as loud sounds). We now also know that infants are capable of learning during their first days of life, that from the moment of birth they begin to explore their world, start to make adjustments to it, and start to take command of it.[1]

Many pediatricians and psychologists were shocked when it was discovered in the 1950s that newborns see well and can perceive forms and patterns during their first hours of life.[2] Yet many mothers (and some fathers) already knew this. When your newborn baby, during his very first minutes, stares into your eyes and keeps his gaze on you as he is moved about, it's easy to conclude that he is seeing you, really seeing you. But the experts said no and told the mothers they were reading too much into their babies' behavior.

There is something else parents seem to know that the experts have neglected. While theorists ponder the nature and origins of intelligence, many parents, quite intuitively, regard their newborns as intelligent beings and begin to play with them in ways that deserve to be called teaching. In other words, in the earliest interactions with their babies, these parents seek to encounter and nurture their developing minds. For example, a mother might walk her fingers gently across her infant's forehead while making a bright rhythmic sound on each step. As she does this, she will probably create various rhythms and patterns with her steps and sounds, repeating some for a while and then introducing new ones (along with animated facial expressions). She may not always be able to put her reasons for doing this into words, but there is clearly purpose in her actions. She is teaching her baby about patterns by introducing them simultaneously to three of his sensory modalities: he feels her fingers, hears her sounds, and sees her lips and face.

As she "plays," she will look closely at him for signs of interest and recognition, she will note his attention span and whether he shows signs of renewed interest when a pattern changes. Her intuitive attempts to stimulate and assess her child's attentiveness appear to be well founded. Research shows that infant attentiveness during the first two years is correlated with higher intelligence test scores when a child gets older.[3]

There is also something else this mother is trying to teach her child by the way she stimulates him. She is introducing him to human *purpose*, trying to convey that her actions are done "on purpose," for his delight. She is teaching him an important aspect of human behavior: people *do* things with intention. The recognition of purpose is, I believe, an important milestone in an infant's intellectual development. During these early interactions, this mother might take her baby's hands and move his arms about in various patterns and rhythms (again with accompanying sounds and facial expressions). Here, too, there is something this mother will be looking for, although, again, she probably won't put it into words. It is an *exchange of purpose*, a sense that her child is *interacting* with her—moving with her or resisting and redirecting her movements in a manner that indicates he recognizes the purposefulness of her movements, anticipates their direction, and is asserting his own intention into the movement pattern. In other words, he is beginning to play.

The exchange of purpose is another important milestone in an infant's intellectual development, and mothers report this kind of recognition as early as the child's third or fourth week. In the terminology of the current framework, these mothers are helping their children discover that there are intentions out there and that intentions *make things happen*.

Parents often do not think of their play with their babies as teaching, but a lot of teaching goes on. I interviewed parents of a 7-week-old boy who said that they didn't try to teach him anything, that he was too young and really didn't do much. At one point in our conversation I was holding the baby and as he was looking at his mother she leaned her smiling face toward his and uttered a lively "Hello." To all of our surprise, the baby voiced a two-syllable gurgle that appeared to imitate her melody and rhythm. The mother's face filled with delight; she laughed and said "Hello" again. The baby grinned, shook his arms with excitement, and uttered more sounds. Such stimulation and reinforcement of speech sounds certainly deserves to be called teaching.

Toward the end of the interview, the father, who was now holding the baby, remarked, "Oh, we're doing something right now that may be a kind of teaching. I've put my finger in his hand and we are having a sort of tug-of-war. I pull his hand a bit and he pulls my finger back. We actually do this a lot and he seems to like it. We started doing it about three weeks ago." Through this tug-of-war game, the 7-week-old baby was learning about alternating his behavior with someone else's—he was learning to exchange purpose.

Research shows that by 4 months of age babies' vocal exchanges with their parents alternate in a give-and-take pattern that is similar to conversational patterns between adults. By 4 months, most babies have had a good deal of practice in communication patterns from the kinds of vocal and physical exchanges that I observed these parents engage in with their 7-week-old.[4]

A baby's recognition of pattern and purpose, and his early attempts at exchanging purpose are certainly not easy events for researchers to measure, but parents know they occur and also know that some parents aren't as good as others in helping their children reach these milestones. Some parents seem not to be very good at "playing" with babies. What these parents don't know how to do is provide a baby with stimulus patterns that he can discern, find interesting, and appreciate the purpose behind. Thus, even during a child's earliest days, parents begin to influence his or her intellectual development—and there are skills they need in order to do this effectively.

To Push or Not to Push?

New parents, concerned about their baby's intelligence, will very quickly come under a lot of pressure. On the one hand, they'll come across programs that promise to transform their infant into a "superbaby" who will read and do math by the age of 3 or 4. And they'll start to worry that their child will be surpassed by others—that their son or daughter will never walk through the portals of an Ivy League college—unless they enroll their newborn in the learning program immediately. From another direction they'll be warned—by psychologist David Elkind, among others—not to "push" or "hurry" their child, that if they place too much emphasis on learning and achievement, he or she will suffer all manner of dire psychological consequences.[5]

Both positions have some merit but are oversold. Yes, some children can learn to read at an early age, but there is no evidence that infants who are given intensive reading instruction (such as flash cards during their first few months), turn out in the long run to be better readers than similar children who learn to read in usual ways at the usual time. Nor is there evidence that the children in these exotic learning programs wind up more intelligent or more successful than others. It isn't impossible. It just hasn't been demonstrated. Given the claims of some of the programs and the length of time they have been around, they should have produced at least a couple of Nobel Prize winners by now—but they haven't.

On the other hand, despite all the warnings about pushing, there is no evidence of any harm to youngsters from introducing them to words, numbers, activity book problems, preschool or after-school classes, or other instructional programs at an early age. Still, no parent wants to be accused of "pushing" a child, and some have become anxious about teaching their children anything at all. Indeed, a few parents that I interviewed, overreacting to the warnings about pushing, refused to teach their children any "school skills" at all—even the alphabet—and were proud of it. (Notably, there were no Asian-Americans in this group.)

Since there is no evidence of dire consequences befalling youngsters who are introduced to instructional programs at an early age, one might wonder what Elkind's warnings are based on. His approach derives from the developmental theories of Jean Piaget, who believed that young children will learn everything they are supposed to learn if they are simply given appropriate playthings and just let play.

Piaget's research, which will be discussed more fully in chapter 3, never dealt in any concrete way with the question of which kinds of parent–child interactions best nurture a child's intellect. Nor did he try to account for why some children are brighter than others. His theory is not about learning or the effects of instruction. It is about "universal" stages of mental development that he claimed all children go through at about the same age, and that neither the timing nor sequence of which are supposed to be influenced by formal instruction. Indeed, Piaget was adamantly against instruction directed at accelerating a child's movement through the stages, although his explanations of why were vague, unsupported statements like, "It appears that there is an optimum speed of development" and "Perhaps a certain slowness is useful in developing the capacity to assimilate new concepts."[6]

Piaget and his adherents, including Elkind and Lawrence Kohlberg,[7] believed that his stages (and the special tasks he used to measure them) encompassed the truly important intellectual operations that children must master, and that children master them in generally the same order and at about the same ages. Yet we know that from a fairly early age children show significant intellectual *differences*—some are much better problem solvers, can do much more and know much more than others.

As any parent and teacher of young children knows, by the age of 5, long before a child has ascended through Piaget's basic stages, these intellectual differences, as manifested on IQ and achievement tests and in everyday activities, can be substantial and a reasonably good predictor of the child's later intellectual attainments.[8] Piaget's "universal" stage theory does not address these differences at all, and so it tells us nothing about why some children are more intelligent than others. Nor does it suggest how to help a child who is lagging behind, nor what special support to give a child who shows intellectual promise. In short, Piaget's work offers no guidance at all for designing an educational program for children.

A number of studies, including one by Elkind, have found only low correlations between children's scores on intelligence tests (IQ scores) and their performance on Piaget-type tasks.[9] Since IQ scores are generally found to be fairly good predictors of children's intellectual functioning, correlating quite well with school performance and to a lesser degree with later, real-world intellectual achievements, it is not clear what use we can make of information about a child's Piagetian stage or his ability to solve Piagetian-type problems. According to Piaget, himself, we shouldn't use this information to formulate any special instructional programs for the child. And, given both the low correlation of Piaget's stages with IQ and the universal nature he claims for his stages, knowing a child's stage isn't going to tell us anything about his or her current or future intellectual successes in the real world—in school or elsewhere.

So, while Piaget and Elkind are certainly right that pushing is not good for children, we need to be clear about what we mean by this highly charged term. Introducing and drawing a child's attention to new stimuli— words, numbers, any kind of stimuli—should never be looked at as "pushing." Encouraging a child to explore new intellectual domains and learn new skills should also not be considered pushing. Too often those who warn parents about pushing seem to have forgotten that a child's greatest pleasure comes from exploring and learning new things. Indeed, the young child's appetite for learning is voracious.

The notion of pushing implies that the child is being introduced to material too soon. But, frankly, we do not have all the answers yet about the best times and techniques for teaching new things to children. Not many years ago it would have been considered pushing to teach a foreign language to a 6- or 7-year-old. Now we know better; young children learn languages with more ease and less pain than older ones.

Pushing occurs when parents insist that a child master something in which she has no interest and which has no intrinsic value for her. Examples would be insisting that a child learn to ice-skate when she has no interest in ice-skating, or that she become a math whiz when her interest in math is not great. A child pushed in this way is likely to sense that her parents' affection and respect for her depend on how well she does on the tasks they assign. Learning under this kind of pressure is an ordeal, far from the natural joy it is supposed to be.

Parents who push in this sense are not likely to recognize and appreciate their child's own intellectual strivings. Because their ambition has little to do with their youngster's passion for exploring and knowing, they are not likely to be sensitive to the moment-to-moment shifts in his or her attention and interest, thus missing many instructional opportunities. Effective teachers—whether they are parents of a toddler or college professors in a classroom—not only lead their pupils down new paths, but are ever alert to, and willing to be led by, their pupils' curiosity and interests.

It is counterproductive to force stimuli on a young child. Children love to learn and parents need to trust this. But children really know what they are ready for. For example, if you present construction toys, such as Duplos or Bristle Blocks, to a 1-year-old, you probably won't arouse a lot of interest. But give them to a 2-year-old and he will work at them with astonishing determination and persistence, as if some basic primitive urge has been tapped.

The parent who makes too great an effort to get his or her child interested in an activity (because other children are doing it, or because it is "educational," or because "our family has always been good at it"), not using the child's interest or lack of it as a guide, may undermine his or her later pleasure in this kind of activity. It may become a stimulus for bad feelings, a symbol of personal failure and mommy's and daddy's disappointment. When this happens often, learning new things becomes a time of tension between parent and child rather than an occasion of mutual delight. Moreover, when children realize that a parent's interest has more to do with having a "smart kid" than with the pleasures of exploration and mastery, they sometimes use this knowledge against the parent, playing dumb as a way to assert their independence or express their anger.

The best that parents can do is introduce new things enthusiastically and then monitor the waxing and waning of the child's interest. When little or no interest is observed, and gentle encouragement does not work, they need to be willing to hold off on that activity until a later occasion. Then it is time to try something else, or follow where the child's own curiosity is leading.

I am not saying that parents should not be selective about what they introduce to their child. On the contrary, all thoughtful parents and teachers are selective in choosing what to present to a child, based on their vision of what constitutes a proper education. But they should also recognize that their child is a unique individual who will develop his or her own interests and inclinations. These should be appreciated and supported as much as possible. Children of any age learn more when they are learning about things that interest them.[10]

Some 3-year-olds have a virtual obsession with drawing and painting (it is wonderful to observe, but as scientists, we do not have a clue as to its evolutionary significance). Other children want to count everything in sight. A parent may have wanted a counter and gotten a painter. He should be patient. His painter may come to love counting too. But perhaps not. Trouble starts when parents fix on particular subject matter or career goals for their children rather than helping them find their way to wherever their own curiosity and intellectual passions lead. It's worth remembering that there is probably no more significant contribution parents can make to their child's mental development than communicating admiration for and pride in his or her own natural strivings.

In addition, parents should not hesitate to share their own intellectual and aesthetic enthusiasms with their children. If they love math or music, or achievement in any area, they should communicate their excitement to their child. Children need to witness the thrill of intellectual and aesthetic pursuits. A parent's excitement may stimulate a child's interest in the same area, but parents should not count on that or make it important. They should be wary of selling too hard or chiding their child for not relishing what they relish. The important lesson is the thrill that attends discovery and creativity, not the specific content area.

They should also be wary of experts telling them what kind of child they ought to bring up. Some parents are dedicated to bringing up children who love science and nature, and they buy mostly "educational" toys and talk a lot about nature and causality and numbers. Other parents want a "well-rounded" child, and devote substantial time to athletic and fantasy play activities. There is no "right" path for every child and every family. Einstein was neither much of an athlete nor the life of the party. What *is* important is how the child responds to what parents present. Is he interested and happy? Those are the best guides, although, there may also be times when parents judge it important for their child to learn something that he does not now find interesting.

There is another important point too often neglected in arguments over what and when to teach children. A child's intelligence should not be defined merely in terms of the mastery of isolated skills like reading and arithmetic. I will illustrate what I mean through a conversation between a parent and a child of 4 years, 2 months. The child had seen the videos of the *Wizard of Oz* and *Meet Me in St. Louis,* both starring Judy Garland, on a number of occasions; she had also seen some other Judy Garland movies occasionally and enjoyed listening to Judy Garland on the phonograph. And she knew Judy Garland had died. On one occasion, as she was watching *Meet Me in St. Louis,* the following conversation took place:

CHILD: Did Judy die because she was old?

PARENT: No. She wasn't very old when she died.

CHILD: Then why'd she die? [She had been told that generally only old people die.]

PARENT: She got sick.

CHILD: Why'd she get so sick if she wasn't old?

PARENT: I think because she didn't take care of herself. I remember reading that she ate and drank all the wrong things, things that weren't healthy.

CHILD: Why? Didn't she know what was good to eat?

PARENT: I think she did but I read that she was very sad, and I guess she didn't think about taking care of herself.

CHILD: She was sad? What made her so sad like that?

PARENT: I don't know, but it makes me feel sad for her.

CHILD: Me too. Why was she so sad? Why wasn't she happy and proud that she had made all those beautiful movies?

I think we'd agree that this was an intelligent 4-year-old. But not because she had learned to read or do sums. She was curious and trying to use information she had learned in order to understand something that puzzled and troubled her. At 4, she was already an interesting, thoughtful person with whom one could have interesting conversations. Eventually reading and math would become tools for her to use to learn more about her world—not isolated, functionless skills. Parents who love and nurture their child's own distinctive curiosity, will find that bringing up an intelligent child is also bringing up an interesting child.

The controversies over "pushing" and the advisability of formal training programs for infants and preschoolers obscures the fact that most of a parent's teaching occurs in informal everyday interactions. What goes on in these continuous and daily exchanges is far more important than whether or not a child spends a few minutes a day with flash cards or activity books. Opportunities for teaching are almost constant and when handled properly can only enrich the time that parent and child spend together.

As an example, a father recorded the many teaching occasions on the afternoon he took his daughter to buy a bicycle on her fourth birthday:

We hurried as we walked the six blocks to the bicycle shop since it was approaching five o'clock and I wasn't sure how late the shop was open. We were both excited about buying her first two-wheeler (with training wheels), and we talked about many things as we walked. I explained that some shops close at five because the shopkeepers (a new word for her) have usually been working since early in the morning and want to go home to be with their families and play with their children. I wanted to give her a sense of the workday for people in stores and also that they were people just like her daddy and mommy, with families and children. I also told her that I should have telephoned the shop before we left the house to find out how late it was open. I wanted her to know that one could do this and that it was good to think ahead. I also explained why I thought the bicycle shop would be open later (because people rent bicycles there and take them on trips that often last until sundown). I wanted her to understand that there is a connection between a store's hours and the products it supplies. As we walked, some stores were locking up. I pointed these out and also noted some that appeared to be staying open later. I asked her why this or that store might be closing or staying open and we enjoyed some nice speculation together.

She knew right away which bike she wanted (based on color), but I had the salesman explain to us the features of each. Happily she had picked the bike that was best for her. She probably would not have been influenced by his descriptions of which brakes and handlebars were the most suitable for her, but I wanted her to understand that there were important criteria besides color.

As we waited for her new bike to be brought up from the storeroom to be assembled, I showed her the name on the sample bike and sounded out the letters with her. Then I pointed out the same name on a big bike and asked her, "What's that word?" She said it correctly. As we approached some tricycles, I mentioned that *tri* meant three and *bi* meant two; she wasn't at all interested. She was more interested in why the bicycles had chains between the pedals and the back wheel. I showed her how pedaling moved the chain and turned the wheel. She liked turning the pedals with her hands (as I raised the back wheel) but didn't want to hear more about the mechanism.

As the mechanic took the bicycle parts out of the box, I pointed out how carefully he arranged the parts so they wouldn't get lost. She watched him assemble the bike and asked a number of questions about what he was doing. I answered some and some we addressed to the mechanic. I pointed out what a handy invention the bike assembly stand was. I said that I bet that some bicycle mechanic just got tired of bending down all day while working on bicycles so he built a stand that lifted the bike up for him.

As she rode home I explained that her leg muscles would get stronger with practice. I pointed out gravel and grease on the ground, slid my foot over them, and explained why these were slippery areas for bikes.

When it was time to turn a corner I called out "Right turn" or "Left turn" to give her practice in these terms. At first I applied slight pressure in the right direction. Then I let her make the move on her own and corrected her if she made a mistake ("Other way"). I told her she had to be very careful when riding near old people and young children since neither could move out of the way quickly and both could be hurt easily. I asked her to observe how slowly they walked. She worked quite diligently at avoiding them, braking as a child or old person was approached and steering carefully around them—and I complimented her on how well she was pedaling and steering and braking.

When we got to our apartment building she buzzed her mother over the intercom to let her know we were back so she could come down to join us. Before a minute had passed she asked, "Where's mommy?" I asked her if she could tell if mommy left the apartment yet. She thought for a moment, looked up at the window, and said "The lights are on. I think she's still there." Then the lights went off and she exclaimed, "She's coming."

On the surface, the event described above is not about teaching and learning; it is about the fun of a father and daughter going to buy a bicycle. But most of the instruction a child receives during his or her first five years takes place while parents and children are engaged in these kinds of everyday activities.

Parents who take their role as teachers seriously realize that they must first become alert to their child's perspective on the world, sorting out what he or she knows and has mastered from what is unknown or confusing.

With this in mind they are ever on the lookout for new stimuli and information to make the world a more interesting and manageable place for their child.

Another parent described the teaching she had done during some hours with her child (6 years, 1 month) in the car:

Jenna and I were singing a song from *Oklahoma* with the term "gas buggy" in it, and I asked her if she knew what it meant. She didn't. I asked if she could figure it out from the meaning of the words. She said, "A buggy is a wagon pulled by horses." I asked what kind of buggy would have gas in it. "One that delivers gas?" she replied. "That's a good guess," I said. "But it was a buggy that *used* gas instead of horses. What kind of buggy uses gas to move?" "We are in a buggy that uses gas to move. It's a car" she replied.

Later we passed the Statue of Liberty and I referred to it as a symbol of what our country stands for. "What's a symbol?" she asked. I explained that a symbol sends a message; it tells us something that goes beyond its simple physical appearance: "When we look at it, in one sense we just see a statue, but it also sends a message to the world that our country is a place where people are free."

Jenna, who was sitting in the back, didn't want to put her seat belt on. I insisted, saying that if I had to slow down quickly, she'd come flying into the front of the car. I explained that the brakes would slow down the car, but that without our seat belts, we'd keep going at 60 miles an hour until we smashed into the windshield. I reminded her how much it hurts when we bump ourselves while walking at only about five miles an hour. That convinced her.

As we came to a toll booth, I asked her if she knew why we pay a toll. She didn't, so I explained that the money is used to maintain the highway: to pay for the maintenance equipment, the concrete and other materials, and the salaries of the workers.

Coming home she asked why the moon appeared to be following us as we drove. I drew her attention to the speed at which objects at different distances appeared to go by. She noticed that the further away things were, the slower they appeared to pass by—and that the distant hill barely appeared to be moving at all. I explained that the moon is much, much further away than the hill, so far away that if we flew there at the speed we were driving, it would take us many months to get there. Because it is so far away, it doesn't appear to be moving past us at all and would continue to "follow" us all the way home.

This parent, like the one in the earlier example, hadn't planned on spending the day teaching. Explaining the world to her child was simply a natural part of their interaction.

Selecting Schools

As more and more children attend daycare centers and nursery schools, more and more parents are faced with the question, At what age should formal instruction begin? Some nurseries boast that they cover the three *R*s with 3- and 4-year-olds. Other nurseries boast that they don't. Which should parents choose? The key factor is what the school means by "formal instruction."

Formal instruction for older children, in grade school, typically means that children must spend time working on material that they wouldn't ordinarily choose to spend time on. They must practice spelling and multiplying when they are not motivated to practice these skills. It is the exceptional teacher who presents these lessons in a manner that sparks the child's interest. Yet most children attend to their lessons and do their assignments anyway. Why? Sometimes they do their schoolwork to avoid being scolded by teachers or parents, or shamed by classmates—that is, to avoid negative consequence. But most do it, I believe, out of trust—because they have come to accept that the things their teachers give them to learn are good to learn, that these are the important subjects to master regardless of interest in them.

Can we expect 4-year-olds to give us the same trust—to spend *hours a day* in "formal instruction," working on lessons that don't interest them because they appreciate that these are good things to learn? I do not think so. If by formal instruction a nursery school means extended periods of teacher-directed lessons, teachers will have to set up a tight system of rewards and punishments to induce their young pupils to cooperate. Learning will then become passionless, with none of the natural joy that comes from following the lead of one's own curiosity. Indeed, in this kind of classroom, curiosity is likely to be troublesome and have to be suppressed.

But these problems should not arise if by formal instruction the school means that teachers spend short periods introducing children to the names and sounds of letters, to numbers and counting, to the names of the days and the seasons, to printing letters, identifying some printed words, to naming new objects and learning new facts about them, and to basic causal relationships (by using simple tools, plants, water troughs, balance scales, magnifying glasses, and other pieces of "science" equipment). In short doses, most nursery-age children will find some or all of these lessons interesting, especially if the lesson is embedded in activities that children enjoy ("Let's paste these cut-out *E*s on the paper while we sing a song with lots of *E* sounds: The wee bee flew from his tree, and sat himself down on my knee, and I could see he wanted my tea, and you can be certain he frightened me").

These can be pleasant educational experiences for nursery-age children so long as the material is presented with no demand that it be learned and no criticism or testing of any kind—no criticism, for example, if a child, upon being presented with the word "eagle," is suddenly inspired to go off and make a clay model of an eagle. Teacher-directed instruction that is locked into a formal lesson plan for the day is not likely to permit such spontaneity. The teacher will have a list of words the class is supposed to learn that day, so presenting the next word on the list will probably take precedence over appreciating a child's imaginative impulses and allowing time for them.

Parents should also be wary of schools that refuse to teach, that won't explain things to a child, even when he or she asks, because they subscribe to misguided "developmental" principles and think *all* children are not ready for such information. These schools often have good intentions but they view children as fragile entities who might be devastated by a little frustration. They forget that when children want to master something they readily endure great frustration, perservering with spirit despite setbacks. Watch a 1-year-old work at climbing a staircase, a 4-year-old putting puzzles together, or a 6-year-old laboring feverishly at a video game. Frustration rarely stops them.

Young grade-school children, too, frequently have difficulty making the transition from self-initiated to teacher-directed learning, and teachers and parents can help by making sure they understand the value of everything they are taught. A child who balks at grammar exercises may come around if he tries to write a letter to a pen pal or his favorite ball player and is helped to see that the reader will not be able to decipher his meaning.

3

Efforts to Explain
Intelligence

It is important to remember that words like "intelligent" and "creative" are only *descriptions* of behavior. They are labels we apply to behavior we consider successful or to people who engage in successful behavior with some consistency. They do not *explain* why that person was able to engage in successful or innovative problem solving. Yet often in child-development and parenting articles and in everyday conversation these terms are used as though they were explanations. Statements like "He was able to solve the problem because he is intelligent" are common. But, in fact, such statements do not tell us anything about why the person was able to solve it. In science, this kind of explanation is referred to as *circular reasoning:* "He solved the problem because he is intelligent. How do I know he is intelligent? Because he solved the problem." We are left with one event (he solved the problem) explaining itself.

A legitimate explanation requires at least two different kinds of observable events: those we want to explain, such as successful problem solving, and some other, prior event, such as some brain activity or some prior learning experiences. Psychologists have tried to explain the nature and development of intelligence in a number of ways. The most influential theory has been that of the Swiss psychologist Jean Piaget.

Piaget's Theory

Piaget's theory attempts to explain critical aspects of intelligence but, as discussed earlier in chapter 2, it does not help us answer the question of why some children are more intelligent than others. Nor does it tell us which neurological, environmental, or educational factors influence intellectual development. Piaget tried to define the key mental operations required to solve the many different problem types that children face. He also specified at what ages children could perform these operations and in what order they emerged. For example, he believed that infants below a certain age (about a year) cannot find hidden objects because they cannot yet bring to mind (or "represent") things that are not in view. Their brains, he believed, are not ready to do that yet, not yet at that "developmental stage."

Similarly, 4-year-olds, he claimed, are not yet ready to integrate information from two dimensions of an object (say, the height and width of a glass of water). So they cannot succeed in "conservation of volume" problems; that is, they will mistakenly believe that a tall, narrow glass has more water in it than a short, wide glass, even though they saw the water being poured from one to the other. Instruction, he believed, would not speed up a child's progress through the stages.

Piaget developed a variety of tests to investigate these and other problem areas and concluded that children proceed through an invariant set of stages, becoming able to solve certain kinds of problems only when they reach the appropriate stage. His framework has generated an abundance of research, much of which does not support his positions. More often than not, the stages he delineated have not been found. Slight alterations in his procedures generally yield very different results. Furthermore, it turns out that instruction *does* enable children to solve problems that his theory says they should not be able to solve.[1]

In general, children understand causality, logic, conservation, classification, other people's feelings, and virtually every other phenomenon Piaget studied at much younger ages than he indicated. In reading Piaget, one comes away with the feeling that he was observing very slow children, years behind normal children.

As one example of this, he said that "At about the age of seven the child becomes capable of cooperation because he no longer confuses his own point of view with that of others." At *seven?!* Other researchers demonstrate cooperation and awareness of another's perspective even before a child's first birthday.[2] Researchers Judy Dunn and Penny Munn of Cambridge University provide an example that shows very clearly a *14-month-old's* recognition of the difference between her perspective and her mother's:

Child has stitches in a cut on her forehead, made the previous day. She "discovers" the stitches halfway through the observation. Child pulls stitches. Mother prohibits her pulling stitches. Child fusses, goes behind sofa, and repeats the pulling of stitches.[3]

Here a father recorded a lovely example of a 5½-year-old with a keen awareness of the difference between self and other:

We were having lunch and I started to talk to Cassie about her earlier refusal to put her toys away when I asked. She reminded me that she had told me she was tired and asked me how I would feel if someone nagged me to put things away when I was tired. Before I could answer she said, "Oh, you'll say you would do it, but that's because you're a grown up. If you were a child you wouldn't say that."

This little girl (still a year and a half from 7) was not only able to assume her father's perspective but could generalize to the perspectives of the typical grown up and child. Her father's next question revealed that she could also shift her own perspective to other, hypothetical circumstances. He asked her if she would have been too tired to play if another child had come visiting. She admitted that she would not have been.

Here is one more example of a young child, a month short of 4, quite able to distinguish her own point of view. She had learned that she, like all living things, would someday die:

CHILD: I don't want to die.

MOTHER: But dying is natural. Everything dies. Flowers and plants die.

CHILD: But flowers are not afraid.

The inadequacies of Piaget's findings are also apparent in his discussion of children's conceptions of causality. In an interesting study of children's understanding of the water cycle (including the relationships between rain, evaporation, and clouds), researchers Robert Kates and Cindi Katz make this point emphatically:

Some of what we have learned differs from Piaget's pioneering inquiry into how children think about the physical world. The most obvious difference is that our children know so much more so much earlier. In one of the few places that we can make a substantive comparison, the differences in our responses and those received by Piaget are striking. In *The Child's Conception of the World*, Piaget (1929) describes the evolution of explanation concerning the origin of clouds:

During the first stage (average age 5–6 for Geneva), the cloud which is usually regarded as solid (of stone, earth, etc.) is conceived as made entirely by men or by God. During the second stage (average age 6–9 for Geneva and Paris) the child explains the clouds by the smoke from the roofs and maintains that if there were no houses there would be no clouds. The artificialism is thus more indirect than in the first stage but is still very systematic. Finally, during the third stage (from 9–10 on the average), the clouds are of entirely natural origin: the cloud is condensed air or moisture, or steam or heat, etc. (pp. 298–299).

In contrast, our four-year-olds are both artificial and naturalistic. They believe that clouds are made out of water and gas, or water and snow but never solids. . . . God may make the rain and snow, and angels make the clouds, but out of natural ingredients. Our five-year-olds never invoke a deity; they believe that clouds mean rain and, at least in part, are made up of evaporated water. It is clear that these four- and five-year-old children offer the more advanced explanations of the six-to-nine-year-olds studied by Piaget in the early part of the century. In our study, the lack of clear evidence of stages in causal thinking is not unique. Nor are our findings that the children know more at an earlier age than those studied by Piaget. There is a substantial body of psychological literature written over the past fifty years that differs with Piaget's conclusions on precisely these questions.[4]

The Kates and Katz study was done many years after Piaget's own research on causality, but similar criticisms were voiced by researchers who were his contemporaries.[5] Even Piaget's descriptions of children's drawings were surprisingly years off the mark, coinciding with what would be expected from his theory rather than with the way children really behave. For example, he said that before the age of 8 or 9 children are unable to draw profiles of faces with only one eye showing, and they cannot correctly draw objects that are partially blocked by things in front of them (he says they draw the whole object, disregarding the fact that part of it would not be visible). Furthermore, he says they cannot indicate perspective by making distant objects smaller.[6] If Piaget's stage theory were accurate, young children should not have the mental ability to do any of these things. But it is not uncommon for 4- and 5-year-olds to do all of them. Moreover, children who are not yet drawing profiles of human faces, will often be drawing profiles of birds, dogs, and other animals. Many other examples of Piaget's underestimation of children's abilities will be found in later chapters.

Turning from Piaget's data to his theory, his central explanatory concept is his notion of *schema*. According to Piaget, schema are enduring mental "structures" that determine our intellectual abilities. These structures change (or "accommodate") slowly with experience as they "assimilate" new information (for example, as the child gains new information about the mutability of substances by pouring water and shaping clay). Until a child possesses what Piaget refers to as the "reversible structure," he cannot understand that the volume of water does not change when poured into glasses of different sizes. Once he possesses this structure, he will have entered a new developmental stage and understand that a substance, any substance, that is merely reshaped can be converted back to its original condition.[6]

According to Piaget, the presence or absence of these mental structures (such as reversibility) are the primary determinants of the kinds of problems that children can and cannot solve, and he sought to elucidate the key structures and the ages at which they normally appear. He acknowledged that the structures are affected by experience but argued that experience alone (say in the form of special instruction) will not advance a child to a new developmental stage. This occurs only when the child's natural neurological development has progressed sufficiently.

Piaget was certainly correct when he said that the effect of instruction and other experiences is dependent on the age of the child. It is obviously true that older children grasp many kinds of concepts (like reversibility) more readily than younger children. On the other hand, as I've indicated, there is also evidence that instruction can advance children to higher Piagetian stages long before they should normally be ready to reach them.

Moreover, even if Piaget's stages turned out to be as fixed and dependent on maturation as he said they were, his notions of structures or schema would not really help us *explain* these facts. Because Piaget did not define his structures in neurological terms, nor in any other terms that are independent of the effects they are supposed to explain, his schema theory appears to be an example of circular reasoning: "The child was capable of solving the problem because he had the schema. How do we know he had the schema? Because he solved the problem." Piaget's other important theoretical constructs, assimilation, accommodation, and equilibration, are also knowable only by their effects, the very effects that they are supposed to explain.

Piaget's contributions to the field of child development have been monumental. His ideas, whether right or wrong, have generated a vast amount of research, significantly enhancing our understanding of children. But his dominance in the field has also led to problems. Advice based on his positions, regardless of how mistaken, makes its way into articles for parents and professionals (including teachers, counselors, and child-care workers), and is frequently accepted simply because of Piaget's status as an authority. Moreover, the focus of the advice is almost always on what children *cannot* do; it rarely emphasizes what they can do or what they might be able to do with imaginative instruction.[7]

More details about Piaget's theory will be presented in later chapters of the book as I discuss specific areas of children's problem solving.

Two Recent Theories: Gardner's and Sternberg's

Howard Gardner and Robert Sternberg, two prominent researchers in the field of human intelligence, have recently presented their own theories of intelligence. Both theorists have the laudable aim of expanding our notions of intelligence beyond the kinds of verbal and mathematical tasks found on IQ tests or in standard academic courses. Their theories have implications for children and education, but unlike Piaget, neither focuses predominantly on the development of intelligence—on delineating the progression of children's abilities as they age.

Howard Gardner has put forward what he calls a "theory of multiple intelligences."[8] He argues that intelligence is not some single entity that underlies all problem-solving behavior, but, rather, that there are many types of intelligent behavior, each produced by its own particular "intelligence." He says there are, in fact, at least seven fundamental, "relatively autonomous human intellectual competences" or "sets of know-how," including linguistic, musical, logical-mathematical, spatial, bodily-kinesthetic, interpersonal, and intrapersonal intelligences. Each intelligence, he suggests, derives from its own brain structure, although he acknowledges that the form and location of these structures are not known.

In other words, Gardner has partitioned the problem-solving domain into these seven major categories, and while a given individual may perform well in one or more of these areas, knowing a person's competence in one area will tell us little about the likelihood that he or she will be successful in other areas. Each develops independently from its own source in the brain, and each, he claims, warrants its own educational program.

Psychologists and educators have long debated whether intelligence should be thought of as a single entity or a collection of separate entities. The dominant position has been to view it as a combination of both—that there is a *general* intelligence that underlies problem-solving ability across many domains, and that there are also specific intelligences that manifest themselves in specific domains, such as mathematical or verbal reasoning. How much of our intelligence is general and how much specific, and which specific abilities are truly fundamental, have also been areas of controversy.

The argument for a general intelligence rests primarily on the fact that children's scores on different kinds of problems on IQ tests are, on average, fairly similar, presumably reflecting some overall intellectual strength that manifests itself regardless of domain. Despite this, Gardner rejects the notion of general intelligence, arguing that since the major domains measured by IQ tests are similar—requiring mostly linguistic and logical-mathematical abilities—it is inevitable that an individual's scores across problem types on these tests will be similar.

I agree with Gardner that intelligence is manifest in many more domains than traditional theories have allowed, yet his own theory appears to be addressing what might be called special sensibilities rather than more basic problem-solving operations. For instance, poets, composers, and choreographers (representing his linguistic, musical, and bodily–kinesthetic domains) must *all* solve problems involving temporal structure; they each create pieces that evolve over time and each must conceive discernible and aesthetically pleasing structures or "progressions" (to borrow a term from jazz musicians). They are each engaging in what I call "imaginative" reasoning (described in chapter 9), despite the fact that the poet works with words, the composer with sounds, and the choreographer with bodies moving through space. In other words, very similar intellectual operations are involved in problem solving across a number of Gardner's domains. It is these operations that we need to understand if we are to explain human problem solving.

As another example, Gardner puts chess players and painters together in the domain of spatial intelligence because they both work with spatial images (so do choreographers whom he places in the bodily-kinesthetic category). But at a more operational level, chess players and painters are solving fundamentally different problems. A painter (like the poet) is likely to be working on "what's out there" problems, seeking to express "truths" about his subject. The chess player is seeking, not truth, but mastery, and is using what I call tactical reasoning techniques (painters also confront tactical problems in their attempts to gain mastery over their medium). The political orator, whom Gardner places in the linguistic category because he uses words, is, in fact, engaging in some of the same key operations as the chess player, such as planning strategies and envisioning counterstrategies.

It is certainly true, as Gardner points out, that individuals differ in their sensitivities to certain kinds of stimuli, that some, for example, grasp musical or mathematical relationships with astonishing ease—and parents certainly want to be mindful of their children's relative abilities in different domains. Moreover, Gardner may be right when he says that such special gifts and talents are biologically based. But his theory leaves out what people actually do when solving problems in each domain, what operations they perform in arriving at solutions. That is something we certainly want to take a closer look at. For instance, categories like "musical intelligence" tell us little about the actual problem-solving behavior and abilities of musical experts. An outstanding composer may not be a particularly talented musician or conductor, and vice versa. Composers, musicians, and conductors have different types of musical problems to solve.

Robert Sternberg, in his "triarchic" theory of intelligence, has also sought to broaden our concept of intelligence. He says that there are "three aspects of intelligence" or three different kinds of mental "abilities." First, there are the cognitive "information processing components," which are the various mental operations we use when solving problems. These include "executive" operations (such as planning ahead in anticipation of problems), "knowledge-acquisition" operations involved in gathering information, and "performance" operations used in reasoning out a problem (such as the steps one must take to solve analogy problems, as in WASHINGTON is to ONE as LINCOLN is to: a. FIVE, b. TEN, c. FIFTEEN, d. FIFTY).

Sternberg's own research has focused heavily on analogical problem solving and he has described a number of requisite operations, including (1) "encoding" (determining relevant meanings of the terms, such as that Washington and Lincoln were both presidents, that they are also the names of cities, and that their portraits appear on U.S. currency); (2) "inferring" (discovering relationships between the first two terms, such as that Washington was the *first* president and his portrait is on the *one* dollar bill); (3) "mapping" (recognizing the relationship between two relationships, such as between Washington and Lincoln and the numbers associated with their positions as presidents or the denominations of the bills containing their portraits); and (4) "applying" (selecting a solution that fits the relationships, which in the present example would be FIVE, since Lincoln's portrait appears on the five-dollar bill and because he was the sixteenth president and SIXTEEN is not a choice). As Sternberg points out, an important benefit of segmenting formal problem solving into its component operations is that teachers can examine precisely which steps in the problem-solving sequence their pupils are leaving out or misapplying.

The second aspect of intelligence described by Sternberg is evident in how well an individual deals with novel problems and how long it takes before the problem solving in these novel areas becomes "automatized"— that is, performed quickly and easily. According to Sternberg, when faced with a novel problem (such as learning "new mathematical procedures"), "more intelligent people will tend to be more adept at responding to the initial novelty and will also automatize the task more efficiently."

The third aspect of intelligence, according to Sternberg, involves how well an individual adapts to and masters his or her environment. Sternberg refers to this third ability as "practical intelligence."

According to Sternberg, these three kinds of mental abilities are relatively independent. A person who has good analytical information-processing skills (Sternberg's first aspect of intelligence) should do well on standard academic problems, but may or may not function well when faced with novel tasks (his second aspect), and also may or may not do well when confronted with real-world problems (his third aspect). Alternately, someone might be what Sternberg calls "street smart" and successful in practical tasks yet may or may not be very competent when it comes to formal reasoning tasks in school or when faced with novel circumstances.[9]

Sternberg maintains that each type of ability deserves to be recognized as a form of intelligence since each involves successful problem solving. His theory, however, appears to offer an explanation for only his first category: formal, analytical problem solving, which, as we have seen, he says is based on going through the proper sequence of "information processing" operations (such as encoding and inferring). But he does not tell us what is required for success on novel or practical tasks. Both clearly depend on many of the same operations as formal tasks (encoding, inferring), but evidently other ingredients are also necessary, otherwise competence at formal tasks would transfer directly to these other areas—and Sternberg claims that it doesn't.

Since he recognizes that a person can be street smart while not being very good at formal information processing, his theory, to be more complete, would need to tell us what unique mechanisms or operations give the street smart person his smarts. It should also try to account for why some individuals perform better than others on novel problems.

Within Sternberg's framework, one obstacle to coming up with a more complete account of problem solving is that the categories "practical" and "novel" are really not precise enough. For instance, TV repairmen and police officers must both confront practical problems, yet the reasoning process required to diagnose why a TV picture is blurry is very different from that required of the police officer trying to quell a domestic dispute. In chapter 9, I describe six different types of reasoning processes that I believe can help us better understand the kinds of individual differences in problem solving that Sternberg and Gardner have been concerned with. For example, the successful TV repairman will go through a sequence of steps that I call "diagnostic" reasoning, while the police officer will engage in a sequence that I refer to as "tactical" reasoning.

Biological and Environmental Explanations of Problem-solving Ability

1. *"Smart" Genes.* There is considerable evidence that genetic factors are involved in intelligence. Many studies report a correlation between the problem-solving abilities of parents and their children, even when the children are adopted and not brought up by their biological parents. In addition, the scores of identical twins on intelligence tests are significantly more alike than those of fraternal twins or nontwin siblings.[10] Still, we do not yet know precisely what is being passed on from parent to child—which genes or biochemical factors or neurological structures.

How much genes contribute to a child's relative intellectual potential is a hotly debated issue in psychology. Without question, however, the evidence is clear that an enriched educational environment will markedly improve the abilities of all children regardless of who their parents were. Various studies have taken children who were disadvantaged in one way or another—economically, culturally, physiologically, racially—and raised their IQs into the average or above-average range.[11]

Correlational studies that demonstrate a genetic contribution to intelligence only tell us that the ranking of children's scores on an intelligence test will be similar to the ranking of their parents' scores. They do not tell us how intelligent any given individual might become with proper stimulation and instruction. Indeed, research shows that the IQ scores of whole populations have improved with improvements in their education, nutrition, and other environmental factors.[12] Thomas Bouchard and his colleagues, in their recent report about the heritability of intelligence and other traits, insisted, correctly I believe, that "This evidence for the strong heritability of most psychological traits, sensibly construed, does not detract from the value or importance of parenting, education, and other propaedeutic interventions."[13]

Some psychologists have argued that because inheritance influences intelligence, racial differences in intelligence must be based on genetic differences between races. But there is faulty reasoning here. For instance, height, like intelligence, has a genetic component: taller parents tend to have taller children. But that does not mean that we can explain current racial and ethnic group differences in height in terms of genes. For example, many immigrant groups, when they first came to the United States were, on average, significantly shorter than resident Americans. Yet, a generation or two later these group differences disappeared, essentially because the children and grandchildren of these immigrants were raised on more nutritious diets than their forebears. Similarly, various immigrant groups scored lower than resident Americans on IQ tests. These differences, too, disappeared as the children of these immigrants reaped the educational and economic benefits of their newly adopted homeland.

In other words, evidence that a trait has a genetic component (as does height and intelligence) and that there are substantial differences between groups on that trait, does *not* mean that the *group* differences are due to inheritance or that they cannot be altered by environmental improvements.

2. *"Smart" Brains.* We know that problem solving is dependent on the brain, and researchers have made headway in understanding which parts of the brain are involved in which kinds of cognitive functions. For example, the left temporal lobe of the cerebral cortex is involved in language processing, the hippocampus is involved in memory.[14] Furthermore, brain researchers and theorists generally assume that specific brain differences underlie differences in people's problem-solving abilities. But the analysis of brain functions has not yet become fine-grained enough to distinguish between the brains of good and poor problem solvers (except, of course,

for individuals with gross brain damage or disease). Brain researchers have not found anything in the brains of geniuses that differentiates them from the brains of anyone else. It is hoped that these differences will soon be revealed through new noninvasive techniques (such as positron emission tomography and magnetic resonance imaging) that can monitor subtle brain activities as they occur.[15]

There are some provocative animal studies by Mark Rosenzweig, Marian Diamond, and others showing that animals reared in "stimulating" environments with lots of different activities develop thicker cerebral cortices and become better problem solvers than animals reared in dull, empty environments.[16] But for humans it makes little sense to evaluate environments in terms of quantity of stimulation. Poor children in our country and around the world live in environments with an abundance of stimulation, such as large, noisy families, crowded communities, and a bustling street life. Yet poverty and the turbulent stimulation that goes with it is certainly not associated with higher intelligence in our country or any other. For humans, quality of stimulation turns out to be more important than quantity (unless of course a child is subject to extreme stimulus deprivation and isolation).

A deprived intellectual environment for human infants is one in which the adults are not helping them discern the significant entities and events in their world, or the important temporal sequences, or the critical causal relationships—and also not helping them acquire the skills and confidence to make desirable things happen. (Obviously, an environment that does not allow an infant to develop properly because of poor maternal or infant nutrition or health, maternal drug use, or similar pathological factors, will have a deleterious impact on the child's intelligence.)

3. *Childhood Experiences.* Researchers are making headway in uncovering the kinds of childhood experiences associated with becoming a good problem solver, and parental behavior seems to be the most significant factor. A number of studies have found relationships between the behavior of parents or other caregivers and various measures of children's mental abilities, such as a child's exploratory behavior, competence with objects, language learning, problem-solving ability, and self-confidence. The important parental factors include:

- responding dependably and approvingly to the child's behavior (to an infant's cries and exploratory actions, to a preschooler's requests and questions) so that she learns that her actions are effective and significant to those around her;
- demonstrating what the child might do with the objects in her environment (such as stacking rings and building with blocks);

- encouraging the child to carry out activities she has observed ("Now *you* comb the dolly.");
- labeling objects and actions for the child ("That's a finger. *Finger.* One finger, two fingers. I'm counting your fingers.");
- providing early *cause and effect* experiences (such as with pull-toys and drums);
- being sensitive to and supportive of her curiosity and assisting her in satisfying that curiosity (such as helping her obtain objects she seeks that are beyond her reach, exposing her to objects that stimulate her interest, helping her past obstacles when frustration mounts, and interfering as little as possible with her explorations);
- giving a young child a lot of attention in the form of holding, looking at, talking to, touching, playing with (such as patticake and peek-a-boo), and presenting toys and objects to her;
- engaging a child in "warm" interactions and conversations, including showing interest and pleasure in what she says and does;
- reading to and explaining stories to her, as well as age-appropriate and instructive videos;
- using a rich vocabulary and increasingly complex, adult-like sentences;
- instructing in ways that help her solve problems on her own and stimulate problem-solving skills, rather than giving her solutions (For instance, as she does a puzzle, saying "See what happens if you turn the piece in different ways" is better than "It goes that way");
- showing interest and delight in her learning and problem-solving efforts, praising small gains instead of criticizing for what she hasn't yet achieved;
- exploring the outside world with her and discussing the things she encounters (on neighborhood walks as well as on trips to zoos and museums);
- engaging her "help" in adult activities (such as dusting, counting coins for the laundry machine, and sorting laundry);
- providing an array of construction toys and playthings (including blocks, paste, scissors, puzzles, crayons, and Legos, among many other items designed specifically for children, as well as common household objects such as mixing bowls and utensils).[17]

So, in answer to the question, Can parents really influence their young child's intelligence? the research evidence says yes.

Since one cannot do much about one's genes or one's child's brain in any direct way, the only practical question for parents interested in helping their child achieve his or her full intellectual potential is, *What kinds of experiences and instruction will foster my child's problem-solving abilities?* The specific answers depend on the kinds of problems the child is trying to solve, that is, on whether he or she is seeking information about what's out there, what leads to what, what makes things happen, or what's controllable. The next four chapters cover these problem types in detail and describe an educational program that derives from them.

4

⌘

What's Out There?

Discovering Phenomena

Colette, writing of her childhood with her mother Sido, offers an evocative example of a parent introducing her daughter to what's out there.

Sido's great word was "Look!" And it could signify "Look at the hairy caterpillar, it's like a little golden bear! Look at the first bean sprout that is raising up on its head a little hat of dried earth . . . Look at the wasp, see how it cuts with its scissors mandibles a bit of raw meat." At sunset she would say, "Look at that red sky, it forecasts a high wind and storm." What matters the high wind of tomorrow, provided we admire that fiery furnace today? Or it would be, "Look, be quick, the bud of the purple iris is opening! Be quick, or it will open before you can see it."[1]

"Look" is a powerful word and parents start using it during their child's first days. Learning what's out there is a lifelong process and it begins when newborns start to distinguish and recognize coherent patterns or "things" in the world, including faces, voices, milk, nipples, diapers, and rattles—as well as their own bodily sensations. (Recall my earlier comment that when focusing on bodily sensations and other private experiences which are not "out" there, it would be more precise to use the form, *What's there?*)

As children grow, parents must introduce them to the names and functions of an incredible number of things, including body parts (nose, eyes); foods (milk, peas); physical characteristics, including shape (triangle), color (red), odor (smelly), texture (soft), taste (bitter), and sound (loud); actions, both simple (look, bring) and complex (cooperate, imagine how she feels); living things (dog, flower); inanimate objects, both natural and man-made (rocks, television); emotions (sad, happy); bodily states (hungry, hurt); relationships between people (friend, aunt); relationships between objects (above, inside);

social units (family, team); jobs (teacher, doctor); places (New York, the ocean); personal characteristics (nice, nasty); national and ethnic identities (Chinese, black); languages (English, Italian); infirmities (broken leg, blind); among many other categories and subcategories.

During early infancy the key processes involved in answering What's out there? are the detection of patterns ("There's a face"), the recognition of similarities ("There's that face again"), and the discrimination of differences ("That's not the same face"). Children perceive and distinguish patterns right from birth, recognizing the solidity of the objects they see and even knowing that what they see should be touchable (they cry when they can't touch a nearby "object" created via an optical illusion[2]).

Far and away the patterns infants show most interest in are the human face and voice. Research shows that from the first week of life newborns respond to faces as distinct entities and prefer looking at them over other patterns, even patterns consisting of facial features in unusual arrangements. A recent study reported that 1-day-old infants will look longer at their mother than at another woman, indicating they can already distinguish between faces. Other studies show that newborns, on their first day, can distinguish different expressions on faces and will even imitate some of the expressions they see.[3]

With respect to newborns' preference for the human voice, researchers report that

> within the first 3 days of postnatal development, newborns prefer the human voice, discriminate between speakers, and demonstrate a preference for their mothers' voices with only limited maternal exposure.[4]

Newborns' sensitivity to the human voice is so keen that by their second day they can distinguish spoken words; they turn their heads toward a speaker emitting a word, stop turning if the same word is repeated a few times, and turn again when the speaker emits a new word. By the end of their first month they have put faces and voices together and get visibly upset in experimental circumstances in which their mother speaks directly to them but her voice comes from a speaker off to the side.[5]

Infants, during their earliest days, will turn and orient toward stimuli to bring them into sharper focus indicating that despite their limited motor abilities they start out life actively exploring the world around them. They also put everything into their mouths and appear to use their mouths to learn about the objects they encounter. Research with infants less than a week old shows that the way they explore objects with their mouths and hands varies with the physical qualities of the objects; they handle soft, flexible objects differently from rigid ones. That they learn to recognize objects from their mouthings is indicated by the fact that by one month they prefer to *look at* an object that they have explored in their mouths but have *never seen before* in comparison to an object that is totally new. As their motor abilities develop their explorations become increasingly fervent, scanning for more details with their tongues, lips, and fingers; by five months they inspect objects by turning them over and passing them from hand to hand.[6]

The fact that newborns start out life able to recognize objects and patterns should not diminish our appreciation of what a complex achievement this is, particularly when it involves visual scanning (as when an infant looks at the parts of a face, one after another). When the infant scans, he takes in parts of the pattern one at a time (for example, focusing on the eyes, then the mouth, etc.). The pattern must then, in some sense, be constructed out of its parts; in other words, the parts must be remembered and integrated over time into a whole.

By 4 months, if not earlier, infants have acquired information, not just about what's out there, but about what things go together, such as the fact that there is a synchrony between a person's speech and his or her lip movements. When shown two films side by side, they prefer watching the film in which the events on the screen are appropriate to, and synchronized with, the sounds coming from the speaker. For instance, they prefer films in which things coming close get louder and in which lip movements are synchronized to speech sounds, rather than films in which what they see on the screen and what they hear do not belong together or are out of synchrony.[7]

By their tenth month children are learning what's out there by picking up cues from others. For example, they will look at something they see their parents looking at and will learn about the desirability or dangerousness of people or things they encounter by observing how their parents react to them. Psychologists call this "social referencing." If a child's mother reacts to a toy or a stranger with fear, he will back off; if mother shows delight, he becomes more likely to approach and play.

Also toward the end of their first year, children begin to look at objects that are pointed to. This is an important milestone for learning what's out there, greatly extending the range of objects that parents can show a child. Understanding pointing is quite an achievement for a child. When he looks in the direction his mother is pointing he is not simply responding to her finger as a concrete stimulus; he has recognized the symbolic and intentional nature of her gesture—that she is sending a message his way and that she wants him to act on it. Children's own use of pointing to bring objects to the attention of others is clearly evident shortly after their first birthday, and some researchers claim that even 3-month-olds point.[8]

Recognizing Categories and Classes and Acquiring Concepts

During the first year, well before language, children begin to recognize and respond to classes of objects; that is, they recognize that sparrows and bluejays are both birds even though they look different in certain ways. When they respond to different birds the same way (say by making flapping movements) and to nonbirds differently (they don't flap when they see dogs or cats), we would say that they have acquired the concept, "bird."

Research shows that when infants acquire concepts they are not simply remembering the different examples they have seen (such as particular sparrows and bluejays), but appear to form an abstract or generalized idea of the objects based on common features (beaks, wings, skinny legs), which enables them to put new objects (say, robins) in their proper categories (as if they were saying, "Hey, those are birds too").[9]

Contrary to the predictions of many cognitive theorists, young children are quite competent at learning categories and classes. Indeed, using increasingly sophisticated techniques, researchers have shown that children as young as 3 months can recognize and distinguish even man-made object classes, such as *A*s and *2*s. For instance, after learning to kick their legs to move a mobile with *A*s on it, they kicked far less when presented with an identical mobile with *2*s on it. Also, the way preverbal infants divide up the things they perceive turns out to be similar to the categories of adults (for instance, they distinguish birds from horses and people from inanimate objects). They also learn and respond to concept names long before they can speak. For example, when a parent says, "Look, birdies!" preverbal children know to look up.[10]

I might note here that Piaget, as well as some psychoanalytic theorists (such as Margaret Mahler), assert that one essential discrimination the child needs to make is differentiating self from nonself. According to Piaget, newborns cannot distinguish self from nonself, and they go through a protracted period learning this difference. There is absolutely no evidence for this assertion, nor has anyone ever come up with a way to test it. Yet one finds Piaget's position echoed over and over in child development and parenting books and articles as if it were a well-established fact, rather than an untested (and probably untestable) assertion.

During the child's second year, with the rapid growth of language skills, concept acquisition accelerates. At first, children recognize classes on the basis of overall similarity ("That looks like a bird too"). By the age of two, toddlers are able to group objects based on specific features ("That's a bird because it has a beak"). They also start to learn concept hierarchies ("Dogs and cats and birds are all *animals*"), and they become aware of special subdivisions within concepts ("We both have families, but *my* family has more children than *your* family''). As language develops children are able to learn increasingly abstract concepts (''Those are *new*'').[11]

Two-year-olds want to know the name of everything they encounter. ''Whazzat? Whazzat?'' they'll ask over and over. Before children turn 3 they will have become quite adept at recognizing and naming common objects and concepts. They will also make surprisingly fine distinctions: When the father of a little girl (3 years, 1 month) described to his wife how he had to *pull* their daughter down the street because she refused to come out of the supermarket, the child corrected him, saying, ''You didn't pull me. You *dragged* me.''

Tests of 4-year-olds show that many of their concepts reflect an accurate understanding of the nature of the objects around them and they can use this knowledge to make reasonable inductive inferences about other objects. They will recognize, for example, that what is true for a red apple (it contains pectin, they were told) is more likely to be true for a yellow apple than it is for a banana or a stereo. In other words, they will use information about an object (an apple) to make reasonable predictions about other similar and dissimilar objects. Other research shows that even 18-month-olds can make such inductive inferences.[12]

In the social realm, the 5-year-old's knowledge of what's out there can be surprisingly sophisticated. Here is a girl of 5 years, 6 months, discussing a classmate:

> I love Nick. Well, I love his outside but not his inside. His outside is handsome but his inside is nasty.

This 5-year-old has recognized that people are made up of parts, not all of which are necessarily compatible. Four- and 5-year-olds also make a serious effort to understand the precise meaning of subtle moral concepts such as lying, tattling, and boasting. These are important notions, both for the way others treat them and for their feeling about themselves. So children this age commonly ask questions like, ''If I tell my friend that I learned to float, is that boasting?'' These kinds of questions reflect the child's growing awareness that in the moral sphere, what is important is the intention behind the act (to harm, to help), rather than the act itself.

Research also shows that 3- and 4-year-olds appreciate the essential differences between man-made and living objects. They will also accurately distinguish and describe different emotional and mental states—other people's as well as their own; three-year-olds correctly use terms like ''sad,'' ''angry,'' ''afraid,'' ''hurt,'' ''know,'' ''understand,'' ''think,'' ''feel,'' ''forget,'' and ''dream.''[13]

The 3- and 4-year-old's quest for an understanding of what's out there can lead to surprisingly thoughtful questions. A child, 3 years, 11 months, asked her father: "Is this real now? When I dream, I think it's real, but it's not. Is it real now? Or am I dreaming? Can I tell if I'm awake?"

The process of discovering patterns and sorting experiences into their valid and functional categories can continue throughout one's life. By adolescence, youngsters are well aware that things that appear different on the surface may share critical features (for instance, French and Italian, which sound very different are both Romance languages, derived from Latin). They will also have learned that things that appear to belong in the same category may actually differ in fundamental ways (although stars and planets look similar to the naked eye—pinpoints of light—they are utterly different kinds of entities).

As youngsters refine and correct their categories, their understanding of the world increases, as does their potential for affecting it. One may become a medical researcher trying to ascertain the main categories of bacteria in order to determine which are harmful and which are likely to succumb to particular medicines. Another may become a lawyer or judge, sorting behavior into significant legal categories (Was the crime premeditated or impulsive? Is begging constitutionally protected speech?). Another may become a safety expert, teaching that all fires are not alike and that each type requires a different fire extinguishing chemical.

Using Logic, Metaphor, and Mathematics to Learn What's Out There

By their third or fourth year youngsters are using deductive logic to learn what's out there. For example, they use logic to place new objects in their proper categories: "That metal box has an electric wire. Mommy said things with electric wires are dangerous. Therefore that must be dangerous." Notice that in this illustration *dangerousness* is not directly observable; it must be inferred from other information. Young children also use deductive logic to make inferences about observable things out there which they haven't actually seen: "The street and the cars are wet. They only get wet like that when it rains. *Therefore* it must have rained." Various studies confirm preschoolers' logical abilities.[14]

Margaret Donaldson, of the University of Edinburgh, studied preschooler's use of logic in everyday situations and found they employed logic more often and more adeptly than developmental theories predict. Here is one of her examples:

It took place shortly after the death of Donald Campbell when he was trying to break the world water speed record, and some months after a visit by a research worker called Robin Campbell to the school where the conversation took place. The speakers were a little girl of five and another research worker.

> **CHILD:** Is that Mr. Campbell who came here—*dead?* (Dramatic stress on the word "dead."
>
> **RESEARCH WORKER:** No, I'm quite sure he isn't dead. (Much surprised.)
>
> **CHILD:** Well, there must be two Mr. Campbells then, because Mr. Campbell's dead, under the water.

This child has put together . . . two quite distinct pieces of information: *Mr. Campbell who came here is not dead* and *Mr. Campbell is dead,* and has drawn a valid conclusion, which she states as a necessary consequence: ". . . there *must be* two Mr. Campbells."[15]

By their early grade-school years, children's conversations reveal their frequent use of logical inferences. As an example, a parent reported that his daughter (6 years, 1 month), upon seeing him eating a cheese sandwich, asked him how come cheese didn't give him a bellyache when milk did. Her reasoning, in syllogistic form:

Milk gives you a bellyache.
Cheese is made from milk.
Therefore, cheese should give you a belly ache.

Another example of logical inference by a young child (5 years, 6 months) stemmed from a discussion of why dinosaurs became extinct. The youngster speculated, "Maybe all the plant eaters became extinct because the Tyrannosaurs ate them all, and then *they* became extinct because they had nothing left to eat."

Research shows that preschoolers have enough understanding of similarities and differences to begin to use and comprehend similes, metaphors, and analogies ("A turtle's home is its shell," "My sore throat is like a street light that goes on and off and on and off," "My belly is out of gas," "My belly hurts. My belly and my supper are having an argument").[16] Metaphors and analogies help children learn what's out there by providing new perspectives on what they perceive ("A machine has to eat too"). Tell a modern preschooler to "fast forward" herself to the bathroom and she'll know exactly what you mean.

One type of analogy is called a *model.* It involves using constructs that are familiar and accessible to explicate something that is not yet understood. For instance, a recent attempt by scientists to understand how black holes affect their surroundings in space employed the familiar notion of a membrane as a model, describing the space around a black hole as a kind of "syrup" that rotates.[17] A child's first model is probably her use of fingers for counting. Ask a preschooler "If you have two apples and I give you two more, how many will you have?" and she will probably use her fingers to find the answer. Her fingers are not apples but she recognizes that they can serve as a model for any counting problem regardless of content.

Counting and arithmetic are ways of learning about and describing what's out there. Other mathematical activities, such as geometry, trigonometry, algebra, and calculus, are also used to describe things and events, including their shapes, sizes, and capacities, and how they change over time, as well as how they compare and relate to other things and events. Mathematics, like logic, is used to deduce quantities and properties that are unknown— symbolized by the notorious x; in mathematical reasoning problems one proceeds from the information given ("One car is traveling twice as fast as another car . . .") to uncover quantities unknown ("What are their times of arrival?").

Many 2- and 3-year-olds can count, and use counting spontaneously as they gather and sort the objects around them. Research shows that 3-, 4- and 5-year-olds are able to add and subtract. I've known 4-year-olds who could multiply. Four-year-olds can also use a ruler quite well for measuring, and a recent study with 5- and 6-year-olds found that without instruction they would use a stick left lying about in order to find out which of two holes was deeper.[18] Children this age will often use their arithmetic skills spontaneously to solve practical problems. One child (5 years, 1 month) said to her father as they prepared for a three-day trip, "We need to bring six books because you and Mommy both read me one each night."

There is evidence that even newborns respond to quantity. In a recent study, babies, one to three days old, responded differently to a two-dot and a three-dot stimulus display, indicating that they could tell them apart. The dots were printed on white cards. When the infants were repeatedly shown cards with the same number of dots (say the two-dot card over and over), their attention soon declined; psychologists call this "habituating" to the stimulus. But attention perked up when a card with a different number of dots was presented, demonstrating that they recognized the new display as different from the one they had tired of.[19]

We have seen that many processes are involved in learning what's out there: pattern recognition, stimulus discrimination, classification, concept formation, social referencing, perceptual learning, logical and numerical abilities, and metaphor comprehension. Psychologists usually study these as separate, unrelated cognitive skills. Here, I am suggesting that they all serve the same basic function, they help us—child and adult—answer the question, *What's out there?* A child is ordinarily able to employ all of them by the age of 4.

Obviously an important role of parents and teachers is helping children learn what's out there—helping them learn the objects, categories, and concepts that make up their world. Parents and teachers do a particularly good job when they also help children learn ways of exploring the world to discover things out there that their elders never knew were out there.

Teaching a Child *What's Out There*

Although this book is not addressed solely to parents, note that in the section that follows, and in similar "how to" sections in other chapters, for the sake of simplicity, the reader is addressed directly, as if he or she were a parent.

Show and Describe Everything to Your Child

As Colette's memoir reminds us, much of teaching a child about the world starts with the word, "Look." Perhaps the best advice one could give a parent is, Show your child everything. Actually "show" is not a strong enough word. One wants to *celebrate* the world for your child, to communicate, as Sido did to Colette, enthusiasm and awe for what's out there. As I've mentioned, the "social referencing" research shows that children's responses to the things they encounter are influenced by the reactions of their parents. Parental enthusiasm tends to spark a child's interest. Parents who are good teachers, like any good teachers, are always on the lookout for what they can show their child, what they can help him or her discover and discern, what new aspects of the world they can reveal to this growing mind. The possibilities are endless. Every room of the house will have different objects to explore and every window will provide a different view.

Research findings certainly support the importance of bringing objects to the attention of babies and young children. Parents who do a lot of "showing" during their child's early months, tend to have higher scoring children when they are later tested for mental and verbal abilities and exploratory interest. Other research shows that preschoolers and young school-age children display more interest in objects, ask more questions about them, and explore them more intensively when an adult directs and supports their explorations with statements like, "Hey, look! Isn't this interesting?" and "Hey, look at that!"[20]

Showing is just the beginning of the process of introducing a child to the things out there. Objects call for exploration. Knowing the world means much more than seeing the world. During his earliest years, your child will want to manipulate, shake, bang, mouth, and take apart the objects you hand him, and you'll see that he will want to do all of this with a passion, wailing when you remove something that has caught his fancy. Research shows that during their early months, infants begin to explore objects in sensible ways, seeking to extract the most information from them: they'll squeeze spongy things, bang hard things, and prefer to bang things onto hard, rather than soft, surfaces. Research also shows that the more opportunities infants have to play with objects (such as different kinds of containers), the more they learn about the functions and limitations of those objects.[21]

Whenever possible, children should be permitted to explore objects with all of their senses (taking safety into consideration, of course). Encourage the full use of your child's senses by revealing the various sensory aspects of the objects you present. If he doesn't bang an object that he has looked at and mouthed, you bang it to expose him to the sound it makes. Then give it back to him. He'll probably copy you and bang it too. You want him to appreciate that the intrinsic qualities of objects are revealed differently to each sense. For instance, plastic objects make different sounds than metal objects.

Try to sense what your child is ready to appreciate but do not worry too much about whether you are right or wrong. Your child will let you know if she isn't ready to appreciate (or even perceive) something you've presented. Don't feel bad or take it personally. Just go on to something else. For example, you may love music and play and sing songs for your baby. She, though, may react with disinterest or may even cry when you begin. You may then discover that your neighbor's baby of the same age perks up whenever music is played. Don't be perturbed and definitely don't communicate displeasure to your child. Just hold off and try again a few days or weeks later. You can only present things, and then you must follow your child's lead. Babies know what they like and you can't talk them into or out of anything.

You'll find that when showing your child objects, even during her earliest days, you will do more than merely present and name the item. When showing a ball you will probably toss it up and catch it. When showing a fork you will find yourself miming eating actions. In other words, introducing your child to what's out there involves teaching various aspects of the items presented, including their function (balls are to toss, forks are to eat with), how they work (you'll turn a radio on and off), their constituents ("See, when you squeeze the orange, juice comes out, and it has a peel that can be taken off''), and their structures (''See how the book is held together by staples'').

Eventually you'll also want to point out limitations associated with the object (''Forks are handy for eating but are dangerous if thrown''), special subcategories (''That kind of cup will break if dropped''), why some objects work better than others (''This knife has a dull edge so it won't cut well''), and even some alternate uses (''We can use the fork to keep the paper from blowing away'').

Among the important things to show a young child are shapes (triangles, squares, circles, etc.). This can begin during infancy with mobiles containing various shaped objects hanging from them and by giving children small blocks, balls, and other objects with shapes that are easy for them to discriminate and for you to name: ''See, that's a triangle'' (as you trace the shape with your finger and highlight the three angles).

Babies and toddlers appear to have a strong and natural interest in well-defined, basic shapes, perhaps because they are easily diffentiated from each other and, therefore, easily known. Toddlers, in particular, love to solve simple shape problems as are found in form boards and shape sorters. They love to manipulate shapes, put them in their mouths, and then find the correct slot for them in the board. Three- and 4-year-olds will generally enjoy more sophisticated shape problems, such as having to make a square or rectangle out of two triangles, or a circle out of two semicircles or four wedges. You can cut the basic shapes out of cardboard and draw the larger forms they have to match (the circles, squares, etc.) on stiff paper, or you can buy a kit at a toy store containing precut shapes and printed forms.

Activity books usually have interesting shape problems for preschoolers and young grade-schoolers, such as finding common shapes (squares, circles, rectangles, triangles) in pictures of everyday objects and scenes. For instance, car tires and headlights are circles; country houses are squares with rectangular doors, square windows, and triangular roofs; apartment buildings are rectangles. Another game with shapes involves asking a child to name everything he can think of that has the shape of a circle (or any other form). Common replies are a bicycle wheel, a drum, and a pizza. You can also explore your home looking for the shapes ''hidden'' in the objects in each room (the refrigerator hides a rectangle, the bicycle seat hides a triangle).

One can use many different formats for teaching about, and strengthening a child's knowledge of, what's out there:

- With a 3-year-old you can play, ''I Spy.'' You select something you see and the child has to guess what it is. Before each guess you provide a hint ("It's round"). Then have the child pick something and give you hints.

- With a 4-year-old, each of you can take turns drawing a quick picture of something and the other one has to make the sound associated with it (a car: "beep, beep"; a duck: "quack").
- Another format using drawing calls for each of you to take turns drawing an outline and some parts of an object (a bus) while the other one has to fill in the missing parts (windows, a sign). The one who drew the object can ask for additional parts to be drawn if he or she thinks of things that the other one has missed.
- A good way to deepen a child's understanding and appreciation of some of the objects around him (and of human creativity) is to play the "Invention Game." Pick an invented object with which the child is familiar, such as the kitchen stove or his thermos bottle, and ask what life would be like if no one had invented it. You can use this game to discuss life in the "old days" before this item was around.
- In a variation of the Invention Game, one asks similar questions about natural phenomena: "What would happen if there was no water?" "What would happen if I had no ears?" "What would happen if there was no sun?"

Children's fantasy play provides wonderful opportunities for teaching what's out there. A child who imagines she's a bird or a princess or a doctor can be reminded to see the world from the perspective of whomever she is enacting, thereby enabling her to learn more about that person's or animal's life. For example, you might say to your little bird as the two of you are flying along: "Here comes a big wind from behind that can carry us along on it. We don't have to flap our wings now. We can just float. Now what do you see below us?"

Your suggestions during these play sessions can also teach her more about the world by focusing her on things that are important to her fantasy character. For instance, as your little doctor is giving an examination you might say: "Don't forget to check his heart. Put your head [or the stethescope] on his chest and listen to the heartbeats. Each beat pumps some blood through the body." Later you can talk about the heart and what it does, show pictures of the circulatory system (children generally love to see pictures of the inside of their bodies), and illustrate the pumping action with a rubber bulb from a baster or a nasal aspirator.

I'd also recommend that you choose names together for all her dolls and stuffed animals. This will make it easier for her to attribute different personality characteristics to each of them, which, in turn, will enliven her fantasy play with them.

Many preschool activity books provide children with practice in attending to the details of common objects. One such activity shows a drawing of an object such as a car plus a few other pictures of the same car with one or more parts missing. The child's job is to fill in the missing parts—which children usually love to do.

When using activity books, there are some things to keep in mind: Children usually find them fun if their parents don't take them too seriously. For instance, in problems like the one mentioned above, some children will fill in parts that weren't in the original picture—they might, for instance, put faces in the car windows. A child who does this will usually know that such additions aren't what the instructions call for but will do it anyway because he enjoys it. Some parents are sticklers about following instructions and discourage these kinds of whimsical though technically *wrong* solutions. At some point your child will have to learn the importance of following instructions carefully, but the preschool and early grade school years are too early for placing limits on a child's imagination, especially when the child's mind is fertile with inventive solutions. Offer help when your child doesn't understand the instructions but give him free rein when he transforms the problem into something else, something he finds more interesting.

A good way to help a child develop proper respect for instructions (in the long run) is for you to read the instructions aloud when you come across them in games, activity books, and kits. You might say, "We need to know how to do this so it'll work, so we better go over the instructions carefully, step by step." You also want your child to understand that instructions aren't sacred, so you may at times want to say something like, "It might work the way the instructions say, but it might be fun to try it another way." Children differ in their commitment to instructions. Some will insist on doing everything "the way it's supposed to be done"; others will be curious to see what happens if things get changed around a bit. These seem to be inborn, temperamental differences, and it is worth respecting them. Both kinds of children can be highly intelligent, although they will probably wind up interested in different kinds of problems and are likely to have different work habits.

As children grow, more and more of what they learn about the world comes from reading—from stories, newspapers, textbooks, etc. This process can begin even before children reach the age of 2. Read, read, read stories to your child. Read with as much expression as you can and use different voices for the different characters. Also explain everything. Talk about the objects, the motivations, the feelings, the thoughts, the preferences and choices, the relationships, the environments, the plans, the actions, the outcomes, the colors—everything. Children want to know all these things. It makes the story more fun for them. One of the reasons they like to hear a story over and over is to master it, to understand what's really going on.

They also like to be asked questions about the story, about things you've told them during a previous reading, or about some aspect you haven't discussed before. Ask them "What do you think will happen?" as a way to heighten the suspense and give them practice in using what they already know to make predictions about what's ahead. To get them to think about characters' motivations, ask them why they think a character did what he or she did. Whether we are children or adults, good fiction teaches us about life. Good films, videos, and plays can serve the same purpose.

Songs and nursery rhymes also provide abundant opportunities for expanding a child's vocabulary and knowledge of the world. For instance, the popular children's song "The Wheels on the Bus" is packed with information (the wheels go round, the wipers go swish, the people bounce up and down).

Support and Encourage Your Child's Explorations

Infants start to explore right out of the womb and keep right on exploring during most of their waking hours. They shift their gaze, they turn their heads, they twist their bodies to bring more of the world into view. Mothers often note that their baby does a lot of looking around while breast feeding. A baby who gets held and carried around a lot gets much more opportunity to explore than one who spends most of his or her day in the crib. A baby who gets picked up and soothed when crying accumulates more hours of alert time than one who is allowed to cry it out on his own.[22]

Be ready to lend a hand when your young child summons your assistance for her exploratory impulses. Babies take their exploring seriously. This was evident in a father's report about his 7-month-old daughter whom he had taken to the window to watch some fire trucks go clanging by. After that, whenever she heard the sound of fire trucks from the street below, she implored him through sounds and body language to take her to the window. She calmed down as soon as he picked her up and headed in the desired direction, and then she watched the scene below attentively.

The positive effect of parental behavior on infant's "exploratory competence" was demonstrated in an interesting naturalistic study of children between 9- and 18-months of age by Jay Belsky and his colleagues. They observed that the more mothers stimulated their children's exploratory behavior, the more focused and competent were their children's explorations. The kinds of stimulation that were effective included drawing the child's attention to objects by pointing at or tapping on them, demonstrating how things work (such as dialing a toy phone), and guiding the child's hands through an action (such as pulling a cap off a bottle). Children who received more of this kind of stimulation, explored and played with objects more competently in the sense that they were more likely to combine objects in their play (putting a block on a toy car), or use objects in appropriate ways (dialed the phone, put pegs in holes), or engage in more sophisticated pretend play with them (such as turning a block into a car or "drinking" from a seashell).

A particularly important finding of Belsky's is that as the mothers, during the course of the study, increased the quantity of exploratory stimulation to their children, the children, before long, began to explore in increasingly competent ways. These mothers not only increased the kinds of physical stimulation described above (such as pointing and dialing) but also started giving much more descriptive information ("The peg goes in the hole," "It's very soft"), more object names ("That's your diaper"), more instructions ("Go get your ball"), and more questions ("Is that your sock?").[23]

As soon as children start to crawl, they begin to hunt for objects of interest to them. Crawlers no longer need everything brought to them. Set them loose and they'll find lots of good stuff on their own. As your crawler leads you to what fascinates him, your enthusiasm and participation in *his* exploration is important. Some recent studies on "responsive" parenting, found that competent and curious toddlers and preschoolers were likely to have parents who allowed them "to direct the focus and pace" of their joint explorations and who permitted "independent discovery of different aspects of the environment."[24]

Starting in their second year, children love to show their parents the treasures they found on their excursions through the house and yard.[25] Your delight and interest in the objects that excite your child and that she brings to show you will communicate that discovering the world out there is a good thing, worthy of admiration. But keep in mind that a child's inclination to explore is not based on parental reinforcement, and you don't need to get in on and make a fuss about every act of exploration. Indeed, there'll be times when you'll want to back off and let your child explore on her own, waiting until your participation is asked for or clearly needed. Exploration is about the joy of knowing, and most of the time your participation in the exploration will serve that end, but you don't want your child to become dependent on your constant participation.

Natural environments seem to bring out the explorer in most children. Three-year-olds usually find beaches places of endless wonder. Woods and streams also supply a plethora of interesting sights, sounds, and smells, as well as marvelous things to touch and sometimes taste (if you come across wild berries, for example). Young children are particularly fascinated by insects and animals. They love to watch anthills and farm animals and sea animals. Even children who are afraid of animals are fascinated by them.

Be prepared for the likelihood that your child's interest in nature won't be the same as yours. Preschoolers and early grade-schoolers like to dig and throw rocks and break off twigs and pile up stones. They won't yet have a sophisticated, aesthetic interest in nature and its beauties; they're more likely to want to roll in it and grasp it in their hands. As much as possible, give your child the freedom to explore his way, which doesn't mean you shouldn't point out things you'd like him to appreciate; nor should you refrain from giving him information about the things he encounters. Just try to make sure you aren't interfering with his own explorations or asking him to appreciate things he isn't ready for. Probably the best thing you can do to support and nurture his interest in nature is to communicate your own enthusiasm for such explorations and your pleasure in doing the exploring together.

You want your child to appreciate that there are always new things to be discovered in the world, from objects one never noticed before to gaining new perspectives on things that are common and familiar. Try playing "Let's Find Something New." The goal is discovery. One might notice that the trees on one side of the street are bigger and healthier looking than on the other side, or you might find spider webs in the recesses of furniture, or you might notice decorative patterns in the brickwork of buildings in the neighborhood, or that older people dress differently than younger people, or that the walls near the bathroom have larger cracks in them than other walls. Any discovery can launch a discussion about what lies behind whatever you've observed (e.g., the walls near the bathroom receive more moisture). Discovering more and more about their environment provides children with an increasing sense of mastery over the world around them. A keen observer is a better problem solver. It also makes life a lot more interesting. It is also a very nice way to spend time with your child.

Communicate your own excitement in discovery to your child. When you read about new discoveries, share them with enthusiasm. Applaud the discoverers past and present. Early in life children's drive for mastery is expressed in actions directed at discovering and manipulating the world around them. But toward the end of the preschool years it begins to get directed toward mastering those tasks that parents define as the important areas of accomplishment. In some families, accomplishment and excellence are defined in terms of outcomes such as making money, winning games, being popular. Success in any of these requires knowing things about the world, but none honors knowing for its own sake. If you communicate to your child that the pursuit of knowledge, simply as an end in itself, is an important criterion of human excellence, you will be channeling his or her mastery drive toward a life of continued exploration. Being an "explorer" (in the broadest sense of that term) will become an ideal and a standard for gauging personal accomplishment.

When a child starts school some parents act as if they believed their job as the nurturer of their child's intellect was completed and that the school was going to take over from here. That's an unfortunate decision. It is enormously helpful to growing minds to know that their parents are interested in what they wonder about and what they are trying to figure out, both in school and out. Moreover, many schools don't have a very stimulating intellectual atmosphere, and even those that do can't always give enough individual attention to students. A student who ponders things that are not part of the standard curriculum or who develops unusual ways of solving standard problems may be overlooked or discouraged.

Outside of school, children pursue knowledge only when their interest is sparked; in school they must be interested in arithmetic at 10:00 A.M., reading at 11:00 A.M., history at 1:00 P.M., and so on. An orderly lesson plan rarely leaves room for the joyful, spontaneous pursuit of children's individual interests. Parents, in one-to-one exchanges with their child, can be responsive, flexible, and encouraging in ways that are difficult for classroom teachers. Parental interest and support can give a child the confidence to carve out his or her own path to knowledge.

There are many things that parents can introduce older children to that the school may neglect; particular schools may be deficient in one area or another. As one of many possible examples, a parent might try to compensate for a school's inadequate history curriculum by helping a child appreciate the connection between the things he or she sees on the TV news and events and decisions that took place decades or even centuries earlier (such as the connection between ghetto family problems and slavery or between Central American conflicts and the Monroe Doctrine). In general, parents and children can pursue knowledge together for their entire lives, starting on day one. The intellectual itinerary will, of course, change as the child gets older, and it won't be long before the child's own discoveries and insights can enrich the parent's knowledge of what's out there.

Another important message parents can convey to children about school is that they don't have to approach their relationships to their courses and teachers passively, that they can and should take responsibility for improving their school experiences even when they encounter "boring" courses or "bad" teachers.[26] In a sense, there are no boring courses, just those one does not now find interesting. Other people certainly find those same topics fascinating. When children are stuck in a course that does not interest them, they can moan and feel sorry for themselves or they can look for elements that might spark their curiosity, and see if their teacher will let them focus on (write a paper on) those elements. For example, a student who doesn't like his geography course, but who likes history, may be able to focus on historical consequences of the geographical facts being studied (such as how rivers, mountains, and other natural land barriers affected historical events).

It is too easy to blame the teacher or the textbook or the topic for being dull, but if a student can't find anything he wants to know then he might have to face up to the reality that it is he, not the subject, that is dull. If children learn that they have a responsibility to bring an inquiring mind to a class, they will soon discover that most subjects become far more interesting, and even an inept teacher will not have nearly as negative an effect.

Label and Talk About Everything

As you introduce the world to your child, and as you participate in his or her discoveries, label everything. And start this labeling right from birth. Research cited above shows that babies can distinguish words during their first week, and before long they can associate words with objects and activities. By giving everything a name you will help your child categorize and differentiate the objects and events of her world, and remember them when they appear again.

Everything the child perceives goes through variations: objects come closer, move away, and are seen from different angles and under different lighting conditions; odors get stronger or fade and come from different directions; sounds too come from different directions and reverberate differently in different surroundings. When the same label is applied across the natural variations of a stimulus, it makes it easier for the child to identify that stimulus as a "thing" with elements that are constant regardless of variations.

Moreover, every "thing" comes in different forms. No two apples are alike, yet they are all apples. When a child hears the word "apple" applied to many different apples it teaches him that apples are a *class* of objects, all instances of which have certain essentials in common.

Keep up a running conversation as you interact with your baby. When you pick him up say "Up." When you take out a diaper show it to him and say, "Diaper. See the diaper." Attach words to all objects and activities and try to emphasize the key words so they stand out for your child.

Parents label things in a variety of ways. Sometimes directly: "That's an umbrella." Sometimes with a question: "What's that? It's an umbrella." Sometimes adding functional information: "It's raining. What do we use in the rain? An umbrella." Sometimes prompting and helping the child to say the word: "Do you know what that's called? An umbrella. Um-brel-la. You say it. Um" (Child says "Um"). "That's right. Um-brel-la" (Child says "Umbweda"). "That's right, Umbrella. Very good."

It's best to reinforce even remote approximations and then merely repeat the word correctly. Children have an intrinsic desire to get it right and are usually doing the best they can. Negative feedback isn't helpful and will probably discourage the child from trying.

Incorporate word lessons in all your interactions. For example, if you and your toddler are playing with doll house figures, you might say, "Let's put the boy in the chair. Can you put him in the chair? Here's the chair. Now you put him in it." If your child does it, you'll know he is beginning to grasp the meaning of the words you are using. Research demonstrates that the more mothers label the objects their child has focused on or points to, the larger the child's vocabulary of object names. Moreover, some recent studies by Carolyn Mervis and her colleagues at the University of Massachusetts show that toddlers learn words best when they are given demonstrations and descriptions along with the new labels: "This is a funnel. It has a hole in the bottom (point at hole in bottom). You can pour water through the funnel (demonstrate pouring water through funnel into glass)."[27]

Once children begin to crawl, they virtually flood themselves with stimuli, exploring everything they can get to. Here too labeling helps inform a child about what he or she is observing. As psychologists Meredith West and Harriet Rheingold discovered, attentive parents label almost everything in sight. They observed mothers of 12-month-olds as they explored a new environment:

> The mothers named not only the toys, the mobile, and the pictures on posters, but many less prominent objects in the rooms, such as the cameras, cushions, microphones, tape markers on the floor, covered electric outlets, the chair, the door sill, and even the floor. They also named small details of the toys such as the eyes, ears, and tail of the dog, as well as the shoe tied around its neck. The mothers also described the colors of the objects, their texture ("It's not as soft as your pillow"), their response properties ("If you touch them, they fly."; "If you wiggle it, it moves.").[28]

Picture books and magazines are wonderful sources for objects to show children and label. Virtually all children love to look at picture books and

magazines and often ask for the names of the things they see that interest
them ("Whazzat?"). They are especially thrilled when they see a picture
of something they possess, such as a toy or a book. They will also ask
questions about activities and emotional states that they see depicted ("Why
she crying?" "Why he running?"). Sometimes they'll ask the same questions the next time you go through the same material. At times this will
be because they don't remember the details; at other times it will be because
they like hearing your story.

Jean Carew and her colleagues at the Harvard Graduate School of Education provide a good example of a mother using a picture book to teach
her young child (age 1) what's out there:

> Sandra points at a picture and Mother says, "Yes, that's a dog." Sandra
> points to another picture and babbles. Mother tells her, "That's right.
> That's an egg. Would you like to eat the egg?" and holds an imaginary
> bite of egg up to Sandra's mouth. Sandra smiles and points to the next
> picture. Mother tells her, "Guitar. Can you pretend to play a guitar?"
> Mother strums an imaginary guitar and sings. Sandra laughs delightedly.
> Mother turns the page. . . .
>   Sandra looks at Mother and points at a picture. Mother says, "Yes,
> teeth. Mama has teeth," and opens her mouth to show Sandra her teeth.
> Sandra says, "a-on." Mother says, "Yes, lion," and demonstrates a
> lion's roar. . . . They look at another picture and Mother asks, "Where
> are the owl's eyes?" Mother points at the owl's eyes, then at Sandra's
> eyes and labels, "Eyes." Mother points to the next picture and says,
> "Shoes. Shoes for your feet," and pets Sandra's feet.[29]

The same authors recorded a mother using clean-up time to teach her
13-month-old the words for parts of her body. The child had just finished
lunch:

> Mother: "Okay, Sonja, that's it for you." Mother brings over a towel,
> saying, "You can come out (of the high chair) now." Mother wipes
> Sonja's face and mouth. Sonja laughs. Mother: "Wash your tongue,
> wash your nose, wash your neck, wash your hands, wash your fingers,
> dry your fingers," as she does each of these actions in turn.

Good teaching, like that described by West and Rheingold and Carew
requires sensitive understanding of the learner, monitoring what interests
him at any moment, and appraising what he is capable of taking in, what
words he can grasp, and what past experiences might be recalled to help
him learn about the things now before him. Certainly empathy is involved
in good teaching: the teacher must enter the mind of the learner, see the
world from his perspective, know his thoughts and questions, anticipate
what will ignite and what will confuse him.

A lot of word learning in early childhood does not involve formal instruction. Young children learn words from the contexts in which the words are used and from how they are used in a sentence. If as you get your child's milk, you say, "Your milk is in the refrigerator. I'll get it," he or she will probably associate the word "refrigerator" with the big box that contains his milk. Parents are often surprised and delighted by the words their children learn simply from listening (including listening to television programs). Research shows that children use context not only through direct references to objects, but also through contrasts. For example, in one study even 2-year-olds learned the meaning of new words which were contrasted with familiar ones. The children were asked questions such as, "Could you bring me the chartreuse [book], not the red one, the chartreuse one." Their learning of the new words, such as "chartreuse," was then demonstrated by their correct answers to subsequent questions.[30]

As your child grows, continue to bring new words into your conversations. By the time children reach 4 or 5 they will commonly ask for the meaning of an unfamiliar word that you've used (What's an "urge?"). Let your child know that you are pleased when he or she asks for the meaning of a word. At any age, if you use a word that you aren't sure your child understands, define it for him (or first ask him if he knows it).

The challenge in providing definitions is in coming up with ones children can grasp. It's easy when you can simply point to an object or show a picture of it, but often that won't be possible. The key is to relate new words to words the child already knows and to keep definitions concrete, creating images your child can picture. For instance, if he asks, "What's an *urge?*" you might say, "It's when we want to have something or do something right away. Remember when you wanted a candy bar after lunch. Well you had an *urge* for a candy bar." As another example, to the question "What's a wedding?" you might reply, "It's like a big birthday party, with music and a cake and presents, except it's not to celebrate a birthday. It's a party to celebrate that a man and a woman decided to get married and start a new family and live together in their own home. Mommy and Daddy once decided to become a family and we had a wedding to celebrate."

There are more than "things" out there that the child needs to learn about. There are also actions: people and animals *do* many things, like run and jump and sit, among a great many other actions. These too need to be pointed out and labeled for your child. One parent I know incorporated action lessons into her daily activities with her 18-month-old. Every so often she would say "Let's run" and they'd run. Then every few seconds she'd switch the action: "Let's walk"; "Let's tiptoe"; "Let's slide"; "Let's spin''; and so on. It didn't take long before her child began to call out the actions, demonstrating her knowledge of them.

Things and actions also have *qualities* that children need to learn about. These include functional attributes such as strong and weak ("That tape is strong enough to hold it"), and aesthetic evaluations such as beautiful and ugly.

The actions people take are connected to the roles they play (father, doctor, waiter). An enjoyable way to teach about these roles is to improvise skits around situations that your child has experienced. You be a shopper and let her be the countergirl. Or you be the waitress and let her be the customer. Ask for items, explain why you need them, be out of some items, offer alternatives ("No we don't have vegetable soup, we have chicken soup"), ask for change.

Children from two on love these kinds of pretend games and play them with devotion. A useful role is to have the child play a "mommy" or "baby sitter" taking care of a child her age, while you play her. It will help her gain an outside perspective on her own behavior. Contrary to what some cognitive development theorists would have parents believe, young children are well able to differentiate themselves from others and reality from appearance. In fact, they are superb and perceptive pretenders.[31]

Learning about the world involves not only learning about the objects and events *out* there, but also about what's *in* there, in the sense of learning to recognize, label, and understand the private emotional, mental, and bodily experiences we all have but which can't be observed directly by others. These private events include bodily pains (such as a toothache), feelings (such as fear and anger), and thoughts (such as recollections of things past and images of intended actions and anticipated events). Teaching children about the world therefore requires labeling the inner world of private experiences.

For example, state the appropriate words when you notice that your child is in pain or afraid or happy and try to describe the experience and its source as precisely as you can ("Bump. Ow, Ow. You fell on your knee. That must hurt." Or, "You've climbed up too high, haven't you? That's scary. You get afraid when you're up that high—and your legs feel funny, don't they?"). Similarly, let your child know about other people's inner experiences ("Uncle Steve has a headache. That's why he is lying down now"). One recent study found that 2-year-olds were better able to talk about feelings if their mothers talked to them about feelings.[32]

Here's a simple but nice example of a mother teaching a 3-year-old child about taking in another's sensory perspective. The child initiated a conversation with the words, "You know, mommy . . ." But the rest of the sentence was barely audible, although from the child's body language she was clearly expressing some important new insight. The mother said, "Do you know what that sounded like to me? I heard, 'You know, mommy, bzm woozy tsoopi yiks.' " The child laughed. The mother continued, "You looked down as you started talking and forgot that my ears are way up here. If my toes had ears I would have heard you fine [the child laughed again]. You were so busy thinking about what you were saying that you forgot to say it loud enough. Now look right at me and tell me again. I really want to hear it." What made this lesson so effective was that the mother gave her child a good sense of what her experience had been like as a listener.

Children also need to be reminded that others do not always have the same information that they do, sometimes because their position gives them a different perspective, and sometimes because they simply haven't had the experience. For example, in a phone conversation, they might say, "Mommy gave me this great toy. Look what it does." They'll need a reminder then that they haven't described the toy and the other person can't see it. With training they will develop this awareness of the difference between what they and others perceive and know.

Recent studies reveal that children as young as 3 have enough awareness of other people's "minds" to recognize that others see things differently from them (sometimes because they are observing from a different position). Moreover, children can make correct inferences about what another knows, based on what that person has or has not observed (for example, that a person who saw an object placed in a box, and who was looking away when it was removed, would think it was still in the box). These findings are in sharp contrast to Piaget's position that children go through a long period of cognitive "egocentrism" and are unable to appreciate the perspective of others until they are between 6 and 10.[33]

As the opportunities arise introduce your child to increasingly subtle and complex inner experiences ("Leslie is *disappointed* because she worked hard to make the team and she wasn't chosen." "Harold is *worried* about his mother who is sick"). Research by Inge Bretherton, Marjorie Beeghly, and others shows that even 2-year-olds are able to grasp the nature of mental states, connect them to their causes, and understand that they are private—not observable by others. For instance, the child in their study who said, "No watch the Hulk. I afraid," recognized the connection between an emotion and its cause. So did the child who said, "I give a hug. Baby be happy."[34]

An enjoyable way to reinforce your child's awareness of emotions is by playing a game in which one of you calls out an emotion (angry, sad) and the other has to make a face and assume a posture that depicts the emotion. Also, when coming across an emotional face in a magazine or picture book, ask your child what the person seems to be feeling and why.

Encourage Your Child to Label and Talk About Things Observed

Toward the end of the first year or during the early months of the second year, most children start to talk, uttering the names of the people and objects they've come to know. Parents usually need no coaching about showing delight at these first words (which usually they alone are able to decipher). Before those first words are spoken, parents have routinely labeled the people and things around the child hundreds of times in various forms ("That's Daddy." "Here comes Daddy!" "See Daddy?"). When the child finally says something that even remotely approximates "Daddy," parents normally explode with ecstasy. While there is no research proving that parents who leap for joy upon hearing their child's first words have more verbal children than those who respond with neutral or sour faces, it is a pretty safe guess that showing delight in a child's early utterances has a beneficial effect.

The child doesn't go from a nonverbal to a verbal being in one grand leap. For months before the first words appear, children use gestures and sounds to express feelings and communicate desires—and attentive parents treat these responses as meaningful communications. One recent study, for example, found that 4-month-olds and their mothers were already engaging in vocal exchanges (such as turn taking) that "were structurally similar to patterns of adult conversation." Other research traces the roots of parent–child vocal communication to the first weeks of a child's life, demonstrating that even 2-week-olds frequently make eye contact during vocalizations.[35]

You'll encourage speaking in your baby if you assume his early sounds are saying something to you and if you enter into a dialogue with him. For instance, if your child babbles some happy sounds while being bathed, respond to and elaborate on his message: "Oh yes, you like the water, don't you? That water feels so good. Pat the water. Water!"

Once children begin to speak, they start to gobble up the names of everyone and everything they encounter. And they delight in playing verbal games to demonstrate their skill. Ask "Who's that?" or "What's that?" or "That's a . . . ?" and they'll chime in with the right word if you've done a good job of labeling for them. If you see that your child doesn't have the word, give it cheerfully and ask the question again. Your child will show delight in having just learned it. Avoid conveying to your child that not knowing the right answer is any kind of failure for him or her.

They need our stimulation but not our criticism or disappointment, as if they weren't trying hard enough or aren't as smart as we would like them to be. With language, as with most other areas of early learning, children don't need prodding. And every child has his or her own rate of learning language—girls, on average, faster than boys—and the range considered normal development is large.

Children's first words are object names (nouns), but it won't be long before they add adjectives and other parts of speech as they become increasingly competent at describing both what's out there and what they'd like out there. The adjective "more" is a common early word, communicating I want *more* milk, *more* piggyback, *more* swinging, or more of any good thing that the child hasn't had enough of. Think of your child's early one-word and two-word utterances as sentences, expressing complete thoughts. When you hear them, expand on them, filling out the unspoken parts. So if your child says, "Up, up," which you take to mean, "Pick me up," put the whole thought into words: "You want me to pick you up? I'll pick you up. Picking up Ronnie."

Similarly, if at the two-word stage your child says, "Sit chair," you might expand on this by saying, "You want me to sit in the chair? All right, I'll sit in the chair." Research shows that young children develop larger vocabularies when their parents respond to and expand upon their speech. In turn, children with larger vocabularies tend to score higher on tests of mental abilities.[36] The positive association between vocabulary and mental abilities in young children is understandable. Children don't learn words by rote (unless their parents have subscribed to a "superbaby" program); they aren't interested in "building their vocabulary." If they know and use a word it usually indicates they have learned something about whatever the word refers to; that is, it is an indication of their increasing mental competence.

You'll be surprised at how well your 2-year-old and especially your 3-year-old will do with complex, multisyllabic words. My own 2-year-old loved to say the word "parmesan," and articulated it well, as she asked for cheese for her spaghetti. Three- and 4-year-olds generally love to play with dinosaur toys and quickly learn to distinguish and name pictures and models of Tyrannosaurus Rex, Stegosaurs, and Brontosaurs, among others. Don't be too insistent about correct pronounciation with young children. If you provide the correct form ("Not skabedi—spaghetti") and your child continues to say it the old way, don't make a fuss. Just say it correctly yourself and give him a reminder every so often of the correct pronunciation; he will begin to say it correctly too after a while.

Here is a good example from Jean Carew of a mother providing a label and then correcting her child's attempt to say the word:

Michael, age two, is watching Mother prepare cake batter. She tells him, "I'm putting in some vanilla." He repeats, "nilla." Mother corrects, emphasizing the syllables, "Yes, va-nil-la, can you say that? Vanilla."

It is important to make a distinction between expansions and corrections. Children's verbal abilities go through a sequence of natural patterns that bring them closer and closer to standard adult speech. They need simple corrections if they mislabel an object, say by calling a tomato an apple. But their progress in sentence structure doesn't depend on formal corrections such as, "No, that's the wrong way to say it. Say it this way." Corrections like this are likely to discourage speech. *Expansions,* on the other hand, don't convey criticism. Rather, they acknowledge what was said, restate it more properly, and fill in missing parts. For instance, if a 4-year-old says, "I wented," give her the correct form within your normal conversation: "Oh, you went. How was it?" If a few such corrections do not work, state the rule, pointing out the irregularity: "We say 'I went' instead of 'I wented' even though 'I wented' sounds like the right way to say it. Sometimes our language doesn't make sense."

It is also important for parents to know that children don't all acquire language according to precisely the same blueprint (contrary to earlier beliefs by psycholinguists). Recent research shows that most start with object terms ("wagon"), and then add related adjectives and verbs ("red wagon," "wagon go"). Others, though, start using pronouns (I, you) very early, along with whole sentences that communicate desires, such as "Stop it" or "I want it").[37] Children who use these pronoun-based sentences almost exclusively, speak well enough to make their needs known, but they don't really talk *about* things, about their features and functions. Their information about the world around them may therefore remain limited. Object labeling and expansions are particularly important for these children.

An effective, and fun-filled way to reinforce a two- and three-year-old's growing vocabulary is to play "Mistake." When you are pretty sure the child has learned the name of something, mislabel it, allowing the child to correct you. Children take great delight in this. For example, you point to a picture of a bird and say, "Oh, there's a cat." The child will usually be eager to correct you (usually recognizing that you made the mistake on purpose as part of a game). If he corrects you, show appreciation. If he doesn't, correct yourself, indicating the features that distinguish the items: "Oh, I'm so silly, that's not a cat; it's a bird. Cats don't have feathers and wings and only two skinny little legs. They have fur and four legs. And that has a beak. Birds have beaks, not cats." I've never known a child who didn't love to play this. As your child gets a bit older, the more farfetched your label (seeing a dog and saying "That's an alligator"), the more likely you'll get a joyful giggle.

Playing "Mistake," aside from being fun and fortifying word recognition, encourages independent thinking and a child's sense of humor. Children love to spot mistakes. There are some delightful books (e.g., *Wacky Wednesday, Oh So Silly*) that have pictures with one or more inappropriate elements, such as a water faucet pointing up or a fish with eyeglasses. Children become positively triumphant when they find these "silly" parts.

Other ways parents can encourage verbal competence are by waiting for words and asking for words.[38] That is, once a child starts to speak, rather than trying to anticipate her every need by interpreting her grunts and body language (as you had to do before she could speak), wait a bit to see if she makes her needs known through words. If not, ask for words; ask her to tell you what she wants, what she sees, what she hears, and what she experiences with all her senses. If she can't, give her the words ("What is it you want? Is it the grapes? Those are grapes. Grapes! Yummy. Yes. Now tell me what you want").

If it's a word you think she knows but can't quite recall, give her a hint ("Guh," "Gr . . ."). If she gets the word from the hint treat it as an accomplishment as much as if she remembered it without the hint. If she doesn't say the word don't make a test of it. Once she knows that you know what she wants, don't refuse giving it to her, insisting that she first pay you with the word. She might take up your challenge and refuse to speak as a contest of wills. She may prefer to give up grapes rather than her sense of autonomy. Even when a child is emotional and expressing herself in wordless cries, ask for words—let her know that you want to help her but you need her to tell you what happened to her and what she needs. Say, "Use your words."

A useful word to teach a 3-year-old is "conversations." For instance, you might say, "I can't get it for you now because Daddy and I are talking. We are having a conversation." Then you can label your discussions with your child as "conversations" ("Let's have a conversation" or "That was a good conversation we just had"), and let him know that you enjoy having conversations with him. When he discovers that he has "conversations" just as grown-ups do, he'll feel very adult and pleased with himself, and he'll want to talk more. Save the word "conversations" for discussions about things or events or feelings. Don't give an order and refer to it as a conversation.

As children approach school age, conversations with them about what's out there can range over virtually any topic. Here's an example from a conversation between a father and his 4½-year-old son:

FATHER: Tim, look at this. It's a horseshoe.

TIM: I've seen pictures of that. (Picks it up.) It's heavy. Does a horse mind wearing it?

FATHER: No, horses have very strong legs so it doesn't feel heavy to them. It protects their feet, just like our shoes do.

TIM: How does it stay on? Does it have a strap?

FATHER: No, it's nailed into the horse's hoof. Horses have thick hooves at the bottom of their feet and the shoes are nailed in.

TIM: *Nailed in?* That must hurt.

FATHER: No. The hoof is made of stuff that's similar to our finger nails and toe nails, except much thicker. When I cut your nails, slicing right through them, does it hurt?

TIM: No.

FATHER: That's because nails don't have any nerves. We have nerves all over our skin which is why when our skin gets cut we feel it a lot. The nerves send messages from our skin to our brain and we go "Eyowww!" But our nails don't have any nerves.

TIM: Do horses' hooves have nerves?

FATHER: No. That's why it doesn't hurt them when the horseshoe is nailed on.

TIM: I bet we don't have nerves in our hair. Otherwise we'd go "Eyowww!" when we got a haircut.

Here's another nice example. A mother and daughter (age 4 years, 9 months) caught a frog near a pond:

NANCY: I want to take it home. We could make a home for it out of a shoe box. I'll poke holes in it so he can breathe.

MOTHER: I don't think the frog would be happy living in a box and we couldn't get frog food now so the frog might starve.

NANCY: Frogs eat flies. We sometimes have flies in the house.

MOTHER: Not enough to feed a frog, at least I hope not. I don't like flies in the house.

NANCY: Me neither. The frog will catch them for us.

MOTHER: There won't be enough flies for a hungry frog.

NANCY: We could leave the screen door open.

MOTHER: Then the mosquitos would come in too and eat us while the frog is eating the flies.

NANCY: Oh no. Wouldn't it be nice if all the flies and mosquitos died?

MOTHER: I'd like that, but then the frogs wouldn't have anything to eat. And a lot of fish that eat flies would go hungry.

NANCY: If they got too hungry we could make them some flies. No, that's silly. We couldn't if they were all dead, because only a Mommy and Daddy fly can make more flies. But how did the first fly get made when there were no Mommy and Daddy flies?

This child, not yet 5, was already quite a good problem solver and her question, "How did the first fly get made . . . ? ," reflected her sudden awareness that there was something missing in her understanding of how flies came to be.

Teach About Locations and Spatial Relationships

The things out there are not isolated entities; they enter into spatial relationships with each other. Some things are inside other things, or next to them, or on top of them, among many other juxtapositions. As babies spontaneously move their playthings about they often seem to be exploring these relationships, placing things on, in, or next to other things with interest and purpose. Many toys are designed to give young children practice in these relationships. Stacking cups, blocks, Legos, and other familiar construction toys will give virtually any child many hours of intensely focused pleasure. As your child manipulates the objects of his world, give him the words that describe the relationships he is creating ("Do you want to put the little block *on* the big one?"). Also, provide demonstrations of the various relationships ("Let's see. I'm going to put the green one *in* the blue one. Hey, Mr. Green, do you want to go in there? Good. In you go.").

Aesthetics enters into the constructions of 3- and 4-year-olds. As they stack their blocks, they make and unmake choices over and over, continually evaluating and improving their growing structures. And they are often quite proud of what they've built and seek your appreciation of their creation. As you praise their efforts, describe what you see ("You put the long one across those two like a bridge. That looks great."). Any artist, even a 3-year-old one, likes it when the details of his or her work are noticed and appreciated. Detailed descriptions also provide you with the opportunity to teach new relational terms, such as "across" in the above example.

Teaching a child about spatial relationships must, of course, go beyond a set of abstract terms like "in" and "on." Most things in the child's natural world are not located in, on, or next to other things in some arbitrary, ever-changing way; rather, they occupy specific locations and have identifying names. Cups go in cupboards; cupboards are in kitchens or pantries, which are in specific dwellings at specific, numbered locales. The more you label the places in your child's environment, the more readily she will develop a mental map of the world about her and feel competent to maneuver through that world. For instance, you can ask your toddler to help you put away groceries: "You put in the things that go on the bottom shelves. The tissues go in the big cabinet. The sponges go in the cabinet under the sink. The soap goes in the bathroom. Would you get me a paper bag from the front closet?" Similarly, on your daily walks point out and label landmarks: "Tommy lives in that building. His window is right above the bank."

Maps and globes illustrate spatial relationships, and preschoolers can be introduced to them and will find them informative if the information is connected to their own lives. For example, if a parent is going on a business trip, a globe or map showing the starting point, route, and destination will usually be of interest. Similarly, if a beloved grandparent lives in a distant city, you can trace the route of her journey when she visits, or the route of a letter mailed to her. Translate distance into concrete time periods, such as "She lives in Baltimore. That's far away. If we got in the car right after breakfast and headed out past McDonalds, and then drove and drove, we'd get to Baltimore just in time for lunch."

You can also draw simple maps together of well-known neighborhood landmarks. The more you let your child fill in, the better. For instance, you might ask, "After we get to the supermarket, do you remember which way we go to the video store? Do we make a right turn (pointing right) or a left turn (pointing left)? Yes [as child points right]. So let's put in a street going off to the right on our map so we can draw in the video store." Then use the map on your next walk and check the accuracy together. Research shows that even 4-year-olds can use maps effectively to learn layouts and locations.[39]

Another important relationship is *part/whole:* all things are a part of other things. Children appear to notice this without any help from us, and they certainly don't need any lessons in taking things apart. Moreover they recognize similarities between objects based on their having similar parts (deer and horses are "closer" animals than deer and snakes).[40]

Parents help their children with part/whole relationships by giving them the appropriate words, such as "part," "piece," "portion," "some," "half," "slice," "segment," "ingredient," "section," "more," and "all," among many others. They also have to teach them about part/whole relationships that won't be obvious to them, such as that all things are made up of atoms; that food can have nutritious ingredients as well as not-so-nutritious ingredients; that our bodies have lungs, a heart, and many other vital organs; and that when some things are taken apart they can't be put back together (alas, poor Humpty).

Some part/whole relationships are based on the functional properties of each part and how each contributes to the whole. For example, a seat is part of a chair and necessary for the chair to function as a chair. An enjoyable way to introduce your child to this notion is to design something together. For instance, if you design a car together, you can "discover" that it will need a way to get it moving, a way to stop it, a way to steer it, a way to back it up, a way to signal which way it is turning, a way to clear the windshield of rain, and many other functions.

Many activity books have part/whole lessons in the form of "What's missing?" problems. There are also some enjoyable children's books (such as *Wacky Wednesday*) that include part/whole lessons. Throughout their school years, children will continue to learn to divide the things they study into their functional and structural parts—for example, the parts of the body (skeleton, organs, etc.), the parts of an engine, and the parts or regions of a country.

Inside/outside is another aspect of objects that children need to learn about. The insides of many things (such as fruit, machines, and animals) usually don't look like their outsides. Insides and outside are usually made of different substances and serve different functions. Whenever possible expose the insides of things to your child and point out the structural and functional differences between inside and outside ("The peel of the orange skin is thick and strong and bitter to protect the inside from bugs").

Researcher Jean Carew provides an interesting example of a father teaching his son about an important relationship: the interposition of one object in front of another:

Father is reading to John, age 33-months, Ezra Keats' story "Goggles." They turn to a picture showing the dog Willy running away with the goggles through a hole in a fence. In the picture the dog's face is half hidden behind the fence. John looks and tells Father: "Doggie face broken." Father explains, "No, it's not broken. It's hiding behind the fence." John looks puzzled. He asks, "Hiding?" Father demonstrates. "See my hand. Now, see it hide when I move it behind the book?" John watches intently. Father continues, "Now, see it come out again. It's not broken. It was hiding." John imitates Father's action several times, passing his hand behind the book and watching it reappear.[41]

Point Out Similarities and Differences

Introducing a child to differences and similarities can start during the early weeks. For example, you can rub a baby's hand over a formica surface as you say the word "smooth" and then immediately rub his hand gently over something grainy and rough as you say the word "rough."

Repeat this a few times, and, if possible, bring the surfaces into contact with other parts of the child's skin (such as the cheeks, which are very sensitive). On each presentation use an animated voice, differentiating your tone for each object (say, by using a higher, more elongated sound for smooth than rough).

After a few presentations show delight in your child's growing "comprehension" of the difference. The word, *comprehension* is in quotes because, in fact, your baby won't be able to communicate to you if and when he begins to appreciate the difference you are presenting; nor will you be sure when he starts to connect each experience with its proper word. Yet, parents who are good teachers do just what I've described: They intuitively give their baby credit for learning whatever it is they are teaching. So, on perhaps the third go-round of presenting the smooth and rough surfaces, they might exclaim, "Yes, that's right, *smooth* (as they present the smooth surface again), *rough* (as they present the rough surface). Yes, now you have it."

Whether or not the baby has really learned anything, the celebration of learning seems to have a beneficial effect. Actually, there is good reason to believe very young children can learn such basic sensory discriminations and connect them to words. As I've pointed out, they can discern words very early (even making such fine distinctions as the sound "pa" from "ba"). And given how well their sensory systems function, it is probable that during their early weeks they can discriminate smooth from rough, hard from soft, warm from cool, and many other basic tactual experiences. There is even evidence that they can visually distinguish objects that they have not seen before but have held in their hands and placed in their mouths.[42]

You can find many kinds of contrasting experiences to present to your child. For babies, use basic sensory qualities employing all the senses. Include color distinctions also ("That's a *blue* ball. Here's a *red* ball. Blue ball. Red ball. Blue! Red!"). If your child isn't interested he'll show you by resisting as you move his hand, or by looking away, or by seeming to look through what you are showing him—or by crying. It is as important to be sensitive to your child's disinterests as his interests. Also, keep in mind that during their first month or two, babies tend to focus on the outlines of objects and faces; it is not until they are 2- to 3-months old that their gaze regularly appears to take in an entire object by focusing primarily on its central features.[43]

Sorting objects with your child is a fun way to focus him or her on similarities and differences ("Let's put all the red checkers in this box and all the black one's in there"; "Let's separate the big spoons from the little spoons''; ''Let's put the furniture here and the utensils there''). The educational value of doing sorting tasks, like any tasks, depends on how parents present information to the child. This was demonstrated some years ago in an interesting study by child psychologists Robert Hess and Virginia Shipman. They observed mothers teaching their children to sort various kinds of objects. They found that the mothers who taught more successfully did not merely give orders about where items should go; nor did they demean or threaten the child over mistakes. Instead, they drew their child's attention to the specific differences that needed to be considered, they presented the task as something fun to do, and they remained encouraging even when the child made mistakes, taking responsibility upon themselves for making the task requirements clearer if the child wasn't getting it.

The authors provide some quotes from the mothers as examples of effective and ineffective teaching (the *a*'s are from effective teachers, the *b*'s are from ineffective ones):

1a. ''I've got another game to teach you.''
1b. ''There's another thing you have to learn here, so sit down and pay attention.''
2a. ''Now listen to Mommy carefully and watch what I do because I'm going to show you how we play the game.''
2b. ''Pay attention now and get it right, 'cause you're gonna have to show the lady how to do it later.''
3a. ''No, Johnny. That's a big one. Remember we're going to keep the big ones separate from the little ones.''
3b. ''No, that's not what I showed you! Put that with the big ones where it belongs.''
4a. ''Wait a minute, Johnny. You have to look at the block first before you try to find where it goes. Now pick it up again and look at it—is it big or small? . . . Now put it where it goes.''
4b. ''That doesn't go there—you're just guessing. I'm trying to show you how to do this and you're just putting them any old place. Now pick it up and do it again and this time don't mess up.
5a. ''No, we can't stop now, Johnny. Mrs. Smith wants me to show you how to do this so you can do it for her. Now if you pay close attention and let Mommy teach you, you can learn how to do it and show her, and then you'll have some time to play.''
5b. ''Now you're playing around and you don't even know how to do this. You want me to call the lady? You better listen to what I'm saying and quit playing around or I'm gonna call the lady in on you and see how you like that.''[44]

Notice that the mothers who were good teachers stressed the principles and operations of successful sorting ("keep the big ones separate from the little ones," "You have to look at the block first before you try to find where it goes"), while the poor teachers stressed blind imitation and treated mistakes as acts of disobedience ("No, that's not what I showed you! Put that with the big ones where it belongs," "I'm trying to show you how to do this and you're just putting them any old place").

In a later study that followed children from preschool to early adolescence, Hess found that children of mothers who instructed more through prompting than commanding turned out to have superior intellectual ability as measured on standard test of mathematical and verbal scholastic apptitude. The effective mothers drew their children's attention to relevant characteristics of the task ("How are these blocks alike?"), rather than telling them what to do ("Now I want you to put the tall ones together and the short ones together").[45]

During their second year babies are ready to learn about similarities and differences that are based on structural and functional aspects of objects, not merely their basic sensory qualities or overall appearance. For instance, they recognize the essential similarities between a sneaker and a terry-cloth slipper. Piaget said children couldn't sort objects into these kinds of "taxonomic" categories until they were about 6, but recent studies show that children make these connections even before they are 2.[46]

During your child's second year you can start to introduce such details as that bird babies come from eggs while dog and cat babies are born "live" right out of their mommies. A 3-year-old can understand that people, cows, and whales, as different as they appear, are all mammals who feed their babies milk from their mothers' breasts (or mammaries). With proper illustrations the 4-year-old can understand the similarities between a skeleton and the frame of a building, that both determine the shapes of the structures they support and enable them to remain upright.

Examples of similarities and differences are available everywhere. Starting when your child is about 2, your everyday rounds through the neighborhood can provide wonderful opportunities for pointing out lots of interesting similarities and differences, such as in buildings, trees, rocks, people, animals, doorways, cloud patterns, shadows, clothing, lettering on signs, and on and on. (Of course, one wouldn't present all of these at once.)

When your child is a little older, you may want to take one or another kind of field guide with you on a walk in the country to help discover similarities and differences in birds, trees and plants (distinguishing evergreens from deciduous trees, ferns from flowering plants), and rocks (distinguishing igneous, sedimentary, and metamorphic rocks, such as, respectively, granite, limestone, and slate).

Look also for unusual similarities. A group of noisy ducks and geese at a pond might be labeled the "duck band." Children generally are tickled by such nonobvious similarities and will come up with some good ones on their own. One 5-year-old referred to the natural history museum as a "dead zoo." Another child, not yet 5, referred to a dog pound as "an orphanage for dogs." The same child, at about the same age, was sharing a swimming tube with her friend. They ran and danced through the house with it around their hips. The child chuckled with self-satisfaction as she exclaimed, "We're dancing in our two-tube," delighted with her own clever wordplay on "tutu."

As you point out differences between things made by people, talk about what the differences are based on. Are they primarily for aesthetic reasons ("He did it that way because he thought it would be prettier") or for functional reasons ("Those windows keep the cold out better")? You want your child to appreciate that many of the things out there were made by people on purpose, for a purpose. You also want to stimulate her thinking about whether the purpose was fulfilled. And even young children can understand that when it comes to aesthetic purposes people's tastes can differ and no one's has priority ("Daddy likes pizza with soft, thick crust. I like pizza with thin, crispy crust. Which do you like better?"). Also, try to describe what your aesthetic preference is based on (e.g., crispiness). That way your child will understand that differences in taste are based on definite qualities that can be perceived and compared (though not always easily described).

If you are aware of a functional principle that lies behind any similarities or differences point it out to your child. You might, for example, point out to a 4- or 5-year-old the many triangles that are found in buildings, bridges, towers, and other structures, and indicate that "The triangle is the strongest structure." You can then demonstrate the strength of triangles by building a structure together, testing its strength (the weight it will support), and then adding triangular supports (buttresses) and testing its strength again. You might want to buy a box of tongue depressors at your pharmacy for construction projects like this.

Point out that similarities and differences in nature's objects are also usually associated with function. For example, the different sizes and shapes of birds' beaks reflect the kind of food they eat. And, while feathers and fur are similar in that both are coverings that provide protection from the weather, their differences are important too: imagine what would happen to a water bird (such as a duck) or an ordinary bird in flight during a rainstorm if its feathers soaked up water the way dog fur does. The giraffe's long neck and the elephant's trunk are conspicuous instances of the relationship between structure and function. And, of course, one finds significant differences between land animals, sea animals, and flying animals.

You also want your child to understand that many important similarities and differences are not at all based on surface features—that things can look different but be alike in some fundamental way. For example a person's home and a snail's shell don't look alike, yet both provide shelter for their occupant. Similarly, oil and wind don't look alike yet both contain energy that can do work for us ("How are a windmill and a gas engine alike?").

Conversely, many things that look similar are critically different in important ways. For instance, dogs and wolves look alike yet are fundamentally different in temperament and trainability. Dolphins and sharks look more alike than dolphins and humans, yet dolphins and humans are more similar in many vital physiological and social characteristics (e.g., both breathe air and nurse and protect their young). Museum and zoological exhibitions usually highlight these kinds of unexpected similarities and differences, as do various illustrated science and nature books for children. Research shows that even 3-year-olds can ignore surface similarities and appreciate more fundamental characteristics (for instance, they recognize that white and brown sugar are more alike than brown sugar and brown sand which look more alike).[47]

In order to describe similarities and differences, you'll need to familiarize your child with a number of terms expressing comparisons, such as bigger, smaller, tighter, thinner, faster, alike, different, and a sizable number of similar terms and their opposites. Preschoolers generally develop a pretty good understanding of these, as well as multiple comparisons such as big, bigger, biggest.[48] In presenting these terms, keep references as concrete as possible so your child can conjure clear images: "Toby is big; Mommy is bigger; Daddy is biggest." "Horses are big; elephants are bigger; whales are biggest."

Sometime during their third or fourth year children become fascinated by similarities and differences between living and nonliving entities. You'll get lots of questions on what it means to be alive, what makes people and animals die, what death is like, and how to be certain whether or not something is living. Three-year-olds, on their own, recognize self-initiated movement as a characteristic of living things, but the vital signs of plants, such as respiration, reproduction, and metabolic processes, are less visible and children, therefore, need more instruction on why plants are alive.[49]

Some questions in this domain can be handled fairly easily: living things breathe, need food, and reproduce. Also, 3- and four-year-olds generally enjoy question/answer games focusing on the category, *alive*. You can ask, "Is a horse alive?" "Is a lamp alive?" "Is the sun alive?" "Is a car alive?" "Is a fly alive?" For each answer explain why it is correct or incorrect. Keep in mind that these explanations needn't turn a game into a dry and formal lesson, which is inappropriate for children this age. Asking your child, "Can you imagine a lamp having a baby?" will convey an essential characteristic of living beings and at the same time give her the opportunity to express a gleeful "No!" as she visualizes baby lamps cuddling up to a large "Mommy" lamp.

While parents generally handle "what's alive" questions with little trouble, many become extremely uncomfortable when their child asks about death and dying. It is difficult to find answers that are candid yet not frightening. Still, these questions should be taken seriously, otherwise you will be communicating to your child that there are domains that are taboo to ask about or perhaps even to think about, regardless of how curious he is about them.

Analogies are based on similarities and a recent study by Marilyn Nippold and Michael Sullivan at the University of Oregon found that children as young as 5 were able to solve analogy problems of the type, "*Dentist* goes with *teeth* and *barber* goes with . . . Is it scissors, comb, or *hair?*" To solve analogy problems the child must compare a relationship (dentists *work on* teeth; barbers *work on* hair), and not look for surface similarities between the parts. Parents can point out analogical relationships to children and also play analogy games with them. Here are some of the analogies from the Nippold and Sullivan study (the correct answer is in italics):

Dog goes with *doghouse* and *bird* goes with . . . Is it sky, *cage,* or duck?

Sled goes with *snow* and *train* goes with . . . Is it *track,* caboose, or plane?

Bird goes with *nest* and *car* goes with . . . Is it *garage,* road, or truck?

Farmer goes with *farm* and *doctor* goes with . . . Is it sick person, *hospital,* or medicine?

Ear goes with radio and eye goes with . . . Is it *newspaper,* glasses, or eyebrow?

I've found that some 4-year-olds, if they are reminded to focus on the relationship between terms, can do these analogies and enjoy figuring them out:

MOTHER: In what way do a sled and snow go together? What's their relationship?

SARAH: A sled rides on snow.

MOTHER: Yes. Now which thing goes with a train in the same way as a sled goes with snow: tracks, a caboose, or a plane?''

An interesting study by Stella Vosniadou and Marlene Schommer demonstrated the value of using analogies for imparting factual information to young children. They read short essays to children between the ages of 5 and 8, covering such technical areas as the causes and stages of infections, the social organization of termite societies, and the workings of the stomach. The *analogical* versions of the stories had sentences like, ''An infection is like a war. . . . Your body fights the infection like a country fights the enemy''; ''Termite societies are like kingdoms''; and ''The stomach is like a blender.'' According to the researchers, children who heard these versions, including many of the five-year-olds, ''retained more information,'' and had ''richer representations'' than those who were just given the facts.[50]

Parents can obviously use similar techniques when providing information to their children: ''A beehive is like an apartment house for bees''; ''The president is like the head teacher.''

Metaphors, similes, and other figures of speech are based on similarities, but not of obvious surface features. ''Be as quiet as a mouse'' is a common expression using a simile. Shakespeare's ''the slings and arrows of outrageous fortune'' and ''a sea of troubles,'' both from *Hamlet,* are well-known examples of metaphor. Imaginative and appropriate figures of speech are one of the foundation stones of great writing and effective speaking. One way to encourage your child's understanding and use of figures of speech is to play word games based on them. For instance, you can give him or her an example of a figure of speech, such as, ''The teacher told the children to be as quiet as mice.'' Then ask, ''What else could she have told them to be as quiet as?'' One 5-year-old came up with ''As quiet as a light bulb.'' Another said ''As quiet as a rainbow.'' A third chimed in, ''As quiet as a clam.''

You will encourage the use of figures of speech if you show your appreciation for them when your child comes up with them on her own. Children often start to use figures of speech spontaneously when they are 4 or 5. Here are some examples:

''There was a traffic jam on the slide'' (at 4 years, 8 months).

''We are weeding the toy chest'' (at 4 years, 10 months).

''My belly hurts. My belly and my food are having an argument'' (at 4 years, 9 months).

''It's an orphanage for dogs'' (at 4 years, 10 months, while watching the movie *Lady and the Tramp*).

Also point out metaphors that come up in everyday speech or that you come across in your reading. You might ask, "Do you know what it means if someone is called a *stone hearted* man?"

Graphs and charts are another way to bring your child's attention to similarities and differences. Children enjoy these. For example, you can make a chart listing the basic food categories along the top and the days of the week down the side; then have your child write in the foods that fall under each column as he or she eats them. Discuss his or her eating pattern at the end of a week. Then see whether the pattern is consistent across a series of weeks.

You might make a bar graph for keeping a record of cloud patterns, creating a column for each basic type (many children's science books have illustrations of cloud patterns). Then each day check the clouds and add a unit to the column listing the clouds you've seen. Compare graphs that were made in different seasons. This should lead to interesting discussions about how much information you need before you can conclude that clouds patterns are different in different seasons.

Describe Concepts and Classes

The world you want to teach your child about is not made up of totally unique entities, each with its own label. Items are grouped together based on shared features. The word "triangle" refers to objects that differ greatly from each other, but all will have three sides and three angles. When a child applies the word "triangle" to all such three-sided forms, we say he or she has learned the *concept* triangle. Similarly, the word "horse" refers to animals that differ in many ways from each other, but all have certain features in common. "Horse" is a *concept* that embraces all animals displaying those features (which are a lot easier to recognize than describe).

Teaching children concepts is an important part of teaching them what's out there. Concepts help them organize their diverse experiences into meaningful units, putting together things that appear to belong together and distinguishing things that seem different.

You teach concepts by:

1. Showing a child different instances of the concept (such as triangles in many different forms and colors) and referring to all of them with the same label;

2. Pointing out the defining features of the concept as well as you can ("See, it's a triangle because it has three sides that meet at three points");

3. Contrasting instances of the concept with noninstances, say by showing a triangle next to a rectangle and labeling both;

4. Testing for learning by seeing if she uses the proper word when encountering new instances of the concept (when she calls a triangle that's unlike any she's seen before "triangle"). At first you might have to ask questions like, "What's that one with the three points?"—questions that remind her of the essential features. Later, a simple, "What's that?" should be adequate. As she gains more experience and her language skills develop, you can ask her to pick out the defining features of concepts ("What makes that a triangle?").

Much of any parent's concept teaching takes place in informal conversations with his or her child. Your child might ask you about the air vents on the VCR or some other machine and you might explain that all machines heat up when they are on and the vents let the heat out so the machine won't overheat and break. In other words, the concept *machine* includes the feature "heat producing." On another occasion, as you read your child a story about a boy who went out for a school team, he might ask "What's a 'team'?" In answering, you will try to provide him with the essential features of the concept *team* in a manner he can understand.

Preschoolers start to use many different kinds of concepts besides those referring directly to *things* as concrete entities. Conditions, such as "health" and "illness," and moral and aesthetic qualities, such as "truth," "justice," and "beauty" are concepts, and preschoolers generally begin to use these notions in their daily discourse. The principles of teaching these kinds of abstract concepts are the same as for any other kind of concept: give examples, describe the essential features, contrast with counterexamples, check on learning with new instances, and correct mistakes. You'll find, though, that the essential features of these abstract notions are generally harder to isolate (philosophers have been debating the essential features of justice, beauty, and other moral and aesthetic concepts for thousands of years).

Concepts referring to bodily states (hunger, toothache) and personal characteristics (greedy, smart) are also more difficult to teach since they can't be pointed to in the same way as concrete objects. They must be inferred from behavior (we infer a toothache when someone moans and holds his jaw). Still, by three, children begin to use abstract and dispositional terms appropriately,[51] though they still make mistakes and need correction (as in the case of a 3-year-old who said "It's not *fair*" whenever she didn't get her way).

The world out there is not only organized into concepts, but the concepts are organized into relationships called classes. Dog, cow, and mammal are all concepts, but dog and cow fall *under* the concept mammal since all dogs and cows are also mammals. In turn, mammal falls under the concept animal in the sense that all mammals are animals. You can start pointing out these kinds of relationships before your child is 2. *Food* is a natural category to start with since young children already know the names of many foods and also know that foods are different from nonfoods. They will readily understand that the concepts, apple, meat, and desserts, all fall under the heading "foods."

Activity books are helpful for teaching classes. They will usually have a page with pictures of foods (apple, banana, cake) and nonfoods, and the child's task is to circle all the foods (or nonfoods). They'll have similar pages with dwellings, vehicles, and animals, among other kinds of objects. Children usually love to do these kinds of tasks. You can also play games with your child to teach class hierarchies, such as "Name all the things in this room that are made of wood."

Psychologist Roger Brown, in a classic paper, pointed out that children learn higher and lower level concepts equally readily. Sometimes they learn lower level, more concrete, concepts first (they learn "apple" and "orange" before they learn "fruit"), and sometimes they learn higher level, more abstract concepts first (they learn "fish" before they learn "bass" and "perch"). Which level they start with depends on which words parents introduce them to first, and this, he suggests, depends on which distinctions parents find it important to communicate to their young children. It is more useful for young children to know the words "table" and "chair" than the more abstract term "furniture"; on the other hand, it is more useful for them to know the word "car" than the brand names Chevrolet and Plymouth.[52]

There has been some controversy among developmental psychologists about children's understanding of class relations. Piaget claimed that before the age of 5, children cannot appreciate the essential features of a class and will lump things together in illogical ways. He also said that before the age of 7 they cannot recognize that a higher level class (flowers) is larger than a subordinate class (primroses). Various studies show that here, as in many other areas, he underestimated children's abilities. He discounted the fact that in their everyday language, young children seem to have a good understanding of class relations (for instance, they know that dogs, cats, horses, etc. are animals), and instead drew his conclusions from how children responded on abstract sorting tasks (sorting circles and squares of various colors) and tricky "class inclusion" problems in which, for example, he would give children 18 brown wooden beads and 2 white wooden beads and ask them whether there were more brown beads or wooden beads. I've found that 4-year-olds can do well on these kinds of questions if you use objects familiar to them ("Are there more chairs or more pieces of furniture?").[53]

Many 5- and 6-year-olds love to make lists. They'll make lists of class-mates, shopping lists, lists of their toys, lists of their favorite animals, lists of birthdays. One parent reported that her child (5 years, 8 months) made a list in pictures of things that needed repair around the home, including a sluggish drain, a leaky faucet, and a bathrobe with a torn pocket. All this list-making reflects children's increasing awareness of categories and classes—of what goes together (such as, "Things that need to be repaired"). Try suggesting some lists to your children that will help them make new connections between things. Some possibilities are things that keep us warm, animals that lay eggs, books that taught me something new, types of jobs, and electrical machines around the house (including battery-operated ones).

Point Out the Transitions Things Go Through

In teaching your child about the world, teach him or her about the regular transitions that things go through: water turns into ice and steam; the moon goes through monthly phases; people age; objects wear out; caterpillars turn into butterflies; puppies turn into dogs; tides ebb and flow; the weather goes through seasonal changes. All of these things retain aspects of their identity as they change in significant ways.

There are many ways to teach about these transitions. Children's nature books often have pictures of caterpillars turning into butterflies and land-scapes changing with the seasons. There are companies that will send you caterpillars and a kit for observing them turn into butterflies (check parenting magazines for addresses). You may have photographs of Grandma taken when she was young. You can demonstrate the transitions of water into ice and steam right in your kitchen. There is also a popular children's story, *The Snow Lion*, about a lion who goes to the mountains to get away from the heat, discovers snow there, and repeatedly packs some in a bag to bring back to his hot friends below; but each time he opens the bag to show them his frosty treasure he finds that his snow has disappeared. Children love to shout out "It melted" in response to being asked, "What happened to the snow?"

Ask and Encourage "What's Out There" Questions

"What's that called?" "Where does the key go?" "Who says 'meow'?" "What's that smell?" "What do cows say?" "What did the dog do when he saw the other dog?" "What did you see at the zoo?" These kinds of questions increase children's awareness of the world around them by remind-ing them of their experiences and drawing their attention to details they might not otherwise take note of. They also stimulate children's language development.[54] Such questions let children know that you are interested in their experiences and impressions of the world.

Make sure your questions cover all the senses, including the various types of bodily experiences such as temperature ("What's the coldest thing you touched today?"), pains ("Does your finger throb?"), and emotionally aroused autonomic sensation ("When you were waiting for your turn to dance, what did your belly feel like?").

The Nobel Prize winning physicist, Isidor Rabi, was asked, "Why did you become a scientist, rather than a doctor or lawyer or businessman, like the other immigrant kids in your neighborhood?" His reply was, "My mother made me a scientist without ever intending it. Every other Jewish mother in Brooklyn would ask her child after school: 'So? Did you learn anything today?' But not my mother. She always asked me a different question. 'Izzy,' she would say, 'did you ask a good question today?' That difference—asking good questions—made me become a scientist!"[55]

Children don't need to be taught to ask questions. But once they start asking them, the kinds of replies they receive can affect their future question asking. Showing interest in and trying to answer your child's questions will certainly encourage questioning.[56] For child or adult, the best reinforcer for question asking is getting useful answers. You should also reinforce your child's question asking with statements like, "That's a good question," "I'm glad you ask when you don't understand something." "You ask such intelligent questions," "I love the fact that you want to know all these things." You want to communicate that asking questions is admirable because it leads to learning.

Parents can also encourage question asking through what psychologists call "attribution" processes. For instance, a father might say to his daughter, "You're an inquisitive girl. Do you know what that means? It means you ask lots of questions because you want to know lots and lots of things. And I think that inquisitive is a good thing to be because you find the world so interesting, and it makes you really interesting to talk to." This father is doing more than just giving praise. He is openly attributing to his daughter a love for learning, giving her a label ("inquisitive"), and identifying that label as desirable. All this is likely to affect her self-concept. She will come to label herself as inquisitive and be proud of it. In general, psychologists have found that attributing desirable qualities to children motivates them to shift their behavior in the direction of those qualities. Children like it when others call them "good" or "smart" and they will try hard not to lose a label they are proud of.[57] A child who enjoys thinking of herself as inquisitive—because she has been described that way by her parents—is likely to keep asking questions.

Three-year-olds can ask a lot of questions. It's wonderful, but also disconcerting for parents who sometimes tire of hearing "What's dat?" and "Why?" a hundred times a day, and who often don't know how to answer questions in a way their child can understand. But the one thing a good teacher never wants to do is discourage questions. Indeed, it's vital that your child sense that you love and cherish his questions. The key to answering them is to give explanations in concrete terms that draw upon what the child can experience directly or already knows. Here's a mother trying to do that in response to the question, "Where does the sun go?":

It goes that way (pointing west). See, the sky is still a little light over there, but it's already dark back the other way. That's because the sun has moved way over there now. When it goes a little further away it'll be dark here, it'll be night. Do you know who lives that way (pointing west again)? Joshua. The sun is going to Joshua's house. It's still night where Joshua lives so he's sleeping now. But when the sun gets there in a few hours it'll bring the day with it and he'll get up. First it's going to Joshua's house, and then it goes further to where Dorothy lives and it'll wake her up. And then it makes a big circle and comes back here and wakes us up.

Later she tried to help her youngster visualize the path of the sun by using a globe and pointing out landmarks that the child could grasp from previous conversations, such as where Joshua lived. By shining a flashlight on the globe she also tried to convey that it is the earth spinning that makes the sun appear to move.

In responding to your child's questions, always admit when you don't know an answer and tell him that you will do your best to find it out. Discuss what you'll do to find the answer, and have your child participate as fully as possible in the research process. You want him to understand that it is okay not to know things, and that looking for answers can be fun. You also want him to learn how to find answers to a question, which might mean asking an expert, consulting a book or encyclopedia, or conducting an experiment of some sort to learn the answer on one's own.

Make Counting and Measuring a Natural Part of Activities

It's hard to tell what an infant learns when a parent playfully counts his or her fingers and toes out loud, as most parents do: "One finger, two fingers, three fingers . . ." As each finger is wiggled, one word stays the same ("finger(s)") and one word varies ("one," "two"). This common exchange may very well spark the child's first awareness of an orderly sequence. In another version of finger counting, parents wiggle one finger, then two fingers together, then three, and so on, as they say "One finger, two fingers . . ." It may be that the child's awareness of counting begins with these and similar number games during early infancy.

Ultimately, for successful counting, children need to learn that each item in a set must be assigned a single term ("one" or "two" but not both), that the terms are assigned in a particular order ("one" first, "two" second, etc.), and that the last number of the count specifies the number of objects in the set (obvious to adults but not to children). They also need to learn counting strategies so they won't count the same item in an array more than once. They can learn all this by the age of three or four.[58]

There are many formats for introducing counting as you acquaint your baby with what's out there. For instance, hold up one ball and say "*One* ball"; hold up two balls and say "*Two* balls." Then repeat a few times. Then add a third ball. You can do the same thing with "One nose, two eyes" as you touch the child's nose and eyes or your own.

When should you begin introducing numbers and counting in this way? Numbers and counting can be integrated into your earliest play with your child, and research shows that children are responsive to, and benefit from, parental instruction in number skills. As with anything you introduce, let your child's attentiveness be your guide as to the appropriateness and timing of your presentations. Two- and 3-year-olds readily learn to count, and by the time children reach 3 or 4, many display a strong interest in counting and will often insist on counting objects they are playing with.[59] Knowing *how many* is another way children master their environments, and it is usually important to them to get their counts right.

Don't be surprised if your child begins a count all over after you've corrected her ("After five comes six, not eight"), and she'll probably be noticeably pleased with herself when she gets it all right. It's not uncommon for 5-year-olds to count to a hundred and beyond, and contrary to some popular beliefs, children have little difficulty understanding the meaning of zero.

Counting things can be a natural part of everyday activities and games, and anything can be counted. For example, during a reading session you might say, "Let's pick three books to read." As you select them count, "One . . . two . . . three." Then when you have them all together, say, "Let's make sure we have three. One, two, three." As you read each, you can introduce ordinal numbers: "This is the *first* book. This is the *second*." As your child learns numbers, ask him or her to do the counting, and provide prompts as needed. You can make the question, "How many are there?" a regular part of your activities with objects. Another effective strategy is to ask your child for help in counting something (such as coins for the laundry machines). Children feel very grown up when they can use new skills to help others. Asking, ''Could you give me two of those?'' is another way to bring numbers into everyday interactions.

Having your child group objects will introduce him to another basic arithmetic skill and provide additional opportunities for counting practice. A peg board is useful (''Put the green ones in this line and the red ones here''). You might also try asking him to put different colored marbles in different see-through bags and then mark the bags with the number of marbles inserted. This will give him practice in associating a set of objects with the proper number. Later put objects in numbered bags that he can't see through and ask for the bag by number.

Activity books and puzzles provide enjoyable number learning-tasks (such as connecting the numbered dots), as well as exercises for children to learn to count and associate written numbers with sets of objects (''Write the number of kangaroos in the picture''). Other common exercises involve following instructions relating to quantity (''Color three balloons red and two balloons yellow''), and matching numbered stickers to numbers printed on the pages.

You'll also find that elevators and numbers on landings in apartment buildings provide opportunities for number learning, as do television sets with push-botton numbers and the brightly colored magnetic number sets made by various toy companies. By the age of 3 or 4, children can certainly learn to identify the written numbers zero through ten and apply them correctly to a set of objects.

Teaching young children these skills doesn't imply that one is ''pushing'' a child or damaging him in any way. On the contrary, if counting is made a part of the natural play activities of children, they pick up counting with ease and joy. If a preschooler isn't ready for counting he won't show any interest in it, won't pay attention when you count objects (such as marbles) for him, and won't make an effort when you ask, ''How many marbles are there?'' He will simply continue playing with the marbles. You *will* be ''pushing'' if you then stop the game and insist that he attend to the counting. It is totally unnecessary to do this, just as it is totally unnecessary to set special time aside to teach and drill him in counting skills. If counting is incorporated into the natural activities of the child, he'll soon discover that it is a useful skill and it will give him pleasure to master it.

Here is a good example of a parent incorporating counting into a game in a natural way:

Let's play a marble game with Minnie and Billie (two dolls). They're going to try to roll their marbles into this cup. First we have to give them each four marbles. You be the official marble dispenser—you give them each their marbles. Ready? Okay, now give Minnie one marble. Good. Now give Billie one. They have to start with the same amount. Give them each another one. That one for Minnie, that one for Billie. Good, now they each have two. Two more to each. That's three for Minnie and three for Billie. One more each. Now they each have four. We'd better count them just to be sure they are both starting with the same amount. I'll count Minnie's: one, two, three, four. You count Billie's. (If counting is still new for the child, the parent will have to speak the numbers and may even have to guide the child's finger from marble to marble; the child will usually say each number after the parent does.)

The card game "Go Fish," which involves matching pairs, is an effective and fun way to teach another basic arithmetic skill, finding identities. Even 3-year-olds can enjoy simple versions of this if parents are very loose about the rules. You can use regular cards (half a deck) or buy one of the versions that base the matching on colors, animals, or other objects. Other simple card games, like "Old Maid," provide practice in matching and counting, such as counting pairs to see who wins.

Blocks provide many opportunities for counting and comparing quantities ("There are three on this side. Put three more there"). Also, many simple board games provide good practice in counting. For example, in "Shoots and Ladders," pieces have to be moved a certain number of spaces and each space is numbered. Dominoes and games using dice give children practice in associating numbers with visible quantities. Bingo provides practice in identifying numbers, as well as in attending to two dimensions at once.

Many traditional children's games incorporate numbers ("You may take three giant steps"). You can also make up an endless variety of new games: "See if you can clap your hands the same number of times that I clap my hands." Then reverse roles. Also try to find a Velcro or magnetized dart game that uses multiples of 10 for scoring (10, 20, 30, etc.). It's a good way to introduce your child to higher numbers.

A handy tool for teaching counting, as well as the names and values of coins, is a coin dispenser—the kind that taxi drivers and outdoor concessionaires use. Children love to insert coins in the correct slots and push the levers to make the coins reappear at the bottom. They will eagerly play fantasy games with you, enacting taxi drivers, concessionaires, and salesclerks receiving coins for purchases and giving change.

There are also fun ditties that provide excellent lessons in counting and also make the idea of zero concrete and visualizable. For instance:

There were five freckled frogs
Sitting on a speckled log
Eating the most delightful bugs,
Yum, yum.
One jumped in to the pool
Where it was nice and cool,
Then there were four freckled frogs.

This is repeated until none (or zero) frogs are left. Three- and 4-year-olds usually love such songs and learn them quickly.

Four-year-olds generally enjoy simple addition and subtraction problems such as, "If there are two ducks swimming in a pond and two of their friends come to join them, then how many ducks are in the pond?" A subtraction problem would be, "There are three birds in a tree. One sees some yummy food and flies off. How many birds are left?" As the child becomes more skillful with these kinds of questions and more familiar with large numbers, use larger quantities. Also, give problems that involve a sequence of events, such as "Barney was gathering seashells. On Monday he put four in his bag. On Tuesday he put in six more. And on Wednesday he put in five more. Then how many did he have in his bag altogether?"

Four-year-olds can also understand the idea of "half" and other partitions or fractions. These are readily taught while dividing objects that you are playing with or eating: "You have half and I'll have half." "There are three of us eating, so we each get a third. See, one-third for you, one-third for me, and one-third for Beatrice."

Young children commonly write numbers (and letters) backwards almost as often as they write them correctly. Don't worry about this—it doesn't portend dyslexia—and don't do a lot of correcting. To most children, whether a number is written backwards or forwards is a minor technicality. The fun and sense of mastery comes from the problem solving, from recalling the number (getting an image of it) and then being able to write down what one saw in one's mind. Too early and too insistent a demand that the child get the minor details right can undermine his or her interest in the more important aspects of the activities.

Once a child can determine quantity, she's ready to master the notions of "more than," "less than," and "same" (or "equals"). Use comparative language in your everyday activities: "Peter, give David the same number of pretzels that you have." "I think the (clay) monster needs one more arm." "We used to have more spoons, but we lost one."

Pegboards are useful for introducing a child to comparisons of quantity. Arrange rows of different color pegs next to each other and *discover* together which has more (or less) and how many more (or less). After your child has mastered quantities in rows, use other configurations such as pegs arranged in squares or triangles.

Another good game for giving children practice in comparing quantities uses playing cards (numbered cards only). You divide the deck in half and both of you turn over one card at a time. On each round, the one with the highest numbered card takes both cards. The game has different names. I learned it as "War." With a five-year-old, try playing this with each of you turning over two cards at a time. The winner of the round is the one with the highest sum. It's a good introduction to adding.

You can combine instruction in comparisons with a lesson in number-writing through the following game: You write a number on a piece of paper and ask your child to pick a bigger (or smaller) number for you to write next to it. Then you ask your child to write a bigger (or smaller) number next to that one. Use your child's errors to clarify his confusion about bigger and smaller quantities.

Preschoolers will also enjoy measuring things and comparing their lengths. Introduce a ruler and a tape measure into your activities. Children especially like being measured: "Your hand is four inches long. See, the four on the ruler is right by the tip of your finger nail. One inch, two, three, four inches. Let's see if your other hand is the same size" (and so on). Demonstrate the usefulness of measuring. "Do you think that will fit in there? Before we put it together, we'd better measure. Uh oh, it is too big. It's seven inches on the ruler, but, see, the space for it is only six inches. It won't fit." And don't forget about liquid and other measurements of volume, which can include filling measuring cups to designated lines and seeing how many spoonfuls of sugar it takes to fill a cup. Bath time is a good occasion for filling and emptying cups to take their measure, and also for learning about flotation and displacement (for example, showing a child what happens to the water in a filled cup when an object is placed in it).

You will of course have to be very patient as you teach your child numbers and counting. He will forget things you were sure he knew. He will tune out or get cranky when you ask for something beyond his ability. He will fail to grasp things that seem so easy and obvious to you. But if *you* lose patience, he's sure to. You will have to simplify games and make sure he wins a lot. And sometimes he will have his own concept of winning: in a matching card game with pictures of animals, it may be more important to him to collect the two horses than to have the most pairs at the end of the game. Similarly, the child may turn your number "lesson" with the pegboard into an occasion for creating designs. When this happens, follow your child's lead. You can't pen up his or her interest when it takes off in unexpected directions. It's a mistake to try.

You may find that your child's preschool or early grade school teacher mistrusts young children's ability to count. This probably derives from Piaget's assertion that children below the age of 7 couldn't really understand the essence of counting. Unfortunately, many educators believed him. Here's how Piaget described it:

> A child of five or six may readily be taught by his parents to name the numbers from one to ten. If ten stones are laid in a row, he can count them correctly. But if the stones are rearranged in a more complex pattern or piled up, he no longer can count them with consistent accuracy. Although the child knows the names of the numbers, he has not yet grasped the essential idea of number: namely, that the number of objects in a group remains the same, is "conserved," no matter how they are shuffled or arranged.[60]

There is considerable evidence that Piaget was wrong—that even 3- and 4-year-olds understand that the number of objects doesn't change when they are rearranged.[61] Try repeating Piaget's study with your 4- or 5-year-old, but ask the child to do the rearranging; that is, after he counts the number of objects, tell him, "Move then around." Then ask, "Now how many are there?" Your child is likely to get it right.

The way the child is questioned makes a big difference in Piaget's conservation procedures. For example, Piaget poured water from a wide glass into a tall narrow glass and asked children which glass contained more water. He reported that children below the age of 7 pick the taller glass (in which the water level is higher) because they can't recognize that estimations of volume must take into account more than one dimension—here, the height and width of the glasses. When I've changed the question to, "Which would fill you up more if you drank them?" I've gotten accurate answers from 5-year-olds. This rewording communicates to the child that she is being asked to judge volume rather than height.

Encourage Logical Thinking

When we say someone reasoned logically we mean that he or she drew (or *deduced*) a correct and necessary conclusion from a particular set of premises. An oft-cited example of deductive logic led to the discovery of the planet Neptune. Astronomers had observed that the planet Uranus had an irregular orbit. So, extrapolating from gravitational theory, they deduced that there must be an unseen mass pulling on Uranus. The theory predicted where to look for this mass and when they looked, there was Neptune. Deductive logic extends our knowledge from the known to the unknown.

One doesn't have to teach children to use deductive logic to make inferences. They do it spontaneously and it is evident in their earliest utterances. A 2- or 3-year-old says "Mama be mad." Implicit in the statement is a deductive inference: Mama gets mad when I make a mess. I made a mess. Therefore when Mama finds out, she will be mad. In another example, a child said, "Doggie get sick." Upon questioning, the logic behind the inference became apparent: Daddy said I'd get sick if I ate garbage on the street. The dog ate garbage on the street. Therefore the dog will get sick.

So parents don't need to teach the fundamentals of deductive logic the way they have to teach the fundamentals of reading or multiplication. Logic is natural to human thinking and research shows that even 4-year-olds can perform fairly well when tested on formal syllogisms of the type:

Every banga is purple.

Purple animals always sneeze at people.

Do bangas sneeze at people?

Other research shows that 4-year-olds are already capable of "transitive inferences" on problems such as:

Peter is the same size as David.

David is bigger than you.

You are the same size as John.

Who is bigger, Peter or John?

Another form of syllogism requires "conditional reasoning" in the form of *if–then* questions, and studies find that first-graders can solve these if the problems are phrased affirmatively:

If there is a knife, then there is a fork.

There is a knife.

Is there a fork? (Yes)

By the third grade, youngsters can do well on conditional reasoning syllogisms using negation:

If there is a knife, then there is a fork.

There is *not* a fork.

Is there a knife? (No)[62]

In all forms of deductive logic, the conclusion is totally determined by the premises. Eleanor Duckworth describes an excellent example of a youngster using his deductive abilities to make known something that was unknown (it also highlights the work of an unusually creative teacher):

Hank was an energetic and not very scholarly fifth grader. His class had been learning about electric circuits with flashlight batteries, bulbs, and various wires. After the children had developed considerable familiarity with these materials, the teacher made a number of mystery boxes. Two wires protruded from each box, but inside, unseen, each box had a different way of making contact between the wires. In one box the wires were attached to a battery; in another they were attached to a bulb; in a third, to a certain length of resistance wire; in a fourth box they were not attached at all; and so forth. By trying to complete the circuit on the outside of a box, the children were able to figure out what made the connection inside the box. Like many other children, Hank attached a battery and a bulb to the wire outside the box. Because the bulb lit, he knew at least that the wires inside the box were connected in some way. But, because it was somewhat dimmer than usual, he also knew that the wires inside were not connected directly to each other and that they were not connected by a piece of ordinary copper wire. Along with many of the children, he knew that the degree of dimness of the bulb meant that the wires inside were connected either by another bulb of the same kind or by a certain length of resistance wire.

The teacher expected them to go only this far. However, in order to push the children to think a little further, she asked them if they could tell whether it was a bulb or a piece of wire inside the box. She herself thought there was no way to tell. After some thought, Hank had an idea. He undid the battery and bulb that he had already attached on the outside of the box. In their place, using additional copper wire, he attached six batteries in a series. He had already experimented enough to know that six batteries would burn out a bulb, if it was a bulb inside the box. He also knew that once a bulb is burned out, it no longer completes the circuit. He then attached the original battery and bulb again. This time he found that the bulb on the outside of the box did not light. So he reasoned, rightly, that there had been a bulb inside the box and that now it was burned out. If there had been a wire inside, it would not have burned through and the bulb on the outside would still light.[63]

There are, of course, differences in children's logical abilities and there are a number of ways parents can foster their child's mastery of logical skills:

1. *Stimulate a child to apply deductive logic to a broad array of circumstances.* By asking a child questions like, "Why do you think that hap-

pened?'' or ''What do you think would happen if . . . ?'' or ''How could you tell if . . . ?'' you spark the deductive process into action. The teacher who set up the electrical wiring problem for Hank and his classmates was asking such a question.

As another example, 7-year-old Claudia and her father were walking in the park where a child was chasing after a helium-filled balloon that was headed for the treetops:

FATHER: Why do you think some balloons rise up into the air and some don't?

CLAUDIA: The wind moves some.

FATHER: But I wonder why the wind doesn't move the others. They look the same on the outside. Maybe they are different on the inside. What's inside balloons?

CLAUDIA: Air.

FATHER: Right. But maybe there are different kinds of air. Where does the air come from that goes into the balloons that rise up?

CLAUDIA: We get it in the store from a pump.

FATHER: Where does the air come from that goes into the balloons that fall down?

CLAUDIA: Our mouths. We blow them up with the air in our lungs.

FATHER: And where do we get the air that we breathe into our lungs?

CLAUDIA: From the air around us.

FATHER: What do you think . . . maybe the air that comes from the pump is different than the air we breathe.

CLAUDIA: Maybe.

FATHER: Do you remember what happens when you mix water and oil?

CLAUDIA: The oil rises to the top.

FATHER: Why?

CLAUDIA: Because it's lighter than the water. We weighed them—remember?

FATHER: I do. What about ice in water? Does it float on top or sink?

CLAUDIA: It floats. Because it's lighter too. Heavier things sink to the bottom, pushing lighter things up. Hey, maybe the air from the pump is lighter than the air we breathe. Maybe that's why those balloons rise up.

FATHER: Exactly, and that lighter air is called helium. The helium-filled balloon, like everything else, is pulled down by gravity, but the heavier air around it is pulled down more strongly, pushing the lighter objects up.

Claudia made a deductive inference: From the general principle, Lighter things rise above heavier things, and the observation that certain balloons rise and others don't, she *inferred* that the balloons that rise have lighter air in them. Obviously, the more information a child has about the world (oil floats on water), the more likely he or she will make a connection between something observed (some balloons rise) and a general principle (heavier liquids and gases sink below lighter ones).

Parents can also use playful questions to stimulate deductive reasoning:

MOTHER: What do you think would happen if people had big trunks, like elephants?

CHILD: We'd have to grow big necks.

MOTHER: Why?

CHILD: An elephant's trunk is heavy. A person would have to have big muscles in his neck to carry it around. Our skinny necks would just break off.

Another enjoyable way to increase a child's sensitivity to logic is through stories. There's an excellent series of *Nate the Great* books by Marjorie Weinman Sharmat. Nate is a little boy detective who uses keen observation and logic to solve problems. *World Famous Muriel* is the heroine of a similar series by Sue Alexander. An older child will enjoy following the logical deductions of Sherlock Holmes and other detective heros.

Telling a child about interesting examples of deductive reasoning should also be helpful. For example, many newspapers recently reported on a marine biologist's surprise when she discovered light-sensitive receptors in the skin of fish that swim far below the depths to which sunlight can penetrate. Starting from the basic premises of evolutionary theory, she deduced that there must be a light source, otherwise the fish would not have evolved mechanisms that respond to light. Her hypothesis was soon confirmed by a deep water diving team that discovered a mysterious light source in the vicinity where these fish swim.

This story, like the story of the discovery of Neptune, can be tailored to children of different ages. Stories about the search for new knowledge are, basically, adventure stories, and even young children can find them interesting and inspiring. Wondering *Why?* and *What if . . . ?* with one's child, and sharing the latest discoveries of what's out there, can be some of the most thrilling moments of parenthood.

2. *Help a child apply logic properly.* It's easy to misapply logic without realizing it. Recall the story of the child who predicted that the dog would get sick from eating garbage because he was told that eating garbage would make *him* sick. Without realizing it, the boy was assuming that children

and dogs get sick from the same things, an assumption that might not be warranted. Applying logic correctly requires that terms be used precisely and consistently.

Advertisements and political arguments provide marvelous examples of the misuse of logic, and parents can use both to further their child's understanding of how logic works (and how it can be corrupted). For instance, the argument in a current automobile advertisement runs something like: "You want to buy a reliable car. We make the most reliable car in America. Therefore you should buy our car." The auto maker hopes the consumer will assume that the most reliable car made in America is *in fact* a reliable car. This may not be the case.

Four- and 5-year-olds are not too young for lessons in misleading advertising. Many will already have encountered toys not working the way a commercial indicated it would, and they can understand an explanation about the profit motive of companies ("They want more money for themselves. Building toys well costs money. So they build them out of junky parts that don't cost them much money and try to fool children into thinking they are good"). Research with seventh- and eighth-graders found that they had already become quite skeptical of advertisers and could discern flaws in the reasoning in ads. A recent study successfully taught children as young as 6 to distinguish "claims" from "facts" in TV commercials so the children could tell the difference between informative and persuasive messages.[64]

When children apply logic to real-world concerns we not only need to make sure that they are sensitive to the precision and consistency of words; we also need to teach them to evaluate the accuracy of the premises upon which the conclusions are based. For example, your child might come home from school and announce, "I'm going to get sick. I have germs in my saliva. I saw them in a microscope in science class." The child is reasoning:

Germs in our bodies make us sick. (premise 1)
I have germs in my body. (premise 2)
Therefore I will be sick. (conclusion)

If the child means that *all* germs in our bodies make us sick, his conclusion that he is going to get sick would be logically correct—but it would not be factually accurate since our bodies contain many germs that are benign and even useful. Logicians are careful to remind us that a conclusion can be both logically correct and factually *in*accurate (and vice versa). In the above example you can see that if either premise is not factually accurate, the conclusion will not necessarily be accurate.

Logicians have identified a number of other factors that undermine the proper use of logic, and parents can be on the alert to make their children aware of these:

- Ignoring the correctness of an argument because we don't like the person making it: "You're a Communist. You couldn't be right."
- Assuming our own argument is valid because an opposing argument has been discredited: "Keeping drugs illegal hasn't worked. Therefore we should legalize drugs."
- Assuming something is true because it hasn't been proved false: "There must be ghosts because no one has proved that there aren't any."
- Assuming something is true because many people believe it: "Gypsies must be dangerous since so many people dislike them."
- Assuming something is true because an authority says it is true: "Even Einstein believed in God, therefore there must be a God."
- Overgeneralizing: "Capitalism has been good for our country. Therefore it will be good everywhere."
- Giving a reason that merely restates an assertion (called a tautology): "Freedom of speech is a good thing because people should be free to speak their minds."

3. *Help children avoid "fallacies," or formal errors in logic.* Logicians have worked out various rules for logical arguments, as well as a number of fallacies or formal errors of logical reasoning. As an example of fallacious logic, an irate child might reason:

Tommy breaks things.
My toy is broken.
Therefore Tommy broke my toy.

Actually whether or not Tommy broke the toy cannot be established from the two premises. With some guidance children can usually understand and correct such basic reasoning errors.

One way to help children learn to avoid fallacies is by giving them practice in logical problem solving. For instance, you can play reasoning games with grade-school children. You might ask, "If trees need water to grow and there is no water in the Gobi desert, can trees grow in the Gobi desert?"

After a while you can present logical reasoning problems in the form of formal syllogisms. You make up a syllogism and have the child tell you if the conclusion follows logically from the two premises (and why she thinks so). In making up syllogisms use both realistic and fantasy content. Here are two examples:

If the timer is up, the lights will go on.
The timer is up.
Therefore the lights will go on.
(The conclusion follows from the premises.)

No gullock birds are lavender.
That bird is not lavender.
Therefore it must be a gullock bird.
(The conclusion does not follow from the premises.)

All mosquitoes are pests.
My friend Herbie is a pest.
Therefore my friend Herbie is a mosquito.
(The conclusion does not follow from the premises.)

4. *Teach specific problem-solving tactics.* In order to solve many kinds of logical problems it is helpful to represent the information visually in a diagram. For instance, most children (and adults) would have trouble keeping in mind all the information contained in the problem:

Louis is shorter than Thomas, but taller than David. David is shorter than Louis, but taller than Carl. Who is the tallest and the shortest?

If we teach a child to diagram the relative heights of the four men, the problem becomes easy to solve. Different kinds of information require different kinds of diagrams. For a question about relative heights a useful diagram would consist of vertical lines of different lengths, each representing one person's height. For a question about electrical circuits one might draw various loops that represent the flow of current. For a question about relative temperatures, one might draw a scale to represent positions on a thermometer. For a question about the transfer of funds between banks, one might draw a flow diagram consisting of boxes to represent each bank and arrows to represent the amounts transferred. For a question about routes, one might draw a map and arrows to represent directions.

Another way to represent information is in a *Table*. Tables use numbers rather than pictures but they too allow us to visualize information, and they come in handy when we have to keep track of more than one thing at a time. Take the problem:

Together Penny, Jill, and Mona have nine rings and six bracelets. Penny has three bracelets and Jill has the same number of rings. Jill has one piece of jewelry more than Penny, who has four. Mona has as many bracelets as Penny has rings. How many rings each do Penny and Mona have?

All this information becomes manageable by setting up a two-dimensional table, such as shown in Table 1, with the three girls' names on one dimension and the two types of jewelry on the other.

Table 1				
	Penny	*Jill*	*Mona*	*Totals*
rings	1	3	5	9
bracelets	3	2	1	6

Truth tables provide a third way to picture complex information. We don't put numbers in a truth table; we put marks to indicate truth or falsity. Try this problem:

Ken, Eva, Sophie, Tom, and Jan each had a different flavored lollipop: cherry, strawberry, mint, orange, and lemon. (1) The girl who had mint is older than Sophie. (2) The boy who had strawberry is in class with Tom and Sophie. (3) Eva hates cherries and gets a rash from citrus fruits. (4) The boy who had cherry is the older brother of the girl who had orange, and they live next door to Jan. Who had which flavor?

If the information is complete enough, a truth table, such as shown in Table 2, will yield the answer. From (1) we know that neither Sophie nor any of the boys had mint (so they get x's on the mint line), leaving Eva and Jan as possibilities. From (2) we know that neither Tom nor any of the girls had strawberry. The only other boy is Ken, so Ken had strawberry. From (3) we can assume that Eva didn't have cherry or the two citrus flavors, lemon and orange, leaving only mint for her. From (4) we know that a boy had cherry, so it had to be Tom; and a girl had orange, but not Jan. The only flavor left for Jan is lemon. The only flavor remaining for Sophie is orange.

Table 2					
	Ken	*Eva*	*Sophie*	*Tom*	*Jan*
Cherry	x	x	x	+	x
Strawberry	+	x	x	x	x
Mint	x	+	x	x	x
Orange	x	x	+	x	x
Lemon	x	x	x	x	+

Truth tables give good practice in sorting out what is known from what is unknown, and what is useful for solving the problem from what is irrelevant. Notice that in the problem above, the ages of the children turned out to be of no value for the solution.

Teach Your Child about Illusions and Other Perceptual Limitations

Researchers have found that by the age of 3, children have already begun to understand the differences between *real* and *not real* and *reality* and *appearance,* and are correctly using the words "real," "really," and "looks like" (in contrast to "is"). For example, they will say things like, "You're not *really* dead, we're just playing," "It's not a *real* bowling ball," and "That [gun] looks *real* but it's not."[65] You can build upon this early awareness that things are not always as they appear, to teach your child that, while we use our senses for learning what's out there, sometimes our senses get fooled. In other words, children need to learn that the way things look do not always correspond to the way things "really" are (or, more precisely, that our immediate perceptions of things do not always correspond to other sources of information about those things). Illusions are an interesting way to introduce children to such perceptual limitations.

For example, with a ruler draw two parallel lines from one side of a paper to the other, about an inch apart and about half way from the top and bottom. Then, from a point between the lines, draw 20 or so straight lines radiating out toward the top and bottom edges of the paper, like spokes on a wheel. The parallel lines will suddenly appear to bow out in the middle. The illusion that the lines are curved is so compelling that your child will want to put a ruler up against them to affirm that they really are straight. You can find other visual illusions in the chapters of psychology textbooks covering perception.

The philosopher John Locke is credited with discovering a temperature illusion, whereby water feels cold to one hand and warm to the other. Prepare three containers of water, one hot, one cold, and one at room temperature. Have your child place one hand in the hot water and the other in the cold. After about 15 seconds, have her place both hands in the container with water at room temperature. The water will feel warm to the hand that had been in the cold water, and cool to the hand that had been in the warm water. Research with this illusion reveals that young children sometimes need help understanding that the effect is based on processes *within* their own bodies (sensory adaptation of one hand to the cold and the other to the heat), and is not due to a peculiar mixture of hot and cold water in the third container. A similar illusion can be set up by holding a light weight in one hand, a heavy weight in the other (both for about 15 seconds), followed by lifting two identical midweight objects, one in each hand.[66]

Another way to help your child understand perceptual limitations is to teach her about color blindness, explaining that not everyone sees the same colors as everyone else. If you can, obtain the cards that eye doctors use to test for color blindness to illustrate these perceptual differences. You can reinforce the idea that what we perceive depends on specific physiological processes by reminding your child how much better she sees in the dark after her eyes have adapted to it—that is, after the chemicals that were bleached out by bright lights have had time to be replenished.

The limitations of our perceptual system are not only relevant to illusions and defects. When we watch movies we are presented with a fast moving series of still pictures and respond to them as if we were seeing continuous motion. Our sensory system doesn't operate fast enough to see each picture separately. Toy stores still carry flip picture books that convey motion when you flip through the pages. Stereoscopes can also convey how our perceptual systems construct three-dimensional impressions out of two-dimensional pictures.

In other discussions make your child aware that there are many kinds of stimuli that other animals can detect which we can't, either because their sensory receptors (eyes, ears) are more sensitive than ours, or because they have sensory receptors that we don't have at all. For instance, bats navigate and detect insects through locating echos, which we can't perceive; dolphins have sonar detectors; snakes have a special heat (or infra-red) sensing organ that enables them to detect their prey in the dark; dogs can hear sounds and smell things that we can't; cats can see in environments that appear totally dark to us; and some birds and worms appear to determine direction by sensing the earth's magnetic field which we are "blind" to.

There are also forms of energy (X-rays, cosmic rays, and other kinds of light) that we can detect only through special instruments, and that, as far as we know, no animal can sense—although perhaps creatures on other planets can. In other words, there's a lot more out there than we can learn about through our unaided senses.

5

∞

What Leads to What?

Discovering Order

During their first days infants begin to recognize that some experiences regularly follow other experiences—that is, that some of what's out there is organized into temporal patterns. There is evidence that they start learning this almost immediately. For example, psychologists have shown that newborns can learn conditioned associations between two stimuli: If a tone is presented to a newborn just before he starts nursing, after a few such pairings he will start to suck as soon as the tone is sounded, without any nipple in his mouth. The child seems to have learned that the tone *leads to* milk, and he sucks in anticipation. Similarly, if a tone regularly precedes an unpleasant odor that the child turns away from, he'll soon start to turn away right after the tone comes on.

A recent study by Christine Moon and William Fifer demonstrated a surprisingly refined ability to discern temporal sequences in newborns between 33 and 77 hours old. A nipple was placed in each infant's mouth and during moments when they weren't sucking they heard one of two syllables ("pat" or "pst"). One of the syllables served as a signal indicating that if they started to suck now they would hear a recording of their mother's voice. The other syllable was followed by silence whether the infants sucked or not. Within a few minutes most infants had learned the association. They were sucking more upon hearing the syllable forecasting mother's voice than upon hearing the other signal, indicating that they had learned the temporal relationship between that syllable and the onset of the voice.[1]

Another example of infants learning what leads to what is provided by psychologists Michael Lamb and Catherine Malkin who report that most 1-month-olds, crying to be fed, will calm down upon the approach of the parent, even before being picked up. The infants appear to anticipate being fed—that is, they have learned that a parent's approach *leads to* milk. Other researchers have confirmed this finding with even younger children.[2]

My own observations and the reports of parents I've interviewed indicate that this kind of anticipation can be evident at least as early as a baby's second week.

Parents often come to believe that their newborns quickly acquire an awareness of how long recurring events ordinarily take, and often make a fuss when goodies are delayed or routines (like diapering) are extended. Researchers are beginning to explore young children's awareness of "duration" and are finding that they do, indeed, have a keen sense of how long events take.[3]

In recognizing what leads to what, the infant discerns more than that different events occur at different moments in time. She apprehends connections between events; events *lead to* other events. In other words, two (or more) events occurring regularly in sequence become a unit: if one occurs, the other is expected to follow ("Here comes that big person. Goody, that means I'm about to be fed"). So newborns, in their search for what leads to what, are quickly able to partition the ongoing flow of events into temporal units or patterns, just as they are able to perceive spatial patterns (such as faces) in their search for what's out there. And once they've learned a temporal sequence, they exhibit surprise when the first stimulus occurs but the second one doesn't follow (researchers have referred to this as the "what happened?" response).[4]

The Learning of Sequences

Psychologists have studied the learning of what leads to what in various formats besides those described above. For example, rhythms and melodies are types of temporal patterns that involve learning what leads to what, and research shows that children can detect and distinguish these by their fourth month. Some studies report that even 2-month-olds can detect differences in temporal auditory or visual patterns made up of sequences of sounds or lights.

An interesting experiment on temporal pattern recognition by 3½-month-olds placed them in front of two screens and projected slides in an alternating pattern, switching regularly from right screen to left screen. The babies' eye movements showed that they soon began to anticipate on which side the picture would appear, thus indicating they had learned the temporal pattern. A follow-up study found that 3-month-olds could also learn to anticipate longer, more complex sequences (such as right-right-left), suggesting a surprisingly early awareness of "numerical" patterns, as if they were following the rule "On the right side, switch after the *second* picture."

A similar study placed 5-month-olds in front of a display with four small windows, one in each corner, and showed them a sequence of four events (for example, a picture of a face appearing in one window at a time in clockwise order). Eye movements revealed that many infants learned to anticipate in which window the face would next appear, some even when tested a week after the training.[5]

Research also shows that 1- and 2-year-olds can imitate a sequence of actions that they've observed, indicating that they have learned which actions follow which others. For instance, in one study, 16- and 20-month-olds were asked to reproduce sequences such as the following:

> The subject was presented with a small wooden board, a wedge-shaped block, and a toy frog. [The experimenter] modeled *putting the board on the base to form a teeter-totter, placing the frog on the end of the board,* and *hitting the board* [thereby causing the frog to "jump"].

The children were quite able to reproduce such sequences. Moreover, if the actions were generally familiar to them (washing a stuffed bear), they could even reproduce them two weeks later.[6]

Studies of 2-year-olds' conversations with their parents demonstrate that children this age have a good grasp of the sequence of events in their normal routines, such as going to the market. For instance, they know you pay on the way out, not on the way in, and they also understand terms (verbs) that refer to the past and future ("Remember when we *went* to the zoo"? "Sit down, *we'll go* in a minute"). Three-year-old children, as most parents are well aware, learn the sequence of events in a story with considerable precision. They are also beginning to use and understand the words "yesterday" and "tomorrow," although sometimes they mix them up; by four they almost always get them right. Nursery-school children routinely learn complex sequences in games, dances, and schedules, and research shows they are becoming good at it.[7]

Other formats for studying what leads to what have imposing names like sensory preconditioning, S–S (or stimulus–stimulus) learning, Pavlovian conditioning, probability learning, and observational learning.[8] Unfortunately there hasn't been a lot of developmental research in young children's learning what leads to what. This is primarily due to Piaget's insistence that children, at least until they reach 18 months, can only learn through their own actions. "Actually," he says, "in order to know objects, the subject must act upon them, and therefore transform them."[9] In other words, he claimed that children couldn't learn a sequence of events merely by observing it. The evidence I've cited above contradicts this assertion (for example, 3½-month-olds learn to anticipate alternating slides).

Further evidence of infant observational learning without action was recently provided by psychologist Andrew Meltzoff. He had 9-month-olds observe novel actions (such as the folding of a hinge, pushing a button, rattling an egg)—actions they hadn't done before. But he didn't let the children touch the objects. Twenty-four hours later he brought them back into the situation, gave them the objects, and found that they repeated what they had seen (but not done) the day before. When a control group of children who had not seen the objects used were given them they did not handle them the same way, indicating that the first group of children had learned to handle the objects simply through observation.[10]

Most parents, too, can cite many experiences showing that children learn sequences through observation. For instance, watch an 8-month-old attend to the front door when the doorbell rings, waiting to see who will enter. If a special person rings the bell in a special way, you'll see him light up with anticipation knowing full well who will walk through the door. In other words, through observation the child has learned what leads to what (that special doorbell pattern will be followed by Aunt May entering).

By learning the order of events a child can anticipate what's going to happen (If A occurs, B will follow). He can then plan his actions more effectively (If A occurs, I'll be ready for B; for example, "It's cloudy. I'd better take my umbrella"). The recognition of temporal patterns also contributes to the child's developing sense of the continuity of past, present, and future. Learning what leads to what is particularly important because it is a central element in the recognition of *what makes things happen*— that is, central to the child's understanding of causal relationships. All cause and effect relationships have at their core a temporal pattern: the cause regularly precedes its effect. But children quickly recognize that not all temporal patterns signify cause and effect. For example, a child may learn that he is taken to the playground on a regular basis right after lunch, but he won't perceive eating lunch as the cause of going to the playground.

Teaching a Child *What Leads to What*

Introduce Your Child to Rhythmic Patterns

Tap out and vocalize rhythms for your baby. Hum, whistle, and sing brief melodies and then repeat them. Then vary them a bit and then repeat the original one. The goal is to provide your child with stimuli that go through changes over a period of time yet cohere as a unitary experience. As described above, infants show early interest in and sensitivity to rhythmic and melodic patterns.

Periodically introduce surprises into the patterns you present, expressing them facially as well as vocally. You want to present these patterns in a manner that enables the child to detect that you are presenting them *on purpose*, for his pleasure—in other words, that you are playing with him. A father described that when his daughter was 4-months-old she responded with delight when he inserted a surprise ending into a verbal pattern. He would make eye contact and repeat a sentence such as "You're pretty," saying it playfully and emphasizing the *p* in pretty. After a few repeats he would start as usual with "You're . . . ," then purse his lips for a *p*, but instead say "silly" or some other new word. He said it was always good for a smile.

Play Sequence Games with Your Baby

There are an endless variety of sequence games you can play with your baby. For example, say to her, "What am I going to touch? I'm going to touch your . . . *nose!* (then touch it). What am I going to touch? I'm going to touch your . . . *ear!* (touch). What am I going to touch? . . ." Do about six such repetitions, giving the word "your" a properly dramatic and playful reading as you circle your finger about before touching. Soon your baby will recognize the pattern and take delight in it.

In a similar game say, "I love your . . . *eyes!* (then kiss them). And so on. In a sequence game of a different type, hold your baby's hands (letting him grasp your index fingers) and pull him forward as you say "Up; then let him down as you say "Down." Repeat this sequence a few times, keeping the timing regular. Then introduce surprises by hesitating briefly or by saying "Up" and waiting for your baby to start to pull on your fingers. Introduce variations, such as repeating "Up, up, up" as you pull up, and "Down, down, down" as you ease him down. The traditional games, "So Big!" and "This Little Piggy" are sequence games that have delighted countless babies and parents.

With children of 3 or older you can tap out a rhythm and hum a melody (pah, pa, pah . . .) and have them try to copy it. Try asking your 4-year-old to create rhythms and melodies for *you* to copy.

Recall the game "Mistake" described in the previous chapter in which you mislabel an object purposely in order to give your child the opportunity to correct you. You can also use this technique to teach behavioral sequences (such as the steps in making a tuna sandwich). For example, as you begin to make the sandwich you might say, "I'm not sure if I remember how to make a tuna sandwich. Let's see. First you spread the mayonnaise all over the plate." The child will interrupt gleefully: "No, you put the mayonnaise on the bread." Then you can add, "Oh, that's right. Good. Now we put the two pieces of bread together and put the tuna on top." Your child will happily correct you again. If the child doesn't catch a mistake, stop and ask about it ("Do we really put the can between the bread? I think we'd break our teeth biting into it"). These kinds of games will stimulate your child to attend more carefully to the details of behavioral sequences, increasing his or her awareness of what leads to what.

Describe the Sequences of Events
That You Engage in and Observe Together

To illustrate, here's something you might do while looking out the window with your baby (babies generally love to look out of windows). Let's say there is a bus stop near your window. As a bus becomes visible, point to it and say "Look, here comes a bus." Imitate its sound if possible to help your child understand what you are referring to. Then provide a running description of what happens, imitating sounds as they occur: "Here it comes. It's going to stop. It stopped. Squeak. The door opens. Clunk. The people are getting on. One on, two on, three on. Oh, one lady getting off. Step, step. Lady off. The door is closing. Boom, it's closed. The bus is going to start. It's starting. Vroom. There it goes. Bye, bye bus."

Do the same thing the next time you see a bus coming. You'll be able to tell if your infant is able to attend yet and if he or she is interested. If not, try again some days later. You are likely to find that your baby will have better distance and motion perception than researchers indicate; they studied babies in laboratories, monitoring their perceptual responses to light bulbs coming on and moving at different distances—they didn't use things like big, bright, noisy buses.

In describing this or any other observations to your child, the purpose is to convey that events occur in orderly and reasonable sequences (the bus comes, it stops, people get on, it goes). The timing and expressiveness of your descriptions and sound effects will help your child parcel what she sees into meaningful units. You'll reinforce the lesson if you can find a way for her to participate in the events she's observed (such as by taking her on a short bus trip from the same bus stop and again describing each step as you engage in it).

Your everyday tasks with your child provide excellent occasions for teaching about sequences. For example, as you go through the steps in the diapering process, describe what you are doing: "A wet diaper. Let's go to the changing table. We'll open this side, then open that side, and off it goes. Old diaper in the pail—plop. Wipe, wipe. Powder, powder," and so on. Again, the purpose is to communicate the orderliness and reasonableness of events.

Be on the lookout for naturally occurring sequences that you can bring to your child's attention. Many parents do this spontaneously. If the doorbell rings, they'll say, "There's the doorbell"; and as they head for the door, "Let's see who is coming to see us." This is teaching what leads to what: doorbells are followed by going to and opening the door and then people appear. The lesson will be reinforced by giving the child the experience of pressing the doorbell (or at least observing someone press it) and having someone open the door for the both of you.

As the child's language ability develops, you can describe sequences before they occur and include events that he or she won't actually observe, yet are important steps in the sequence. For instance, in a restaurant: "The waiter is going to give us a menu which is a list of all the different food they cook here. We'll look at the list and then tell him what we want to eat. He'll write down our order and give the cook the piece of paper. The cook is in the kitchen behind that door. He'll cook it and when it's ready the waiter will bring it to us." Giving the child a glimpse of the activity in the kitchen will make the connections between events clearer.

As your child gets older and more and more familiar with what's out there, you can introduce her to the temporal connections between an increasingly wide array of events. For instance, if a new building is being built nearby you can point out the sequence of steps that the construction must go through: digging the hole, installing the foundation, building the frame, putting in the plumbing and electrical lines, constructing the walls, inserting the windows, etc. As the building nears completion you can talk about the changes that will soon take place: "It is dark and empty now, but what will we see and hear and smell when people start to move in?" (lights in the windows, the sounds of people and dogs, delivery and garbage trucks, the smells of cooking, etc.)

In the following example, a parent helps a child understand a sequence of events involving the space shuttle:

CHILD (Seeing a TV news story on the space shuttle's slow trip from the hanger to the launchpad): Why do they move it from one place to another, and why do they have to drive it like that? Doesn't it have an engine?

PARENT: Yes. But it's a rocket engine, which gets very, very hot and has a lot of fire and smoke coming out of it—kind of like the air shooting out of a balloon, but very hot. Even hotter than the fire on the stove. So before they can start the engine they need to bring it to a special place that won't burn, and that's called the launchpad. They build the shuttle in a big building and then they use that giant wagon to take it to the launchpad—very carefully and slowly so it won't fall over.

Children continue to learn about what leads to what for the rest of their lives. They learn the steps that go into electing a president, and that there are good reasons why painters add colors to white and not the other way around, and that a touchdown is followed by a chance to kick an extra point, and that solar activity waxes and wanes in regular cycles.

When appropriate, express the connection between events in general terms: "Whenever you feel sick, we take your temperature." "Whenever we get into the car we put on our seat belts." "We always brush our teeth before going to bed." In addition, always provide the reason behind this regularity: "When we sleep, those teeny-tiny germs that try to dig into our teeth start to grow if they can find some food to eat. Sometimes little bits of food stick to our teeth, like sticky candy, and sometimes bits squeeze between our teeth, so we brush our teeth to keep those germs from finding any food at all."

Use Books and Videos to Teach What Leads to What

Children's books and videos provide many opportunities for teaching what leads to what. Story characters pack their bags before going on a trip, birds sit on eggs before their babies hatch, geese fly south when the weather turns cold. Such sequences transcend the particular characters or narrative in the text; they are not simply a series of arbitrary occurrences, but depict the order in which things happen naturally. Ask questions that prompt the child's understanding of such sequences: "If they didn't pack their bathing suits what would they do when they got to the beach?"

Three-year-olds enjoy making up their own stories for a parent to write down. A nice device is to fold a sheet of paper into book form and write the story as a book. Take it quite seriously, putting down the title, author, and date. In telling the story, the child will need reminders such as, "And what happened next?" or "What about the cat? Did he get out of the box?" Encouragement with lines such as "I can't wait to find out what's going to happen next" will be helpful.

Making up stories helps children focus on the logical and natural connections between events in time and space, and on the relationship between characters' motivations and actions. But don't expect total sense from a 3-year-old and don't be perturbed if your child borrows heavily from stories he has heard before, or if he breaks off the activity before achieving anything that seems to you to be a complete story. Even when children have only come up with a fragment of a story, they usually experience great pride when parents read the story aloud to them and to other members of the family.

Use Songs, Poems, and Nursery Rhymes for Teaching Sequences

Many songs, poems, and nursery rhymes contain lessons about what leads to what. "The Eensy Weensy Spider," for example, describes a sequence of events that is both orderly and reasonable: the spider crawls up, the rain comes, it gets washed out, the sun dries the water, and the spider ascends again.

In children's songs, successive stanzas typically repeat some aspect of previous stanzas and then add some new information. For instance, in "The Little White Duck" each stanza adds a new creature to the pond, until the last, a snake, empties the pond of everyone but himself. The song depicts a sequence that children readily learn. Sequences are also described in many nursery rhymes: "Little Miss Muffet sat on a tuffet eating her curds and whey. . . ." When teaching songs, poems, and nursery rhymes to children help them picture the sequence described. Sometimes children simply learn to repeat the words by rote, but it's much more fun for them, and more educational, when they picture the events in the story or song.

There's a lesson on what leads to what inherent in rhymes, whether in songs or poems. The set-up line of a rhyme creates an expectation that a similar sound is coming soon. When it does come in the appropriate place, we—adults as well as children—take delight in it, particularly if it is a well-chosen word that advances what is being communicated. Here is one of my favorites (from a song in *My Fair Lady*):

There he was, that hairy hound from Budapest.
Nowhere have I ever seen a ruder pest.

By the time they are 2, most children love rhymes. They seem to recognize the constraint that rhyming places on the rhyme maker and appreciate that something special has been achieved. Read lots of rhymes and sing lots of songs to your child, and let her listen to recordings of rhymes and songs. You want to support her appreciation of the achievement of successful rhymes. Also, make up rhymes for her. These can be very simple: "I got in the car and drove very far." Some of the time let her see you struggling to overcome the constraint; then you can share in each other's delight when you succeed. And don't be surprised when she recognizes that you've made a bad rhyme.

When she is 3 or 4 she'll probably try to make up her own rhymes. You can encourage this by making it easy for her at first—by asking her to fill in a rhyme that you've begun. For example, you start with, "We walked to the store and opened the . . ."; then ask her to find an ending that rhymes. If your child has trouble give hints. Then try reversing roles, keeping in mind that most 4-year-olds will only be able to give you an opening phrase ("We walked to the store . . ."), not a full set-up for the last word. By 5 or 6, many children will be able to make up good rhymes and enjoy doing so.

Remind Children of Past Events and Help Them Anticipate the Future

An infant can make temporal connections only between events that occur closely in time. Years later that same person, now grown, may contemplate the connections between events that span billions of years. He or she may study the relationship between the "big bang" that initiated our universe 20 billion years ago and the eventual burning out of all the stars billions of years hence. Another may chart the geological record back to the dawn of the earth and tell us where our tectonic plates are taking us now. A third may ponder the truth or falsity of Karl Marx's dialectical history of human societies. To these growing minds, the past and the future continually expand toward infinity in both directions.

Parents spark this expansion when they remind their young children of what they experienced yesterday and last week and last summer, and describe to them what will happen later today and tomorrow and next week and next summer. Researchers Joan Lucariello and Katherine Nelson found that mothers who frequently referred to and asked questions about past and future events—who *remembered* and *planned* with their children—had children with a greater awareness of what they called "temporally displaced" events.[11]

Remembering and planning with a child embed the here and now of his or her experience in an expanding continuity of recollections and anticipations. Parents can remember and plan with their child by providing the information about the past and future themselves ("Remember that storm when we were out on the boat?" "We are going to the zoo tomorrow." "If it doesn't rain, let's go on a picnic") and by asking questions that stimulate the child's thoughts about the past and future ("Do you remember what happened when we were out on the boat?" "Let's plan what we are going to do tomorrow." "What if it snows? What would you like to do then?").

By keeping the past current, parents stimulate their child's memory, help him grasp the temporal order of events, and help him categorize things that go together across a much broader base than simply what he encounters in front of him. Saying, "Remember how different the grass felt at Uncle Bob's," encourages a child to notice, categorize, and differentiate aspects of his environment that he might not otherwise pay much attention to. Children love these kinds of conversations and they love to remember things that you've forgotten ("What was the name of that dog we played with in front of the supermarket? I can't remember. Do you?"). You can begin to talk about the past during a child's first year.

By talking a great deal about what is coming up in the future—later today, later in the week, and beyond—parents provide their children with a sense of the movement of time and how long things take, as well as giving them the pleasure of having things to look forward to.

Parents also need to foster their child's awareness of the relationship between the present and the future. One way to do this is by making plans with him, particularly if carrying out the plan is made contingent on the child fulfilling some action ("If you help clean up now we can go to the fair later"). Such plans, both short- and long-term, provide a child with concrete experiences for understanding *If . . . then* relationships—If we do this, then that will happen. Also ask questions about *If . . . then* relationships ("If A occurs, what will follow?").

You can discuss *If . . . then* contingencies with 2-year-olds ("If you take the medicine, your cough will get better"; "If I let you have a cookie now, you can't have one later"; "If we plant these seeds now, grass will soon grow"). *If . . . then* relationships will play a central role in the child's thinking for the rest of his or her life—whenever he or she seeks to explain or gain control over some occurrence.

With 3- and 4-year-olds you can begin to expand their awareness of time beyond their own lifespans. You can do this by placing the concrete experiences of the present moment in an extended temporal framework. For example, when listening to Mozart you might say, "This music was written a long time ago, long before Daddy was born; even long before Grandfather was born. But it was so good that people still like to listen to it." Here are some other examples: "This building was built before there were any cars or electric lights. People used to ride through this gate up to the door in carriages pulled by horses and a man used to go around and light candles in each room so people could see." "When Grandma was a little girl there were no supermarkets. And her Mommy grew up on a farm far away from any stores. She couldn't go to a bakery for bread. She used to bake it herself every morning and I'll bet it tasted delicious."

Books and films depicting earlier eras are very useful for helping a child visualize other times and places. You can also extend a child's vision into the distant future:

> Just a few years ago, around when Cousin Jenny was a baby, people went to the moon for the first time. They took a rocket plane there and got out and walked around and brought some rocks back which we can see in the museum. For a long, long time people had wondered what was on the moon and wanted to go there, but they didn't have a plane that could take them there. And now people have gone there. Someday, maybe when you are Jenny's age, people will go to Mars, which is much further away than the moon. And someday, maybe when you are Grandma's age, people will make a plane that can go all the way to another star. Maybe, you'll be one of the people to make that plane or go that far.

Here too books and films will help. Keep in mind that when children learn about events that will take place long after they are gone, they are reminded of their mortality (and their parents' mortality as well) and may need comforting. This is as likely to be true for the 15-year-old as the 5-year-old. Their parents often need comforting too.

For a child to make sense of today and prepare for tomorrow, he or she needs to know what happened yesterday and many yesterdays before that. As George Santayana cautioned, "Those who cannot remember the past are condemned to repeat it." It is useful to know what happened before because it may happen again. Indeed, some things happen over and over in cycles. Children come to recognize cyclical patterns by the time they are 3 or 4. They see that their family does different things on weekdays and weekends, across many such cycles. They learn that the seasons affect activities and experiences in similar ways year after year, and that there is a ski season and a baseball season and a hurricane season and a flu season. In school they'll learn about the recurring ice ages and economic depressions of the past and wonder whether the next one is just around the corner.

Parents can point out these cycles, using books and calendars as visual aids. There are a number of children's picture books that are based on the changing seasons and one can easily find calendars that show scenes that typify each month. As children become aware of unpleasant events that run in cycles (like hurricanes, influenza outbreaks, and economic depressions), it is important to stress the positive side of the knowledge—that by being able to anticipate unpleasant events we can better protect ourselves from them and perhaps even prevent their recurrence.

As your child grows, introduce her to historical events and try to connect them with today. Celebrations of national and religious holidays provide many opportunities for this. Today's Supreme Court justices hotly debate what Jefferson, Madison, and the other founding fathers *really* meant when they wrote the Constitution. The Monroe Doctrine still influences the relationship between the United States and Latin American countries. Our major religions began in faraway places thousands of years ago. Teaching children about these connections helps them recognize the continuity of their own lives with the distant past (what Jefferson did 200 years ago affects what we do today). Teaching them about evolution helps them recognize connections that go back to the dawn of life.

You can convey large lengths of time through illustrations. For example, you can draw a one inch line and say, "That line represents how long since you were born." Then draw a longer line: "That line represents how long since I was born. Then draw a very long line: "That line represents how long since George Washington lived. Now if I was to draw a line from here to McDonald's, that would represent how long it's been since the dinosaurs were alive."

6

∾

What Makes Things Happen?

Discovering Causes

From her first day of life, the child, herself, starts to make things happen, and she can adjust her behavior, such as her sucking rate on a nipple, to make some things happen more often and other things less often. She also observes other people making things happen. They make things happen *to* the child, say by touching and lifting and singing to her, among many other kinds of contact. We can see babies react to much of this contact, seeming to notice who is doing what to her.

Before long the baby will also observe that people make things happen to the other people and things around them ("Whenever that lady yells 'C'mere darling,' that big guy shows up. And whenever she lifts that gate, I hear that same terrible squeak"). A baby will also observe that objects are involved in making things happen. Objects act on each other ("Whenever my stroller bumps the chair, it moves"); objects also act on people ("Whenever that thing on the big guy's wrist goes beep, beep, he looks down at it"). The baby will also learn that he or she is one of the people that objects have an impact on ("Oh no, that powder container is falling toward my head again").

The question, What makes things happen? is obviously concerned with causality. A fairly recent, but already classic, study by Lois Hood and Lois Bloom shows that at about 24 months of age, children's conversations reflect quite a sophisticated awareness of cause and effect. Two- and 3-year-olds make causal statements of various kinds ("I'm putting medicine on the lamb's leg cause he had a booboo." "Don't ring the bell either . . . Jenny will wake up." "You can bring me my puzzle . . . very careful so pieces don't fall down"). Children also ask causal questions

("Why you wrapping it around?"); and they answer causal questions (Adult: "Why are you taking off your socks?" Child: "Because it's not cold outside").

In another important study, Inge Bretherton and Marjorie Beeghly report that 28-month-olds are adept at using causal statements in connection with various kinds of mental states and emotions ("You better get shirt so you won't freeze." "Maybe Gregg would laugh when he saw Beth do that." "I nice? I get to ride horse again?" "Grandma mad. I wrote on wall"). A more recent study by James Byrnes and Michele Duff found that 3-year-olds are already using the causal terms "if" and "because" spontaneously and accurately ("My other shirt is wet . . . cause I played in the water"—from a child of 2 years, 11 months).[1]

Parents of 2- and 3-year-olds will not be surprised at reading these kinds of causal statements by children and may wonder why these studies are so important. The reason, as the authors of these studies point out, is that their findings are diametrically opposed to the conclusions of Piaget, who said that children have little understanding of causality until they are about 7.

Piaget studied children's causal understanding, as well as their ability to understand another person's point of view, in very circumscribed ways. For example, he studied causal understanding by asking children such questions as why a nail sinks to the bottom of a beaker of water. To study children's understanding of the causes of someone else's inner experiences he asked them to describe what someone sees who is looking at the same objects they see, but who is seeing them from a different position (that is, viewing them from a different angle). From young children's inadequate answers to these kinds of questions he mistakenly concluded that they had little comprehension of causality in general and little understanding of the effect of viewing perspective on anothers' experiences. Because of the dominance of Piaget's theory his conclusions were widely accepted for years. Now, along with the three studies mentioned above, there are a great many research reports, in virtually all the areas that Piaget studied, that confirm that children understand far more than he gave them credit for.[2]

Indeed parents of 2- and 3-year-olds know that children this age not only understand causality, but that they are genuinely obsessed with learning about causes. "Why?" is their favorite word. They want to know what makes everything happen. Everything! And their *why* questions are appropriate to the kinds of events they are asking about. When people make things happen, they ask about intentions ("Why you doing that?"). When human agents are not involved they ask about mechanisms ("Why that happen?");

and they hardly ever confuse the two. Research shows that it is rare for a child, whether he or she is a 3-year-old or in grade school, to attribute intentions or desires to inanimate objects (despite Piaget's claim that they do).[3]

By the age of 5 or 6, children's understanding of causality can be astonishingly sophisticated. Here is a parent's report of a conversation with a child of 5 years, 2 months:

> As I turned the dishwasher on, Lydia said "We've had that dishwasher for a long time." I replied, "Yes, almost as long as we've had you." Then I joked, "I love the dishwasher and I love you. If I could only keep one—you or the dishwasher—and had to get rid of the other, which do you think I would keep?" She answered, "You would keep both . . . because we'd get rid of the president or the mayor who made the law that said you had to choose." I had explained to her recently about the difference between a government with a king and one in which the people select their leaders.

Lydia apparently asked herself how such a silly rule or law could have come about and then used what she knew about how laws are *caused* (the government makes them) plus her new information about how people in our country become government officials (they are selected and removable by the people) to find a way out of the dilemma her father had posed. When psychologists set out to study children's understanding of causality they do not usually monitor these kinds of naturally occurring conversations (the three studies described above are exceptions). If they did, they'd be surprised at how well young children understand and use causal reasoning.

Children's Understanding of Causal Principles

The research cited above demonstrates that very young children recognize causal relationships. But another question that psychologists have asked is, When do children begin to use and understand *causal principles?* In other words, at what age do their observations of cause and effect in specific situations get transformed into a more general understanding of a causal relationship which they expect to hold in any situation. For instance, after observing such events as baseball bats hitting balls, waves moving boats in the water, and themselves moving various objects, they might conclude, that, in general, *the stronger the force applied to an object, the faster and farther it moves.* The process of deriving a general principle from particular instances is called "induction" or "inductive inference."

Causal principles are useful because they enable the child to predict what will happen in new situations, making it easier for her to bring about desirable outcomes. For example, a child who understands the principle, *The greater the force, the greater the movement (or acceleration)*, will know to look for ways to increase the force when she wants to move something too heavy to push (and she might just reinvent the lever).

A child's behavior may indicate that he understands a causal principle even though he cannot describe it in words. For instance, before he can describe the relationship between force and acceleration, he will deal with objects in ways that show he recognizes this relationship. His understanding and descriptions will ordinarily start at a concrete level ("When I push the ball harder, it goes faster"), and then become increasingly general ("When I push things harder, they go faster"); and sometimes will reach the point of a universal law ("The greater the force, the greater the acceleration, for *any* force applied to *any* object").

Telling children the general principles that others have discovered is, of course, an important part of child rearing and education. When a mother tells her 3-year-old son that it hurts people's feelings when you take things from them, she is communicating a general principle—one she doesn't want to wait for him to discover on his own. Years later, when his science teacher communicates Ohm's Law to him, $i = v/r$, (an electric current equals the voltage divided by the resistance), she too is sharing a general principle with him, one that he can put to good use long before he may be ready to discover it on his own.

Here's an example of a child of 4 years, 9 months expressing a causal principle (years earlier than one would expect from current theory). As her mother described it:

> Claire's summer friend, Annie, was visiting and we went to the neighborhood playground. Annie didn't know any of the children, but joined in the games easily. Soon the two girls were playing with different children at opposite ends of the playground. I saw Claire leave her group a few times to check on Annie. When she saw Annie was doing fine, she went back to her own activities. I complimented her for being so concerned. She explained: *"You know Mommy, children's feelings can be hurt when their friend ignores them because they have another child to play with."*

Here, Claire was enunciating a causal principle that was guiding her actions, something she believed held for children *in general*. As another example, I've found that 3-year-olds can understand and use the causal principle, "If at first you don't succeed, try, try again," which expresses a causal relationship between effort and success. Here's another example from a child of 4 years, 8 months:

I was reading her a version of *Sleeping Beauty* in which one of the good fairies gives the baby the "gift of wisdom." She was familiar with the Disney version in which wisdom is not one of the gifts. She asked, "What does 'wisdom' mean?" I answered that it means very smart. She smiled and replied, "Not smart enough to not touch the spinning wheel."

The principle behind this child's statement might be phrased, "Smart people know what to do to keep out of danger." The father had given her information that was inconsistent with this principle (Sleeping Beauty was wise, *yet* got fooled into touching the spinning wheel). Recent research confirms that 4-year-olds are able to detect such inconsistent information.[4]

In the Bretherton and Beeghly study mentioned above, the causal statements of 28-month-olds were sometimes expressed as principles, and sometimes seemed to imply an underlying understanding of a principle. For instance, the child who said, "I'm hurting your feelings, 'cause I was mean to you," seemed to understand, as a general principle, the causal relationship between being mean toward others and their feelings being hurt.

Other research provides some examples of causal principles used by 6- and 7-year-olds:

(Explaining to mother about accidentally hitting another boy), "And I tried to go up to Jim to play with him again, but he won't come near me. . . . When a kid isn't really your friend yet, they don't know you didn't mean to do it to them."

(Explaining to mother why he wouldn't sit where another boy had been), "Well, that's the way I manage my feelings when something bothers me."

(Explaining to a friend why another child didn't respond to the friend's attempts at comforting), "Well, that's all right. Sometimes when I hit you and then I want to comfort you, you push me away because you're still angry."

(After child broke her arm she asks her mother not to tell her grandmother about it) "No, don't tell her. Don't tell anybody; it just makes people feel bad if you tell them. Makes them feel sad."[5]

In searching for causal principles both scientists and ordinary citizens often look for broad patterns in the relationship between causes and effects. For example, the statement, "The hotter the water, the cleaner the wash," is asserting a relationship between a *range* of temperatures and *levels* of cleanliness, not just between a specific temperature of water and a particular level of cleanliness.

"The more sugar added, the sweeter the taste" similarly expresses a relationship between two varying quantities. When we know the relationship between different amounts of one thing (such as heat of water or amount of sugar) and different magnitudes of another thing (such as cleanliness or sweetness), we have a lot more information than knowing only that a single event leads to a particular other event. Scientists call such relationships between varying quantities "functional relationships" and describe them with graphs and in mathematical terms. For instance, Einstein's famous $E = MC^2$ is the mathematical expression of a functional relationship that says the greater the mass (M) of an object, the more energy (E) it contains.

Actually, there are three kinds of causal connections that children learn about, each with its own mechanisms. They are:

1. The causes of physical events, such as a bat hitting a ball;
2. The causes of emotions (and certain other psychological states), such as crying, in response to an insult; and
3. The causes of actions, such as making a phone call, writing a sonnet, or running for President.

We'll cover each of these separately, first discussing the nature of the causal connections, then the evidence for children's recognition of these connections, and then how to foster a child's understanding of each type of causality.

The Causes of Physical Events

There are four criteria we ordinarily use in judging *physical* causality, and, as we'll see, young children seem to recognize all four.

1. Causes precede their effects (for example, the ball moves *after* the bat hits it).

2. The cause must in some way "bump into" the effect (the bat must *hit* the ball to make it move, or hit something else that hits the ball). In other words, there must also be some spatial connection between cause and effect; this tells us the "mechanism" of causality, *how* the energy of the first or antecedent event was transferred to produce the consequent event. A tenet of science, from Descartes to present day quantum mechanics, is that there can be "no action at a distance"—and this holds whether the objects under study are as massive as galaxies or as tiny as electrons inside an atom.[6]

Some causal "bumpings" are apprehended immediately through perception, as when we see a bat hit a ball. Others require investigation, as when medical researchers seek the cause of a new disease. Indeed, some of the most outstanding achievements in science have been discoveries of previously unknown entities that mediate causal connections (an example is the discovery of DNA as the medium through which offspring inherit characteristics from their parents).

3. More forceful "bumps" are expected to produce larger effects. In other word, the more energy transferred from the causal event, the greater the effect that follows—a heavier or more rigid bat, a harder ball, or a more forceful swing should move the ball farther. (Sometimes, though, we attribute causality to the *absence* of an entity or force that is normally present, as when we say that the airplane crashed because it ran out of gas. On further analysis, though, the actual effect [falling to the earth] is always the result of present and positive forces [the pull of gravity].)

4. We use one additional criterion when judging causality: *regularity*. If A really is the cause of B, then whenever A occurs B should follow (if other conditions remain unchanged). Our confidence in A as the cause of B will be weakened if A occurs and B doesn't follow (if a medicine that appeared to cure one person doesn't work for others, we would suspect that the first person got better for some other reason). Scientists always look for regularity when searching for causes; research findings must be replicated before they are accepted. Scientists also recognize that they can never be 100 percent sure of a cause—that regularity never means certainty. Einstein expressed this vulnerability to new evidence in the statement, "No amount of experimentation can ever prove me right; a single experiment may at any time prove me wrong."

In determining causes we distinguish between those that are *necessary* and those that are *sufficient*. For instance, oxygen is a necessary cause of combustion, in the sense that things don't burn without oxygen, but it is not a sufficient cause because the mere presence of oxygen won't produce combustion on its own. In contrast, a sufficient cause does produce the effect on its own. For a given substance oxygen *plus* a critical temperature would be a sufficient cause of combustion since together they do cause the substance to ignite. In many cases a sufficient cause is made up of a combination of necessary causes. Not all sufficient causes, though, are necessary. A bat hitting a ball is sufficient to cause the ball to move, but a bat is not needed to make a ball move.

Children's Understanding of the Causes of Physical Events

Research during recent decades has shown that during their first 5 or 6 years, children become responsive to the basic elements of causality that

I've just described. Psychologists Merry Bullock, Rochel Gelman, Renée Baillargeon, and their colleagues found that 3-year-olds, when asked what made something happen, consistently selected a prior event as the cause of a later event. For example, children never say a jack-in-the-box popped up because of an event that happened after it popped.

In addition, when the children had to choose a cause from two prior events, they chose the one that appeared to make physical contact with the later event (the one that appeared to bump into the jack-in-the-box). In other words, these young children seemed to understand the idea of transfer of energy and mechanism. The children also took amount of energy into consideration: a ball rolling toward the jack-in-the-box was selected over a light moving toward it as the cause of its popping up. A more recent study demonstrating 5-year-olds' awareness of energy (and inertial) effects found they understood that the heavier an object sliding down a ramp, the further it will move something it bumps into at the bottom of the ramp. They also understood the converse—the heavier the object at the bottom of the ramp, the less it will be moved by something sliding into it.[7]

Research also shows that 3-year-olds are adept at picking out the correct order and causal mechanism when shown before/after pictures. For example, when shown pictures of an intact cup and a broken cup, the children correctly selected a picture of a hammer to insert between them. Also, the children's explanations of causal mechanisms were properly "mechanistic"; they did not attribute intentions to inanimate objects, disconfirming Piaget's assertion that preschoolers rely on animistic explanations. Other researchers also report that children rarely give animistic explanations. Indeed, it is evident that even during their earliest months children recognize the difference between people and inanimate objects as causal agents. For instance, infants will smile and vocalize toward people in ways that they don't do to objects. Babies will try to get a person to pick up something they want; they'll never try to get a chair to do it.[8]

I suspect that when children do give animistic explanations, attributing intentions to the wind or feelings to furniture, it is because of the training they've received rather than anything intrinsic to their thinking. Children's stories are filled with animistic images, from clouds having conversations, to angry trees that try to grab little girls, to little engines that strive to do good deeds. Religious stories are another source of nonnaturalistic causal explanations. Parents also sometimes encourage animistic thinking by the explanations they give: "The moon comes out to tell little children that it's time to go to sleep." Reminding children that engines and other objects don't really talk or think or strive to do things won't undermine their pleasure in such stories.

By the time children reach 2, they have had a lot of experience with cause–effect relationships and already appear to understand that all events have causes. Moreover, when a cause isn't obvious (for example, something moves but they didn't observe what moved it) they look for a causal mechanism (such as something or someone that might have bumped into the thing that moved). In other words, the 2-year-old is already a confirmed determinist, recognizing that things don't just happen for no reason. Indeed, some researchers claim to have demonstrated that even three-month-olds are determinists—for instance, that they show what appears to be surprise when a familiar object seems to move on its own.[9]

Other research shows that preschoolers' understanding of causality is already keen enough for them to recognize when events are random in the sense that one can't make precise predictions of them (for instance, they recognize the impossibility of predicting which colored marble will pop out of the hole in a rotating bingo-type cage filled with different colored marbles).[10]

As to when children begin to use regularity information in determining causality, studies of 3- and 5-year-olds show that even children this young recognize the importance of regularity: In the tests, one event consistently preceded an effect while a second event preceded it only occasionally. For instance, moving a lever on the right side of a box was always followed by a light on the box going on, while moving the left lever down was followed by the light going on only when the right lever was moved down at the same time. When asked which of the two levers caused the light to go on, the children picked the right one, the one that consistently preceded the effect.[11]

In an early and interesting study of 6-year-olds, Louis Long and Livingston Welch found that with some hints and practice, children this age could use regularity information to determine which of several potential causes (such as various foods eaten in different combinations) was associated with an effect (getting sick). To solve these kinds of problems the children had to use, intuitively, what logicians call inductive inference. In this specific case they used "Mill's Joint Method of Agreement and Difference" through which they sorted out which one food was *always* there when the illness occurred and was *never* there when the illness didn't occur.[12] (Obviously, the children didn't know the name of the procedure they were using or that it was named after John Stuart Mill, who codified the various methods of inductive inference.)

The few other studies in this area confirm that grade-school children can take regularity (or "covariation") information into account and that their use of regularity information improves with training; that is, they learn to consider not just the confirming information (such as how many got sick of those who ate the food) but also the disconfirming information (such as how many of those who ate the food *didn't* get sick).[13]

Teaching a Child about Physical Causality

Demonstrate and Point Out Cause/Effect Occurrences

The possibilities for doing this are endless and will vary with your child's age. Here is a simple example that illustrates the idea; it can be done with a 6-month-old. Put two large checkers or similar discs (such as plastic hockey or knock hockey pucks) on a table. For safety, use large discs and be prepared for your child's attempts to put them in his mouth. Place your baby on your lap near the checkers and in a position to see them. Then holding one checker bump it into the other one. Repeat this a few times, sometimes changing the angle of approach (thus sending the one being bumped off in different directions).

Next, using a finger, flick one checker into the other; repeat this a few times too. Mix in a few misses. Then add another checker and try to set up a chain reaction; again, miss some of the time. Verbalize what is going on in the form of a game: "Now I'm going to try to hit the checker. Flick. There it goes. Bump! I hit it." Then let your child move the checkers about. At first you may have to guide his hand to push the checkers, but give him as much freedom as he wants to move them on his own in whatever way he wants (recognizing that he may discover that knocking them off the table is much more fun than knocking them into each other).

This simple activity captures core aspects of physical causality, such as force and the transfer of energy, and very young infants appear fascinated by observing and making objects bump into each other. If you play the game on different surfaces you will be adding a lesson in friction.

For another activity that provides a basic lesson in gravity, put your baby on your lap and place an open box on her lap (a shoe box will do). Then put a ball in the box—preferably a whiffle ball—and gently tip the box back and forth so the ball rolls from end to end. (Here again be ready for the baby's inevitable attempts to mouth the ball.) Next, put the box in the baby's hands and guide her into tipping it in different directions to make the ball roll. On some occasions try to stop the ball in the middle of the box. Soon add a second ball and later a third. Your baby will enjoy watching and listening to them rumble back and forth and click into each other. After a while make a hole on one end of the box so she can watch the balls fall through it one at a time. Try placing her hand under the hole so the ball falls into it. In this simple activity with balls, as in the one with checkers, your child will be exploring basic physical processes.

During their infancy, toddler, and preschool years children learn about physical causality largely through their own endless experimentation. Their parents' job is primarily to provide them with mobiles, sand, water, blocks, balls, marbles, rope, construction toys, balloons, trucks, pull-toys, drums, funnels, xylophones, harmonicas, stacking cups, sifters, straws, rubber bands, marble and water shoots, things that float and things that sink, padlocks and keys, and various kinds of tools. With these they will then spend joyful hours learning about gravity, force, balance, and other physical phenomena. Toys that demonstrate transformations of energy are particularly useful (such as water and sand wheels in which flowing water or sand turns a wheel).

While children don't need formal instruction during their explorations, parents can be helpful in a number of ways. These include:

- Displaying interest in the child's explorations and delight and amazement at whatever he or she makes happen.
- Applying verbal labels to the objects and events in the play: ''The *round* ones keep *rolling* away.'' ''Look at it *squirt* out.''
- Coming to the rescue when frustration mounts: ''That big block just won't stay up there. Maybe if we put a brace on this side it'll stay.''
- Encouraging new possibilities: ''I wonder what will happen if we put some sand in the balloon and then blow it up and shake it?''

Sometimes it is best to reveal new possibilities without describing them— simply by doing something in the child's view and then letting him ''discover'' the rest on his own. For instance, you might set up a pendulum (a weight hanging from a rope will do) so that it swings close to the ground. Then, while playing with it, you might casually place a ball in its path. Your child is likely to want to recreate the impact of the weight smashing into the ball and will discover some practical aspects of centrifugal forces as she learns to position the weight for maximum impact.

You can provide a lesson in balance by placing a long block across a can and balancing small blocks on each end. Encourage your toddler to pick up one of the small blocks and note his surprise and interest when the other end tumbles down. You can provide a lesson in tensile strength by fastening a napkin across the open top of a coffee can with a rubber band and piling blocks on top. See how many it takes before the napkin gives way. Try it again with another kind of paper. Talk about what you are doing as you do it ("That's five blocks and it hasn't ripped. Now put another block on top and let's see if it can hold six blocks").

Generally, children's explorations take them through three levels of understanding of causal relationships. At first their understanding is limited to what they have experienced directly ("That floats; that doesn't"). Then their understanding generalizes to an intuitive, but not yet verbalizable, grasp of the physical principle at work ("That piece of wood should float; I'm sure that rock won't"). Finally they may reach the point where they grasp and can describe the underlying physical principle ("Objects float if they weigh less than an equivalent volume of water"). *Your explanations will make it easier for your child to gain an understanding of the causal mechanisms.*

Unfortunately, many teachers of young children have been influenced by Piaget's position and take a strong stand against explaining causal relationships to children (among many other things that they won't explain), even when the children ask. Piaget's position is summed up in his statement, "Every time you teach a child something you keep him from reinventing it."[14] But we don't want our children to have to rediscover everything on their own. And, contrary to Piaget's beliefs, children learn without having to take actions (see the discussion of this in chapter 5); and they learn from explanations (as demonstrated in the study by Barbara White and Paul Horwitz described below, as well as by other research cited in this chapter).

Giving your child explanations does not preclude his making discoveries on his own; nor does it mean that you should simply give information without encouraging him to make inferences about possible causes. For instance, all children enjoy observing a blown-up balloon go zooming off when the air is allowed to rush out of it. By the time children are about 6 many can gain an understanding of the mechanism at work—if it is explained to them. If parents wait until they discover it on their own, it may be a very long wait.

You can begin the explanation of balloon flight by stimulating your child to think about the problem: ask her why she thinks the balloon goes flying about. Her explanation will probably not be accurate, although I've known 6-year-olds who figured it out without any assistance. You'll find that children this age can understand that air has been squeezed into the balloon, and they can perceive the "strength" of squeezed air by pressing in on a filled balloon and feeling the resistance. You can explain that "The air we breathe is actually made of tiny pieces (or molecules) of air, and that each piece tries to keep a certain distance away from the other pieces. If pieces are squeezed together, they move apart as soon as they are released, just as a sponge expands as soon as you stop squeezing it, or a spring pops back up after you stop pressing on it."

"In a closed balloon, the air pushes out in all directions at once (you can draw a picture to illustrate this), so the balloon doesn't go anywhere (demonstrate this by having your child place his hands inside a sturdy plastic bag and then push them out in opposite directions; the bag will expand but not go anywhere).

"Now if we open one end of the balloon by releasing the stem, the little pieces of air, still trying to expand, rush out of it. The pieces of air on the other end are still pushing against the side of the balloon, moving it in that direction (illustrate this by cutting a hole in the plastic bag so one of your child's hands can come out of it as he moves his hands apart; the hand remaining inside will move the bag in the direction opposite the hole)."

After the demonstration with the bag, see if he can explain the similarity between what he experienced with the bag to what happens in the balloon. Also point out that rockets work on the same principle: The gas in the rocket expands when heated. Some of it rushes out the open back end; the rest pushes on the front end, moving the rocket forward.

On their own, children are likely to assume that the balloon (or rocket) moves forward because the column of gas rushing out the back hits up against the surrounding air, which then pushes the balloon (or rocket) forward. They'll recognize the inadequacy of this answer, at least for rockets, if you remind them that rockets work in the vacuum of space where there is no air.

Obviously, physical causality is happening everywhere. When the trees bend in the wind, point out the connection between the force of the wind and the degree of bending. You might also point out how the extraordinary flexibility of trees protects them from snapping in half as the wind blows them. Try demonstrating the value of flexibility by comparing the effect of pressure on a wooden and a plastic toothpick.

Your child will quickly let you know whether your explanations are clear. If not, try another approach, using something she is already familiar with to help her understand the new ideas. For instance, a 5-year-old asked her father why men get bald. Her father recalled reading of recent evidence that a particular protein was missing from the hair follicles of balding men. He also knew that his daughter was familiar with tulip bulbs, so he explained:

Scientists aren't sure why men get bald but one came up with a good idea recently. You know how a tulip grows out of a bulb? (She nodded yes.) Well each hair on our body grows out of a similar little bulb called a hair follicle. People get bald when these little bulbs stop growing hair. This scientist found that a chemical that's usually inside that little hair bulb is missing from the ones that stop growing hair. Maybe if they can put that chemical back inside the bulb it will start growing hair again. So the scientist is trying to figure out how to get the bulb to make that chemical again. She is also trying to make a cream with that chemical to rub on the head.

Here's another example of a parent explaining something new by drawing a parallel to something familiar. The child was 5 years, 1 month:

I was reading Larry a story in which the protagonists were maneuvering some rapids in a canoe. I asked him if he knew why the water moved so fast at the rapids. He said he didn't. I pointed to the rocks in the picture and said that the water was moving fast because it had to squeeze between the rocks. He had a blank look on his face. I reminded him of how we made the water come out faster and more forcefully from the garden hose by placing our fingers over the nozzle. I explained that our fingers made the water rush out faster by forcing it to squeeze through a smaller opening. The rocks in a stream do the same thing; they get in the way of the flow of water, forcing the water to squeeze between them, thus making it flow faster.

As one father discovered, sometimes the child will find the analogical connection for you:

Robin (4 years, 7 months) asked why her grandmother's hands shook (she suffers from Parkinson's disease). I explained that the muscles in our hands and arms are controlled by our brains and I drew a diagram to show her the connection between brain and arm muscles. I continued, explaining that usually our brains only send messages to our arm muscles when we decide to move our arm, but that grandma's brain was sending messages even when she wasn't thinking about moving—so her hand was moving even when she didn't want it to. Robin then said, "Oh, I understand. The brain is sending teeny letters to the muscle that tell it, 'Move, move'."

If you can't come up with an explanation that your child can understand, tell her you'll try to think of one and try again later. Also, don't get discouraged or punitive if your child tunes out. It's probably because you are giving more details than she can comprehend, such as too many new terms or too many steps in the causal sequence. You can ask for her attention and let her know that some things take a while to explain. You can also let her know that part of a mommy's and daddy's job is to help their children understand the things around them and that you love explaining things to her. But don't make a fuss if she has lost interest (or loses it again quickly) and wants to go on to something else.

In whatever environment you are in with your child, be on the alert for opportunities to reveal cause/effect relationships. Bring your child's attention to how doors lock and open (how the hinges work and how the doorknob moves the bolt in and out of the slot on the doorframe), and talk about how birds fly by pushing the air with their wings and how fish swim by pushing the water with their fins and bodies (which wriggle from side to side).

Explain the cycles of the washing machine (first the clothes spin in soapy water, then new water comes in to rinse them), and point out the hoses that bring the water in and out. Also describe what happens to the water in the dryer and where the water vapor goes—if possible letting your child feel the vapor as it disperses in the air (she'll feel it turn back into water on her hand). If your child hears about an earthquake on the television news, try to illustrate for her how the surface of the earth is made up of moving plates that bump into and slide under each other, causing the land at the surface to change shape (you can use your hands, a blanket, or pieces of paper as a model).

Share whatever facts you know about causality with your child but don't hesitate to admit when you don't know how something happens. It is just as useful to wonder aloud about how it might have been caused and to speculate with your child on possible reasons. You definitely want to encourage your child to speculate on reasons. Your library and bookstore will have children's books on science, nature, and technology that describe and illustrate how things happen. Some are appropriate for children as young as 4 and 5—ages when children are asking lots of causal questions.

Many causal explanations require a lot of preliminary information before they can be understood. For instance, children often ask why they need inoculations when they aren't sick. To understand how an inoculation prevents illness, the child would need to know the following: (1) Germs (or tiny bugs that can't be seen) get inside our bodies and make us sick. (2) Medicine kills germs. (3) Our bodies make medicines on their own that kill germs. (4) Sometimes our bodies can't make enough medicine fast enough to kill off the germs that get inside us. Only when these four pieces of information are grasped can a child understand the way inoculations work: (5) The vaccine contains dead or weakened germs that can't harm you but that get your body's medicine factory going. Then if live germs of that same type get inside you, your body has lots of your own medicine ready to gobble them up.

Try to be aware of the information your child must have in order to understand your explanations and make sure you present each step along the way—although not necessarily all at once. When a child doesn't understand an explanation try to ascertain whether it is because some essential steps in the causal analysis have been left out.

Also, be careful about giving false causal information for the sake of some other agenda. For instance, a friend told his son that the reason they couldn't get a puppy was because they already had a cat and cats and dogs fight. Now this friend knew very well that it is not difficult to get a cat and a puppy to adjust to each other, but he didn't want to be seen as a bad guy or to give his real reason: a puppy involves a lot of work. Misinformation like this tends to backfire. Either the child remains misinformed (an unfortunate result), or he'll learn the truth and mistrust his father's explanations in the future (another unfortunate result).

Describe the Physical Principles Underlying Causal Relationships

By 5, children can understand general physical principles; for example, that substances expand as they get hotter. For instance, explain that the reason the concrete in the sidewalk is divided into squares with spaces between them is to leave room for expansion in summer. For similar reasons the doors in the house sometimes stick in the warm weather. And that's also why we can open a tight bottle top after running it under hot water. And even our bodies expand, which is why our shoes feel tight when our feet get hot. You can point out that even highways and bridges are built with spaces along the roadway to leave room for expansion; otherwise the road buckles. And show your child how a thermometer uses the very same principle: the mercury expands as it is heated and fills up more of the tube. Ask your child to tell you when he or she comes across other examples that might express the same principle.

Other important physical principles are the notions of energy and gravity. Your child will understand on an experiential level that it takes energy to move, as well as to lift or push something. And he or she will also understand that it takes more energy to run than to walk, and more to run fast than slow. The reason it takes energy to move oneself or anything else is because gravity is pulling everything down toward the center of the earth, and things (objects, persons) are able to move only when there is enough energy propelling them to overcome the downward pull of gravity.

Furthermore, once something is moving, it only stops when some other force stops it. For example, a car will stop when we take our foot off the gas pedal because gravity pulls it down. It will also stop if we apply the brake, which sets up a counter force. You can illustrate the notion of inertia by demonstrating that the faster the car is going, the longer it takes to come to a halt, whether it is slowed by gravity or the brake. Explain that that's why the faster you go, the more room you leave between your car and the car in front of you. Point out to your child that he or she has had direct experiences with inertia when running: it takes longer and more effort to slow down when running fast than running slow.

Children are usually surprised when they learn that all objects fall to the earth at the same speed, regardless of their size or weight (except for the effects of air currents and friction). Their intuitive understanding is that heavier objects will fall faster (adults have the same intuition). One way to explain why they don't is to imagine gravity in the form of an invisible spring stretched between the earth and each object falling to it. When objects fall to the earth they are really being pulled (gravity is a *force*). The heavier (or more massive) the object, the stronger the spring (or force of gravity) pulling it.

At this point your child may ask, "If heavier objects are pulled by stronger springs, why don't they fall faster?" The reason is that the stronger springs are pulling heavier things. It takes a stronger spring to accelerate a heavy object to the same speed that a weaker spring accelerates a lighter object. So while it is true that the force of gravity is greater for heavier objects, this stronger force is needed in order to overcome the inertia of the heavier objects.

Another interesting question for children to ponder is where we get our energy to overcome the force of gravity. You can explain that it comes from the food we eat—that tiny bits of the food are carried in our blood to our muscles, which are like large rubber bands that pull our body parts back and forth when we decide to move. Without the food the muscles get weak and can't pull very hard. When we run, we use up more of the food than when we walk. You can draw a parallel to the energy used in a car—that cars get their energy in the form of gasoline which gets heated in the engine, and the heat (which is produced as little explosions) moves the pistons up and down (like pedals on a bike), turning the wheels. When we step on the gas pedal, we are sending gas into the engine faster, making the wheels spin faster.

Obviously these descriptions do not depict the actual processes (such as the function of actin, myosin and ATP in muscles, and the pistons and crankshaft in cars), but they are accurate enough to allow a child of five or six to grasp the underlying causal mechanisms and energy exchanges. Once these mechanisms are grasped, more accurate terminology and depictions can be provided.

You might rig up a simple pulley to show a child how one can use gravity, which pulls everything down, to help lift something *up*. Children are usually fascinated by pulleys, apparently tickled by the fact that one pulls a rope in one direction to make something attached to it move in the opposite direction. Pulleys can also be used to demonstrate the usefulness of counterweights, here again demonstrating gravity at work. On one end of the pulley, place a counterweight that is heavy enough to balance the weight of the object to be hoisted. Then a slight downward pull on the counterweight side will be sufficient to lift the object easily. Elevators use a similar mechanism of pulleys and counterweights, saving a great deal of energy that would otherwise be needed to lift the cab and passengers. For a demonstration you can use small pulleys from the hardware store, some cord, and hand weights of five and ten pounds.

Since children can't see energy, it is not easy for them to grasp the idea that one kind of energy can get transformed into another kind. The great practical value of this notion is also not apparent to them. Therefore, whenever possible introduce them to instances of energy getting transformed, and show how we use these transformations to make things happen. For example, you can hold a piece of paper over the spout of a steam kettle to demonstrate how heat can make things move; this can be followed up with a description of how steam engines use the very same principle to make locomotives and steamships move. You can make the causal connection clearer by explaining that the steam in these engines (which are essentially great big kettles) flows into the pistons which are something like the pedals of a bicycle. The pistons move, just as the steam from the kettle moved the paper. The pistons, like the pedals of a bicycle, are connected to wheels; so when the pistons move, the wheels go around, carrying the locomotive down the track or the ship through the water.

Be aware that there are some seemingly "natural" misconceptions that youngsters (and grown-ups too) have about physical causality. One that I've already mentioned is that heavier objects fall at faster speeds than lighter ones. Another misconception is revealed in their belief that if a ball rolls through a spiral tube it will continue to roll in a spiral path after leaving the tube. They seem to believe that a force that affects an object (the ball) somehow stays with the object even after the force is no longer being applied (after it leaves the tube). Recent research by Barbara White and Paul Horwitz has shown that with carefully structured instruction, sixth-graders could learn the principles governing such physical events and have their misconceptions corrected. For instance, after training, one boy explained why the ball would go straight after leaving the tube:

STUDENT: Because what happens while it is being spiraled around and pushed around doesn't have anything to do with what it does once it's free.

INTERVIEWER: Can you think of another way of saying that?

STUDENT: When it leaves the tube, there is nothing pushing on it and so it just keeps going straight.

The youngsters learned to consider the "Newtonian" forces acting on objects and to think of the forces as "impulses." A push on a ball is a single impulse. It sets the ball in motion and doesn't do anything after that. Gravity pulling an object down acts continuously, which can be conceived of as a new impulse added every moment. In an interview, one of their sixth-grade trainees demonstrated that he "got" this notion of impulses:

INTERVIEWER: Imagine that we throw a ball straight up into the air. Describe what happens to the motion of the ball.

STUDENT: It will start going up at the speed you threw it up, and then it will gradually slow down, and there will be a second when it is stopped in the air, and then it will start coming down, and it will gradually speed up.

INTERVIEWER: Can you explain why that happens?

STUDENT: Because going up the gravity keeps pulling, adding another impulse down, and that will eventually stop the ball, and then going down it keeps adding another impulse down which makes it go faster and faster.[15]

The researchers report that sixth-graders receiving the instructions not only performed better on tests of Newtonian principles than untrained peers, but better than a group of high-school physics students. Here is an example of imaginative instruction producing extraordinary and unexpected results.

Point Out Unexpected and Nonobvious Cause/Effect Occurrences

Here's an instance of a parent pointing out a cause/effect connection to a puzzled child (who was 4 years, 4 months):

We were in the waiting area of the bank during one of their regular afternoon electric organ concerts. Rick saw the man playing what to him must have simply looked like a piano, but the music was coming out of the speaker to our left, many feet from the organ. He walked to the speaker, looked at it and then at the musician. A puzzled expression was on his face. During a break in the music I took him around to the back of the organ and showed him the wires coming out of it and we traced the speaker wire around the room to the speaker. I explained that when the musician hit the keys the sound went into the wire and came out through the speaker. I reminded him how our phonograph at home worked the same way, sending the sound from the turntable through wires to the speakers some feet away. He seemed satisfied with the explanation.

The causal connections in electrical appliances (from organs to toasters to telephones) are certainly not obvious to children. Point out these connections and draw simple diagrams showing electrical and telephone lines coming down the street from the power station, then entering the different buildings and going into everyone's home.

It will be helpful to show the child the inside of an electrical wire and, as a starter, you might describe electricity as something that flows down the wire making it very hot. Point out the glowing, hot wires in toasters and light bulbs, and show how they are connected to the electric flow at the outlets. You might explain that when the switch on an appliance is off, the electricity can't flow into it because there is a gap in the circuit. Turning the switch on moves a piece of wire into the gap, completing the circuit, allowing the electric current to flow through.

A diagram depicting telephones might show how your own phone is connected by a wire all the way to the phone company and from there to the different people you call. Pick one or two friends or family members whom you call frequently and whose homes your child has visited: "See, when we call Laura and Richard, we speak into the phone and our voice is carried out of this wire, which goes out of our building and then under the streets all the way to the telephone company's building; there it connects to another wire going all the way to Laura and Richard's phone."

Diagrams and picture books will also make it easier to satisfy your child's curiosity about how the unobservable parts of his or her body work. For instance, you can play a little game with your child that illustrates that bodily reactions take time to occur. Have him rest his arm on a table, extending his hand over the edge. Dangle a dollar bill between (but not touching) his thumb and forefinger. These two fingers should be about a half-inch apart, poised to grasp the bill when you let go of it. Hold the bill vertically with half above and half below his thumb and forefinger, then release it without signalling when.

The child won't be able to close his fingers in time to grasp the bill and will be surprised at his inability to do so. He'll probably enjoy trying over and over again. With the help of a diagram you can explain that when you release the bill, before he can grab it, a message has to go from the bill to his eye, and then to his brain and down his spine, and out his arm, and to his fingers—and that all this takes longer than the time it takes for the bill to drop out of reach. Along with the diagram, use your finger to trace on his body the route the message must travel through his nervous system.

Children usually find demonstrations of their reflexes interesting—that their leg jerks involuntarily when their knee is hit in the proper place, that they can't keep their eyes open when you clap your hands near their face. Chart out the "wires" in their body that control these mechanisms. Also explain the importance of pain receptors and reflexes by discussing the dangers everyday environments pose for children born without these receptors.

The task of explaining unobservable body functions is made easier by drawing parallels to familiar objects—for instance, by pointing out that blood flows all through the body in little tubes that are like straws or hoses. You can demonstrate the pumping action of the heart with a bulb baster or even a plastic food bag filled with water. Also, by dissolving a sugar cube in water you can illustrate how our digestive juices break down our food into tiny pieces, too tiny to see and small enough to enter our blood stream and be carried to all parts of our body. Have the child taste the sugar water so he'll believe that the sugar, though unseen, is still in the glass.

A fun way to illustrate the function of sensory nerves in the skin is to play a game in which the child must guess whether you've placed one or two fingers on different parts of his body. Some areas, like the back, have few touch receptors, so two fingers pressing on the skin about an inch apart are both likely to be affecting the same receptor, making it feel like one finger pressing. Other areas, such as the lips, have many receptors, making it easy to tell that two fingers are pressing.

You can give a child a sense of his body's feedback mechanisms by pointing out how perfectly the liquid in his nostrils is controlled when he is in good health. Children have a lot of direct experience with the liquid in their nostrils: too much and they have a runny nose, too little and the nose feels dry and burny. Explain that our bodies have sensors that monitor the liquid and adjust the amount produced to provide just the right wetness for comfortable breathing and to catch any particles or germs that we might breathe in. When we are sick the feedback mechanism gets disturbed and our bodies make too much or too little.

You might want to check the science and nature section of your toy store for kits and models that demonstrate anatomical and physiological functions.

What makes plants grow? is another question that children often ask. You can buy seeds (such as beans) to demonstrate the life cycle of plants. Children enjoy observing the seeds send out roots (for bringing in water) and shoots that develop leaves to exchange air and catch sunlight. The plant uses the sunlight, air, and water to make its food in the form of carbohydrates (which are sugars and starches). Plants, unlike animals, *make* their food internally, out of hydrogen and oxygen taken from the water (H_2O) and carbon taken from the carbon dioxide in the air (CO_2). Of course, before children can understand how plants make food, they will have to understand that water and air are made up of a combination of elements (such as oxygen, hydrogen, and carbon) and that carbohydrates are made from some of the same elements (for example, one carbohydrate is $C_6H_{12}O_6$).

You can underscore the importance of plants to our survival by pointing out that animals (including human animals) also require carbohydrates but can't make them. They are the source of energy in all our cells, so we must get them directly by eating plants, or indirectly by eating other animals that have eaten plants and stored the carbohydrates in *their* cells.

If you grow plants from seeds and put a couple of drops of food coloring in the water you can see the color rising up in the plant as it takes the water in. Your library or bookstore will have well-illustrated books that explain how plants propogate through pollination, the production of fruit, and the distribution of seeds.

A difficult concept for children to comprehend is that light travels from a source to an object and from the object to our eyes, and that it takes time for light to move from place to place. Children obviously can't see light moving, but they can begin to grasp the notion with reference to vast distances. For example, you might tell them that the light from the stars they see took a very long time (sometimes hundreds of thousands of years) to get from the star all the way to their eyes, and that the light from some stars we see through telescopes might have started with an explosion on the star millions of years ago, so long ago that there were still dinosaurs on earth (or even before there was an earth). When a child's awareness of time is sufficient, you might explain that the light from the sun takes eight minutes to reach the earth.

Creating shadows with objects or hands is an enjoyable way to convey that light travels from a source and can be interrupted. Flashlights are also excellent for learning about light and the reflectivity of different surfaces.

A lightning storm provides another opportunity to teach about the time it takes for light (and sound) to travel. The roar of thunder always comes after the flash of lightning, although at their source they occur at essentially the same time (the lightning instantly heats the air around it causing the air to expand rapidly; we hear this expansion as thunder). You can explain that we see the lightning first because light travels much more quickly than sound; the light travels *through* the air, but the sound has to *push* the air. Children often find it interesting that you can tell whether the storm is moving toward or away from you by the number of seconds between the lightning and the thunder: if the interval is diminishing, the storm is headed your way; if it is increasing, the storm is moving off.

Another confusing question for children is where the water comes from when they turn on the kitchen and bathroom taps. Show your child the pipes that bring the water to the sinks and describe where these pipes originate (such as in reservoirs and wells), and how the water gets from these sources, sometimes more than a hundred miles away, all the way to our homes. Here again, diagrams and illustrated books can make the paths clear. Look for books that describe the entire sequence of steps in the water cycle, from the evaporation of ocean and lake water, to the formation of clouds, to rain and snow falling on a reservoir or other water source, to the water being piped to our homes and businesses, to the runoff and drainage that returns it to the ocean or lake.

Encourage Thinking about Cause/Effect Relationships

You can do this by the questions you ask. One type of question starts with some event and ponders what might follow from it: "What do you think would happen if . . . ?" A second type of question asks what could have caused something that already happened: "Why do you think that happened?" With 2- and 3-year-olds, one's questions will naturally pertain to their everyday experiences: "What do you think will happen if we lean that block over the edge of the table?" "Why do you think that card falls off the shelf every time the door opens?" "What do you think will happen to the water if I open the plug?" "Why do you think the drawer won't open?"

To answer these kinds of questions the child has to use things she knows to infer something she doesn't know. She knows that things that are not supported fall. If she pictures that the block leaning over the edge will not be supported, she should be able to predict that it will fall. She knows that the wind blows things. If she also knows that the door swinging open creates a wind, she may realize that the card is blown down by the wind created when the door is opened. Her inferences can be checked by experiments—by leaning the block over the edge, or by placing something between the door and the card so the wind no longer "bumps into" the card.

As children get older, more complex and technical questions can be asked. For instance, you might ask, "When it rains where does all the water come from?" This can lead to a description of the water cycle: rain water runs off into streams and rivers, and then into lakes and the ocean. The water on the ground and in the lakes and oceans evaporates and rises into the air, eventually coalescing into clouds that are mixtures of water droplets and dust. When the water droplets get too heavy they fall to the ground as rain or snow, starting the cycle over again.

You can demonstrate some of these processes, such as water vapor turning into droplets on a cool surface or in cool air (the air at cloud level is cooler than at ground level); and that two or more small drops coalesce into larger, heavier drops; and that weighting water drops with a bit of dust (or baby powder) causes them to run down a surface more readily.

A walk with a child can be used to get him or her to recognize and think about the impact that different aspects of the environment have on each other. "Why are some streets more windy than others?" "Why do trees grow better on one side of the street?" It's less important to know the right answer than to explore hypotheses together ("Do you think the trees on one side get more sun?") and to analyze how each hypothesis might be tested.

By 5 or 6, children can ponder speculative questions like, "What do you think would happen if the traffic lights stopped working?" and "What do you think life would be like if there were no electric machines?" Children won't necessarily rattle off correct answers, but will respond to a dialogue that narrows the questions down for them: "If farmers didn't have trucks how would we get our food?" Here again their task is to use what they know to infer what they don't know. They know that cars and pedestrians stop and go according to the color of the traffic lights. From this they can foresee that without traffic lights, cars are likely to crash into each other and to run over pedestrians trying to cross the street.

One father reported that he liked to ask his daughters questions designed to stimulate their thinking about the basic needs of human survival. He would usually begin, "What if we were on a deserted island . . . ?" He might continue" . . . and winter was coming. How might we prepare to stay warm?" Or "How would we try to make sure we had enough water to last through the dry season?"

Some other questions dealing with familiar events are, "Why do you think the radiator gets hot?" "Why do you think the water bubbles and boils when we heat it on the stove?" "Why do you think the days are longer in the summer than the winter?" "Why do you think yeast makes cakes rise?" "Why do you think the plants over there are growing better than these?" Clearly, one can wonder about the causes of anything, and just as clearly, wondering is an activity to encourage in a child.

Be alert for news stories that can spark causal conversations. A few years ago there was a well-publicized search for the Loch Ness monster. A parent and child heard the news report announcing that no monster was

sighted. The child wondered if there still might be a monster hiding somewhere. The parent acknowledged that this was possible, that they hadn't
proved that the monster doesn't exist. Parent and child then explored the
reasons why the search might have failed even though a monster might
have been there. The reasons included: they searched in the wrong places;
the monster had a hiding place such as a cave; and the monster is well-
camouflaged.

Teach Inferential Thinking Skills for Discovering Cause/Effect Relationships

When children (or adults) wonder why something happened, there are
questions that can help find the cause. The daily news provides us with
many examples of detectives, physicians, ecologists, and structural engineers
using inferential reasoning to establish causal relationships:

1. *What was present when it happened that is usually not present?*
   Example: When people come down with an unusual illness, such as
   Legionnaires' disease, epidemologists look for the presence of a mi-
   crobe that is ordinarily *not* present in that environment.

2. *What was absent when it happened that is usually present?* Example:
   A bridge might collapse because rivets that are usually present have
   fallen out.

3. *What has happened that is similar to this and for which I already
   know the cause?* Example: If fish are discovered to be dying in a
   lake, ecologists will check the acidity of the water since high acidity
   has previously been implicated in the death of fish in lakes.

4. *Was there anything that appears to have changed that might be
   the cause?* Example: To a detective in search of the perpetrator of a
   hit-and-run accident, a car with a bloodstained bumper and a broken
   headlight will suggest a likely suspect, particularly if someone saw
   the vehicle clean and intact a short time before the accident.

5. *What could have caused something of that magnitude to happen?*
   Another way of phrasing this question is, What could have bumped
   into this, transferring this quantity of energy? Example: When an
   airplane blows up, investigators study the size of the hole and the
   heat and force of the explosion to ascertain whether it was a bomb
   and, if so, the type of explosive used.

6. *Are there any auxiliary effects that may reveal the cause?* Example:
   If a physician is treating someone for a drug overdose but isn't sure
   which drug was abused, he or she can narrow the possibilities by
   checking whether the patient's pupils are dilated or constricted.

7. ***What causes can be ruled out?*** Example: When something has been stolen from a store, police routinely check the doors and windows for forced entry. If no forced entry is apparent, it increases suspicion that it was an "inside job."

8. ***Are there any unique linkages between the effect and its cause?*** Example: Ballistics experts can determine from the shape of a bullet which gun it was fired from. Similarly, in paternity suits genetic analysis can determine the child's natural father.

Each of these questions attempts to narrow the possibilities as to what made something occur (but none guarantees a correct answer). These kinds of questions can be a regular part of parents' causal dialogues with their children, even with very young children. In fact, parents and children use these kinds of analyses all the time. If a child has a bellyache after the circus a parent might suggest that it was due to eating the cotton candy— "because you're not used to all that sugar." This is an example of number 1 above. As an example of number 2, if a child scrapes her knee in the park she might say to her mother, "I told you I should wear long pants."

Here's a dialogue that illustrates number 3:

CHILD: How come Barry's cat, Ribbon, wouldn't play with me?

PARENT: Do you remember when Uncle Sam came over and tried to play with you? What happened?

CHILD: His voice frightened me, and he bounced me too hard. I ran away from him.

PARENT: Well I think *you* were too loud and rough for Ribbon. So he got frightened and ran away, just as you did.

CHILD: I didn't mean to frighten him.

PARENT: And Uncle Sam didn't mean to frighten you. But you couldn't tell that from the rough way he was playing with you. And Ribbon couldn't tell that from the rough way you were playing with him.

As an example of number 4, a child might complain to her mother about her brother, "You gave Billy and me ten marbles each yesterday. Now I have only six. I want you to check Billy's marble bag to see if he took mine." As an example of number 5, a kindergartner might surmise who was (and wasn't) responsible for throwing over the playground equipment: "I think it had to be an older kid because a little kid couldn't have lifted it."

Illustrating numbers 6 and 7, a child might assert her innocence with the statement: "I didn't touch your perfume. You can smell my hands." As an example of number 8, a child might complain, "That cat must have been sleeping on my pillow again; it's covered with fur."

Parents can have their children make a list of the eight inferential questions and keep them in a handy place. Then whenever a causal problem is encountered, they can check the list to make sure they're covering all relevant questions. Also, when either parents or children come across a causal analysis in a newspaper, magazine, or detective story, they can note which of the questions, if any, led to the discovery of a cause. They might also discover that the list is incomplete and new questions need to be added.

Teach Experimental Techniques for Investigating Causes

Causal explanations need to be tested. If a physician believes a particular microbe causes a disease, she will try to confirm her belief through an experiment. Similarly, an ecologist will seek experimental confirmation of his belief that fish die in highly acidic water. Experiments are not always possible (one can't pull the moon around to confirm that it really does affect the tides, and one can't give people a fatal disease to confirm a theory of its cause). But when experiments are possible, they can support or disconfirm a causal explanation, as well as rule out competing explanations.

Preschoolers are not too young to understand the purpose of an experiment. For example, a parent reported that when their cat came down with a mysterious illness, the veterinarian explained that they would try a series of treatments, starting with the one he believed was most likely to succeed; each treatment was to be tried for a prescribed period of time. The veterinarian was experimenting. The parent explained this to her 4-year-old who seemed to understand the trial-and-error nature of the strategy. The child participated in administering the medicine, marking off the doses and days on a calender, and monitoring the cat for signs of improvement or decline.

Parents can also introduce experimentation in more formal ways. For example, you can plant seeds in different pots and vary aspects of the environment—such as amount of water or sunlight, soil quality, or spacing—to see which factors lead to healthier plants. Preschoolers can understand the goal behind such procedures (to discover what produces healthier plants) and the purpose of the experimental strategies. Use the word "experiment" to define what you are doing; it will help the child grasp the overall concept that encompasses the different steps in the procedure.

Four- and 5-year-olds can also come up with *hypotheses* on how to bring about some desirable end. I told my daughter, who was then 4 years, 10 months, about a boy I was working with who had stolen a bicycle. I explained that I had to figure out a way to keep him from stealing again.

She thought for a moment and said, "I have an idea. You can give him a T-shirt that says 'It's wrong to steal' on it. Then he'll be reminded not to steal wherever he goes." She took her idea very seriously and twice during the next few days asked if I had made up the T-shirt. I explained that he wouldn't wear that kind of a T-shirt and we couldn't force him to. She said she would try to come up with another idea—and she did.

Parents can present problems from work or any other domain to their children and ask for help in solving them. For example, the owner of a pizza shop told his son that customers weren't throwing their empty soda cans in the recycling barrel, but were putting them in the garbage barrel, which required an unpleasant sorting job. He asked for some ideas. The boy proposed that he attach a shoot shaped like an elephant's trunk to the soda can barrel. "People will notice that," he suggested, "and enjoy seeing their cans slide down the shoot." These kinds of problem solving sessions lead to interesting and pleasant exchanges between parents and children, and often to good ideas.

Sometimes experiments produce results that seem clear and easy to interpret: One can count the number of soda cans in the barrel before and after attaching the shoot. But often, experiments to establish a causal connection must be designed very carefully and the results interpreted with caution. For instance, experiments often require one or more *control* or comparison conditions to rule out alternative explanations. Experimental controls can be understood by children by about the age of 5 or 6. Picture the following dialogue:

CHILD: Do you think we should give Willie [their kitten] vitamins?

PARENT: There are vitamins in his cat food.

CHILD: But maybe he could use extra vitamins. I want him to grow up strong and healthy.

PARENT: Well, we could give him extra vitamins. But if he grows up strong and healthy, how could we tell if it was because of the extra vitamins? Maybe he would have grown up that way anyway, just by eating his regular food. Or maybe he would have grown even stronger with just the amount of vitamins that are in his food. Maybe extra vitamins are bad for cats.

CHILD: I don't know how we could tell. But I'd like to give him vitamins anyway. I know. Mary has Willie's brother. If we gave Willie vitamins and Mary didn't give her kitten vitamins, we could see who grows up healthier. Then we could tell if the extra vitamins made a difference.

PARENT: Great idea.

This child had discovered the importance of a comparison condition to rule out a competing explanation. Obviously, if one were to actually carry out an experiment on the effect of vitamins on cats one would want to have more than one cat receiving each treatment: getting versus not getting vitamins. Since any single cat may become healthy or unhealthy because of a great many factors, it wouldn't be possible to tell if vitamins really had an effect unless many cats were compared. So one would want to use a representative *sample* of cats. The next section of the dialogue makes this point:

PARENT: You know, some cats are just born to be stronger or better jumpers than others. If one cat turned out to be a stronger or a better jumper, I don't think we could tell if it was due to the vitamins or because it was just born that way.

CHILD: Is there any way to tell?

PARENT: You know what we'd have to do? We'd have to have a bunch of kittens that we gave the vitamins to and a bunch that didn't get them. Then we could see which bunch turned out better. We wouldn't expect all the ones that were born to be good jumpers to wind up in the same bunch.

Often experimenters are faced with the question of deciding how to measure the effects they are interested in. For instance in our cat experiment one would need a clear and reliable way to measure the strength and health of cats:

PARENT: How could we tell which cats were stronger and healthier?

CHILD: Well if some cats got sick a lot or died, or if some jumped higher than the others or ran faster, then we'd know.

PARENT: What if they all seemed pretty healthy but the ones we gave the vitamins to jumped a teeny bit higher than the others—do you think we could tell if it was because of the vitamins?

CHILD: I don't think so, not if it was just a teeny bit.

PARENT: You think it would be easier to tell if there was a big difference?

CHILD: Yes.

Here the child was learning an important element in interpreting the results of an experiment: the larger the difference between comparison treatments, the more likely the effect was due to the treatment. But there is still another important factor we would use in deciding whether a difference is really due to the treatments:

PARENT: What if all the kittens that got the extra vitamins turned out to be very strong and healthy and all the ones that didn't get vitamins turned out to be weak and sickly, then we would be pretty certain that the vitamins helped, wouldn't we?

CHILD: Yes. Then it would be easy to tell.

This last point introduces the notion of *variability*. If every kitten in the vitamin group turns out healthy and every kitten in the other group turns out unhealthy, that would indicate very small variability within those group, strongly supporting the beneficial effect of the vitamins. The smaller the variability within groups, the more likely a difference between the groups is due to the treatments.

As your child confronts causal questions throughout his or her school years, stress the value of using experiments to find answers, and introduce the elements of well-designed experiments, such as proper control treatments and carefully defined measurements. Research shows that these are notions that grade school children can understand.[16]

When you read about interesting experiments in the newspaper, such as on a new medical treatment or a new educational program, share the information with your child and discuss the experimental strategies. Sometimes the articles will describe a disagreement between scientists over the interpretation of research findings. Discuss this too. For instance, many scientists feel that higher temperature readings during recent decades indicates that the earth is getting warmer. But some scientists question this conclusion, arguing that the areas around the weather stations from which the readings are taken have become increasingly urbanized over recent decades and the temperature increases reflect local conditions and not global weather changes.

Teach about Coincidences, Superstitions, and the "Law of Large Numbers"

How would you explain this? A mother dreams that her son, a soldier in Viet Nam, is wounded and she soon receives word that her son was indeed shot that day. Many people find meaning in these kinds of occurrences, explaining the dream in terms of extraordinary premonitory or communication powers. Yet the dream seems far less extraordinary when one considers that there were millions of soldiers in Viet Nam, most with mothers, many of whom on any given night had a nightmare of her son being shot. Given the number of soldiers who were shot every day, by chance we would expect a certain number of these to coincide with a mother's nightmare.

There may be forms of communication between people that have not yet been discovered, but many of us are too ready to accept causal linkages between events that are better explained as coincidences. Given that it's hard enough to get someone standing just a few inches behind you to find the exact place on your back that needs scratching—despite intense efforts to send a clear message—the chances of being able to send and receive messages to and from vast distances is pretty slim. We do our children a disservice by neglecting to teach them about the law of large numbers, which says that very unlikely events happen some of the time just by chance.

Superstitions are also based on spurious causal connections. If you break a mirror, you'll have seven years of bad luck. If you wear your "lucky" shirt, you'll score more points. Some children readily adopt superstitious beliefs—sometimes because they are taught them by "authorities" (such as an older child). There is a good deal of evidence that false or superstitious beliefs, once in place, are not easily disconfirmed, so it's best to discourage them as they arise.[17] They foster notions of causality that are the opposite of what your child needs in order to understand what makes things happen and what he can control.

Teach That the Search for Causes Is an Ongoing Process

Children tend to assume that adults know why everything happens— that all the answers about causality are in. So it is useful to teach them that there are many things that happen that we don't yet know the causes of, and that there are people who devote their lives to uncovering why these things occur. "Illness" is a good topic to convey this information because children are often interested in understanding the causes of illness and how medicines work.

Point out that for certain illnesses (such as measles and strep throat) there were no medicines to cure or prevent them until very recently; there was nothing we could take to kill the tiny germs that cause them. But that doctors and scientists worked very hard for years and finally found medicines that worked. Also indicate that there are some illnesses (such as colds) for which there are still no medicines, but that doctors and scientists are trying to develop new drugs for them.

Preschoolers can comprehend that the search for causes is an ongoing process and that all the answers are not in. A father reported that his daughter (5 years, 1 month) asked why she found cats and dogs and certain other animals so cute. He answered that he wasn't sure, but he knew that scientists were working on it by showing children pictures of parts of dogs and cats to see which specific aspects they find cute. The daughter replied, "Are they also showing parts of rats to find out why people *don't* find them cute?"

You can give your child a good sense of the ongoing search for causes by sharing information from the science pages of newspapers and magazines and by watching television science documentaries together. It is also helpful to read biographies together about eminent scientists so your child can be inspired by their stories, by their curiosity, perseverance, and dedication to uncovering what makes things happen.

The Causes of Emotions (and Other Psychological States)

When we want a child to understand what makes things happen, we don't just mean what makes physical events happen. Another important question is, What makes emotions happen? The causes of emotions, like the causes of physical events, precede their effects. We get sad *after* hearing bad news. We get angry after being insulted. We get nervous after we start to think about an upcoming exam.

Emotions arise as involuntary reactions to various stimulating circumstances. But emotional stimuli do not simply pass their energy on in the direct way the causes of physical events do; the magnitude of a person's emotional reaction isn't based on the energy that "bumped into" him or her. A whispered "I love you" can produce a far greater reaction than a shouted "Hello, how are you?" Similarly, two fingers raised in a "V" for victory sign can set a crowd of thousands cheering. And a snake, not moving at all but poised to strike, will engender a far greater emotional reaction than a friendly dog prancing about. With such symbolic or linguistic events—events with "meaning"—we expect the psychological significance of the event, not its physical magnitude, to correspond to the size of the emotional reaction.

One way to think about the physical mechanism underlying emotional events is by analogy to the mechanism in an elevator. One may push the buttons for the third and thirteenth floors with equal force, but each sets off a different mechanism involving very different amounts of energy. In an analogous way, symbolic stimuli ignite what appear to be preestablished emotional mechanisms, leading to various kinds and degrees of emotional arousal (fear, anger, joy, etc.).

Ethologists refer to the mechanisms underlying emotional arousal in animals as "releasing mechanisms"—a term that well conveys the sense that the emotional mechanisms are prewired into our systems and ready to fire when the appropriate stimuli are presented. The physiological circuitry underlying some emotional reactions have been uncovered.[18] In humans, the stimuli that arouse emotions are far more complex than in animals and are continually being modified by experience. For instance, we must learn the meaning of words and gestures before we can respond to them emotionally, yet the releasing mechanism notion may still apply.

Children's Understanding of the Causes of Emotions

Children start to recognize and respond to the emotions of others during their early months.[19] They also show an awareness of the causes of emotions at a very young age. For instance, Bretherton and Beeghly, in the study discussed earlier, found that 2-year-olds are both aware of and concerned with emotions and their causes—and they talk about emotions with surprising clarity. The following are some examples they recorded:

"I give a hug. Baby be happy."

"Mommy exercise. Mommy have a good time."

"Maybe Gregg would laugh when he saw Beth do that."

"Grandma mad. I wrote on wall."

"It's dark. I'm scared."

"You sad, Mommy. What Daddy do?"

"I laugh at funny man."

Notice that in some of these statements the child is not merely describing an emotional reaction he or she has observed, but is predicting specific emotional reactions to particular arousing conditions (as in, "Maybe Gregg would laugh when he saw Beth do that"). Inferences like this reflect quite a good understanding of the connection between an emotion and its cause.

If parents incorporate emotional explanations into their conversations with their children, emotional understanding becomes evident well before a child reaches 2. A father reported that his 18-month-old daughter refused to give him back the cat's comb (which she had run off with) so he couldn't continue combing the cat. But when he told her, "It makes Wendy [the cat] sad," she brought it right over. Another parent said that her 17-month-old wouldn't stop shaking the table at a restaurant. But she calmed down when her mother explained, "The coffee is hot and it will burn Mommy if it spills." In both these incidents, the child's response reflects her recognition that her actions can produce painful feelings in others.

When children don't understand what led to an emotion, they will often ask for an explanation. A father reported that as he was scolding his child of 2½ for playing with food at the dinner table (as he had done many times before), she got a puzzled look on her face and, instead of reacting with her usual defiance, asked him why he got angry with her when she played with food. He realized then that during the many occasions when he had reprimanded her for playing with food, he had never made clear to her why it bothered him.

Parents of 2-year-olds are often surprised at how much their children know about emotions and their causes. One parent reported that her 24-

month-old protected her from all kinds of harm, not allowing her to sit or stand near the edge of a dock or to put her finger where it might get caught in a door. She also protected others whom she cared about. On one occasion she insisted that her babysitter not sit sideways on a carousel horse, calling out, "Don't! You'll fall." During the next few months she also began to protect those around her from more subtle forms of emotional distress. One afternoon she and a cousin of the same age were playing with an aunt who wanted a rest from their hectic games. When the cousin insisted that the games continue, the child intervened with a forceful "Aunt Becky is tired. You leave her alone."

The father of a 32-month-old reported an incident in which he pulled his daughter off the monkey bars in the playground and carried her home because she wouldn't leave when he asked. She had just mastered climbing to the top of the apparatus and was very pleased with herself. A short while later she was still upset. Her father asked if she was angry. She replied, "Yes, because you weren't nice to me. If I stopped you from doing something you liked, you'd be angry too." Her answer shows a clear understanding not just of what led to her own emotion, but of the general principle that people get angry at those who interfere with their pleasure.

Children this age are also becoming skillful at purposely provoking emotions in others through both words and actions. They'll comfort someone who is hurt, give gifts, and say things to make others feel good or bad, such as telling a playmate "I don't like you. You can't come to my house ever again" or "You're nice. You can play with all my toys."

Various studies show that 3- and 4-year-olds are not only able to predict emotions from prior causes, but are generally adept at explaining the emotions they observe. For example, in one study preschoolers responded to questions about playmates' emotions with explanations such as, "He is sad because he misses his mother" and "He is mad because she took his airplane." This same study also found that children this age could come up with suitable strategies for changing someone's bad feelings, here again reflecting considerable awareness of the causes of emotions. Other research shows that by the age of 5 or 6, children's understanding of basic emotions— their causes, the behaviors they are likely to spark, and their own ability to influence them—is not very different from that of adults.[20]

Here is an example of a child, 4 years, 9 months, applying her understanding of the antecedents of emotions to make a younger child (age 2) feel good:

The children were chasing fireflies in the backyard. The older child complimented the younger for being good at catching fireflies, which wasn't so. Later she explained why she had said it: "He really wasn't good at it but I wanted to make him feel good."

As they gain social experience, children become aware of a wider array of emotional states and their causes, including many that are quite subtle. A 3- or 4-year-old, for example, may use the word "proud" appropriately, recognizing the relationship of pride, not merely to success, but also to one's effort to do something well. Research with 5-year-olds found that they understand that a person's emotional reaction to another's behavior is not simply based on the surface aspects of the behavior but takes into account the intention behind the person's act. For instance, if asked how someone would react to being stood up by a friend, children this age recognize that the reaction would depend on what the person thought motivated the friend's failure to show up. If the friend didn't come because she suddenly took ill, they say there would be little anger—in contrast to a great deal of anger if the friend decided to stay home to watch TV without bothering to call. Other research shows that children this age realize that different individuals may react with different emotions to the same event (for example, two children might react very differently to a cat sitting down next to them); they also know that sometimes people hide their emotions.[21]

Here's an example of a child (5 years, 3 months) displaying a sophisticated understanding of what leads to fear by describing what *doesn't*:

> I woke Bea from a nightmare but she didn't remember what had frightened her. I asked if she was afraid now. She answered yes, but couldn't say of what she was afraid. I smiled and asked, "Of everything?" Then she smiled and said, "Not of everything, silly. Could you imagine someone yelling, 'Eek, a caterpiller'? That would be so silly. They don't have anything to hurt you. They're only sticky. Or what if someone went into their garden and yelled, 'Eek, a butterfly'?" She laughed heartily at the image.

Emotions are one of many different kinds of psychological states (such as feeling hot, cold, tired, hungry). Each of these states has its own causal factors—and just as with emotions, young children understand and talk about the causes of these other states. Bretherton and Beeghly recorded instances of such causal connections in the conversations of 2-year-olds:

> "You better get shirt, so you won't freeze."
> "Take bubblebath, Mom, to get warm."
> "Me ski. Thirsty."
> "If I eat poison, it will make me sick."

Here's an example of a child (6 years, 2 months) who had an insightful understanding of the connection between emotion and action:

We were watching the movie, *Oliver,* and Chrissie asked why Nancy stayed with Bill, who was so mean to her. I explained that sometimes people love people who are mean to them and can't seem to stop. I added that I had never felt that way and didn't really understand it. She said that she did understand it—that she loved a boy in class who was mean to her. She added, "People are wrong when they say, 'If I were you, I'd do it different.' If they were really you, and felt what you felt, they'd do the same exact thing as you."

Teaching Children about the Causes of Emotions

Discuss the Causes of Emotions

Discussions should cover the child's emotions, your emotions, and other people's emotions. Children often have trouble putting their feelings and the causes of their feelings into words. Parents can help by providing words and explanations.[22] For example, if you see that your child is sad, describe what you see: "Your face looks sad." And try to connect the feeling to what might have caused it: "Is it because Mommy burned her finger?" Also try to make your child aware of the bodily sensations that go along with emotions: "When you are sad it feels funny in your chest and throat, doesn't it?"

Always be open to your child correcting you. The child may say "I'm not sad" or may acknowledge the sadness but deny the cause you've suggested. If you don't judge your child's emotions, he or she is not likely to try to hide them from you. Parents who say things like, "Oh, big boys aren't afraid and you're a big boy so I know you're not afraid" are likely to force emotions underground, often to the point where the child denies his feelings even to himself. Children need to feel that any and all emotions are natural and not to be judged, not even by Mommy and Daddy. Certainly if a child is to gain control over his actions (for example, to learn not to hit whenever he's angry) he needs full recognition and acceptance of his emotions (such as his anger) and an awareness of their causes (such as who he is angry at and why).

Ask your children about their feelings and what caused them, and try to help them delineate the specifics of their experiences. For instance:

PARENT: Did that movie frighten you?

CHILD: I think so . . . a little.

PARENT: Which part was scary?

CHILD: I'm not sure.

PARENT: Was it when the children got lost?

CHILD: Yes. They couldn't find their way home.

PARENT: Most children get scared during that part. It's scary to think about getting lost. Did you worry about that happening to you?

CHILD: Well I don't think I could find my way home if I were out by myself somewhere.

PARENT: That's why we never let you out by yourself. When you are older, you'll know how to find your way home, just the way I do; just the way Larry (his older brother) does. Then you'll want to go out by yourself.

CHILD: I guess so, but not for a long time.

You can start to label your child's feelings and connect them to causes even before he or she is a year old. For example, when your crawler hurts himself, point to the bruise and say, "Ouch." Once the child learns "ouch" you can ask, "Where's the ouch?" whenever he appears hurt. You can do the same thing with the word " 'fraid" when you observe that he is afraid (say upon climbing too high in the playground). Once your child has learned an emotional word through its connection to his own experience, you can apply it to others. For instance, if he pinches a playmate who starts to cry, you can point to the spot he pinched and say, "Ouch!" thus conveying that he has caused in someone else the same bad feeling that he has when he experiences an ouch. Similarly, if he frightens a pet, you can point to the animal and say, " 'fraid," to convey that he has caused the animal to feel what he feels when he is afraid. Do the same with other emotional words, both positive and negative.

Share your own feelings with your child and explain their causes. Verbalize what makes you happy, sad, angry, frightened, etc. Obviously parents need to be selective in discussing their emotions, holding off on information that would be unnecessarily frightening or confusing. But many feelings can be talked about, starting with those generated by the child: "I feel happy when I see you and Bobby having so much fun," "I don't want you to hide from me in the store because I get frightened when I can't see you. If you need me I won't know where you are," "Yes, I get angry at you when you kick me and try to hurt me on purpose."

During an emotional scene with your child you may not be able to provide a clear explanation of your feelings. Take time to talk about it later. It will be good for your child's understanding of emotions and for your relationship. Here are three incidents that illustrate this point:

I was making a toy for Elton (19 months) and fastening the parts together. He kept yanking at the pieces and the diagram and wouldn't stop when I asked him to. I got mad and plopped him into his playpen and he started to cry. I let him stay there awhile, then took him out and explained why I was angry—that I like to make things carefully so they come out right, and that he must learn to wait when he watches me make something or he won't be allowed to watch. I told him I know that this is hard for him and apologized for being so abrupt with him.

I got angry and scolded Leah (20 months) for crayoning on the wall for the second time in two days. She was defying me and I realized that I had set this up as a power struggle because I had never explained to her why I didn't want her to crayon on the walls. So I told her that I realized this and explained that Mommy and I try hard to make the house look pretty (a word she knew). I reminded her of the "pretty" curtains that Mommy had made for her room and the "pretty" paint that we all selected for her walls. I said that the reason I didn't want her to crayon on the walls is because it makes the room not look pretty anymore. I'm not sure if she agreed with my aesthetic judgment but she seemed to appreciate my giving her the respect of an explanation. She didn't crayon on the walls after that.

Eric (5 years, 1 month) was unfriendly to my elderly aunt even though I asked him to treat her nicely. He didn't understand why I was upset with him and asked, "Why do I have to? I don't like old people." I reminded him of the photographs he'd seen of my aunt as a sparkling young woman and explained why I loved my aunt, describing how she took care of me and always tried to make me feel good when I was a child. I told him that now that she was alone and frail I wanted to take care of her and make her feel good, that I especially wanted to make sure she knew she still had a family that loved her. I continued that since my son is part of our family, it is important to me that he make her feel good too. I stressed that it hurts me when I see her hurt and that a few simple actions on his part could make a huge difference to her. We went over the actions (saying hello, smiling, reciprocating her hug) and on our next meeting with her he carried them out and told me it made him feel good.

As you and your child go through the day together, there will be many occasions for discussing emotions. At one moment you might say, "I get angry when people drive that way because they could hurt someone."

Sometime later, while watching a nature documentary together, you might express feelings of sadness about the hunting of elephants for ivory.

Try to help your children understand the feelings of the people around them, and the causes of their feelings. Sometimes children will ask for explanations. For example, a father reported that his daughter (5 years, 4 months) asked why her friend Liz was always angry at her mother even though her mother was nice to her. Liz's parents had divorced a year earlier and the child lived with her mother. The father explained that Liz might blame her mother for breaking up their family and forcing her daddy to move out and that children often feel hurt and frightened when their parents divorce.

In the following conversation a parent explains to her kindergartner what a new teacher might be feeling:

CHILD: Mrs. Robbins (the new teacher's aid) yelled at me.

PARENT: I know. She told me. She said you didn't pick up what you dropped, even after she asked you to.

CHILD: I know, but she didn't have to yell and get so angry.

PARENT: Perhaps not. Today is only her second day as a teacher and she might be a little scared, afraid she won't do a good job and the children or other teachers won't like her. Grown-ups get scared too. I think after a few days she won't get so angry, especially if you help her feel good during this first week by being helpful to her. If you're nice and she keeps yelling, then we'll have a discussion with her to find out why, just like our family discussions.

Remind your child that people don't always feel the same way about things. Something that frightens one person may give another pleasure; one person will get angry over an insult while another will see it as silly or pathetic and fluff it off. This is important to teach in the context of the child's own emotional reactions, pointing out that others—his or her friends, for example—often feel differently about things. One child may, for instance, get upset whenever she doesn't go first in a game. Another child may not care as long as she gets her turn.

Often parents keep the feelings of adults a mystery to their child, sometimes to protect the child, sometimes to protect an adult. For example, parents will usually not want to explain that the reason a neighbor is upset is because of his or her spouse's marital infidelity. Yet some explanation is usually possible, such as that the neighbor and spouse are arguing over something. Observing strong but incomprehensible emotions in others can be frightening to children. Some sensible explanation, even if it only approximates the truth, is better than none.

Story books, videos, and films are excellent for teaching about emotions and their causes, providing many opportunities for discussions and questions about what characters are feeling and why. Make questions about emotions a regular part of your reading sessions ("Why do you think he ran away?" "Why do you think he got angry?"). Give your child's answers a lot of respect even if they miss the mark ("Yes, that might be why"). Then offer your explanation as another possibility ("Another reason he might have gotten angry is because he was jealous"). If you don't put your child on the defensive, he will usually recognize that your explanation is more accurate and not feel compelled to insist on the answer he gave.

Help Your Child Predict Emotions

As children learn about the causes of emotions, they should become skilled at predicting emotions—other people's as well as their own. Parents can stimulate their children to anticipate the emotional outcomes of various events by asking them to think about the feelings that are likely to arise from these events. A parent might, for instance, ask, "What do you think Uncle Larry will feel if he wins the lottery today?" Or, "What will your brother feel if you don't share that with him? What would you feel if he had one and didn't share it with you?" Or, "What do you think I feel when you do that? Do you remember how you felt when someone did that to you?" "Before you do that you better think about how you'll feel if it breaks."

As children approach 5 or 6 they begin to recognize *personality differences* in people's emotional reactions, making distinctions between reactions that seem intrinsic to the person ("It's nothing you did; he's just a grouch") and those that derive from specific stimuli ("He doesn't usually get angry but you pushed him too far"). Five- and 6-year-olds' discussions of emotional events include such enduring personality characteristics ("Robby had no reason to be angry at her. He's just always angry at everyone"). Children this age also begin to recognize temporary factors that affect an individual's emotionality ("Don't ask Mom now; she and Dad just had an argument").[23] Parents can assist here by noting people's enduring and personal characteristics when they appear to play a role in their emotional reactions.

The Causes of Actions

As we've seen, young children certainly know that people's actions cause things to happen, but do they understand what causes lie behind the actions? In other words, do they understand what makes people take the actions they do? When we, as adults, seek to explain actions or sequences of actions a new causal factor comes into play, fundamentally different from the ones we've discussed: We ask what "motivated" the action or, alternatively, what it sought to accomplish.

Actions are unlike any other events. We never ponder the motive or goal of a ball that has moved after being hit; nor do we seek the motive of a finger that has jerked reflexively after a pin prick, or even of a sad emotional reaction to a loss or rejection. But actions—from going to the refrigerator to going for a Ph.D.—appear to us to be a product of motives. Other events are all reactions to the past, but we take actions to change the future.

We feel we understand the cause of an action only when we can answer the following questions:

1. What was the person after?
2. Why was he after it?
3. Why did he take that specific action to get it?
4. How strongly did he want it?

For instance, let's say we observe a youngster deliver a valentine card to a classmate. In answering the four questions, we might find that (1) his immediate goal was to make the classmate aware of his affection for her; (2) his reason was that he hoped she would eventually become his girlfriend, (3) he used the card as a way to communicate his feelings because he had learned that she likes such gestures (or perhaps it once worked for him with another girl); and (4) it was very important for him as evidenced by the fact that he went out in a blizzard to deliver the card.

We do not experience actions as having the same kind of automatic quality as other events, including emotions. An apple *must* fall in accordance with the forces acting on it; similarly, we don't choose to be angry when insulted—the emotion happens *to us* upon encountering the proper releasing stimuli. But actions, as we experience them (and as we observe them in others), have a voluntary quality about them, as if we could remake our choices and redirect our behavior anytime (and we attribute the same freedom to others). We experience prior events as *influencing* our actions, but not as *determining* or *triggering* them through some direct or indirect transfer of energy from outside. The driving force or energy behind our actions appears to lie *within us* as biological and psychological systems. We seek out desirable ends and avoid undesirable one; it is our nature to do so. In other words, we experience ourselves as self-initiating systems, and we assume the same of others.

Our actions, at least those we call "purposeful" or "intentional," start with a vision of a desirable end-state. We act to achieve that end. External stimuli signal which actions are likely to be successful (a green traffic light says "You can go safely"), and past successes and failures guide current choices, but external events don't compel actions to occur in the way they compel reflexes and emotions to occur.

The voluntary nature of actions is so much a part of the way we experience and explain them, that we even have a term for the rare occasions when actions don't seem to be voluntary: we say the person had an "irresistible impulse," implying that he couldn't help himself from acting the way he did—and we don't then hold him responsible for his behavior in the same way we usually do. Actions performed under hypnosis are also commonly described as involuntary—not under personal control nor based on personal motives (some psychologists, though, have argued persuasively against this "captured-mind" conception of hypnosis[24]). Certain forms of brain damage and electrical brain stimulation also seem to eliminate the voluntary aspect of actions.

Behavior that appears to be "unconsciously" motivated also cannot be said to be voluntary in the same sense as consciously motivated actions. In particular, we lose the possibility of self-control when we have misconstrued our own intentions; we can't tell ourselves to alter our direction when we aren't aware of where we are headed. People mislabel and deny their intentions primarily because they are ashamed to admit them, even to themselves ("I did not want to hurt her feelings. I just wanted to explain to her that she was wrong. I'm not the kind of person who intentionally tries to hurt people's feelings"). We may not accept a person's denial if we have strong evidence to the contrary—if, for example, he continued his tirade long after his point was made and stopped only when the other person cried. In this case, we would say that his behavior was under the control of consequences of which he was not aware (seeing the other person in pain).

For some behaviorists, most notably B. F. Skinner, the consequences controlling our behavior are the significant causal factors under any circumstance; our conscious intentions are never determining elements. The voluntariness of behavior, they argue, is an illusion. Yet, when we consciously envision a goal and the actions we consider taking to reach it, we can usually alter our behavior at any point along the way. It is this experience of options that underlies our sense that our behavior is self-initiated and voluntary. Indeed, the process of choosing our behavior, of envisioning alternative courses of action before selecting one, is often far more time consuming than the carrying out of the action itself. Without envisioned outcomes this process of evaluating actions in advance is not possible; nor is there any opportunity for self-control. We cannot control our behavior unless we are aware of the actions we are about to take. I maintain that the envisioning of outcomes has a significant causal impact on our actions. In other words, the causes of actions (of "operant behavior" in Skinner's terms) that are taken *after* the envisioning of outcomes are very different from those taken without such prior conscious experiences. It is doubtful that evolution would have burdened us with so much anticipatory thinking if it didn't have any causal significance for our actions.

Children's Understanding of the Causes of Actions

Research by Thomas Shultz and others shows that young children do recognize intentions as causes of their own and other people's actions. As expressed by Shultz and Diane Poulin-Dubois, "Infants can distinguish between the causal powers of social and nonsocial objects by the end of their first year." Two- and 3-year-olds will ask about intentions when they don't understand why someone does something ("Why you do dat?"). They'll also explain their own behavior in terms of intentions ("I left it open because I wanna watch it [the TV]"). Three-year-olds can already distinguish between intended actions based on true and false beliefs ("He thinks balloons are there but they're not").[25]

Also by 3, children verbalize the distinction between intended and accidental outcomes (a distinction they appear to make much earlier). They will defend themselves against accusations by exclaiming, "Not on purpose." A child this age will also react differently to a playmate who accidently steps on her foot than to one who steps on it intentionally. The 3-year-old can also understand the difference between intended outcomes and mistakes (such as errors in tongue twisters) in which the outcome turned out different from the intention. They also recognize that some behaviors, such as reflexes, aren't intended.

Three-year-olds not only recognize intentions, but they make moral judgments based on them, judging some "good" (such as wanting to help someone) and others "bad" (such as wanting to take someone's belongings). (Piaget said these abilities don't develop until the child is about 7 but here again he was years off.)[26]

Children as young as 2 not only use intentions to explain and anticipate actions, but recognize that others do the same. So they will hide their intentions when they want to fool others, for instance, in games. A child might say, "Give me the ball. I'm not going to throw it"—and after she gets it burst into laughter as she throws it. Children use deception even before they are 3.[27] Their first lies are often to prevent parents from interrupting their activities:

PARENT: Is your diaper wet?
CHILD: (Involved in playing) No.
PARENT: (Approaching for the wet finger test) Let me check.
CHILD: (Wriggling away) No . . . not wet.

The wriggling reveals that the child knew the diaper was wet but said the opposite. The lie reveals that the child understood the parent's intention: to whisk him or her away to the changing area for a new diaper.

Children also hide their intentions when planning to do something forbidden. For instance, a little girl (3 years, 2 months) who never wanted to sleep with the door to her room closed, told her father, "You can shut the door tonight, Daddy. It's okay." By having the door closed, she thought she could get away with turning on all four lamps in her room for the night.

The children in these incidents clearly recognized the privacy of their intentions, that other's couldn't know them unless they revealed them. One child (5 years, 4 months) expressed this awareness directly during an argument with her mother over the fact that she was awake way past her bedtime. She interjected that "Grownups don't always know what children are thinking," and went on to explain that she wasn't awake willfully— that she couldn't simply fall asleep because her mother wanted her to; it was out of her control.

Here's an amusing anecdote in which a youngster (4 years, 9 months) asked a friend about her motivation and received an unexpected reply that made her laugh:

Julia came over and said, "You know what was funny? I asked Lizette why she was sucking her thumb and she said, 'Because it's time to!' "

In another incident illustrating a young child's sophisticated awareness of intention, a father reported that after observing his daughter (5 years, 5 months) and her playmate get into a series of squabbles he said, "You girls are very competitive." His daughter asked what that meant and he explained that they both wanted to be better than other and beat the other at whatever they were doing ("My bathing suit is prettier"). His daughter replied, "I'm not." Her friend followed quickly with an assertive, "AND *I'M* NOT!" His daughter walked over to him with a twinkle in her eye and whispered, "She's doing it now, isn't she?"—clearly recognizing the competitive intention behind the playmate's assertion.

In another incident that demonstrated a child's awareness of her own intentions, a father reported that his daughter (5 years, 10 months), who had been trying unsuccessfully to get his attention while he was busy, finally succeeded by dusting his hair with a feather duster. He started to scold her but caught himself, saying, "I'm sorry. You didn't know it was dirty and that you shouldn't play with it that way." A minute later the youngster came to him and said, "I want to apologize because I think I did know it was dirty and that I shouldn't put it in your hair."

Parents, upon questioning, generally believe—I think correctly—that their infants recognized intentions during their first months. They also report that well before 12 months, their babies could tell the difference between intentional and accidental behavior directed toward them. For example, babies react differently when they are hurt accidently (as when their hand is hurt during dressing or diapering) than when they are hurt intentionally (as when their hand is slapped to keep them from touching something).

Babies, like the rest of us, pick up intention from tone of voice, facial expression, eye contact, and body language—and parents make an effort to communicate their intentions by varying these elements. Try tickling a baby with a straight face, a monotone voice, a stiff body, and no eye contact. You'll get a very different reaction than the normal one. Our intentions are often revealed through our emotional expressions (imagine your reaction if your dentist, drill in hand, came toward you with an angry or gleeful look on his face). Research shows that by 10 weeks, if not earlier, babies are able to differentiate a number of different emotions in faces, such as joy, anger, and sadness, and they react differently to them, mirroring the expressions to some degree.[28]

Children's awareness of their own intentions and the connection of those intentions to actions can have interesting effects. Here's an example from a child of 4 years, 2 months:

My child doesn't like to lie, so she will refuse to make a promise if she knows she doesn't intend to keep it, even though not promising is a giveaway of her intention and gets her in trouble. For example, I was scolding her at bedtime for making her usual fuss and then left the room in a huff and shut the door, which was usually left open. She pleaded for me to open the door, saying "Give me another chance." I opened it and stated I would leave it open *if* she promised not to make a fuss the next night. "I want you to promise to control yourself" I said. Instantly, she gave her promise. But then she explained in a teary voice, "I can't promise, Mommy. I don't want to control."

In another incident a child, just turned 3, corrected her father about an intention of hers:

I told her I wanted to cut her fingernails, but she said no. I said they were too long and that I was going to cut them now because she had scratched me a few times while we were playing. I took her hand and pulled it toward me. She pulled it away. I took it again and pulled it toward me firmly. As I pulled, she gave in—I believe, because she saw a stern and determined look on my face. As she gave over her hand I said, "Thank you." She retorted sharply, "No, you did it. I didn't do it. You took it"—thus, letting me know I was forcing her, that she only stopped pulling because she knew I was stronger.

Here's an example of a 5-year-old's (5 years, 7 months) fine-honed awareness of the intentions of her friends:

I told Joanna that I didn't want to plan an outing with her friend Lana because Lana was always whining and having tantrums. Joanna protested, saying "She's one of my best friends." I asked her why she wanted to spend time with Lana, given her inevitable fits. She replied, "Because she never tries to hurt my feelings. Kimmy or Bea don't have tantrums, but sometimes they do things to hurt my feelings."

Young children's statements about intentions also reflect an awareness of the dynamic aspect of intentions, such as how badly someone wants something and how far they'll go to get it. Parents often hear children say, "I really, *really* want it—more than I wanted the other one," or even, "I'm going to keep yelling until you give it to me." Statements like these demonstrate an understanding that intentions can be pursued with varying quantities of passion and persistence. As another example, a father recorded this conversation between his daughter, Jocelyn (3 years, 11 months) and a playmate, Erica:

ERICA: I need that broom.

JOCELYN: You don't really need it. You just want it.

Research confirms that young children recognize the dynamic aspects of intentions. In one study, 3- and 4-year olds correctly understood such terms as "tries hard," "likes to," and "wants to." Moreover, they also understood the implications of "good at," indicating that they recognized that the outcome of an action was affected not just by intention and effort, but by ability as well.[29]

Teaching Children about the Causes of Actions

Communicate about Intentions—Yours, Other People's, and the Child's

Communication about intentions can begin during parents' first interactions with their babies. Essentially, you want your child to understand that you are doing things *on purpose*. This can be communicated by the way you touch her and give her things, the rhythms you create via sound and touch, the sounds and words you utter to accompany your actions, the surprises you provide, the repetitions and variations you present, and your eye contact and facial expressions.

There are so many subtle ways that parents can convey to babies the purposefulness of their behavior:

- For instance, if you notice that your baby needs you to support her head or release her arm from under her body, try to make sure she notices you noticing. You can do this via comments and facial expressions ("I see that your arm is stuck"). As I've noted, research shows that during their first weeks infants are sensitive to parents' vocal and facial expressions. So by making your noticing obvious to your child, he or she will quickly get the message that you've observed her need and are acting *on purpose* to help her.

- Even holding a baby in your arms and dancing to music can communicate to her that you hear what she hears and that you are moving her on purpose to keep time with the rhythm. The purposefulness of your movements will come through more clearly if you include some playful variations and surprises in your dance.

- Common parent-child games can communicate intention. Touch your baby on the nose and say "Beep." She'll probably laugh. Do it again, and she'll laugh again—and you'll laugh in response to her laughter. Then she'll wait for your next touch and beep. She'll watch your face to see the particular look that signals your action. Touch her nose twice accompanied by two beeps, and you'll get a bigger laugh. As you play this, you'll be engaging in a dialogue, with anticipations, reactions, surprises, and mutual delight.

- Your reactions to events that you've noticed she has observed will communicate both your awareness of her experiences and the purposefulness of your behavior. Examples would be turning your head toward and commenting on a sound she's heard ("What's that?"), or tapping on a mobile she is staring at ("Is this what you're looking at? See, it moves and goes tinkle, tinkle").

You also want to let your infant know that you recognize that *she* is doing things on purpose. Your responses to, and comments upon, her explorations and entreaties can convey this. For instance, after she swipes at and hits a mobile, you might say, "Boom, you hit it. Hit it again. Boom, you hit it again."

This kind of interaction quickly develops into a behavioral dialogue in which parent and child purposely alternate their behavior and are aware of each other's intentions to do so (otherwise known as "playing" with each other). As another example of a parent and infant exchanging purposes in this way, recall from an earlier chapter the story about the father and baby having a finger tug-of-war, taking turns pulling and letting the other pull.

An effective way to initiate a dialogue is by imitating your child's sounds, facial expressions, and gestures. It communicates that you have noticed what she's done (even if it was only a reflexive burp), that you prized it and found it worth commenting on. Soon she'll make an effort to repeat the behavior *on purpose* in order to get you to imitate it again or respond to it in some other interesting way.

Repeat your imitations a few times in a lively manner. Your expressions of delight and surprise at what she's done or uttered will usually fix her attention on you: "Blup? *Blup!* Did you say 'Blup'? Blup is a great sound. Blup, blup, blup." After a while, try some variations: "Blup, blup, blip. Can you say that? Blup, blup, blip." It won't take long before you'll see her moving her mouth trying to enter into a dialogue. Research shows that parents and infants do frequently imitate each other,[30] letting each other know, in essence, "I noticed that, found it enchanting, and this is what it looked (or sounded) like. Now what do *you* have to say to that?" A dialogue has thus begun.

As soon as your child can understand language, explain intentions to him—why you and others (and the child too) are doing the things you do. Take the time to explain the common actions that are a part of your everyday behavior. Here are a few possibilities:

- Explain why you read the labels on the food containers in the supermarket: "Because I want to know what is in the things we eat to make sure we are eating only foods that make us healthy."
- Explain why you are taking so long looking through the birthday cards: "I want to find a card that will make Daddy laugh when he reads it."
- Explain why you are putting him in his room: "You hurt my feelings when you do that and I don't want to be with you now."

Obviously the list of actions to explain could be endless.

Ask your child to come up with explanations of people's actions. Questions like, "Why do you think she did that?" can open up interesting discussions of motivation. For example:

MOTHER: Why do you think Fred pushed Regina when she was showing him how to do a cartwheel?

CHILD: He was angry, I think. He wanted to hurt her.

MOTHER: Could be. What might have made him angry? Did she do anything that might have made him angry?

CHILD: I don't think so. But she's his little sister and he doesn't want her to be able to do something better than him.

MOTHER: I think you are right about that. I think you really understand what was bothering him. Do you know what that feeling is called? It's not exactly anger.

CHILD: Was he jealous?

MOTHER: Yes. Jealousy is a little different from anger, although they both sometimes make you want to hurt someone. What do you think the difference is?

CHILD: When you're angry it's usually because you think the person tried to hurt you on purpose, but when you're jealous it's just because they can do something better than you—but they didn't try to hurt you.

MOTHER: So I wonder why he pushed her if he was jealous?

CHILD: Maybe to let her know that even though she could do a cartwheel better than him he could still beat her up if he wanted.

MOTHER: Sounds right. He wanted to let her know that he was better than her in something more important than cartwheels as far as he's concerned—fighting.

Also ask about the intentions of the characters in stories, films, and television programs: "Why did the Wizard yell so much and make such a fuss when Dorothy asked him questions?" "Why did the boy practice running every day?" "Why did Robin Hood put on that disguise?" A child can't make sense of a story without understanding the intentions behind the characters' actions. Indeed, you'll find that even without your prompting, your child will make an effort to link actions to intentions. One of the reasons that children are so fascinated by witch stories is, I believe, because they keep trying to grasp why the witch does the bad things depicted. Witches are presented as embodiments of evil with no comprehensible motivation, except the immediate intention to do harm. The fact that they can't be understood adds to their scariness. (Bruno

Bettelheim and other psychoanalytic theorists would find this explanation far too straightforward.)

Young children are likely to assume that story characters have intentions even if they can't decipher what they are. As they grow older and gain confidence in their understanding of human motivation, they become less willing to make this assumption and lose interest in stories in which the intentions are unfathomable. They will also find it troubling when they can't understand the intentions of real people they encounter, particularly those who, like witches, might be dangerous (for example, many years after his death, scholars still try to comprehend what drove Hitler to pursue his evil ends). "Why would someone do that?" we ask whenever we come across bizarre and terrifying behavior.

In fact, our need to understand actions in terms of intentions is so compelling that when we can't attribute actions to a person's conscious intentions we formulate unconscious ones ("The reason he washes his hands so many times a day is because he feels dirty as a result of his unconscious sexual thoughts"). We even look for intentions in our deities: "Why would God let that happen?" And because the events of the world do not conform to any orderly pattern of intentions we say, "God's will is unknowable"; that is, God has intentions, but we can't grasp them.

As children gain experience with actions and motivations, parents can explain increasingly subtle intentions to them. Here's an example from the father of a boy of 5 years, 5 months:

> We were in a restaurant and Gordon wanted a refill of his water glass. The waitress passed near us a number of times but I couldn't get her attention because she never looked our way. I mentioned that the waitress walks as if she were blind, and he asked what I meant by that. So I explained that she walks without seeing anything around her—almost like a blind person—except that she does it on purpose, probably so she won't have to work so hard getting lots of extras for customers, like more water or more bread and butter. We watched her walk by a few times and he understood what I meant.

Children also need to learn that people sometimes hide their intentions by communicating a different intention in the form of a *bluff*. Here's an incident between two 3-year-old girls:

> When my daughter, Erin, was 3 years, 9 months, we rented a summer cottage next door to a family with a girl who had just turned three. The children became fast friends, but on a few occasions I heard the other child say that if Erin didn't go along with some request, she'd leave and go back to her cottage. Erin, who hated to see her playdate

end, would start to cry and give in. One evening I explained to Erin
that her friend really didn't want to leave, or intend to leave, but used
the threat of leaving because it got her what she wanted. I suggested
that on the next such incident she tell her friend she could go if she
wanted or stay and work out a compromise, such as taking turns.

On the next such occasion, Erin managed to hold back tears and
said what we had worked out. Her friend looked shocked, turned back
twice as she headed for the screen door and finally left. Erin was
devastated. Her dad's plan hadn't worked. I went to the door and saw
her friend standing on the porch, looking befuddled. I asked if she wanted
to come back in. She said yes and entered. Erin pulled herself together
promptly and the children quickly worked out a compromise plan ("You
choose the first game; I'll choose the second"). That was the last time
the friend threatened to leave, and for Erin it was, I hope, a useful
lesson in calling someone's bluff.

An enjoyable way to teach a child about the causes of intentions is
through role playing: "Let's play that you are mommy and I'm you."
Children between 4 and 7 usually love this kind of play. As your child
enacts other people, her understanding of their needs, feelings, and goals
will increase and she is likely to become more toward sympathetic toward
them. Steer the scenarios to typical conflict situations, but keep the event
playful by enacting a humorous caricature of your child (for example,
you might start by caricaturing your child saying, "No mom, I'm not
cleaning up my room!").

Some intentions are very confusing to children. For instance, research
has shown that it takes some time before they understand the causal relationship behind "displaced" anger and aggression. An example of displaced
anger would be a parent who, after an unpleasant day at work, has a
tantrum at home over some ordinarily innocuous behavior of his or her
child or spouse. While 2- and 3-year-olds have a fairly good understanding
of the direct and observable causes of anger in those around them, displaced
anger appears to them to come from nowhere. By four, children are beginning
to gain some understanding of displaced reactions.[31]
Parents can help by explaining the real antecedents of these outbursts,
whether the outburst came from the parent, from someone else, or from
the child himself. For instance, a parent might say, "I shouldn't have
yelled at you before. You didn't do anything wrong. I had an argument
at work and I was still angry when I came home. Next time I'm feeling
that way, I'll let you know and I'll try not to be a grouch, but in case I
am you'll know it's not your fault."

Children also need help connecting behavior to outcomes that are delayed. Some instances they might come across are (a) an older child practicing piano scales over and over to perfect her fingering; (b) an aunt studying every evening to pass the bar exam; (c) a neighbor lifting weights to develop a better body; and (d) parents depositing money regularly to pay for their child's college education many years hence. The payoffs for such actions are not readily visible. Discussing the links between these kinds of actions and their ultimate goals will help a child make sense of them and also extend his or her grasp of time into the distant future.

Include in your discussions of actions, explanations covering roles and other defining characteristics of people—such as profession, nationality, and religion ("He does it because he's a fireman; that's his job and he's been trained to put out fires," "Japanese people bow when they meet people because in their country that's the way they are taught to be polite and respectful").

In explaining human actions to your child don't neglect aesthetic, moral, and mastery motives. We take actions to create beauty, to help others and achieve ideals, and to increase our control over the people and things around us. Psychoanalytic theories have downplayed these three categories of motivation, explaining such pursuits in terms of "primitive" unconscious reasons, which are usually less laudable. Freud's essay on Leonardo da Vinci, which attributed his paintings to unresolved Oedipal strivings, launched this highly constricted vision of human motives.[32]

Freud claimed that curiosity and moral and aesthetic concerns are by-products of infantile sexual pursuits. Despite the lack of evidence supporting these theories, they have had a significant impact on both psychology and our general culture and have led us—both theorists and the general public—to underestimate the importance of aesthetic, moral, and mastery goals in our explanations of human actions. Yet these are among the most powerful human motives. It is *intrinsically* satisfying—for both children and adults—to create a splendid work out of one's imaginations, to comfort someone in need, to live up to ideals, to figure out how a piece of the world works, and to make things turn out the way one planned. You needn't assume any deeper, darker motives. Nor should you worry that you might be providing your child with explanations that depict human pursuits in too rosy a light. A lot of human motivation certainly is selfish and ignoble, but a lot isn't. Your child needs to learn about both.

Include in your explanations the factors that lead to strong motivation and persistence ("He worked hard to get a good education because he was very poor as a child and wanted to make sure he could get a good job with a high salary so he could feel secure he'd always have enough money to live comfortably," "She worked hard to get a good education because she loved learning new things about the world and wanted a job that would allow her to continue to learn new things every day," "She kept trying because her older sister had won that contest a few years earlier and she wanted her parents to think as much of her as they do of her sister"). Point out that different people can engage in similar behavior (working hard for a good education) for very different reasons (for economic security, for love of learning).

Also try to give your child an understanding of the human motivation behind economic activities. At a young age, children become aware of store sales, auto rebates, and other buyer incentives, and they also learn that some things are too expensive to buy (or need to be saved for). But they are usually confused about how prices are set for goods. Try to give them an idea about costs and profits. Also introduce them to the law of supply and demand: When there isn't enough of a product to meet the demand of everyone who wants it, sellers can raise their price so that only those who are willing to pay more get it. Conversely, when a seller can't sell his goods at the current price, he can charge less to try to attract more customers.

Some children conclude that the law of supply and demand means that only the rich can have the really good things—which certainly has some truth in it, but sometimes it is only true for a while. You can explain that in many cases, when there isn't enough of something desirable to go around, the sellers make more of it (or something similar to it) to sell at a cheaper price to the many people who want it. Point out that many of the appliances in your home were once only affordable to the rich. You might also explain that with fixed commodities that one can't simply make more of, like land, the law of supply and demand gives the rich a definite advantage.

Use Games to Teach about Strategies and Intentions

In many competitive games, success depends on being able to figure out one's opponent's strategy (or plan of action), which requires inferring the intention behind each of his or her moves. In chess, for example, a player might set up a trap to capture his opponent's queen by sacrificing one of his men as bait, hoping that the opponent, in his eagerness to take off a man, won't notice the trap. But if the opponent does perceive the trap, he can counter with a strategy of his own.

Four- and 5-year-olds can begin to appreciate such concealed strategies in games. Parents can help by reminding children to look for strategies before making their moves. You might say, "Wait. Before you move, think about why I might have moved there." It will also help if during the early phases of teaching a child a game, you put your strategies into words ("Ah ha, if I move between your two pieces, you'll only be able to move one away and I'll get to capture the other one"). I'd also recommend that during these early phases you show the child strategies and traps that he failed to recognize and let him replay his moves ("Whoops, you took off my man but left an opening for this guy to be kinged. Do you want to try that move again?").

This kind of instruction calls for great sensitivity to the child since a number of factors must be balanced. First, for the child to want to keep playing (especially a young child), the game needs to be fun *as a game,* and not turn into an endless lesson. Second, the child needs to be able to replay moves in order to experience the positive outcomes that follow from figuring out his opponent's strategy. Third, some of the time the child needs to experience the negative consequences of failing to consider his opponent's strategy; that is, some of the time the option to replay shouldn't be given.

It will also help if *you* fall for your child's strategies some of the time, thus reinforcing his efforts to plan his moves. For instance, as your child starts to think ahead, planning two or three moves in advance, you might suspect that he is thinking, "If I move there, he'll probably protect that man, thus exposing his queen." If you sense this kind of a strategy, some of the time let him take your queen. Then, as he gains increasing experience with the game, make it harder for him to beat you.

Help Your Child Learn to Predict Actions

It is easier to understand the intention behind an action when we know the context from which it arises. For instance, a child might be baffled by seeing his friend act in an unusually disrespectful manner toward his father. The friend's motivation might be clarified by information that the father reneged on a promise to him, or embarrassed him in front of family members, or abused his mother. Any of these could have motivated the boy to want to hurt his father's feelings, to get back at him for the pain he caused. The context, or instigating circumstance, clarifies the action. Conversely, when we know the instigating circumstance (the father reneged), we are often able to make an accurate prediction of the type of action that will follow.

Research shows that even 5-year-olds can provide insightful predictions of future behavior from information about a person's past experiences (for example, that a child who has been bitten by an animal is less likely to comply with a request to feed it).[33] Insightful, accurate predictions of actions are obviously useful, allowing us to prepare for the action in advance.

You can encourage your child to make predictions by the information you give and the questions you ask. For example, after the two of you observe a serious fight between two playmates, you might ask, "Do you think that's going to make a difference in their friendship? How do you think that's going to change the way they treat each other from now on?" Similarly, you can discuss what happens when people are lied to or when they discover that a secret they confided has been revealed. Young children's comments will usually be concrete, reflecting their everyday concerns and limited experience. For instance, in answer to a question about what might follow from a fight, a child might say, "They won't invite each other to their birthday parties." You can then offer more general statements that cover a range of specific outcomes, "That's right, when someone thinks another person has been mean to him, he doesn't want to spend time with that person or share his special days, like birthdays, with him."

Help Your Child Overcome Biases about Actions and Intentions

A great deal of research has shown that in our attempts to understand the causes behind people's behavior, we are subject to biases, construing some actions and intentions as too positive (a "halo" effect) and others as too negative.[34] Often this occurs because we tend to assign people to categories and then anticipate behavior from them that is consistent with the category. Our age-old prejudices are sustained by this mechanism (this group likes to get drunk, that group is cheap, another group is violent). When we have a negative bias against someone, no matter what he or she does, no matter how benign the behavior appears on the surface, we are likely to attribute it to an underlying sinister intention.

Moreover, we usually treat people in accordance with these biases and often drive them into displaying the very behavior that we expected. For instance, if we expect someone to behave aggressively (because he belongs to the wrong race, religion, political affiliation, school, etc.), we may treat him in ways that provoke him into aggression, thus confirming our prediction. Social scientists call this a *self-fulfilling prophecy*.

Obviously, some of the time our categories and expectations are functional. In an encounter with a band of neo-Nazis, few would argue that some caution would be warranted. In many instances, though, it would be helpful to remind ourselves and our children of the adage, "You can't tell a book by its cover." Parents will want to discourage their child from jumping to unwarranted conclusions about others' intentions, particularly when based on negative group stereotypes. At stake is not just the child's accurate understanding of the causes of actions, but also the quality of life in the community. Some recent research by Steven Neuberg of Arizona

State University is hopeful in that it found that when people are encouraged to form accurate impressions of others, they can put aside earlier negative expectations.[35]

Group stereotypes are not the only reason for biased interpretations of intentions. For example, it's not uncommon for 5- and 6-year-olds to attribute nasty intentions to a child who can do things they can't, misconstruing the other child's skills and successes as purposeful affronts ("She's just showing off because she wants to make me feel bad"). The child feels bad because of the other's behavior so she assumes the other child *wanted* to make her feel bad. It doesn't take a lot of correcting to get a child to recognize the difference between showing off to deliberately make someone feel bad and causing pain unintentionally because someone envies you.

Appreciating Science—The Systematic Study of Causes

Young children often show an interest in science, but as they advance in school, too many find it tedious or boring. This may be because science is often presented as a set of odd phenomena ("See the copper penny get shiny"; "See the string stick to the ice"). Few students develop a sustained interest in science from these demonstrations. Real science starts with curiosity about events in the world, with *wondering why*. Wondering why is something children can appreciate because they do it themselves. Indeed, as physicist I. I. Rabi observed, wondering why is one of the things that children and scientists have most in common. He referred to physicists as "the Peter Pans of the human race."[36]

To the scientist, science is an adventure, a continually unfolding mystery story. The facts and procedures of science are only valuable insofar as they bring one closer to solving the mysteries. When science instruction is not tied to the great mysteries, most children don't muster enough interest in the facts and procedures to make the effort to learn them. Without the questions, children can't appreciate the passion of scientists. A television interviewer asked the Nobel Prize-winning physicist Richard Feynman what he really wanted to know. Feynman began to answer, "I want to know . . . ," then paused with a puzzled expression on his face. After a moment he smiled and continued with an emphatic, "Everything!"

Children often have trouble understanding what scientists do—as do many parents. Actually what scientists do shouldn't be all that baffling because, essentially, they do what children do: they try to discover what's out there, what leads to what, what makes things happen, and what's controllable. They just do it more systematically, often using special observing devices, such as microscopes, telescopes, and X-ray machines, to see things that aren't otherwise visible.

Math, which for many children and their parents is the "scary" part of science, is essentially a tool for scientists to describe their observations as precisely as possible. It is much more useful to describe how fast birds fly in miles per hour than in terms like "fast, faster, fastest." Scientists also use math to describe causal relationships. For example, a mathematical description of the relationship between wingspan and flight speed is far more precise than the general statement, "As wingspans get larger, birds fly faster."

The best way for parents to introduce their children to science is by doing with their children just what scientists do: observe, classify, and look for causal relationships between the classes. For example (sticking with our birds for the moment), upon seeing a bird, draw your child's attention to some specific aspects of it, such as its color, size, speed, or type of beak. These are all classes. Then, when you see another bird, discuss how it is similar or different from the previous bird with regard to one or more of those aspects. The next step is to "wonder why"—that is, to remark, "I wonder why that kind of bird flies so much faster?" Or "I wonder why they have beaks that are so much longer?" At this point you are doing science together.

Encouraging a child to "wonder why" is among the most valuable gifts a parent can give. And don't worry because you don't have answers to many of your whys. Generating hypotheses on why is what's important; it ignites a child's imagination. "Maybe those birds have larger beaks because they eat a different kind of food, or build their nests using bigger twigs, or have to fight more to protect themselves, or. . . ." Even 3-year-olds will chime in with plausible suggestions when parents "wonder why" with them.

You or your youngster can find answers to some questions in a book, or from an authority (a science teacher), or by doing your own research. It is worth pursuing an answer as often as is practical. You want your child to feel that *wondering why* is important, not just idle chatter. You also want him or her to experience the pleasure of finding answers. So follow up on "I wonder why . . . ?" with "Let's see if we can find out."

Children should understand that even though we learn much of science from books and teachers, ultimately *nature is the only authority*. This is an important guiding principle of science. Everything in science is open for question, even facts and laws that seem established beyond doubt. Disagreements among scientists are settled, not by reference to authorities, but by going to the source, Nature herself, and taking a look.

7

⚭

What's Controllable?

Developing Mastery

The question "What's controllable?" is really an extension of the question, "What makes things happen?" But here the child's concern is "What can *I* make happen?" Little by little children gain increasing control over their physical environments, over the people around them, and over themselves. To cause things to happen—to be a cause—is intrinsically rewarding for human beings.[1] Once we have set our sights on effecting some outcome, whether it be to get a ball in a hole or send a rocket to the moon, a motivational process is set in motion that drives our actions toward the achievement of that outcome. This is especially true of young children. Indeed, one of the most thrilling things to witness in young children is their impassioned and relentless pursuit of ends. One of the saddest things to witness is the crushing of this passion by unsupportive parents or teachers.

But when do children start to make things happen? An ingenious study by Anthony DeCasper and William Fifer indicates that newborns start to make things happen during their very first days. In the authors' words:

> By sucking on a nonnutritive nipple in different ways, a newborn human could produce either its mother's voice or the voice of another female. Infants learned how to produce the mother's voice and produced it more often than the other voice.[2]

In this study mothers read to their children "shortly after delivery." The next day the infants were given a nipple that was hooked up to a tape recorder. For half the infants, speeding up their sucking rate activated a recording of their mother's voice, while slowing their rate activated a recording of a different female voice. For the other half, slowing down activated their mother's tape, while speeding up produced the other female voice. Almost all babies altered their sucking rate to hear their mother's voice more often than the other voice. This is an extraordinary finding, demonstrating that before their third day, babies can adjust their sucking rate in order to control outcomes that have nothing to do with the normal functions of sucking such as nutrition and oral gratification. Nor were these brand new arrivals sucking reflexively. Rather, they were regulating their sucking rate—faster or slower as the situation required—in order to hear mommy's voice again.

Now, a newborn's reflexive behavior also makes things happen. Her cries bring attention and care. Her sucking brings nourishment. Poke her foot with a sharp object and she'll withdraw it. These and other reflexes do alter the environment, but they aren't what we ordinarily have in mind when we talk about *controlling* the environment and making things happen. Reflexes lack *intention* and they don't readily adjust to outcomes, two important aspects of behavior that we think of as making things happen. Sucking to hear one's mother's voice strikes us as a fundamentally different category of behavior from jerking one's foot back from a sharp object. The foot withdrawal appears automatic and stereotyped while the alteration in sucking rate appears intentional and adjusts to the behavioral requirements (it can be faster *or* slower).

Many studies show that from their first days of life, infants embark on the process of learning what's controllable by adjusting their behavior to outcomes. One experimental demonstration of the newborn's ability to adjust to outcomes showed that 1- and 2-day-old babies will learn to turn their heads to the side for sweet drinks; they'll even learn which of two sounds (tone or buzzer) signals that the sweet drink is available. They don't bother turning when they hear the sound that signals no drink.

In a more complex task, 2-month-olds learned to roll their heads about on a pillow in order to make a mobile move or turn on a light (their head rolls activated a switch). Two-month-olds will also quickly learn to shake their leg to move a mobile connected to it by a string. In fact, contrary to expectations, after a bit of practice they move only the leg that connects to the mobile; before this study it had been thought that infants this age couldn't control one side of their body independently of the other. In a variation of the mobile procedure, an infant kicked more for a red mobile than a white one, revealing an early aesthetic preference. In another example, 3-month-olds learned to suck on a nipple more forcefully and more frequently when such sucking produced visual displays from a slide projector—and they sucked more for novel stimuli than ones they had seen before.

Harriet Rheingold demonstrated that at 3 months, babies are adjusting their behavior not only to gain control over the physical environment, but over the people around them as well. For instance, they will vocalize more when vocalizing produces "social reinforcement," such as smiles from an adult who also touches their bellies and makes sounds back.

It may be that purposeful behavior begins with the baby's discovery during the first hours of life that closing and opening her eyes makes the world disappear and reappear. Research shows that as early as 2 months of age, babies display delight in making things happen—in discovering that they can move something, knock it down, bang out a sound, or make a parent fetch what they have tossed away.[3] The other day I watched an 11-month-old make a high pitched "yee" over and over because each time it caused a little dog to yip. He appeared to have a great time controlling the dog. He watched it attentively, always waiting until it calmed before setting it off with another "yee."

Intending Things to Happen

In the last chapter, in the section on the causes of actions, I proposed that intentional behavior starts with a vision or image of a desirable end-state and includes anticipatory images of the actions one might try as a way to bring that state about. We "try out" the action in the convenience and safety of our thoughts and, depending on what we "see" and "hear" (in our mind's eyes and ears), we may reject the action ("I'd better not say what I'm thinking now"), modify it, or "observe" that it is likely to succeed and worth a try. It is certainly far less dangerous and taxing to try out behavior in our thoughts than in the real world.

Thus, whenever we engage in an intentional action we are, essentially, testing an hypothesis: we are making the prediction, "If I do this, that will follow"—and we are putting it to the test. All active problem solving is based on such predictions ("If I clear fractions, I can find the answer," "If I keep turning left, I can get out of the maze," "If I enclose the filament in a vacuum, it will burn more slowly"). When we reach a dead end with a problem it means we can not envision any more actions worth trying—we have no more hypotheses about how to reach the goal.

The importance of envisioned outcomes may readily be seen by trying to imagine playing chess without being able to picture moves and outcomes before you actually reposition a piece. All your moves would then be purposeless, random. In actuality, a chess player's imagery is the most important part of the playing, and the most time consuming.

Because of envisioned outcomes we can even prepare our self-instructions in advance and teach our children to do the same. For instance, a parent might say to a child, "Whenever you are about to hit someone, remind yourself to walk away and count to ten." But how does a child know he is "about to" hit someone? He knows because before he hits, he pictures himself hitting. So, the parent is actually asking the child to monitor his aggressive imagery and if any occurs, to take it as a signal to engage in some pacifying self-instructions ("Walk away and count to ten").

Self-control based on envisioned outcomes and self-instructions is certainly evident in the 2-year-old who says to herself, "No," as she is on the verge of reaching for a forbidden object. Research shows that 2-year-olds guide their problem-solving behavior (for example, on puzzles) by talking to themselves, and these anticipatory self-instructions improve their performance.[4] Such anticipatory self-control—that is, engaging in one behavior in order to make another behavior more (or less) likely, probably begins in infancy (though, obviously, without words). I've seen a 3-month-old, whose mother kept trying to stop him from sucking his thumbs (an unnecessary lesson for a child this age), tuck his thumbs into his fist as he brought his hands toward his mouth.

Three-year-olds can even use formal principles for self-control. For instance, a child this age can learn that when frustrated over a task (say with building blocks) and envisioning doing something destructive (flinging them), to remind herself, "If at first you don't succeed, try and try again." A child who does this has learned that she can gain control over outcomes by starting with a deliberate act of self-control.

Here's an instance of self-control in a child of 2 years, 6 months (reported by her father):

> Rae and I were playing with Legos. After some pleasant interactions she started to get a bit cranky and bossy, complaining about what we were building and who was to do what. Suddenly she said, "Put me in my crib. I'm not feeling friendly." I complied and soon she fell asleep. This was a very unusual request since ordinarily she disliked spending time in her crib and was placed there only as a last resort when she was very disobedient (with explanations that if she couldn't be nice, she couldn't be with people). The only other times she'd asked to be put in her crib were on a few occasions when she was receiving some serious scolding; it seemed to be a way for her to gain control over the situation since she would have probably been put there anyway. This time, though, I wasn't scolding or criticizing her at all since her behavior was not that bad. But she seemed to be anticipating that she was about to do things that I'd dislike and she apparently wanted to avoid a conflict.

This child appears to have gone through a sequence of stages in the acquisition of self-control: First, her parents put her in her crib when she wasn't "nice." Then she asked to be put in the crib when she was being scolded for not being nice. And finally, she asked to be put in as a way to prevent herself from doing something not nice (or not "friendly," as she put it).

A child's capacity for self-control becomes even more effective as he learns to identify the *circumstances* that precipitate his envisioning particular outcomes. For example, if a child recognizes that he doesn't feel friendly and gets nasty mostly when he's tired or after he's had a failure experience (failed an exam, struck out in baseball), then on the next occasion of fatigue or failure, he can anticipate his aggressive thoughts and remind himself to be on the alert for them or decide to stay away from others until his bad feelings pass.

It is obviously hard to tell when an infant begins to envision and consciously intend to bring about outcomes. In the DeCasper and Fifer study, did the newborns have an anticipatory image of their mother's voice as they adjusted their sucking rate? With older children we would certainly assume that they did. These babies were clearly engaging in operant behavior, adjusting to outcomes, but we can only speculate about whether their behavior was purposeful in the sense that the infants had images of the outcome desired.

In truth, though, we can never be certain of anyone's imagery, child's or adult's (except our own). We can only infer such private experiences from various behavioral cues, some of which are quite subtle, such as the timing of reactions, changes in pupil size, redirections of gaze, a cock of the head, and slight shifts in facial muscle tone and posture. Most researchers who study infants do not record these kinds of behaviors. One researcher who did was Piaget. His observations of his 3-month old daughter, Lucienne, appear to catch her anticipating outcomes and, hence, engaging in what I am calling purposeful behavior. Here is Piaget's description (with some comments in brackets added for clarification):

At [3 months, 5 days] Lucienne shakes her bassinet by moving her legs violently . . . which makes the cloth dolls swing from the hood. Lucienne looks at them, smiling, and recommences at once. These movements are simply the concomitants of joy. . . . [in other words, Piaget is not yet attributing intention to them—although he isn't certain and wonders] does she keep this up through consciously coordinated circular reactions [his term for behavior that adjusts to outcomes], or is it pleasure constantly springing up again that explains her behavior? [That is, is her continued movement simply a joyful reaction to the swinging dolls, in effect, swinging them unintentionally, or is she shaking her bassinet *for the purpose of* swinging them?]

The next day . . . I present the dolls: Lucienne immediately moves, shakes her legs, but this time without smiling. Her interest is intense and sustained and there also seems to be an intentional circular reaction.

At [3 months, 13 days] Lucienne looks at her hand with more coordination than usual. In her joy at seeing her hand come and go between her face and the pillow, she shakes herself . . . as [she had] when faced with the dolls. *Now this reaction of shaking reminds her of the dolls which she looks at immediately after as though she foresaw their movement* [italics added]. She also looks at the bassinet hood which also moves. At certain times her glance oscillates between her hand, the hood, and the dolls. Then her attention attaches itself to the dolls which she then shakes with regularity.

At [3 months, 16 days], as soon as I suspend the dolls she immediately shakes them, without smiling, with precise and rhythmical movements with quite an interval between shakes, as though she were studying the phenomenon. Success gradually causes her to smile [note, now the smiling comes from "success" at moving the dolls, not simply from seeing them move]. This time the circular reaction is indisputable.[5]

As described in the italicized sentence above, Piaget judged that Lucienne "foresaw" the movement of the dolls. This is then an example of what I am calling intentional behavior, behavior that attempts to bring about *envisioned* outcomes, behavior with a conscious goal. Note that Piaget's description of Lucienne being reminded of and foreseeing her dolls' movements contradicts his theoretical claims that infants younger than 12 to 18 months old are not aware of objects that are out of immediate view—that they do not have what he called "object permanence." He based his claim largely on his observation that very young children do not search for an object that has been hidden under a cloth or cup. A number of researchers, using various procedures have found substantial evidence *for* object permanence in children as young as 3 months. T. G. R. Bower and his colleagues demonstrated that infants who fail to reach under the cloth for a hidden object, *do* reach for an object that was dangled in front of them and then "hidden" by the lights going out in the room. Bower also reports that infants who "fail" Piaget's under-the-cloth test will reach for an object hidden behind a screen: "All the infants without exception, were able to remove the screen to get at the object." According to Bower, contrary to Piaget's claim about object permanence, "out of sight was not out of mind." Bower's conclusions have been supported by many other studies, including those which show that infants can anticipate recurring events and show surprise when objects hidden behind a screen seem to have disappeared when the screen is removed. Children could not anticipate something if it did not exist for them, nor could they show surprise at its disappearance.[6] If you want to test object permanence yourself, try locking a 9-month-old crawler in her room; you'll find out very quickly whether she thinks you and the world she cannot see beyond her door has ceased to exist for her.

Piaget is not the only researcher to have noticed indications of forethought and envisioned outcomes in infants. For instance, Rose and Albert Caron reported anticipatory behavior in 3½-month-olds in a learning task. The infants could activate a sound and light show by turning their heads to the right in the presence of one stimulus pattern (the sight of a checkerboard pattern and sound of a chime) and to the left in the presence of another stimulus pattern (a bullseye paired with a buzzer). The children readily learned which way to turn in response to which pattern—but the researchers found something even "more impressive": the infants seemed to "understand" that each stimulus pattern was a *signal,* telling them which way to turn:

> This was evident from their deliberate inspection of the [stimulus patterns]. For example, a baby might start to turn in the incorrect direction, hesitate, recheck the stimulus, and then change direction.[7]

According to Caron and Caron, these infants were "problem solving." Were they, then, envisioning outcomes as they hesitated, rechecked, and changed direction? When adults or older children hesitate, recheck, and change direction we ordinarily infer that they are aware of their goal and foresee the effects of their actions. There is nothing special about these infants' behavior that should lead us to a different conclusion.

As babies grow into toddlers and preschoolers they become increasingly able to anticipate and work toward *delayed* outcomes, including those that take a series of actions to produce. For instance, many 18- to 24-month-olds are already efficient at stacking nested cups and correcting their mistakes in a manner that shows their awareness of the stepwise nature of the task.[8] Three-year-olds can play games that require a sequence of steps leading to a delayed outcome, such as the card game, "Go Fish," which entails matching pair after pair of identical cards, lining the pairs up, and counting them to see who has more at the end of the game.

With increasing age children come to envision outcomes further and further into the future, setting more and more distant goals for themselves (when the goals are sufficiently lofty we call them "ideals"). Here again the envisioning of outcomes is clearly an important notion. The very act of *formulating a goal* has an enormous impact on one's behavior. When a child sets her sights on getting an A in class or making the team or saving money for a video game, her behavior will change markedly from that moment on; from then on, she will select and evaluate her actions on the basis of whether or not they bring her closer to her goal. The significance of goal setting was described well by psychologist Edward Locke and his colleagues. Based on their research in work settings they concluded:

Goals affect performance by directing attention, mobilizing effort, increasing persistence, and motivating strategy development. Goal setting is most likely to improve task performance when the goals are specific and sufficiently challenging. . . . [and when] feedback is provided to show progress in relation to the goals.[9]

Robert Browning expressed the importance of goals far more succinctly in his stirring lines:

Ah, but a man's reach should exceed his grasp.
Or what's a heaven for?

(from "Andrea Del Sarto")

Learning Body Control to Make Things Happen

An important step in learning to control the environment is learning to control one's own body, a process that begins during the first weeks as infants learn to control their hands and lift their bodies. T. G. R. Bower has shown that babies as young as a week old reach for objects.[10] A 3-week-old is becoming a master at sucking his fingers. A 3-month-old will have "discovered" his hand visually and spend a good deal of time looking at it as he moves it about and brings it toward his mouth. He will also watch his feet as he moves them about. At this age he is working hard to lift up his head and chest and to sit up for a better view of the world. Soon he will be working hard at crawling, then walking, then running, and on to many other physical skills. The quest to gain more control over his body will continue into adulthood. An Olympic athlete practicing to perfect a move is, essentially, continuing a process that began in infancy.

Children don't learn to control bodily movements simply for their own sake. They use their new skills to make things happen in the environment around them. For instance, during their second month they spend increasing amounts of time reaching and grasping for interesting objects. At first there are a lot of swipes and misses. But healthy babies never give up. And over the next few months they will get better and better at contacting and grabbing the objects they reach for, and they will exhibit delight over their successes.

By 4- or 5-months, children have already become quite adept at grasping and manipulating objects and will start to hold their bottles on their own and use thumb and forefinger for manipulating small objects. By the middle-to-late months of their first year another milestone is reached: children start to use "tools" to make things happen, such as pulling a string or manipulating a stick to bring a toy closer. Over the next months and years tool use will become increasingly important as the child's motor coordination becomes incredibly precise, unmatched by any species.[11]

Learning to Use and Influence Others to Obtain Ends

As children improve at making things happen they also become more adept at using others to do for them what they can't do on their own (such as retrieving or opening things). This too is a way to gain control over outcomes. Psychologist Barbara Rogoff and her colleagues report such attempts in children as young as 4 months. By 9 months babies are sending all kinds of signals requesting help from their parents. They entreat and pull and plead with sounds and gestures. Over the next year they start to use other adults as well to help accomplish their ends. Before their first birthday children not only use adults but can coordinate their behavior with an adult's to achieve some end; they'll exchange objects with grown-ups, wait for an adult to set something up for them, and alternate turns.[12]

Rogoff cites an example of a 9-month-old attempting to get an adult to work a jack-in-the-box (note this child's object permanence):

> The baby began by pushing the box across the floor towards the adult, and patted the top of the box when the adult asked "What?" The adult responded to the baby's actions as a request, and asked "Should we make Jack come out?" The adult tried to get the baby to turn the handle (an action too difficult for this 9-month-old), and the baby responded with a series of frustrated yet determined moves—whining and fumbling with the box—that expressed his desire to have the box opened. Finally the adult began to turn the handle and the baby immediately relaxed. The adult asked sympathetically, "Is that what you wanted?" and the baby stared at the handle and let out a big sigh of relief.[13]

As soon as their skills permit, infants demand a more active role in making things happen. Rogoff provides another example and here again the object of play is a jack-in-the-box:

> Initially the adult performed all aspects of manipulating the toy (turning the handle to get the bunny out of the box, and pushing the bunny back into the box), while the baby concentrated solemnly on the actions. In the second episode of play with the jack-in-the-box, the baby attempted to push the bunny back in the box, and the adult encouraged, "Close it up," while helping the baby push the lid down. In the third episode, the baby began to participate in cranking the handle, and in the fourth episode the baby seemed to demand some independence in managing the handle while the adult encouraged this involvement.

The adult in these episodes provided demonstrations, instructions, and assistance. She stimulated the child's interest, supported his mastery efforts, and then moved more and more out of his way as he became ready and able to proceed on his own. This process of continually gauging and extending a child's skills has aptly been called "scaffolding" and it is at the core of all good teaching. The teacher must be:

- committed to the child's autonomy, taking pleasure in his or her mastery efforts.
- sensitive to what draws the child's attention and arouses mastery motives (such as a crank that turns).
- aware of what the child is currently able to do and not able to do.
- willing and able to break down what has to be learned into units that can be mastered.
- attentive to cues from the child that signal that he or she needs assistance or should be encouraged to persist unaided.
- ever on the lookout for stimuli that will teach the child something new.

To illustrate this process with a basic early mastery task, consider the problem of infants in our culture trying to master crawling. At that time in their lives many infants are spending all their time on smooth surfaces such as their plastic-coated cribs or playpens. In addition, their feet are typically covered with socks or pajama bottoms. This combination (socks on a smooth surface) makes it very difficult for them to dig their toes into the surface to get a good push with their legs. Mom's or dad's hand tucked behind the foot that the child is trying to push off with will help a lot. And a little push on that foot when the struggle forward is too frustrating will keep the mastery activity going. If it is truly a *little* push, it will give the child the sense that it is her own effort that is moving her forward.

Learning to get others to help is only one form of social influence that babies must master. Throughout childhood and adulthood they will need to develop social skills for making friends, for forging cooperative work and play relationships, and, eventually, for creating a happy family of their own. By 3, children can already engage in cooperative tasks, such as building things together and matching objects in games ("I need a big one. Do you have a big one?").[14]

Children's intentional efforts to alter emotional states are evident in 1-year-olds and probably begin even earlier. Here's an example of a child, not yet 2, frightening her sister intentionally as her mother was describing the sister's fears to a researcher (who recorded the incident). The mother was saying:

"Amy [the sibling] is really frightened of spiders. In fact there's a particular toy spider we've got that she just hates." [Just then the] child runs to next room, searches in toy box, finds toy spider, runs back to front room, pushes it at sibling [who] cries.[15]

Here's an example of a child, just turned 3, trying out her skills at changing someone's feelings. Her father reports:

> I was angry with her and wouldn't play with her. First she tried, "Daddy, I'm nice now." I'd been a sucker for that one before so this time I wanted to make it a bit tougher on her. Then she did a little jig saying, "Watch. This is funny, daddy. Are you happy now? Smile, daddy."

Other research shows that by the age of 5, children are well aware of what it takes to produce positive and negative feelings in others.[16]

Learning What's Controllable Through Observing Others

Between 6 months of age and their first birthday children increasingly learn to control things around them by observing others and imitating what they do. Pile something up for them or knock it down, and they will do it too. If they see you open a cabinet, you can be sure they will try to open it as soon as you close it. By 12 months, they will remember something they've seen you do even if a few minutes or a few days pass before they get a chance to copy it.[17]

An important area of observational learning is, of course, language learning. As babies hear the speech of adults their babbling changes to sound more like the language they hear. French and English babies start out babbling with the same sounds; but before long their sounds reflect the language of their parents and they begin to engage in give-and-take exchanges, making their needs known through directed sounds and gestures. Recent research shows that 18-month-olds will learn new words and verbal forms, such as the meaning and proper use of "me" and "you," just by observing their parents speaking and pointing to each other.[18]

By their third year, children are not only actively engaged in controlling their physical and social environments, but they can use their newly developed language skills to describe what they are after and what they want others to do to help.[19] Moreover, when what they are after is the acquisition of a new skill, watch out! They are likely to pursue it with dedication and purpose. Barbara Rogoff described an experience with her 3½-year-old daughter that illustrates this nicely:

> I was getting ready to leave the house, and noticed that a run had started in the foot of my stocking. My daughter volunteered to help sew the run, but I was in a hurry and tried to avoid her involvement by explaining that I didn't want the needle to jab my foot. I began to sew, but could hardly see where I was sewing because my daughter's head was in the way, peering at the sewing. Soon she suggested that I could put the needle into the stocking and she would pull it through, thus avoiding

sticking my foot. I agreed and we followed this division of labor for a number of stitches. When I absent-mindedly handed my daughter the needle rather than starting a stitch, she gently pressed my hand back toward my foot, and grinned when I glanced at her, realizing the error. The same child at 4 years of age asked me, as we worked in the kitchen, "Can I help you with the can opener by holding onto your hand while you do it? . . . That's how I learn."[20]

By 3½ years of age this child already had a good idea of how she learned and she was able to make very specific suggestions about how her mother could help her. Psychologists call this kind of knowledge "meta-knowledge": knowledge of how one goes about acquiring knowledge.

Making Plans

By the age of 3, it is clear that children don't merely act—they plan. In games they begin to plan a series of moves in advance.[21] And they plan ahead in everyday activities as well. A 3-year-old girl will insist on wearing a particular dress on a visit to a playmate because she knows that the playmate has the same dress and they will enjoy looking alike. She'll also ask, "Can we go to the carousel tomorrow?"—seeking a commitment today to increase the likelihood of a desirable activity tomorrow. And she'll negotiate for future outcomes: "If I eat *all* my broccoli can I have *two* cookies?"—again with the goal of making desirable events more likely. Planning involves not only envisioning the desired outcome *before acting,* but also envisioning the actions to be taken *before taking them.* For instance, a 3-year-old in a hurry to get to the playground might say, "I'll eat fast, then go to the bathroom, then put on my overalls, and then let's run all the way to the slide."

Of great importance is the child's growing ability to plan for distant outcomes that will occur in totally different settings. A youngster who anticipates the fun she and her playmate will have wearing the same dress is planning for and imagining outcomes that don't depend on current stimuli since the fun with the playmate will take place in another setting at a later time.

As another example of this kind of long-term planning, as I was dressing my daughter, just turned 3, for a visit to her friend, Sammi, she said, "Don't forget to remind Sammi about the rule about playing with toys." We had a house rule (adopted by Sammi's parents too) that once a child picked a toy to play with, she could use it, by herself if she wanted, for as long as she wanted. This saved a lot of arguing, and paradoxically, led to a lot more sharing. Based on past experience, my daughter was anticipating (envisioning) that Sammi would insist on playing with the toys she had chosen, and she was setting a plan in motion (envisioning her daddy stating the rule upon arrival at her friend's door) in order to prevent this kind of interference with her fun.

Parents of 4-year-olds know that their children generate lots of plans ("Mommy, I have an idea"). They have plans for activities and plans for projects, with definite outcomes *in mind,* clearly visualized. And often these outcomes are truly original ("Let's make a wagon with a point in the front so it looks like a rocket ship"). The young planner has also begun to formulate hypotheses: "If I do this, that will happen." And, as research shows, 4-year-olds will revise a hypothesis if the outcome doesn't turn out as predicted.[22]

The hypotheses of 4-year-olds can be surprisingly sensible, applying what they've learned in quite novel ways. When a 4-year-old overheard a conversation about a child who was afraid of cats she suggested that he'd get over it if he were made to stay with a cat for a long time. "If he is frightened for a long time and can't run away," she reasoned, "he'll learn that the cat won't hurt him."

Here is an example of a child of 5 years, 8 months who understood some very subtle (and perhaps profitable) aspects of planning. As her babysitter was teaching her how to play poker she said:

If I get a royal flush I better not go "Ah, ah" [simulating excited sounds and gestures] or you'll fold and I'll have wasted a great hand.

This youngster was already getting a handle on the fine art of bluffing.

Thought Experiments

Certainly by 4, and often younger, children will *think before they act.* By this, I don't mean just planning out actions for later outcomes; I mean delaying an action that could be taken now until the child has worked out the best plan "in her head." Children do this by first imagining alternative actions and outcomes, and act only after they have "seen" (in their mind's eye) which action produces the desired outcome. In essence, they use thought experiments to covertly test hypotheses of the form, "If I do A, B will follow." Children who act without this kind of forethought are labeled impulsive and are generally poor learners and problem solvers.

Indeed, one could make a good case that there is no more important human ability than our capacity to "act" and make mistakes within the safety of our minds. Here we have what could be the survival value of consciousness. Those of our ancient ancestors who were good at "thought experiments" were most likely the ones who survived long enough to pass on their traits ("If I run that way that sabre-toothed tiger is certain to have me for lunch, but if I can distract him by throwing some rocks over his head, I should be able to make it to the cave").

Thinking before acting is a form of self-control and, like any form of self-control, its purpose is, ultimately, to increase control over outcomes. By thinking before acting one has a better chance of coming up with problem-solving strategies that are likely to succeed. Children who remind themselves to think before acting provide themselves the opportunity to engage in a number of useful problem-solving strategies, including:

Making a plan and evaluating each step: "Before building that tree house, I'd better figure out where the ladder will go and how I'll support it";

Sorting out what is essential from what isn't: "The ladder to the tree house needs to be 10 feet tall but needn't be made of wood; a rope ladder would work";

Imagining alternative courses of action and the positive and negative aspects of each: "A rope ladder would give me privacy since I could pull it up but it has to be tied properly or it might slip off while I'm on it. A wooden ladder is sturdy and easier to climb but it might sink into the soil after a heavy rain";

Estimating the probabilities and risks for each alternative: "Since it usually rains only a few days during the summer and the soil dries quickly, the wooden ladder would be okay. On the other hand, if I use the rope, I can prevent it from slipping off the tree house by nailing it to a plank after tying it to a branch";

Breaking down the problem into more manageable steps: "I want something sturdy *and* I want privacy. Rope isn't as sturdy as wood but it may be sturdy enough, and it will give me privacy";

Looking for parallels to situations that they or others have maneuvered through successfully before: "I've seen that rope rots in water, and since it will rain, perhaps rope is a bad idea. But I've also seen plastic coated clothes line that doesn't rot; perhaps I can use that";

Seeking advice: "I'll ask the man in the hardware store if there is rope that doesn't rot."

"Metacognition" and "Transfer of Training"—Or Learning to Control Outcomes by Reminding Yourself of What You Already Know

When we instruct a child who is struggling with a problem to "stop and think" we are reminding her that she already knows some things that can help her solve the problem:

1. She may know specific things pertaining to the *content* of the problem (such as knowledge of the behavior of sabre-toothed tigers), and/or

2. She may possess tactical knowledge about how to best proceed with these kinds of problems (such as reminding oneself that one should always

have a *back-up plan:* "In case the tiger turns and spots me running, I'd better note which trees along my path I can scoot up").

When a child instructs *herself* to stop and think before acting, it indicates that *she* knows something about her own problem-solving process—she knows she will increase her chances for a successful solution by taking some strategic mental steps first.

Psychologists use the term "metacognitive skills" to refer to people's knowledge of what to do to enhance their own learning and cognitive performance. Recall the description above of the young girl who asked if she could hold her mother's hand when she operated the can opener—because, as she explained, "that's how I learn." This child understood something about her own learning process *across* problems. Similarly, a youngster who has once discovered the value of defining terms in an intellectual task (such as on an exam), may remind herself to define terms on subsequent problems ("So, I'm supposed to write an essay on 'intelligence.' Well, what do I really mean by 'intelligence'—what events does the term refer to?").

Psychologists also attach the prefix, *meta,* to various specific cognitive areas to denote knowledge of one's own mental strategies in those areas. So "*meta*memory" refers to knowledge of what to do to enhance one's memory (such as reminding oneself to create a visual image for each word on a list to be remembered).

The application of metacognitive knowledge starts with the recognition that there are similarities across problems regardless of how different they appear on the surface. For example, a college football player might realize that he can learn historical facts for an upcoming exam with the same memorization strategy that he uses to learn the quarterback's play signals. Both tasks involve memorization and both become easier if the young man knows what his best memorization strategies are.

Psychologists who study learning use the terms "transfer of training," "generalization of learning," "learning to learn," "learning set," and "analogical transfer" to describe the application of knowledge gained in previous problem solving situations to new ones. The application of metacognitive knowledge (such as "I remember things best when I write them down") to new problem solving tasks is an instance of this kind of transfer. Research shows that when children are taught to think about and apply their metacognitive knowledge as part of a general strategy of problem solving they become better problem solvers.[23]

In general, when a child recognizes that a new problem is similar to one he's already solved, he can then approach the new problem with techniques he learned while working through the earlier one. A child who has learned to rotate the three-dimensional pieces of a shape sorter may recognize that the same strategy will help with a two-dimensional picture puzzle. A child who is faced with how to spell the word "receive" may pause before he writes his answer and remind himself of the rule, "*i* before *e*, except after *c*"—a rule that applies across a great many words. A child adding decimals, may tell himself, "Line up the decimals before adding columns." A budding creative writer, might revise a passage after reminding herself, "Don't mix metaphors." Each of the self-instructions becomes then a behavioral rule for improving one's problem solving.

In an early (1908) experimental demonstration of the value of rule transfer in problem solving, boys who had been taught about the refraction of light in water were better at hitting an underwater target with darts than boys who had not received this instruction. The training primed them to take account of refraction when aiming. These boys were not simply carrying forward the effects of practice; they had learned a behavioral rule or principle, *in words,* that they could then apply to a new task. When we use verbalized principles to guide our behavior psychologists refer to our actions as "rule governed." More recent research using different problems (hitting a target by banking correctly off a wall) confirms the value of such verbalized principles ("Whenever a ball bounces [off a wall], the side angles it makes are alike").[24]

In another recent study of transfer, Maria Crisafi and Ann Brown demonstrated that children as young as 2 could successfully apply a problem solving strategy that was told to them ("You play them all the same way") to solve similar problems that on the surface appeared different (getting candy from candy machines that looked very different from each other and required very different kinds of tokens to operate). Three-years-olds in this study who were not told the strategy but who were encouraged to verbalize their own strategies after each try, were far better able to solve subsequent problems than children who had not put their strategies into words. Stating the problem-solving steps in words apparently helped the children recognize the similarity from problem to problem.[25]

Another recent experiment that confirms the value of teaching children to remind themselves of specific strategies and rules was aptly titled, "Rules as Tools." Psychologists Michael Pratt, Jennifer McLaren, and Garth Wickens taught first-graders to communicate information more effectively by instructing them to remind themselves of two communication rules. The children's task was to describe something to someone who had to act on the information. The communication rules they learned were, "First I'll figure out all the different things my clues could mean to you" and "Then I'll tell how the one I mean is different from the rest." By reminding themselves of these rules, the children became less likely to say things like "It's the big one" when three of the visible items were equally large.[26]

Every domain of human activity has evolved its own set of problem solving tactics, rules, or principles—*If-then* statements describing the procedures or action sequences that lead to successful solutions. The good teacher passes these on to students or helps them rediscover them. A ballet teacher might instruct her students that they will move more gracefully if they imagine moving through liquid. A writing teacher might suggest the frequent use of active verbs. An arithmetic teacher will remind students to always check the sign (plus, minus, etc.) before computing. A science teacher might say, "Always look for the exceptions to the theory; they'll lead you to a better theory." And a baseball coach is sure to tell his batters, "Never take your eye off the ball." Each of these promises good results if the tactic is followed. Once students can verbalize such tactics they can use them to guide their own behavior, no longer needing reminders from their mentors.

Without the passing on of problem solving tactics from teacher to pupil we would all have to reinvent the wheel and every other useful human invention. On the other hand, creative problem solvers are ever reevaluating the adequacy of the problem solving principles that have been passed down to them, looking for exceptions and alternatives. Rodin rejected the notion that beautiful sculpture had to adhere to the triangular form. Einstein rejected Euclidean geometry as the framework for gravitational physics. Kandinsky rejected the position that the goal of a painting had to involve the depiction of objects.

When established principles are replaced or supplemented by a new set, new behavior emerges. When Darwin expounded a new principle on the origin of species (Look for adaptive fitness, he said, not divine purpose), it launched a vast amount of research in biology that would have made no sense before. When Merce Cunningham contended that dance could be about movement itself rather than movement to music, it opened up possibilities of choreography that could not have been conceived before. When the physicist, Louis Victor de Broglie demonstrated that electron particles were also waves, it paved the way for the exploration and exploitation of the atom in ways that would have otherwise been inconceivable. In each of these examples, the innovative products stemmed from the rejection of an old principle and the assertion of a new one.

Formulating Behavioral Rules

Not only are children able to use problem-solving rules or tactics that are taught to them, but research demonstrates that as their language abilities develop they begin to formulate their own rules for successful responding,[27] that is, like the scientist, once they have solved a problem, they try to come up with general strategies and principles that can be applied to new problems of the same type ("If ice melts when it is warmed and butter melts when it is warmed, perhaps all solids melt when warmed; so I'll warm this rock and see if it melts").

Ann Brown and Mary Jo Kane demonstrated this process of induction from particular instances to general principles in children as young as 3 and 4. In one part of their study, 4-year-olds were told about a hawkmouth caterpillar that changes its looks to resemble a poisonous snake—but they weren't told why the caterpillar goes through this change. Some of the children were then asked why a caterpillar would want to look like a snake *and* what he could do to stop the big birds from eating him. These youngsters concluded on their own that the reason the caterpillar changed was to defend itself by mimicking a more dangerous animal. The children who induced the general principle, *mimicry promotes self-defense,* were then able to solve similar problems, such as why a crested rat will transform its appearance to look like a skunk. Children who did not verbalize the general principle were unable to explain why the rat would want to look like a skunk. The authors also note that children who formulated the principle on their own did better than those who were told the principle by the researchers (although other studies haven't always found this).[28]

Effective teachers are ever searching for ways to help students discover problem-solving tactics. At the Bauhaus, the famous German school of architecture, new students were asked to design and build a tepee. The purpose was to have them discover on their own—presumably so they would truly understand and never forget—the basic principles of structure and support.

Educators refer to this kind of teaching as the "discovery method": students are given the problem and told to find the solution on their own. But the teacher does not simply abandon responsibility for instruction. He or she must select and sequence the problems with care, give prompts and hints when appropriate, and then determine whether the students have in fact discovered the correct principles and can apply them to new problems. Unless the Bauhaus architectural students were able to induce usable principles of design from their experiences with the tepee, any lesson they learned would be useful only for building more tepees.

The discovery method is important primarily when the *process of discovery* is a central part of the lesson. There is no need for every ballet dancer to rediscover the principle of "spotting" as a way to keep one's balance while pirouetting. On the other hand, a mathematics teacher might want to help students "discover" the Pythagorean Theorem since the "work" of mathematicians requires knowing how to discover mathematical principles. The Bauhaus was dedicated to innovation in architecture, so there too it was probably useful to spend time fostering students' exploration of fundamental principles.

The Joy of Mastery

Child researcher John Watson noticed something interesting as he studied 2-month-olds learning to roll their heads to turn on a light or move a mobile. He observed that the infants were not only able to adjust their behavior to control outcomes, but that they appeared to *enjoy* doing it for its own sake. The infants in his study began to smile and coo as they learned to activate the mobile and light. Watson recognized this joy in controlling outcomes as a general characteristic of children:

> . . . one day someone begins playing a game with the infant. They touch his nose each time he widens his eyes, or they bounce him on their knee each time he bobs his head, or they blow on his belly each time he jiggles his legs, or they make sounds after he makes a sound. . . . As the specific game is played more times, the infant experiences an increasing awareness of a clear contingency, and with that, vigorous smiling and cooing begins.

This early pleasure in having an impact on the world is expressed by the 18-month-old in the familiar plea, "I want to do it myself," and a few months later in the emphatic, "I can do it!" By 2, children display pride in their successes. The 2-year-old not only wants to put on her own shoes and zip up her own jacket, but wants to participate in doing the things she sees her parents doing: she wants to help cook and dust and vacuum. Actually, the 2-year-old wants to do everything; she is dedicated to *making things happen*.[29] She will take everything apart (and try to put some things back together); she is an insatiable builder with blocks, Legos, and any other construction items she can get her hands on; she will turn switches on and off and bang on pots, drums, and piano keys, taking delight in the effects she produces. Interestingly, 2-year-olds are also developing a good sense of which tasks are beyond their ability and will ask for help when that is the only way to produce a desired outcome.

One facet of the young child's drive to control the world around her is, as every parent of a 2-year-old knows, the vigorous resistance to being controlled by others. The 2-year-old demands autonomy and will continue to demand it in varying degrees throughout childhood and adulthood.[30] As an example of this demand, a child of 3 years, 11 months explained to her parents that the reason she ran away in the department store was because "I wanted to be boss of myself."

By the time children reach 3 or 4, they not only want to master whatever they encounter, they also want to be ready for anything that *might* come along. This is expressed in an avalanche of "What if . . ." questions: "What if a robber tries to steal our cat?" "What if a car hits us?" A child this age would subscribe to the adage that to be forewarned is to be forearmed.

Since the early days of psychology, researchers have been studying the learning mechanisms through which children acquire problem-solving skills and knowledge of the world around them. But it is only during recent decades that they have paid much attention to this "drive" to learn about and master the environment. We humans, child and adult, derive great pleasure from discovery and from success at tasks that we have set for ourselves. Psychologists have referred to this drive as a motive for "effectance," "mastery," and "competence," among other terms.

In the dominant psychological theories, including psychoanalytic theory and most major learning theories, exploratory and mastery behaviors were consigned to the service of supposedly more basic survival and reproductive motives such as hunger and sex. The assumption was that if the basic motives were fulfilled the person would remain quiescent. These theories were definitely not based on the observation of children. After children have their "basic" drives met, it is then time to explore and play and learn what's controllable. Exploration and play have built-in rewards and are not engaged in for external ends. As psychologist Robert White observed, the 1-year-old who insists on holding the spoon to feed himself gets a lot less food than if he let his mother feed him. Yet, insist he will.[31]

Although exploration and play do not arise from the so-called basic drives, they are not idle behaviors in children and no child takes them casually. Moreover, they certainly do have survival value—they are ways children acquire knowledge and skills, and it is safe to assume that the skillful and knowledgeable are the most likely to survive in times of crisis. Psychologist Leon Yarrow and his colleagues at the National Institute of Child Health and Human Development have provided evidence that young children who explore more do indeed grow up to be more skillful and knowledgeable. In a series of studies, these researchers found that infants who explored more at 6 and 12 months of age turned out to be more skillful and knowledgeable on tests of mental development given during early childhood.[32]

Infants' and young children's motivation to learn about and gain control over their environments is so strong that they will learn (and show delight in learning) totally arbitrary connections between their behavior and outcomes. This was demonstrated by John Watson who taught his 2-month-old son that by looking at the correct one of two fists held in front of him he could make it open and close. At first the child looked at both fists equally and not much at either. Within a few training sessions things had changed: The child now looked attentively and primarily at the "contingent" fist, the one that his gaze seemed to open and close; and after the fist closed he would look away and quickly look back to make it open and close again. He even learned to switch his gaze to the other fist when Watson switched which hand would open.

When Watson complicated the task even further so the child had to look at one fist in order to make the other one open, the boy learned that too. After he learned this, according to Watson, at the next session:

. . . [his] apparent delight and "ready attention" was so marked that [I] noted the feeling of confronting a "sophisticated" subject.

Watson regards the increased speed with which this 2-month-old child learned new variations on the game as an example of learning to learn:

. . . as a result of the preceding contingency experiences, the infant gained in ability to learn contingencies.[33]

As I noted above, learning how to learn, which research by Watson and others indicates begins in early infancy, will remain a central factor in a child's intellectual development. Watson's baby seemed to recognize that when he failed, when his old behavior no longer produced the desired effect, this was a signal that the rules of the game had changed and it was time to explore alternatives to discover the new rule. An early study on discrimination learning in 6- to 12-month olds reports similar findings— the babies had "learned to learn."[34]

Children as Problem Seekers

From Watson's description, his baby had clearly developed confidence in his ability to discover whatever new rule daddy might devise, behaving as though he believed he would again be able to control that fist. And he had fun in the search. Many psychologists have stressed the importance of being able to maintain confidence in the face of setbacks and failures. The successful problem solver construes failure, not with a sense of helplessness, but as a signal for renewed and revised problem-solving efforts. With this kind of confidence a child continually sets his sights on new challenges to be mastered; he becomes a problem seeker, not just a problem solver.

Maintaining confidence in the face of failure is a prerequisite for creativity. Many great problem solvers—Einstein, Michelangelo, Van Gogh, among numerous others—have commented on the agony of the setbacks that must be endured and accepted if one is ever to reach the ecstasy of achievement.

Over the years, psychologists have referred to this confidence—the confidence that one can control outcomes, reach one's goals, make pleasing things happen and displeasing ones cease—as a high sense of "self-efficacy," an "internal locus of control," a high level of "frustration tolerance," and a high "generalized expectancy of success." It might also be called the *"I think I can* attitude."

Research shows that children (and adults) who don't believe they have much control over outcomes tend to set their sights low, achieve little, and experience high levels of depression. There are ways that parents can help their children develop a positive feeling of personal power and the conviction that they genuinely can control outcomes. One way is by keeping children's level of frustration low enough to prevent their giving up, yet high enough so they get used to the hard work of overcoming obstacles. A recent study reports that by the age of 4, children already recognize that greater effort leads to better outcomes, and they believe that effort itself deserves to be rewarded.[35]

Psychologist Albert Bandura, among other researchers, has demonstrated an association between a high sense of self-efficacy and high goal setting; that is, those with greater confidence in their ability to control outcomes tend to strive for more challenging goals. Other research, in turn, has found that individuals who regard striving for challenging goals as an important personal value, score high on a measure of "life satisfaction" or subjective well-being. In other word, adults who have retained their childhood commitment to mastery and exploration tend to lead the most fulfilled lives.[36]

Similarly, children who view problem-solving tasks in terms of what they can learn from working on them (a mastery goal) rather than as a test of their ability, handle frustration better, set higher goals for themselves, achieve better solutions, and have more fun than those who approach problems from a "test" perspective, as merely a measure of their level of achievement. Other research shows that parents of children with a "mastery orientation" tend to encourage their children's curiosity, independence, and persistence, as well as their selection of challenging achievement goals. They are also likely to be involved in their children's educational activities and be responsive to their emotional needs.[37]

Teaching Children *What's Controllable*

This section might be called, "Bringing Up a Powerful Child." Parents consider many things when they interact with their babies; they attend to their safety and comfort and try to provide stimuli that will attract their attention and interest. I suggest that parents need also to strive to give their children a sense of power over their environments, including the people in them. Let me note, though, that helping children gain power or control over people does not mean "spoiling" them by giving them anything they want regardless of whether they have earned it; nor does it mean neglecting their moral instruction in fairness and sensitivity to others. Addressing these issues here will take us too far from our central concerns, so I will refer the reader to my book on moral development, *Bringing Up a Moral Child.*[38]

Provide an Abundance of Mastery Experiences

Children will acquire an expanding awareness of what they can control only if their actions do, in fact, bring about what they intend to bring about. Practice in making things happen will give them both the confidence to set high goals and the skills to achieve them.

The value of such practice even for infants was demonstrated in a study of 4- to 10-month-olds (aptly titled, "Learning to Control the Environment in Infancy"). Babies who were given practice at learning to make things happen (for instance, pulling a string produced colored lights on a screen) were better at learning new contingencies (such as pressing a panel to turn on music) than age-mates who didn't have the practice. As the researchers, Neal Finkelstein and Craig Ramey put it, the babies with practice at making things happen "appeared to become more competent and efficient learners in new situations . . . [and] were subsequently better able to determine the relation between their behaviors and environmental events." Other research supports this view: lots of two-way "dialogue" between mothers and infants (which gave the infants practice in making things happen—to their mothers) was associated with better performance by the infants on a subsequent contingency task (fixing their gaze on a spot produced a sound and light show).[39]

Whereas successful practice enhances subsequent learning, a study of 3-month-olds demonstrated the detrimental effects of frustrating and disappointing experiences. The infants first learned to move an appealing, ten-component mobile by kicking their legs. Then, for some, a simpler and apparently less appealing two-component mobile was substituted, leading to tears and other signs of frustration in many of these babies. When tested a week later with either mobile, most of the babies who reacted with frustration appeared to have forgotten how to make it move, while those who had not had the frustrating experience retained what they had learned.[40]

Parents can stimulate and foster their child's mastery behavior in many ways. Right from the start try to let your baby know that her actions have an impact on you and that you are alert to her intentions. Whenever she appears to be after something—to lift her body or roll over or bring something into view—parents should monitor to see if some help is needed; and if it is, they should provide the least assistance necessary for the child to achieve his or her goal. In other words, as pointed out earlier, they should "scaffold" their assistance, giving more or less help in response to the child's changing abilities.

An interesting study of how effective parents actually do scaffold their assistance was carried out by British psychologists David Wood and David Middleton. They asked mothers to teach their 3- and 4-year-old children to assemble a pyramid out of specially designed, interlocking blocks. The researchers observed the mother's techniques as they presented the various steps toward a solution, and then observed which children could assemble the blocks correctly on their own. Mothers' instructions ranged from very nondirective ("That was good." "What are you going to do next?"), through pointing out specific requirements ("No, you need one with a hole, don't you?"), to direct interventions and demonstrations (such as, putting blocks to be joined near each other or demonstrating how blocks are connected).

Interestingly, what was important was not how directive or nondirective a mother was but her ability to gear her instructions to the moment-to-moment learning needs of her child. The most successful mothers, the ones whose children did best on their own in a later test with the blocks, appeared to be following the instructional rule: "Increase help when the child fails and give greater latitude when he succeeds." The researchers characterize successful teaching as an interactive, "dynamic, problem-solving activity" in which the tutor tries out "various instructional hypotheses, relinquishing initiative to the child when he succeeds and taking over more task operations when he fails." Other researchers have confirmed the relationship between parental scaffolding of instructions and child competence.[41]

Parents can set up countless occasions for mastery experiences. You can provide objects for your infant to reach for and grasp during her first months. You can play gentle tug-of-war games with a 2-month-old. You can be sensitive to your 3-month-old's increasing contribution to routine activities like diapering and dressing, noticing how he now assists the endeavor by adjusting his torso and limbs in anticipation of your behavior. Leave time for his movements and let him know you notice and appreciate his help.

You can teach your 2- or 3-month-old about causality and about herself as an initiating cause by looping one end of a string around her wrist or ankle and fastening the other end to a bell or chime hung securely overhead in her eye view. Studies show that she will quickly learn to pull the string to produce a sound—and will remember the maneuver even a day later.[42]

Try placing your 4-month-old on her back and give her your thumbs to grasp as you hold her forearms in your hands. Gently pull her to a sitting position (as you say "Up"). Then let her down (saying "Down")—and repeat the sequence a few times. You will feel the baby participate in pulling herself up and lowering herself down with all her strength. If you weren't helping by pulling her arms forward she'd never make it all the way up or maintain any control on the way down, but if you provide the minimum force necessary so her own muscles can contribute their fullest, you will see her face light up with joy in what to her is a great accomplishment.

You will probably find that your own facial expressions and verbalized "Up" and "Down" reflect her effort and sense of accomplishment ("UuuuuUP"). Effective parents do this intuitively and it probably highlights for the child the effort and endurance required to accomplish the task. It also lets the child know that she has an adoring and empathic fan.

Continually look for new ways to set up mastery experiences. For instance, put a 6-month-old in a Sassy Seat at a table and place a dish towel in front of him with a favorite plaything on it just out of reach. The baby's natural reaching behavior will shift the towel and move the plaything and he will soon learn to pull the towel to obtain the toy.

Try a similar set-up with a small toy truck or wagon. Place the truck in front of him with a piece of apple on it (or any other food he likes and can pick up). After he eats the piece, place another piece on the truck but move it just beyond reach. Place in his hand one end of a sturdy cord that is attached to the truck. If he doesn't pull it in (which he is not likely to do), help him by guiding his hand. Soon he'll begin to pull it on his own, learning that he can move things by moving whatever is attached to them.

Also give your 1-year-old experience in knocking things down, such as a few light blocks. Build them up and guide his hand so he knocks them down. Build them up again, counting the number of blocks as you do. He'll soon start knocking them down on his own—with great delight. A while later he'll be able to build them up on his own too, and will still take delight in knocking them down.

During the latter part of the first year, your baby is likely to enjoy search games in which you hide a plaything under a cloth or cups (starting with one cup, then two, then more). If necessary, during the early rounds leave a little piece of the toy showing to help him locate it—again with the aim of building his sense of power to make things happen. Make a fuss, of course, when he finds the object, and you might also communicate how very hard you are trying to hide it from him but that he is just too smart for you to fool.

You will also find that at about 8- or 9 months, your baby will begin to search spontaneously for things dropped or accidently covered up and hidden from view. Making something reappear is a thrill for babies this age and research shows that even children this young search in sensible ways (contrary to Piaget's claim that they forget instantly that out-of-sight objects even exist). Children enjoy search games well into their second and third years and you will find that they search in increasingly systematic and logical ways, checking locations in a more orderly fashion (each location checked only once until all are checked) and only where objects are likely to be.[43]

Babies' mastery skills are also enhanced by playing with toys that do things. The traditional rattle is a great toy for learning about making things happen, as are activity boards, pull toys, drums, pianos, xylophones, toy tools, stacking cups, blocks, balls, toy phones, music boxes, and countless other playthings that fill the shelves of toy stores. The key is to select toys that allow the baby to have a reliable impact on something, to learn the connections between actions and outcomes. Many objects around the house can serve the same purpose. A collection of pots, pans, and spoons will delight any baby. The other day I watched a 6-month-old enraptured for many minutes as she manipulated the movable handles on a dresser drawer.

Guide your 1-year-old's hand to the various switches around the house that make things happen: light switches that turn lights on and off, elevator buttons that open and close doors, touch-tone telephone buttons that make sounds, radio dials that turn on voices, among others. You will also find that flashlights are wonderful for teaching children about light (it can be directed, the circle of light changes size with distance, and it produces shadows when blocked). Elevators are useful for teaching numbers (pushing 2 leads to the floor with the 2 on it, pushing 3 leads to the floor with the 3 on it).

Another way to increase your toddler's behavioral repertoire is by making requests and suggesting actions to her, such as "Bring me the spoon, please," "Put the socks on the dolly," and "Let's turn all the cups upside down." Two-year-olds generally love to fulfill these kinds of assignments. As Harriet Rheingold and her colleagues have shown, young children usually carry out such commissions "with alacrity and enthusiasm"; they learn new behaviors through them, and then incorporate the new behaviors into their later play. Rheingold concluded that for the young children she studied, "the achievement of fitting their actions to the words of another was enjoyable; the pleasure resided in the accomplishment."[44] In other words, the children's motivation was mastery.

Little by little, make the assignments more complex, requiring two or more steps (for example, "Poor Teddy looks cold. I think you should put his sweater on. Then put him in bed and cover him with your blanket"). You may have to lend a hand if your requests are beyond your child's ability. And, of course, don't be critical if he or she doesn't carry out the requested actions or modifies them. The goal here isn't obedience.

As your child grows, he or she will show increasing interest in making things with sand, construction toys (Legos, Tinker Toys, Lincoln Logs), and moldable products such as clay and Play Dough. All of these provide mastery experiences involving assembling, transforming, combining, and separating, as well as fantasy play with the products (castles, cabins, cars). And it is wonderful to watch children manipulate these objects in fervent and thoughtful ways as if they were fulfilling some primal urge. Much of the time, let your child construct his own creations, even if he doesn't use the product as intended (he may roll the Lincoln Logs about instead of building with them). Some of the time make suggestions as to what he or the two of you might make, but don't insist if he isn't interested. Some of the time you might start making something on your own and wait to see if he becomes interested and joins in.

Your child will also show increasing interest in doing things for herself, including buttoning her own blouse, zipping her jacket, putting clips in her hair, pouring ketchup on her food, switching lights on and off, and squeezing toothpaste from the tube. Allow her to do as much as possible that is safe for her, recognizing that she will be slow and make lots of mistakes. Teach her to accomplish her goals by breaking down each task into steps and going over them patiently ("Line up the bottom edges of the blouse before you start to button. Then find the bottom button and bottom hole and put them together.").

As your child's skills increase, include her in household projects like making salads, cleaning up, baking, making popcorn, watering plants, planting a garden—everything. Take time to teach her the proper way to do these things, emphasizing that some ways are more effective than others. But take into consideration that she is a novice and may not remember everything you've told her, that her physical abilities are still limited, and that she may not be able to resist trying it *her* way. Try to make sure that she understands the project and isn't just following along mindlessly. For example, talk about what goes into a salad, what the options are, and what variations you enjoy. Discuss the spacing of plants or why some get more water than others.

Children's everyday play also provides them with many lessons in making things happen. For instance, a lot of learning takes place while dressing and undressing dolls and setting up their environments. Children get practice in fine motor skills (getting Barbie's clothes on and off isn't always easy); they get to work on balance problems (to keep the dolls from falling over); and get to exercise their aesthetic preferences. Play with trucks and other vehicles provides many lessons in practical physics. Fantasy play, in which children enact roles (mommy, daddy, doctor, mailman) and play out scenarios, helps them better understand the actions and obligations associated with each role. One should never underestimate the learning that takes place when children are "just playing."

Try to provide easy access for your child to the objects she uses regularly, such as her toys, books, and clothes. Place them where she can reach them. If there are lights in her area that turn on with a pull chain, add a cord so she can turn the lights on and off by herself. Teach her how to turn lamps on and off. You will, of course, have to remind her (more than once) that with freedom comes responsibility, that objects have to be handled properly and respectfully, and that some things are dangerous (for example, that light bulbs in lamps can burn her). You'll also have to remind yourself (more than once) that her mishandling of objects is a natural byproduct of her inexperience and her need to explore things in her own way "just to see what happens."

Construction Projects

When your child is between 2 and 3, construct something useful together. You want your child to understand that we make things not just for play but to produce objects to use. You also want her to appreciate that most of the things she encounters were built *by people,* for themselves or others to use. When my daughter was about 2½ I told her we were going to build a stepping stool to make it easier for her to reach things. I drew a picture of a rectangular box and compared it to a shoe box (which she discovered was too weak to stand on). I told her we would make it out of strong wood and that I'd need her help.

We counted out the number of boards we'd need and went to the lumber yard. She watched the man cutting the boards and we bought screws, nails, and stain (she picked the tint). I had her help me with each phase (holding the ruler, marking the spot on the board where we'd have to cut, helping turn the screws, sanding, staining). Her interest flagged at times and sometimes her own agenda intruded (she enjoyed sliding the nails and screws down a tilted board), but we eventually completed a simple, sturdy box which she used proudly as a stool for the next three years. At around the same time she and her mother went through a similar procedure, sewing a dress together that she could wear and a matching dress for her favorite stuffed animal.

As your child grows, building projects can give the two of you many enjoyable hours and lots of problem solving and mastery experiences. All manner of material can be used including wood (balsa, tongue depressors, popsicle sticks), cloth, clay, paper, buttons, spools, plaster of paris, colored tapes—virtually anything. You can improvise ("Let's build a bird feeder out of tongue depressors," "Let's make a cereal man") or buy kits with prepared materials and instructions. There are many good project books to be found in libraries and book stores.

When using prepared kits, make the reading of instructions a part of the enterprise. Children need to learn that successful construction requires an orderly approach to a project. Since instructions will often take you a while to figure out and are frequently too complex for children to follow (especially since they usually want to start handling the materials immediately), you can avoid some difficulty by studying them first in private and then reading them to the child with whatever modifications seem necessary for his or her understanding.

By the time a child is 5 or 6, introduce some projects that involve batteries, lights, and motors. So many of our daily activities involve using electrical energy and motors, and children should not grow up feeling mystified by and estranged from the technology that is all around them. The fundamentals of basic electrical mechanisms and motors are truly not hard to understand and can be introduced at a young age with simple kits that can be purchased in toy and hobby stores. When children master a circuit and make a light come on or a buzzer buzz, they become more at home in the highly technological world they live in.

Whatever the project, remember to have the child participate in any way she can, and don't worry if her interest and attention drift in and out. As you work, speak about why you are making it, what purpose it will serve, and how you plan to go about it. And whenever obstacles arise, discuss how you think you can overcome them. It is important to put plans into words for a child. It is also important to demonstrate that obstacles are cues for renewed problem solving, not for falling apart or giving up. When the project is done, enjoy it together.

Making Plans

You want to give your child experience in formulating and carrying out plans. Plans are, essentially, *If . . . then* statements: If I do this,

this, and that, then the outcome I desire will (or is likely to) happen. There are many natural events that your child can participate in planning, such as a party, a vacation trip, a visit, a busy day that needs careful scheduling, a picnic, a sports schedule, a construction project, among others.

Good planning involves setting a clear goal, selecting a way of reaching it, anticipating what you'll need at each step along the way ("The weather is changeable there so let's take sweaters"), working within realistic constraints ("All we have to spend is $10"), and taking into consideration that each step might not go smoothly ("In case the subway isn't running, let's find out what bus will get us there"). It is also worth considering whether you should have a written copy of the plan with you as you carry it out, in case you forget some aspects of it ("We planned five games for the party; let's check the list for the order we worked out").

Try to include children in planning sessions as often as possible so they get practice in working through the steps of good planning. A central aspect of planning is estimating the likelihood of events: What's the probability of rain, or that the plane will be on time, or that there'll be a gas station along that route, or that some guests will be late? Research shows that by the age of 6, youngsters are sensitive to probability information and can make accurate probability estimates (they'll know, for example, that the chance of picking a desirable candy from a bag of mixed candies depends on the ratio of desirable to total candies in the bag).[45] Ask them questions to stimulate their thinking about probabilities and how to tailor plans accordingly.

As you are carrying out a plan with your child, look for opportunities to refer to it in order to reinforce the message that good outcomes are a product of good plans. If things aren't going well, reevaluate and update the plan if possible to convey that the commitment is to the goal and not to the plan. Afterwards, talk about what went right and wrong, and what you'll need to take into consideration in future planning. Children generally enjoy planning, and research shows they recognize the value of good plans at a young age.[46] They also appreciate the respect their parents show them when they are included in making plans.

Besides making actual plans with your child, the two of you might enjoy planning hypothetical events in a game format, such as "If you were going to live on a desert island for a year and could only take 10 things with you, what would you take?" You might also try *planning a city*. You are urban designers and your assignment is to plan a new city from scratch. You might begin by making a list of things that the people who live there will need: dwellings; places to get food and other supplies; terminals for deliveries of supplies; means of transportation into, out of, and within the city; manufacturing and business areas; garbage disposal sites; energy and water supplies; places for vehicles; drainage and sewer systems; places for communication, education, entertainment, and recreation—and so on. Then try to map out where each function should be located, using such criteria as convenience, safety, and aesthetics.

Skill Learning

During the grade-school years, mastery activities increasingly take the form of *purposeful skill learning*. Children start to take music lessons, and they strive to perfect athletic skills, and drill away at the multiplication table; in pottery class they try over and over again to "throw" their clay onto the center of the potter's wheel; in English classes they go over lists of words for proper spelling. All of these endeavors require sustained attention and practice. What makes them different from the persistent mastery efforts of the young child (say at opening a latch) is that adults now determine what's worth mastering and how to go about it. The music teacher determines which scales are to be practiced and how much time should be spent on them; the gymnastics coach decides which moves are to be practiced and controls how many times each is gone over.

Most children adjust well to these new forms of learning, particularly when they are motivated to learn the skill. Many, though, at some time or other, need encouragement to keep plugging or to meet the instructor's demands. Children do need to understand that drilling is an unavoidable aspect of most skill learning, a natural part of the mastery process.

Parents are often confused about how to handle a child who doesn't want to practice enough. A useful question then is, *How important is it for the child to learn this skill?* And also, *Must it be learned now?* It is counterproductive to pressure a child who has lost interest in playing the piano to practice scales. On the other hand, multiplication and other arithmetic skills are clearly central to a child's education and not so easily tossed off. Sometimes a learning task that is currently difficult and boring for a child will be handled easily a few weeks or months later.

But, unfortunately, most school curricula do not accommodate the individual pace of each youngster, so parents will usually have to insist that material be mastered at the time the school says it must be mastered. Sometimes the child's cooperation can be gained by a clear, straightforward explanation of why the assignment is important. If this doesn't work, it may be necessary to make access to some desirable activity contingent on fulfilling the school assignment ("First finish your homework, and then you can play").

Sometimes parents get upset at their youngster's lack of perseverance even when the skill involved is not particularly important; they worry because their boy or girl seems to switch interests quickly, bounding toward new enthusiasms before making much headway in old ones. Actually, it is quite natural for children to switch interests quickly; when their interest is aroused in an activity, they are too inexperienced to foresee their reaction to later phases of the instruction.

A child may plead for piano lessons after learning to bang out "Twinkle, Twinkle, Little Star" on the keys, and may promise with total sincerity to practice, practice, practice. But in reality he or she has no idea of what practicing entails and verbal explanations by the parent ("You'll have to sit for an hour and practice scales every day") can't really convey what the experience will be like. Parents should expect this kind of sampling and switching of activities and need only be concerned if their child seems unable to sustain any interests at all. If that occurs it may be remedied by altering aspects of the instruction. The pace may need to be slowed so less practicing is required during the early stages of learning; or the assignments might be adjusted to permit more intrinsic satisfaction (such as more time devoted to banging out songs); or parents might join the child during practice sessions, providing timely pep talks and reinforcement.

Provide Lots of Success in Learning

This is accomplished by paying close attention to what your child is ready for, and by breaking down what has to be learned into small steps. If you ask a 2-year-old to copy the letter *A*, he's not likely to even try. Nag at him to do it and letters may become a negative stimulus. But ask him again a year later and he'll probably be interested in trying—and if during the preceding year letters have been a regular part of his experience, he'll probably succeed.

One way to promote success is by breaking down tasks into easier steps. For example, you can simplify the task of copying letters by drawing part of the letter and asking your child to complete the rest. Then draw part of it again, but leave more of the letter unfinished. Or you can draw the letter with dots and ask your child to draw over the dots; then do it again, but with fewer dots. Psychologists use the term "fading" to refer to this process of gradually removing cues (fewer dots) as the learner becomes ready to take on more of the task.

Your enthusiasm and glee at your child's successes and partial successes are important, but let the natural reinforcers that a child experiences in mastering a task take precedence over your praise. Remember, children love to learn. They love it for its own sake. Don't make learning about pleasing mommy and daddy. Your joyful, "Look at that! An *A*. You did it!'' in response to your child copying an *A* is better than "I'm so pleased" or "I love you because you're so smart.'' There is evidence that too much emphasis on external reinforcers, such as the wrong kind of praise or paying a child money for good grades, can undermine the natural, intrinsic reinforcement of learning something new.[47]

Parents can also help their child experience success by keeping the criteria of success reasonable. A 3-year-old who prints an *A* that is, in truth, barely an *A*, still deserves great credit: "You're doing it. Yes. That's an *A*.'' Then you can try a simple correction: "See the top. Make the two lines meet on top.'' If you sense that your instruction isn't welcome at that moment, don't push it—at least not with a young child. Go back to a positive response over what the child has accomplished. You'll have many more opportunities to introduce the correction. Older children do, of course, have to learn to attend to and appreciate the importance of corrections, which often occurs spontaneously when they begin to recognize the value of accuracy and precision. A child will, for instance, become more concerned about the quality of his lettering, and more accepting of correction, when he realizes that people can't read what he's written to them.

Instruction doesn't always have to be direct and obvious, particularly with children who resist formal explanations and corrections (which many children do). I once tried to show a 3-year-old who loved to draw faces that noses are below the eyes, not between them (children often draw them too high). She wasn't interested in being corrected and that was fine with me. The next day while looking at a picture book with faces I asked her where the artist had drawn the nose. She pointed to the nose. I then asked her where she would draw it. She placed her finger *above the nose,* between the eyes.

As we continued reading I asked the same question about another face and she gave the same reply. We didn't discuss it further. I didn't comment on her responses and gave her no formal instruction. The next day when I looked at her drawings the noses were in their proper place and she seemed delighted with her depictions. It wasn't critical that she learn where to draw the nose at that time. But the opportunity was there and it turned out to be easy to help her—and it gave her great pleasure.

Help Your Child to Persist at Learning Tasks Despite Frustration or Criticism

Some years ago Abraham Korman did a series of studies demonstrating that when you convey to people engaged in challenging tasks that they really can accomplish them, their effort and level of accomplishment increase.[48] Successful athletic coaches operate from this "can do" framework, setting high expectancies and reinforcing them through pep talks and timely prompts. It's a useful framework for parents too. Help your child set challenging though realistic goals. Then when you see his drive giving way to discouragement, rouse his spirit with some inspiring words and, if needed, a practical suggestion or two.

Parental pep talks can save the day for a teen as well as a toddler, but you also want your youngsters to be able to give *themselves* a pep talk when frustrations start to mount. In other words, you want to help your child learn what to say to himself at these dark moments. Research shows that you can do this by actually teaching and modeling useful self-statements.[49] For instance, let your child see you having trouble accomplishing something and getting frustrated over it. Then let him hear you tell yourself something like, "Calm down. I'm getting upset. That won't help me solve it. I need to figure out why it's not working so I can try it another way." You might also relate anecdotes about yourself and others that describe positive outcomes from persisting in the face of frustration.

You can also use more direct instruction to teach children what to say to themselves when frustrated. Even preschoolers can learn the old adage, "If at first you don't succeed try and try again." And if you remind them of it at least a few times when they appear thwarted and discouraged, they will soon learn to remind *themselves* of it when frustrated.

Children also learn persistence when they are introduced to longer and more complicated problem-solving tasks in a gradual way so that they can get used to working for increasingly delayed and uncertain payoffs. Parents can also gradually increase the length of time they allow a child to experience failure before coming to his or her aid.[50]

And don't forget to praise a child for his hard work and persistence and to remind him after he succeeds that he "got it" because he worked so hard. These various "frustration tolerance" lessons work best when parents remain calm and enthusiastic during their child's setbacks, stressing the joy of the challenge rather than momentary success or failure. You want to convey that hard work and frustration are a natural part of the process of trying to accomplish anything really worthwhile.

Also prepare your youngster for the discouraging and disparaging comments of others, of those who say "It can't be done" or "*You'll* never do it." Provide examples of people who persisted in the face of criticism and setbacks, both famous achievers (Edison, the Wright brothers, etc.) and ordinary people whom the child knows (grandpa, Aunt Betty). Convey that everyone has a *right* to make mistakes and that no one has the right to ridicule anyone's efforts. Children, even 5-year-olds, can understand the notion of rights and take them seriously. Once this framework of rights is established, parents can use it to fortify their child after he or she has been ridiculed by a friend. Parents can say something like:

> You know that real friends don't act that way; at least they shouldn't. Real friends are on each other's side. And if *you* want to be a real friend you have an obligation to let your friend know that that's the way you expect the two of you to treat each other.

This approach encourages children to recognize "put downs" as inappropriate and unfair, not to be accepted as valid assessments of their abilities. You can reinforce this message with Edgar Alan Guest's inspiring poem, "It Couldn't Be Done" (the first stanza of which follows):

> Somebody said that it couldn't be done,
> But he with a chuckle replied
> That "maybe it couldn't," but he would be one
> Who wouldn't say so till he'd tried.
> So he buckled right in with the trace of a grin
> On his face. If he worried he hid it.
> He started to sing as he tackled the thing
> that couldn't be done, and he did it.[51]

Point Out Examples of Mastery and Inventiveness

One way children discover what's controllable is by learning how others—from famous inventors to nameless craftspeople—have made things happen. Point out and discuss the way common objects are made and how well they fulfill their purpose. When possible, compare different objects of the same type (a manual typewriter vs. an electric typewriter vs. an electronic typewriter) and try to define the problem that each innovation was designed to solve. Highlight the striving and effort behind improvements and laud the ingenuity of the accomplishments. You want your child to recognize that the everyday objects we take for granted are actually somebody's solutions to problems.

You can inspire your child to appreciate human inventiveness by recounting humankind's long struggle to solve the same basic problems, such as the need to communicate over long distances. Smoke signals, telegraph keys, and telephones don't look alike but they are all solutions to the same problem. Hieroglyphics don't look like writing but both convey messages. A donkey in harness doesn't look like a truck but both have been used to transport supplies—and owners of both have had to consider that both run out of fuel, overheat, and wear out with use. Your library and bookstore will have many good books describing the lives and struggles of famous inventors. Children usually love these stories.

Discussions of inventiveness can also arise during everyday conversations about common items: "See how much faster our new push button phone works than the old rotary phone. Somebody in the phone company must have said, 'I bet I can figure out a way to make dialing faster,' and invented push button dialing. And look how much better this coiled cord is than this old one."

The goal of such conversations is, again, to sensitize your child to the fact that *people* make things, that it takes thought and effort (that is, problem solving) to make them well, and that making things well is a worthy goal. It is also useful to point out when something is not made well (such as a toy that malfunctions), perhaps because it wasn't thought through sufficiently or the maker didn't care about quality (caring more for quick profits, perhaps). You might then, try to figure out together how it might have been made better. The Consumers Union's children's magazine, *Zillions,* is a good source for learning about the quality and defects of products, as of course is their excellent magazine, *Consumer Reports.*

Keep in mind that not all worthy inventions are "modern" or a product of Western technology, as the following story illustrates:

> During the summer, Phillip (5 years, 10 months) had his first experiences with row boats and canoes, and he was not completely satisfied with either. He preferred canoes because they were fast and quiet, but he could feel that they were easy to tip over and he was somewhat uneasy in them. The rowboats were stable, but slow and noisy (they had aluminum hulls).
>
> In early fall I was reading a natural history magazine and came across a photograph of a canoe with pontoons used by South Pacific islanders. It was the perfect solution: fast *and* stable. The pontoons were attached to beams that lay across the top of the canoe so they only made contact with the water when the canoe tipped. That way they added safety without extra friction, except when needed. I showed the photo to Phillip and we talked about the ingeniousness of the invention. Then, on his own, he added pontoons to his toy canoe, using chopsticks and popsicle sticks.

Magazines such as *National Geographic, Natural History,* and *Smithsonian* provide many examples of inventiveness by non-Western peoples who have come up with ingenious devices to help them survive in environments very different from our own. The National Geographic nature series on television is another excellent source, as are many Nova specials and other TV nature programs.

Human inventiveness is not limited to the production of material things. We also invent institutions (democratic government) and behavioral practices (the Dewey Decimal System used by libraries, algebra, one-way toll booths at bridges and tunnels). There are also countless strategies that all of us invent or adopt to improve our lives. There's a good way to sweep a floor and a good way to splice electrical cords. Communicate enthusiasm for these kinds of "inventions"—both major and modest ones. And when confronted with obstacles or problems, share your solution attempts with your child and invite him to join you in thinking up solutions.

As your child becomes aware of or participates in different institutions, point out the problem solving attempts that are embodied in its organization and rules, including the policies in your own family, the regulations of the little league team, the organizational hierarchy of a corporation, and the Bill of Rights of the U.S. Constitution. Suggest, and ask your child to suggest, organizational and rule changes that might produce improvements in those institutions.

You want to convey that organizational structures, rules, laws, policies, etc. are means to ends, and that it is legitimate and worthwhile to evaluate whether those ends might be better served by other practices—or even whether the ends themselves are worth pursuing. Should the rule on the team be that everyone gets an equal opportunity to play regardless of ability? Or should the best players play the most? Obviously, it depends on what one believes the goal of playing should be. Parent and child can have interesting dialogues around these kinds of questions.

You may also find it interesting to evaluate common proverbs. Proverbs are rules for effective action, describing tactics for improving our lives. When we remind ourselves of a proverb to help us make a decision we are engaging in rule-governed behavior. But all proverbs may not be useful. Indeed, sometimes we come across two seemingly wise proverbs that appear to contradict each other. Perhaps each is wise in only some situations. Evaluating proverbs can give your child practice in analyzing and validating rules. Here are a few contradictory pairs:

Nothing ventured, nothing gained. / Better safe than sorry.
Absence makes the heart grow fonder. / Out of sight, out of mind.
Many hands make light work. / Too many cooks spoil the broth.

Together, think of situations in which each of these constitutes good advice, and other situations in which each seems wrong. Evaluate whether they are truly contradictory.

An interesting way to teach about human inventiveness is to take a common substance like water and point out the many different ways people have put it to use. Aside from drinking it and bathing in it, we use it for power (via steam engines, water wheels in mills, hydroelectric plants, and, someday, fusion reactors), for transportation (by boat), for building (in concrete), for irrigating plants, for cooking (boiling), for cooling heated products in manufacturing (such as molten steel), for heating (in radiators), for fighting fires, for sleeping (water beds), and for pressing our clothes (with steam irons), to name just a few.

You can do the same thing for air, pointing out the many ways we make air work for us: windmills, compressed air in pneumatic machines, and the air bubble in a carpenter's level, to name just a few.

Another way to give children an appreciation of human inventiveness is to teach them how common objects are made. Children ordinarily find this interesting and will often ask questions about how the objects they come across came to be. Since causal connections are involved in the making of things, your explanations of how things are made also become lessons in causal relationships. For instance, you might explain to a child that the wool in his sweater started out as the hair on a sheep; that sheep get haircuts (called shearing) in the spring; that their wool is then spun into yarn and then dyed and woven or knitted into clothing, blankets, and carpets. Obviously it will be helpful if he can witness any of these processes. You can readily find good children's books that describe and illustrate the making of common objects, such as sweaters, bread, cheese, furniture, steel, paper, etc. Look for books that describe the processes by which raw materials are turned into the many useful products around us. If the book has information about the history and evolution of the manufacturing processes, so much the better.

Give Your Child Experiences with and an Understanding of Tools, Machines, and Other Products That Make Things Happen

We use tools and machines to help us make things happen. In one way or another they augment our muscle power or sharpen our senses by transforming or amplifying energy. Before your child is three get her safety scissors and help her learn to use them (expecting it to take a while). A toy tool set will give her practice in using a hammer, screw driver, wrench, and clamp. Include lots of experience with various "fasteners," such as tape, string, glue, paper clips, twist ties, rubber bands, and brass fasteners. Also introduce instruments for amplifying sensory input, such as a magnifying glass, binoculars, and a stethoscope (many project books describe how to make a toy stethoscope).

As your child's manual skills improve add experiences with staplers, hole punchers, sand paper, springs, pulleys, wheels, and as many different kinds of real tools as possible (considering safety, of course). Provide patient instruction on how to use each instrument properly, and include lessons in the proper care and the dangers of each. Also, a visit to a crafts fair will introduce your child to many specialized tools and provide her an opportunity to observe people making lovely and useful things.

Present tool use as problem solving and hypothesis testing: "We need to hold those together. Maybe string will work. No, we'd have to make the string very tight and the pieces might break. I think we can use the hole puncher to make a hole in each piece and then use a fastener." Ask your child for her solutions and let her try them out.

Whenever possible, demonstrate or let her try out alternative instruments that were designed to solve the same problem. As an example, perhaps you (like me) possess a few different kinds of instruments for removing corks from wine bottles (mine include a traditional corkscrew, a corkscrew with a lever attached for easier extractions, a pump that injects air into the bottle to force the cork out, and a pronged gizmo that enables one to twist or rock the cork out). By demonstrating these different solutions to the same problem you help your child understand that tools are a product of creative thinking and that the search for better solutions need never end. Other instruments you could use to teach the same lesson are different kinds of razors, different kinds of toasters, and different kinds of light bulbs (incandescent vs. fluorescent).

Children are more likely to use tools creatively if they have some understanding of the mechanisms underlying different tools. To engineers there are only a few fundamental mechanisms underlying the many different kinds of tools and machines we use. One way to help a child understand this is to point out the essential similarities between what are ostensibly very different instruments. The lever is one such basic "machine" or mechanism. Levers help us move things that are beyond our strength, whether we are trying to dislodge a boulder with a stick, pry the lid off a jar with a can opener, open a bucket of paint with a screw driver, pump water from a well, lift a car with a jack, squeeze orange juice with a hand juicer, remove nails with the claw end of a hammer, turn bolts with a wrench, or clip toenails with a clipper.

All these instruments are levers comprised of a handle end and a working end (and the "fulcrum" upon which the lever rests). All operate similarly: the long, handle end of the lever moves through a much larger arc than the short, working end—so the small, steady force needed to move the handle a long distance gets concentrated at the working end into a large force traversing a small distance.

Other basic "machines" are the *wedge,* for cutting, splitting, and separating (including knives and axes, and also the keystone at the top of an arch, which keeps the sides from collapsing in on each other); the *wheel and axle,* for transporting things with far less friction and therefore less effort than dragging them; the *screw,* for boring, fastening, moving, and lifting; and the *ramp* (or inclined plane) and the *pulley*—both used to make it easier to raise and lower things.

With your child try to discover the basic mechanisms in whatever tools and machines you use or come across. For instance, when we turn a knob or a faucet handle, tighten a clamp, or activate a propeller (as in a motor boat), we are using a screw; clocks and phonograph players are both built out of wheels on axles. The spring is another ubiquitous device, and it's worth noting some of its many applications. You won't have to look far to find them: springs are in ball point pens, mattresses, wind-up toys and watches, self-closing door hinges, scales, guns, shock absorbers, and various kinds of switches.

When using an instrument or a machine draw your child's attention to efficacious aspects of its design ("See how the handle tapers to provide a better grip") and try to reveal how it works. For example, you might point out the arrangement of gears in an egg beater, or the rubber belt that turns the carpet beater in an upright vacuum cleaner (notice that the gears and the belt both alter the direction of force).

We use many other products to make things happen that aren't usually classified as tools or machines. For example, we use paper in many forms, for many uses: for cleaning, as a medium for writing and printing, as containers, for wrapping, for blowing noses, etc. Take your child on a tour of the house to find all the types of paper products and how each is especially designed to fulfill its function. Tissues are soft and absorbent, which makes them good for our noses, but useless for writing upon with a pen. Waxed paper is good for wrapping foods, but won't make a good coffee filter. Point out these connections between structure and function.

Parents don't need great mechanical skill themselves to convey an interest in and respect for tools and machines as problem solvers. Fortunately there are a number of well-illustrated books on *how things work*—some geared for young, grade-school children (such as *Joe Kaufman's Big Book About How Things Work,* a Golden Book). These provide cut-away and blow-up illustrations of many of our common devices, along with clear descriptions of their mechanisms. Any parent, whether handy or all-thumbs, will find these books useful for teaching about tools and machines.

Many of the things we (children and adults) want to make happen turn out to be difficult. We want to fix a clock, or cure a mysterious illness, or make a faster computer chip, or paint the images we experienced in a dream, or win a chess tournament, or figure out which financial investment offers the highest return. Each of these requires some skill in problem solving in that particular domain. Chapter 9 provides a discussion of the major domains of problem solving (diagnostic, inductive, inventive, tactical, imaginative, and mathematical) and how parents can foster the requisite skills for each. First, though, we will consider the core skills of reading, writing, and arithmetic.

8

ↄ⳹ↄ

Core Mastery Skills

Reading, Writing, and Arithmetic

Parents often ask when they should start teaching their children reading, writing, and arithmetic. It's the wrong question. These skills are best learned by incorporating them into children's normal, everyday activities, from their earliest years, and not through formal lessons beginning at a particular age.

Mastering these skills early in childhood is often considered an indication of intelligence, in the sense that it shows an ability to learn quickly. By late childhood, though, most children will have mastered these basic skills and they are no longer, in themselves, considered signs of superior intelligence. There are some studies that have found an association between learning to read early (mastering basic reading skills before first grade) and later academic and intellectual achievement. In one study, early readers stayed better readers in comparison to peers over a six-year follow-up period and showed superior academic skills. Other research found a correlation between high IQ and early reading—though by no means all, or even most, high IQ children learned to read early.[1] It is a safe bet that a child who develops basic reading, writing, and arithmetic skills early will evince high intellectual achievement later. But it is also important to remember that many high intellectual achievers were not early readers.

Reading

Reading involves a number of component skills, all of which must be mastered:

- Children must be able to recognize letters and know their sounds (that is, they must learn "phonics").
- They must be aware that the beginnings and endings of words are indicated by spaces.
- They must be able to sight read common words without sounding them out (called the whole word or "look-say" method of reading).
- They must be aware of the left-to-right direction of writing, and that when they come to the end of a line they continue by going back to the left side of the next line.
- They must understand the meaning of the individual words, as well as such symbols as the comma, period, and question mark.
- They must be able to understand the meaning of phrases, sentences, and groups of sentences, and not just words in isolation.
- They must be able to react to a written piece as a whole, perceiving the links between its parts, such as between successive incidents in an emerging story plot or between premises and conclusions in an essay.

If children are deficient in any of these skills, their reading will suffer.[2] There has been a longstanding debate among some educators about whether phonic (sounding out) or look-say (whole word) skills are more important in learning to read. This debate is as sensible as arguing about whether the right foot or the left foot is more important in learning to walk. Children can't learn to read without both. They must, of course, know the sounds of the letters, but our language is too irregular to rely solely on sounding out words. For instance, the same double vowel in the words "book" and "soon" are pronounced differently. Sounding out words is a slow, uncertain process, as you can experience yourself by reading the chemical compounds in cosmetics and processed foods. Few of us will feel confident sounding at the word, "coelanth."

On the other hand, children who only know words by sight and who cannot sound out new words can only read those words they have already learned. You can experience this problem if you try to read a medical dictionary with unfamiliar words. Try "chorioallantois"; if you don't know the sound of "ois," you won't be able to pronounce it. Similarly, try reading French or any foreign language whose sound rules you don't know. You won't, for example, be able to read the French word "nouveau" if you don't know that "eau" is pronounced "oh" (more or less like the vowel "go"). A recent longitudinal study of children's reading development through fourth grade, found that those who entered first grade with little ability to sound out words were the most likely to become poor readers.[3]

Introduce letters by the time your child is 2, if not sooner. Point them out in books, on signs, on doors—everywhere ("That's an *A*. Oh, there's another *A*"). Enthusiasm will help. Magnetized letters, alphabet form boards, and blocks with letters are very good for teaching letters, since children are inclined to play with them and they provide manual as well as visual information. Start with the capital letters, and once your child has become familiar with them, introduce the small letters. Your child is likely to learn the letters quickly, which is quite an achievement when you consider how long it would take most of us as adults to learn a totally unfamiliar alphabet.

Teach the names of the letters and the sounds ("Thats a *T*. T . . . T . . . Tommy. That's your name, Tommy. See the *T*. That word is *T*ommy." Oh, and look here. Another *T* . . . for *T*able. This is your *t*oy *t*able. Oops, there's another *T* word . . . *T*oy. Tommy's toy table"). It will take a lot of repetition, but try to make letter teaching a regular and pleasant part of your interaction. However, don't let it interfere with other interesting things you have to discuss with your 2-year-old, and avoid switching the focus to letters when he or she is engrossed in some activity.

When letter lessons are integrated into children's activities, they want to learn letters, just as they want to learn everything else. For instance, when working on a form board together, ask for a letter ("Can you give me a *B?*"). Your child will want to know what letter to give you in order to proceed with the activity. Give instruction gently no matter how many times you have to give them ("It's that one with the two curves. Here, feel those curves"). Before asking for the letter, you might put it where it will be noticed easily.

Look for opportunities to teach the letters and their sounds. You might make an Alphabet Book together, looking for pictures of *A* things, *B* things, etc., to paste on the appropriate pages. You can play Pack the Suitcase: "I'm putting an *A* thing in: an apple. You put a *B* thing in"—and so on. When you read to your child, point out letters and sounds every so often ("Look, there's a *P* for 'Peter' and a *P* for 'put' "), but it's best not to do this the first time you read a story. The alphabet song is an enjoyable way to learn the sequence of letters, which will be important later in using things like dictionaries and telephone books. I've never met a child who didn't love the alphabet song.

It should be apparent that the opportunities for letter and phonics instruction are endless. The same goes for words. Point out signs that you pass regularly ("See that word, *shoe*. S, H, O, E. This is a shoe store. We buy shoes here"). One of the first words read by my child was "pizza," a sign we encountered with some frequency. Many story books will have pictures of streets with shops, such as bakeries and groceries. Point out the signs, as well as the items (breads, cakes) in the window. When you come to those signs again ask, "What does that say?" Your child may not remember the word, but will look at the picture of the breads and cakes in the shop window and give you the correct response. If necessary, point his attention to the items in the window. This is a good way to give him an understanding of what written words are and to get him started identifying them.

Print your shopping list in large letters and read it together as you look for items, matching the word on the list with the word on the package. Build words with blocks or magnetized letters ("Let's write *cat: C, A, T* spells *cat*. Let's find a *C* and put it down. Then put an *A* next to it; then the *T*. Great! You wrote *cat*. Can you read that to me? Hey, you can read! Shall we write, *pussy* next to it for *pussy cat?*").

In some reading sessions, underline or highlight a particular consonant sound whenever it appears at the beginning of a word on the page. Remind your child of the sound ("That's an *L*. It's pronounced, 'Luh.' Can you say, 'Luh'?"). Then ask her to make that sound whenever you point to the underlined letter as you read the words on the page. Whenever she says "Luh" you fill in the rest of the word and indicate the whole word to her ("*Love*. See, *L, O, V, E,* spells *love*"). This will help her grasp how words are formed on the page, introduce her to the left-to-right pattern, and give her the good feeling that she is participating in the reading process.

Do the same thing with whole words, underlining a given word ("the" or "dog") whenever it appears. Follow your reading with your finger, and have her read the underlined word when you stop and point to it. Rebus books, in which pictures are substituted for key words (a picture of a house appears instead of the word "house"), are also useful for teaching a child about the left-to-right word pattern. You can also base a lot of reading and writing instruction on *names*. Most children love to read names: their names, parents' names, friends' names, pets' names, cartoon character names, etc. Ask your child to draw pictures of real people and story characters and write their names in. Then have her read the names. You can also make lists of names under interesting headings: family, friends, stores, among others. Another useful reading exercise is to have your child dictate a short story to you (two or three sentences), and to read it back. Children like to see their words in print and enjoy reading them back.

Keep your eyes open for interesting word games that will get your child reading whole words. For example, write action words on cards (jump, hop, skip, dance, bend), then have her pick one and act it out. You must guess the word. The first few times through, someone will have to help her with the reading, but soon she'll read all the words on her own. After a while, add new cards that contain short sentences (Walk back and forth; I am a monkey; The ballerina is here).

For another game, mark four sets of index cards with different colored crayons, two cards per color. Turn a pair over and write words that are opposites (in, out; up, down; on, off; big, little). Do this for each pair, then shuffle them and set the cards out randomly, word side up. Your child must match the opposites and check if he is right by turning the cards over to see if they have the same color.

Word Bingo also teaches sight vocabulary: Write 16 basic words, one each, on small cards, and place them in a bag. Then draw a 4-space by 4-space grid on a few larger cards and write the 16 words in the spaces, arranging them differently on each card. Each player gets one of these "bingo" cards. Then pick one word card at a time from the bag and each player puts a penny on the matching word on his or her bingo card. The first player to fill a row, column, or diagonal, wins. Simple commercial board games that require reading ("Go back 2 spaces") will also contribute to your child's sight vocabulary.

When it comes to sounding out new words, you'll find that your child will master the consonants before the vowels since the sound of a consonant differs much less from word to word than the sound of a vowel. Children gradually learn the range of sounds associated with a vowel letter (an *e* might be "ee," "eh," "uh," or silent), but when encountering a new word they do not know which of these particular vowel sound to make. Indeed, sometimes two words are spelled exactly the same but the vowel is pronounced differently, as in "wind" (The wind blows; Wind the clock). Two vowels together are especially unpredictable, as in *lead, heard, hearth, head,* and *fear*.

There are some rules for vowels that work most of the time, as when a final *e* changes a preceding short vowel to a long vowel (*bit* to *bite*), but most of the time you will simply have to supply the vowel sound ("This time the *i* is pronounced 'ih' "). The consonant blends (*th, sh*) also take longer to master, as do the highly irregular letter combinations, as when *ph* is pronounced "f." Extra time will also be required for letters that indicate two different sounds (*c* can be pronounced "s," as in center, or "k," as in cat). At early stages of reading, children often rivet on the first consonant and guess the rest of the word. They need reminders to work through the word letter by letter.

One problem you may encounter with consonants is the extra sound that children frequently add on, as when *T* becomes "tuh" and *P* becomes "puh." These "uhs" often make it hard for children to recognize the word they are sounding out, as when "rabbit" becomes "ruhabuhituh." The sound, "rabbit," may not leap out of all that. Children usually need reminders to keep the consonants crisp and to blend them with the vowels that follow. Silent consonants, such as the *l* in "half" and the *gh* in "night," also cause problems. Tell your child that we have a pretty crazy language, so there are extra things to learn. Children enjoy exercises like, "Name three words that begin with B." Or, "Tell me the first letter in the names of the seven dwarfs." Generations of young girls have enjoyed playing "A my name is . . .", which provides an excellent lesson in phonics.

Word-family exercises, using lists of words with the same spelling and sound pattern (sat, hat, fat, cat), provide phonic and whole-word instruction simultaneously. You can find word-family exercises in many activity books or you can make them up. Another exercise to try consists of writing some simple words on a paper (cat, dog, etc.) and then asking your child to assemble those words out of magnetized letters. At first, allow him to look at the written page. Later, ask him to do it from memory. If necessary, give hints: "What animal barks?"

Activity books and magazines will have many other letter and word exercises and games that most children enjoy. Try them. If your child has fun with them, don't let any "expert" talk you out of them. Some experts are adamantly against parents teaching their children to read. If you ask them why, I don't believe you'll get a reasonable reply.

Good readers generally come from homes in which they were read to a lot. That's how they discovered the wonders that books contain. Reading to children motivates them to want to read so they can have access to those wonders whenever they want. It also conveys that reading is not about word mastery, it is about the evocation of ideas and images through an expanding progression of words.

So make reading a daily activity with your child, and make sure he understands the content by asking him questions and explaining any aspects that may be unclear. Also provide the meaning of new words and encourage him to stop you whenever there's a word or anything else that he doesn't understand. Research shows that open-ended and complex "what" questions when reading ("There's Eeyore. What's happening to him?") have a beneficial effect on children's language abilities.[4] As his familiarity with words increases, you can improve his vocabulary by pointing out common word elements (prefixes, suffixes)—for example, that the words triangle, tricycle, and triceratops all contain the same prefix because the objects they refer to all have something in common involving the number three.

Most children's books have illustrations to help the child picture the events that the words describe. But some events will not be depicted and children have to fill in gaps with mental pictures. Check that your child is picturing the events properly. Even when there are lots of illustrations, there are still important elements in a story that the reader must fill in, such as characters' motives and feelings—and sometimes children need help with this. Consider even the simple narrative, "Tommy took Mindy's hat. Then she pushed him down." The reader must fill in that Mindy was upset about her hat being taken, which motivated her to attack Tommy. Even young children make these kinds of inferences and can generally make sense of a narrative if story content covers material within their experience.[5]

Content outside of their experience confuses them unless the author (or a parent) fills in the missing elements. For instance, if a story character is afraid of giants, but the child hasn't learned the convention that giants are mean, he may be confused about why the character hides and runs away when the giants arrive. You can get an idea of the inferences your child is making by asking questions ("Why is the boy hiding?").

In a sense, each fact in a narrative is a clue and the reader must infer a cohesive story from the entire collection of clues. To make sure your child is apprehending the facts in a story, discuss the feelings of the characters, their motivations, the environments they are in, their strategies and actions, their obstacles and outcomes, their values, their senses of humor, their relationships, and anything else that seems relevant. Also, if the story has a point of view, discuss that too. And, when appropriate, connect the content of the story to similar experiences that your child has had. Another way to tell if your child is building a cohesive and logical narrative is to ask him periodically what he thinks will happen next. This will let you know if his expectations reflect the events already described.

Some parents reported that their children enjoyed it when they occasionally inserted illogical content into familiar stories, such as ". . . and then they put the milk in the oven to freeze it." Their children enjoyed catching them.

Little by little have your child read some words and lines in a book you are reading to him. Obviously, use simple books to start, especially ones that have words he knows and perhaps has already learned to read by sight. At the early stages, you read the book first, or use a book that you've already read to him a number of times, so he's familiar with the sounds of the words. Keep in mind that simple books don't have to be uninteresting. Dr. Seuss' *Hop on Pop* and *Big Fish, Little Fish* are imaginative early readers to start with. You will need a lot of patience as your child learns to sound out words. Be very encouraging and show excitement over his progress. Since you're likely to be thrilled as your child actually begins to read, this shouldn't be too difficult.

Give sound hints when he gets stuck ("That's a 'guh' "), but allow enough time for him to come up with sounds he has learned but can't recall immediately. In any kind of instruction, hints should give the least information necessary to prompt the right answer, but there are many kinds of hints, including some that incorporate humor. For example, if your child reads "father" as "frather," you can ask "Am I your frather?" (or "Is daddy your frather?"). You'll get a laugh and provide a hint at the same time. One mother said her child gained practice reading by reading to his stuffed animals. Some of this reading might have been reciting memorized text, but she said he followed the written text word by word and learned to associate the sound of the words with its appearance on the page.

It is extremely important that you make sure your child makes sense of the passage and is not just reading words. After he's read each word in a sentence, have him go back and read the entire sentence again so he can hear it for sense. Young children often do this spontaneously; they want to understand the content of the reading material. Children who learn to read through formal instruction in classes that stress word mastery at the expense of meaning, sometimes focus on showing that they can read each word and need reminders to assemble meaning as they proceed from word to word.

Instruct your young reader that whenever he doesn't understand what he is reading, to go back over it; and if that doesn't work, to read ahead a bit to see if a fuller context will make the meaning clearer. If neither works, he should ask for a clarification and show you, if he can, exactly where in the text the meaning broke down. Research confirms that children can learn the strategies of going back and ahead in search of missing meaning, and their reading is improved by them.

In addition, ask questions to make sure your youngster has understood the topic and main points in an essay or article he has read ("It's about people wanting to save seals; they were saved by groups who went to the Arctic to protest the killing"). Children who don't spontaneously reflect on the topic and main points of what they read can learn to do so with some reminders and practice.[6]

As another reading exercise, type up the words to a brief, simple song and teach it to your child from the typed copy. Before she has memorized it completely have her use the typed copy to remind herself of the words. It's also worth mentioning that children love to type. If you have a typewriter or a computer, work with your child on typing notes, lists, letters or anything else. Here again your patience will be crucial.

Another enjoyable activity that is useful for teaching both reading and writing is to write a brief story together (just a few simple sentences at first). It can be pure fiction or based on some experience of your child. If your child can write letters, let him do the writing with your help; otherwise, you do it with his help. Then have him read it back. Have him read it to others too. He will enjoy being an author—and don't worry if it is more memorized than actually read. Just check to make sure he can actually read all the words.

Children's reading comprehension grows as their vocabularies grow. You can help build your child's vocabulary by defining new words when you come across them, providing connotative as well as denotative meaning. The sentence, "A lark is a bird," provides the simple denotative meaning of "lark." In literature, a reference to the appearance of a lark may also *connote* the end of a long night, since larks begin to sing at sunrise. You can also build vocabulary through your daily conversations. Talk about the things the two of you observe and do together and help her find the words to answer any questions you ask. Also encourage her to discuss what she's done, thought, or felt, and you tell her about your observations and feelings, as well as interesting things you've done or discovered.

As your youngster's reading progresses, try to make him aware of the stylistic aspects of stories, including the use of metaphor and other figures of speech, the careful selection of words for precise effects, the use of rhythm, repetition, and other structural elements to convey mood, the employment of irony to promote a point of view, and many other literary devices.

When your child starts school, continue to show an interest in her language and reading skills. Go over her assignments and read some of her school stories together. Make clear that you want to continue to share in her learning, that it delights you.

The reading "lessons" described above are all enjoyable activities for children—which does not mean that there is no frustration encountered. When introduced early, letters, words, and reading become a natural part of the child's day, not chores to learn, as they frequently are when children start to learn to read in large first-grade classes. The child masters reading the way he or she masters speaking, climbing the stairs (lots of frustration here), throwing a ball, learning to operate the VCR, and many other everyday accomplishments. Swiss children ski when they are 3 (not daunted by the fact that they fall down a lot) because skiing is taught to them as a natural activity; similarly, children who grow up in homes with swimming pools can usually swim when they are 4 or 5. Contrary to what many educational authorities believe, children are not daunted or devastated by the natural frustrations of mastering challenges that they are motivated to master.

By introducing these lessons early, *without setting any criteria for how fast learning is supposed to take place,* parents actually save their children a lot of frustration. Reading becomes a natural, comfortable activity for them, and they tend to start reading early and use it as a tool for pleasure and learning. Indeed, research on early readers shows that their parents engaged in precisely the kinds of activities I've described: they read to their children every day, pointed out words on signs, taught sight (whole-word) vocabulary, taught the names and sounds of letters, played letter and rhyme games, constructed words out of letters, listened to their children read and helped them sound out words, and used workbooks.[7] The same "natural" approach will work for writing and basic arithmetic.

Writing

When reading and writing are learned together both are acquired more easily. Before children can write they need to be able to control a pencil or pen. So, during your child's second year, whenever she seems ready, start giving her lots of experience with writing tools and paper, as well as chalk and a chalkboard, crayons, markers, etc. Let her doodle and scribble to her heart's content, and occasionally steer her toward making lines and circles. Letters are made out of lines and circles so encourage her to copy these in various orientations.

Draw two dots about an inch apart and ask her if she can connect them. Draw a circle and ask her to make a big circle around yours or a little circle inside it. Make a circle family, with lots of babies of different sizes. Draw sets of lines and ask her if she can draw one more or one less (good counting practice here). In other words, look for game formats to stimulate her line and circle drawing. Connecting the dots is another format that most children enjoy (and it teaches them counting, as well).

When she is about 3, help her write brief messages with magnetized letters ("I love mommy"). Children also enjoy using press-on and "sticker" letters. Allow as much free exploration as she desires with these, but some of the time use them for writing messages or lists to be used. You want to encourage her to use writing for communication.

An enjoyable technique for giving a child an understanding of writing is to use *hieroglyphics.* Cut out a lot of pictures of people, places, and objects, spread them out in front of the child, and ask her to make up a story using the pictures (with a little help from you as needed). As the story proceeds have her paste the pictures, from left to right and from line to line, across a piece of paper. Then have her look at the pictures in sequence and "read" the story to you. Share her story with others so she can feel like a proud author.

Next give her practice in writing letters. It's a slow process. Sometimes she will work with enthusiasm; sometimes she will give up or refuse even to try. Take it all in stride, without pressuring her. Assume she wants to master it and is doing the best she can. Try again a day or two later, perhaps with a different format. Give her letters to copy. At early stages, you draw the letter lightly and ask her to go over it. Or make it with dots or dashes and ask her to go over them. Different children are responsive to different formats. Try a lettering stencil (with thin letters); some children enjoy practicing with them.

Most children love to write their names and those of family members, so introduce these early in the training. Try writing a name with magnetized letters and see if she can copy it on to paper with a pencil. Before long, have her write simple signs ("Maria's Room," "Doll House") and messages ("We went out") by providing a sample alphabet for her to copy and pointing out which letters to copy in what order.

Show her how to hold the pencil but be very flexible. If she works comfortably with her right hand, encourage her to use it. If she clearly prefers her left, let her use that. For quite a while, her letters will be distant approximations to the real things. Regard them as gold. Some of the time, show her the more correct way, pointing out precisely where she made her errors ("It's great but next time bring that line up to here"). If you feel she is being too careless, ask her to write a letter, word, or message over "so it's easier for me to read."

Remind her of the spaces between words. If she seems not to care about the spaces, don't make a fuss. She'll put them in eventually. Keep in mind that for a while she will be at the "baby talk" stage of writing and treat her accordingly. Workbooks have many writing exercises that most children enjoy. When using them, don't stress the proper way of constructing a letter (this line first, that next) until later.

Also, expect your child to write letters (and numbers) backwards almost as frequently as the correct way. Here, too, save serious corrections until the basic skills are mastered. It is not a sign that he or she is dyslexic (unless the problem persists well into grade school despite instruction). Occasional corrections, such as, "That one's backwards," or "That one is made this way," will sensitize her to orientation without arresting her inclination to write. Try to give her mnemonic associations to help her remember a letter's direction: "The *buzzing B's* are flying toward the *C's*" may help a child who knows her A, B, C's and can picture the two loops of the letter *B* as two bees flying toward the next letter.

As she learns to write whole words, have her write some items on your shopping list, or have her make her own shopping list. When she no longer needs a sample to copy but can write from memory, dictate the letters very slowly at first and help her with them if necessary. As she gains proficiency, dictate two or more letters at a time in increasingly larger chunks at increasingly faster speeds.

One of the truly great innovations in writing instruction is *Invented Spelling*.[8] Once children have learned to associate sounds with letters, they write whatever they think. They will invent their own spelling, of course, getting the consonants right much of the time, but will often leave out vowels or put in the wrong ones. Here's an example: "Wee wnt to da zu." When your child starts to bring you his writing you'll see pride and excitement in his face. If you sound out what he's written you'll usually be able to read it (and he'll fill you in when you can't make something out). Your excitement over his writing will encourage him to do more.

By 5, many children have mastered the sound–letter association and are therefore capable of writing. Encourage your child to write notes, lists, letters, captions, labels, directions, stories, project ideas—everything. Do not correct spelling yet. If your child is worried about proper spelling, encourage him to just write it the way it sounds. Give him the spelling if he insists, but continue to encourage him to write it his way. Once children realize that they can write, they do it with escalating relish and frequency.

Try a daily diary or journal (as they call it in school). Also make mailboxes in the home for notes that members of the family write to each other. Pick a theme (Trips we've taken) and have him write a few lines on a number of different aspects of it; then bind each page into a book and select a title together ("The Child's Travel Guide"). In sum, keep looking for opportunities to induce your child to write.

At first, children don't always follow the left to right rule in their writing; nor do they always leave spaces between words. For a while, do as little correcting as possible. Just delight in the writing, even if reading it is like following an errant treasure map all over the page. As your child gets comfortable with the basic writing process, provide reminders about the proper structure ("We start on the left, which is the side of the page closest to the hand without the pencil").

Children's spelling begins to improve naturally as their reading skills develop. When they think they know the proper spelling of a word but have some doubts, they'll ask ("Does kettle start with a *K* or a *C*?"). Once your child has become a "writer," you can begin to give the correct spelling when asked. Also begin to correct some spelling errors (starting with familiar words) as you read his writing, but continue to keep the focus on the message. One way to do this is by writing a list of misspelled words and asking him to correct them on his page. It is also time to introduce a "first" dictionary.

Sometimes (but in my experience, infrequently) a child who is used to invented spelling will resist learning correct spelling, usually because he is pouring out his ideas on the page and doesn't want the flow interrupted. When this happens, pick certain writing projects to stress the importance of spelling, such as a letter to grandma ("She is used to reading words that are spelled correctly so she won't be able to read what you've written her"). Use the same argument if there is resistance to improving penmanship; writing must be easy to read. Make the transition to correct spelling as easy as possible by providing the corrections most of time yourself and only sending him to the dictionary occasionally (unless you sense that he prefers to look words up in the dictionary).

Expect his writing to contain the same grammatical errors he makes in his speaking ("They wented"). Here again, when you give corrections keep the focus on making his message more readable. In time, children's writing begins to differ from the way they speak. For example, by early grade school, children will employ more complex phrase structures in their writing than in their speech.[9]

Before long your child will start to undertake longer pieces, either because he likes to write or because they are assigned in school. Longer pieces require more careful planning. Many writers find outlines helpful. You can introduce him to the process by trying to formulate one together. With regard to the quality of his writing, of supreme importance will be his willingness to rewrite. Make sure he understands that serious writers spend most of their writing time revising—that it is a natural part of the writing process. Go over his pieces and discuss areas that he is not satisfied with, as well as places that you feel could be improved. As an interested and sympathetic reader, you may suggest or prompt ideas that spark his desire to go back to the piece and make it better.

As his writing ability develops, encourage him to try different forms of writing, such as poetry, dialogue, a "profile" of an interesting person, a "feature" on something he feels strongly about, or a journalistic article on a local "news" or sports events. Also try to sensitize him to stylistic possibilities. The quality of the material he reads will have an influence here.

Arithmetic

In chapter 4, I described ways of introducing a child to counting and other basic quantitative concepts (such as *more than* and *less than*). In the next chapter, I will cover more complex mathematical problem solving. Here I'll present some techniques for teaching children the four basic computational skills: addition, subtraction, multiplication, and division.

Before getting to specific techniques, let me stress two things you will need if you are to help your child master and enjoy arithmetic. They are patience and a positive attitude. Arithmetic skills, like most skills, are acquired slowly, through lots of practice. You will need to balance moving ahead to new material with going back over old material. You will also need to be sensitive to when it is time to stop a frustrating lesson and when it is time to encourage your child to go on making an effort despite frustration.

You must also have faith that your child *can* truly learn and enjoy arithmetic, and must never convey that arithmetic is a dull chore that must be endured. Arithmetic is puzzle solving and children like puzzles. Arithmetic is useful and children like to gain new competency skills. Any normal child can become skilled at, and comfortable with, basic arithmetic computation. Evidence is accumulating that an important reason behind the poor performance of American children in mathematics, compared to Asian and European children, is the failure of American parents to place a sufficiently high value on mathematical achievement and to set high standards and expectations for their children's mathematical competence.[10]

Addition and Subtraction

Researcher Martin Hughes has shown that 3- and 4-year-olds can begin to learn computational skills but need help making the transition from concrete to formal problems; that is, a 3-year-old who can give the right answer to, "How many bricks is two bricks and one brick?" will often be baffled when asked, "How many is two and one?" "One what?" the child may ask.

Hughes was able to help youngsters with this transition by putting objects ("sweets") in a number of identical tin cans, one in the first, two in the second, and so on. When the cans were closed and shuffled, the children obviously couldn't tell which can contained which number of objects. This was solved by having them place magnetic numbers on each can to represent the number of objects inside. Then the children shut their eyes and Hughes changed the number of objects in a can, indicating the change by placing a message on it in magnetic numbers and signs, such as "+2." The children had to figure out how many objects were now in that can—a task they were able to accomplish with some guidance. This process enabled them to begin to talk about the changes in purely formal terms, in terms of numbers rather than objects.[11]

In general, the learning of computational skills needs to proceed on two fronts, the concrete and the formal. You can incorporate concrete lessons into daily activities:

"We have to put out table places for two grown-ups and two children. How many places do we need?"

"I received three letters and daddy got one. How many more letters do I have?"

"You have five dolls but only three dresses for them. How many more dresses do we have to buy?"

"That candy was five cents and I gave the man ten cents. How many cents should he have given me back?"

Start with small numbers and small differences and gradually build up into two- and three-digit numbers. Children often like these kinds of computational challenges, but you'll have to be very patient and encouraging. When your child isn't sure of an answer or gives a wrong answer, get him to try to solve it by counting:

You're not sure? Well, I think it'll be easy for you if you count them. Daddy has one place, so put one finger up; mommy has one also. Right— another finger. How many is that? Good. Keep holding up those two "grown-up" fingers. Now, Mary has one place and you have one place. How many is that? Right. Keep holding up those two "children" fingers. Now how many places is that altogether? How many fingers do you have up? Right. So we need four places. Two places for grown-ups plus two places for children gives us four places altogether. That's because two plus two is four. Two fingers plus two fingers is . . . how many? So if we have two of anything and add two more, how many will we have altogether? Hey, let's write that down. (Making marks) Here's a mark for daddy and one for mommy and next to them we'll put $1 + 1 = 2$. Now here's a mark for Mary and one for you and we'll put $1 + 1 = 2$ here also. How many marks? Right, four. So if we write $2 + 2 = \_$, what number should we put down? Great, you write it here.

Notice in this explanation the progression from concrete to formal computation (from table places to numbers), as well as the alternation of information and questions. Do a lot of these kinds of computations in various forms. Some enjoyable ways of extending the lessons are by setting up a play store, playing simplified versions of Monopoly and other board games that require computation, playing target games in which scores on successive throws are added, and playing dice and card games that require computation. In a board game with numbered spaces (such as Shoots and Ladders), you can ask computational questions: "You were on four and the spinner landed on three. What number do you jump to?" As with reading and writing, the goal here is for your child to become totally at home with computation, to regard it as a natural activity—like skiing for a child raised on a Swiss mountainside.

An important computational technique for youngsters to master is *counting-on*. If you ask a 4-year-old to add 4 plus 3, he will typically count out on the fingers of one hand, "One, two, three, four," and stop. He will keep those fingers up and then count "One, two, three," as he puts up three fingers on the other hand. Then he'll count all the upright fingers.

This method (called "counting-all") isn't very efficient. Parents can teach him a better approach called the "counting-on" method. This consists of stating the larger of the two numbers to be added (in this case, "four"), and then *counting on* from there ("five, six, seven")—putting up one finger as each number is voiced. This is a faster procedure for addition, but obviously more complex since the count doesn't correspond to the number of fingers up: he says "five" as he puts up one finger, "six" as he puts up two fingers. Moreover he must remember to stop the count when the number of fingers up corresponds to the number to be added ("three" in the current example).

The child must also understand that a stated number (*"four"*) is *always* the final count word when counting that many things, as in "There are four cats," making it unnecessary to count the number of cats. This is the crucial insight for mastering counting-on. Research with first-graders demonstrated that they could learn counting-on procedures in a single lesson.[12] Younger children can also learn it, but it will take more reminders.

Subtraction can be handled with either a *counting-down* or a *counting-up* procedure. Before children can count backwards (a very useful skill), it is often easier for them to subtract using a counting-up procedure (for instance, they figure out *8 − 3* by verbalizing "four, five, six, seven, eight" and putting a finger up for each stated number). When subtracting *9 − 1*, this isn't very efficient; counting up requires eight steps, while counting down requires one. This is why it is important to give a child practice in counting backwards.

An effective way to help children make the transition to adding written numbers is to write out an addition problem (*5 + 6 = __*) and ask them to make dots under each number, corresponding to its quantity (five dots under the number *5*, six dots under *6*). Then ask them to count all the dots together and insert the total after the equal sign. A similar procedure can teach subtraction. In the problem *6 − 4 = __* the child makes six dots, then crosses out (or puts a circle around) four and places the number for the dots remaining in the proper place. After some practice this way, the child should no longer need the dots.

You can continue this procedure with two-digit numbers (such as *25*) by teaching your child to put lines under the number in the tens' place (under the *2*) while still putting dots under the number in the ones' place (under the *5*). Then when he adds (*25 + 13*), he adds the dots and lines separately and puts their quantities in their proper places.

The hundreds' place can be represented by squares and the same system used. Representing numbers this way is useful for learning carrying since a sum of more than nine dots means you add one or more extra lines in the tens' place. Similarly in subtraction, you can't take four dots from three, so you have to take a line away from the tens' place. The dots and lines are useful for providing children with a concrete understanding of computational concepts. For similar ends, many schools use Base Ten Blocks and Cuisenaire rods.

As you introduce your child to larger numbers and to addition and subtraction with borrowing and carrying, look for any consistent errors that indicate that he or she doesn't really understand basic concepts such as the meaning of the one's, ten's and hundred's places. Children can learn to follow the procedures by rote (such as borrowing in subtraction) without really understanding what it means.[13] And keep in mind that children frequently forget a procedure that just yesterday they appeared to know well. Each time they relearn it, though, they learn it faster. One recent study found that checklists were useful for children who made the same subtraction errors consistently. For instance, one child's list had the following steps that the child had to check off:

1. I underlined all the top numbers that were smaller than the bottom.
2. I crossed out only the number next to the underlined number and made it one less.
3. I put a *1* beside the underlined number.
4. All the numbers on the top are bigger than the numbers on the bottom.[14]

When you give your child story problems make sure he or she understands how to translate the story into numbers and operations. Children often make systematic errors on story problems, giving a "correct" answer to the wrong question. For example, they see the word "more" and assume it is an addition problem, which it may not be ("Tom had three marbles and Bill had five. How many *more* did Bill have?") Sometimes changing the wording of a problem will help a child understand what is being asked. For example, one study found that nursery school children had trouble with the problem, "There are 5 birds and 3 worms. How many more birds are there than worms?" But most were able to solve the problem when the question was changed to "How many birds won't get a worm?"[15]

Another study, using addition and subtraction story problems, reported marked improvement by children who were taught to diagram the information described in the stories by setting up a kind of flow chart with boxes depicting, say, the number of toys each person started with, the number they wound up with, and the direction and quantity transferred between them.[16]

In making up story problems, try to vary the format to give your child practice in the various math patterns, including:

Combining: Tom has four stickers. Alice has three. How many do they have altogether?

Changing: Kerry had eight pages in her looseleaf. She put in five more. How many did she have then?

Comparing: Tom had seven marbles. Bill had three less. How many marbles did Bill have?

Separating: Two brothers had nine toy soldiers. One brother took four toy soldiers to school. The other brother stayed home with a cold. How many toy soldiers did the one who stayed home have to play with?

A good formal problem is to work out all the ways a number can be constructed. For example, the quantity four can be constructed out of *4 + 0, 3 + 1, 2 + 2,* and *1 + 3*. Children often need to be shown that *3 + 2* and *2 + 3* are equivalent (as are *3 × 2* and *2 × 3*). Mathematicians call this the "commutative property" of numbers: $a + b = b + a$. As your child becomes more adept at adding, play "Double it": Pick a number from one to ten and have your child continue to double it as far as she can go.

There are many good arithmetic workbooks (such as the *Golden Step Ahead* series) with story and number problems that your child will enjoy using. Also, encourage her to make up problems for you to solve. Her growing understanding will be reflected in the quality of the problems she devises.

It will also help if you give her an appreciation of the practical importance of arithmetic skills. Let her see you adding and subtracting bills, balancing your checkbook, dividing a recipe, and engaging in other everyday arithmetic activities. Talk about the importance of accuracy and how easy it becomes with practice. As the child's skills develop, let her check the bill in a restaurant or a cashier's receipt. Children who are interested in sports, will enjoy computing batting averages and other player and team statistics. The more children appreciate the practical value of arithmetic, the more motivated they are to master it.

Multiplication

You pave the way for multiplication through repeated counting problems: "Holly, Molly, and Polly are hens and they each have 4 chicks. How many chicks do they have altogether?" Explain that $4 + 4 + 4$ is four, three times (or 4×3). Illustrate it also by drawing three groups of four chicks. As in adding and subtracting, give problems and explanations in both concrete and formal terms. Formal problems can be worded, "How much is three, three times?" When beginning you might have your child solve it by arranging three sets of three pennies and counting the total. Drawing rectangles on graph paper is another way to give a child concrete experiences with multiplication concepts (three boxes down and four across makes a rectangle of 12 boxes).

The process of repeated counting can be expedited with practice. Set ten pennies out in pairs and ask your child to count them by twos. Build up to 100. Also arrange sets of five pennies and ten pennies and help your child learn to count by fives and tens. Then work on sets of three, four, and so on. Children learn to count to 100 by twos, fives, and tens with little difficulty. The other numbers require more practice. (Once your child learns to count by fives, she'll make great strides in learning to tell time.)

With increased skill in repeated counting, multiplication problems become easier. But it's still a long climb to solve 8×9 by counting eight, nine times. Moreover, since children are more confident counting by twos than nines, they tend to approach 9×2 the long way, by counting twos. Eventually, the multiplication table needs to be memorized. Here again, work books are useful, especially for learning to solve written multiplication problems.

Star Count is a multiplication game from Peggy Kaye's *Games for Math*.[17] It's played with a die and paper and pencil. Each player throws once and draws on paper a number of large circles equal to the number on the die. Then each player throws again, and draws a number of stars in each circle based on the roll of the die. So if a player throws a three, he draws three circles. If his next throw is a six, he draws six stars in each circle, 18 stars in all. The player who has the most stars wins. In the dialogue draw the child's attention to the repeated sets (three sets of six). Also write out the formal multiplication notation on the page.

As children become more familiar with multiplication, try Multiplication Bingo. Each player writes along the top row of his or her card any five numbers between one and twelve (leaving the far left space empty). They put in a different set of five numbers down the left-hand column (leaving the top space empty). Then pick out numbered cards (1 through 144) from a container. All players check to see if it can be placed on their grid by multiplying one of the numbers along the top of their card by one of the numbers along the side. Numbers that can be placed are pencilled in at the proper spot on the grid. The first player to fill a row, column, or vertical wins. Before children have the multiplication table memorized, give them a copy of it to check if a number fits their grid.

One of the complexities of multiplication story problems is that they involve different kinds of quantities. When you multiply two like things, such as one length by another length, the answer is an *area,* not a length. Similarly, when you multiply unlike things, such as miles and hours, the answer is a new entity, miles per hour. This can make multiplication troublesome. Researchers Pamela Thibodeau Hardiman and Jose Mestre have grouped multiplication problems into four types based on how they link quantities.[18] It is worth being aware of these in case your child has trouble with them:

Compute: Ellen needs five party hats. Each hat cost ten cents. How much money does Ellen need?

Compare: Mary has four marbles. Bill has three times as many. How many marbles does Bill have?

Combine: Diane has four different skirts and three different blouses. How many different outfits can she make?

Convert: Kay drank two glasses of water in an hour. Each glass held eight ounces of water. How many ounces per hour did Kay drink?

Try to bring multiplication into everyday activities, for both practical reasons and play. A practical question: "We have four muffin tins which each hold six muffins. How many muffins can we make?" A play question: "Can you tell me how many windows that side of the building has without having to count all the windows?"

Division

Children generally find division the most difficult form of computation although they can usually understand it conceptually since they have had many experiences dividing things, such as pizzas, cakes, clay, and toys. Introduce division through concrete operations: "If we have eight slices of pizza and there are four people sharing them, how many pieces will each one get?''

Presenting division as *sharing* gives children a concrete conceptual framework. You can give them physical practice in division as sharing by setting out an egg carton or ice tray and bunches of beans or pennies. Then ask, ''If you have 16 pennies and want to give them to four friends to share equally, how many will each friend get?'' Each of the four friends ''lives in'' one of the spaces in the egg carton or tray and your child must put his pennies into those spaces until he has four equal amounts.

Another way to think of division is as repeated subtraction. For instance, the problem ''What is *14* divided by *2?*'' can be restated as ''How many 2s can we *take out* of *14?*'' Still another way of conceiving division is, ''How many twos can we *squeeze* into 14?'' I tend to like this last way, especially when working on formal, long division problems. Try all three forms of explanation and see which your child finds the most helpful.

You can illustrate division as repeated subtraction through the Leapfrog game, using graph paper. Fill in a row of boxes to correspond to the number to be divided (say fourteen boxes), and write the word ''Home'' at the beginning of the row. Then tell your child the number to divide it by (say two), which determines how many boxes the ''frog'' must leap on each jump. The problem is to figure out how many jumps the frog must make to get home (seven in this example). Write the numerical operations to the right of the row. Introduce both forms for symbolizing division problems and use workbooks to gradually build more sophisticated skills, such as remainders. In teaching division, as well as addition, subtraction, and multiplication, make sure you teach how to check if answers are correct (for instance, for checking an answer in division, multiplying the answer and the divisor should produce the number that was divided).

When your child starts to multiply and divide fractions be aware of a particular difficulty many children have. Your child will have learned that when multiplying two whole numbers (except one and zero), the answer is always larger than either number. But when multiplying a whole number by a fraction (say $1 \times \frac{2}{3}$), the answer is always smaller than the whole number (in this case it is $\frac{2}{3}$). You can explain that when we multiply a number by one, we get the same number ($6 \times 1 = 6$). When we multiply it by more than one, we get a larger number ($6 \times 2 = 12$). *And* when we multiply it by less than one (a fraction), we get a smaller number ($6 \times \frac{1}{2} = 3$).

Similarly, in division, when dividing one whole number by another, the answer is always smaller than the number being divided ($6 \div 3 = 2$). But when dividing a number by a fraction (say $1 \div \frac{1}{2}$), the answer is always larger than the number being divided (two in this example). The "squeezing" image may help the child picture what happens when dividing by a fraction. A number divided by one will always equal that same number because that's how many ones can be squeezed into it. But we can squeeze many more $\frac{1}{2}$s into a number than ones, twice as many. We can squeeze two $\frac{1}{2}$s into the number one, and ten $\frac{1}{2}$s into five. With any number less than one (any fraction), we can squeeze more of them into a number than we can squeeze ones into it. That's why dividing a number by a fraction always gives an answer that is larger than dividing it by one—that is, it gives a number larger than itself.

There are many other aspects of arithmetic, including remainders, percentages, and decimals. Your child will cover all of these in school, but you should try to stay abreast of his or her progress and help out as much as you can. Try to find out exactly how your child's teacher approaches arithmetic so you can coordinate your efforts (and don't let teachers convince you that you should leave it all to them). United States students score among the lowest of all industrial nations on mathematics tests. Yet U.S. parents are far less involved with or concerned about their children's math progress than parents in other countries.[19]

Parents of daughters should be aware of the cultural bias against women pursuing mathematical interests (as well as science interests). The cultural stereotype is that girls don't do well in math—or aren't supposed to; that mathematics is not a "feminine" activity. During grade school and early high school, girls actually do very well in math, as well as boys and often better, especially if they don't feel that math is inappropriate for girls. In more advanced high school and college math, females, on average, do not do as well as males, and no one is sure why.[20] It is very difficult to sort out cultural from biological influences. In any case, there have been a number of outstanding female mathematicians and there is no reason to stifle a young woman's mathematical potential by causing her to feel that as a female she can't possibly succeed in math or that such interests make her less feminine.

9

❦

Problem-Solving
Strategies for
Mastery

Educational theorists and practitioners have long sought a set of problem-solving or reasoning strategies that could be applied across a variety of problem types. Essentially, they ask, Do good problems solvers—whether they be mathematicians, auto mechanics, physicists, plumbers, or playwrights—use similar problem-solving strategies? It has proved a difficult question to answer, first because there are so many different kinds of problems, even within a particular craft or profession, and second, because successful problem solvers are often not very good at describing the steps they go through in solving problems.[1]

We can make some headway on this question by dividing the vast number of problem types into a few basic, functional categories, and then examining the strategies that are applicable to each category:

Diagnostic Problem-Solving: Finding Causes and Cures

Diagnostic problem-solving strategies are applicable to such areas as selecting the correct treatment for an illness, repairing an engine, debugging a computer program, or solving a murder mystery. A youngster whose Walkman doesn't work is faced with a diagnostic problem, as is one whose best friend refuses to talk to him. In diagnostic problem solving one starts with an unexplained event and tries to figure out what caused it by reference to *already known factors*. For instance, in trying to explain why a Walkman doesn't work one doesn't look for strange and exotic forces; one uses what one knows about tape players or similar electrical and audio devices to pinpoint the defect in this particular machine.

The main strategy in diagnostic problem solving is to formulate and test hypotheses about what might have produced the event in question. For instance, there can be many reasons why a Walkman fails to work: the switch is off or broken, the battery is drained, something is jammed in the mechanism, an electrical connection is severed, the tape isn't inserted properly, etc. The diagnostic problem solver asks, What do I know about the makeup and operation of this object (the Walkman) or objects like it, that might reveal what caused this event (malfunctioning of the Walkman); in other words, which of the various possible causes is the correct one?

Sometimes diagnostic problem solving is a straightforward, trial-and-error procedure involving testing the most likely or most accessible factors in descending order: First, check if the switch is on; if it is, check the batteries next (because they are more likely to be defective than other components); if the batteries are okay, try a different tape (which is easier to do than taking the machine apart); and so on. In such cases, one knows a number of possible causes and checks them one at a time.

Sometimes no hypotheses spring to mind and a much more stepwise inferential process is required, starting with broad questions, with the focus narrowing on each succeeding question. For example, in trying to understand why fish are dying in a lake, an ecologist might start with the broad question, "Are they being poisoned by toxins, made ill by microorganisms, or suffocating from a lack of oxygen?" If toxins are found, the next question might be, "Are they natural or man-made?" If man-made, he might inquire, "Are they airborne, being dumped directly into the water, or derived from contaminated drainage or runoff?" In this example, the diagnostic reasoning began with the effect (The fish are dead) and proceeded backwards toward the source of their demise.

Clearly, good diagnostic skills require a systematic method of inquiry, which research shows even 4-year-olds can learn. Psychologist Mary Courage used a form of the game 20 Questions to teach preschoolers and young grade-school children to seek information systematically—that is, to start with a broad question ("Is it one of the red houses?") and to narrow the focus with each additional question ("Does it have windows?").[2] When young children first play 20 Questions, their main strategy is guessing. But with patient instruction and lots of examples on how to divide the range of possible answers (Is it man-made? Is it a machine? Is it made of metal? Do we use it in the house?) they begin to adopt the broad-to-narrow strategy.

In sum, the successful diagnostic problem solver says to herself:

1. What probable causes am I aware of?
2. I'll test those causes in an orderly sequence.

3. When I don't know any specific probable causes, I'll look for a possible cause based on what I know about these kinds of events and divide the range of possibilities systematically ("Is it a toxin or a micro-organism?").

4. I'll proceed backwards through a sequence of inferences until the initiating condition is reached.

5. Since the more I know about these kinds of events, the more likely I am to come up with an accurate diagnosis, I'll acquire as much advance knowledge as possible.

Item 5 applies to all the problem types covered in this chapter: the more information one has about the domain in which one is trying to solve problems, the better one's chances for coming up with a solution.

Parents can foster successful diagnostic problem solving by encouraging their children to follow the steps just listed when faced with events that they can't explain. Parents can elicit probable causes ("Why do you think there's no hot water?") and should also suggest some reasons of their own ("Maybe the boiler needed fixing and was shut off or maybe it ran out of oil"). They can prompt their children to test hypotheses in an orderly fashion ("No, don't take it apart yet. Let's check out the easy things first. Let's see if a fuse blew").

When no obvious explanations appear, they can stimulate thought about possible explanations ("I'm not sure why the refrigerator door sticks. There's no glue holding it and the hinge moves easily. Ah, but notice that rubber insulation around the edge. Have we ever seen rubber stick to a surface before? (If no answer) Hey, remember how those rubber darts work? That's right, they stick through suction. Check if something similar might be happening to the door").

Parents can also point out interesting examples of successful diagnostic problem solving in fiction (especially good detective stories), in science (the tracing of acid lakes to industrial pollutants emitted hundreds of miles away), and in news reports (as when Nobel physicist Richard Feynman dramatically demonstrated the fatal defect in the O-rings on the Challenger space shuttle by putting a sample ring in ice water).

Two- and 3-year-olds are not too young for diagnostic explanations if the causal mechanisms are simple and concrete: "The doll's leg falls off because the little hook is missing on this leg. See, look at the other leg. It has a hook that keeps it in place. This leg lost its hook so it falls off." Children this age are not too young to be encouraged to come up with diagnostic explanations on their own: "This leg falls off, but that one stays in. See if there are any differences in the two legs that might explain why.''

Inductive Problem Solving: Discovering the Undiscovered

Inductive problem solving, like diagnostic problem solving, starts with something that needs explaining (such as the orbits of the planets), but standard explanations and known entities are clearly not sufficient. One must come up with something new: a new entity or phenomenon (the atom, the gene, the big bang, tectonic plates, quarks); or a new understanding of already known entities (the helical structure of DNA, the disease causing properties of bacteria); or a new framework for organizing what is known (Copernicus' placement of the sun at the center of the solar system, Einstein's notion of curved space-time, Mendeleev's periodic table of chemicals).

In science and technology, inductive problem solving is especially valued and is often the basis for Nobel prizes. Einstein's theory of relativity, Watson and Crick's discovery of DNA's double helix, and Louis Pasteur's germ theory of disease are three notable examples that had an enormous impact on how we think about and function in our world. One could cite many other such discoveries, both major and minor.

Children can be introduced to some famous examples of inductive problem solving by their early school years. The "discovery" by the ancient Greeks that the earth is a sphere and not flat is one such example which young children can begin to grasp (it was first asserted by Philolaus in about 450 BC and gained acceptance through Aristotle's writings about 100 years later).

Note that I placed quotation marks around the word *discovery* in the previous paragraph; this is because the spherical shape of the earth was arrived at by inductive reasoning, not perception (unlike the way the word discovery is used to describe, say, a biologist coming across a new kind of butterfly or an archaeologist unearthing a new fossil). The word discovery is used in the rest of this section in the same way; it refers to uncovering new entities or events (the atom, the gene) through reasoning, not perception. Ultimately, of course, all such conjectured entities must be verified by perception (sailing all the way around the earth was one way to verify its spherical shape).

Children often find discussion of the shape of the earth interesting because the world looks flat to them, just as it did to the ancient Greeks. But certain observations don't coincide with a flat earth: How does the sun go down on one side of the earth and manage to get around to come up on the other side? How come one never gets closer to the place where the sun sets no matter how far west one travels? And why does a ship's mast appear on the horizon before its hull? A globe will come in handy in these discussions, as will the story of Christopher Columbus's search for a westward passage to the Indies.

Check your library and bookstore for books on this and other famous "discoveries" and the men and women who made them. Isaac Asimov's excellent *How We Found Out* series provides many examples (book number 16 is *How We Found Out the Earth is Round,* published by Longman).

Other areas that grade-school children can begin to understand are the discoveries of dinosaurs (no one had any idea what kind of creatures those huge bones could have come from), of germs (no one knew what caused diseases and why they spread in characteristic patterns), of vitamins (sailors on long trips became ill with scurvy, except if they ate fruits or vegetables, but no one knew why), and of X-rays (discovered in 1895 by W. C. Roentgen who wondered how rays from his cathode tube were passing through walls and other solid objects).

Also make your child aware that there are still many mysteries to be solved, such as how millions of brain cells store and retrieve information; or what dinosaurs were really like (more like birds or more like lizards?); or what led to their extinction; or what signals the cells in an embryo to start making heart cells, muscle cells, or brain cells; or what led to the ice ages; or what makes some babies friendlier than others; or what is in the middle of the earth; or what makes some cells become cancerous; or what led to the formation of galaxies in the early universe. The science sections of popular magazines and newspapers frequently have clearly written, well-illustrated articles on these questions and report any progress toward answering them.

Obviously children aren't going to solve these problems but they can be introduced to the style of thinking that has solved similar problems in the past. Among the useful questions the inductive problem solver asks are:

1. *What happens if I change some assumptions?*
For instance, Newton replaced the assumption that all moving objects naturally come to rest with the assumption that moving objects stop or slow down only when they encounter an opposing force, such as gravity, friction, or another object.

2. *Can I apply some facts or principles from other areas of knowledge?*
The English chemist, Robert Boyle, found that air could be squeezed into a smaller and smaller space. How could that be explained? Other things, such as sponges and bread, could be compressed because they had spaces between the solid parts. So, *by analogy,* Boyle, in the late

1600s, proposed that air too is made of solid parts and spaces. The solid parts were the basic elements or *atoms* of air.

3. *Is there a better way to define or group the events?*

A famous example from chemistry was the development of the periodic table of elements. By midnineteenth century, chemists had distinguished a great many different elements but didn't understand what determined their properties. In 1869 the Russian chemist, D. I. Mendeleev, published his "periodic table," which ordered the elements according to their atomic weights and arranged columns so that elements with similar properties fell into the same column. There were some empty spaces in the table because there were no known element to place in them, but Mendeleev predicted that those elements would be found and he even described the properties they would have according to their position in the table—and he was soon proved right. Years later other scientists demonstrated that elements with similar properties (those that fall in the same column) have similar atomic structures.

4. *Might there be some unknown entity behind the observed effects? And if so, how can I learn about it?*

By the end of the nineteenth century it was known that bacteria caused infectious diseases, but for some infections no bacteria could be found. What then might be the cause? Filtering the infectious agents revealed that the unknown entity must be much smaller than bacteria—a thousand times smaller and with very different properties. The unknown entities were called viruses but it was not until the 1930s that fine enough filters were available to trap and remove them from the infectious body fluids. Researchers knew they finally trapped a virus when, after pouring the fluid through finer and finer filters, they reached the point at which the fluid was no longer infectious.

Once a new entity or formulation is proposed it leads to the prediction of new events. If these events are actually observed they lend support to the reality and usefulness of the new conception. For instance, Edwin Hubble's theory that the universe started with a big bang was supported by A. A. Penzias and R. W. Wilson's observation of uniform radiation coming from all parts of the sky—presumably the leftover radiation that would be expected if the big bang did actually occur. Sometimes observations doom a proposed entity. This was the fate of the once widely accepted notion that all of space contains an "ether," a kind of invisible fabric embracing all matter. In a famous experiment in 1887, Albert Michelson and Edward Morley failed to find the effect that the ether was supposed to have on the speed of light—and the ether was soon abandoned as an explanatory concept.

Inventive Problem Solving

In inventive problem solving one wants to construct something specific that hasn't been made before (for Edison it was a light bulb; for Marconi it was a radio), and known methods won't work. Note that in inventive problem solving one's primary aim is not to explain anything (unlike diagnostic and inductive problem solving).

Some much-publicized current inventive problem-solving projects include efforts to make a more energy-efficient automobile engine, a faster computer chip, a fusion reactor, and a machine that will type out accurately what a person dictates into it. But the products of inventive problem solving need not be machines. The Peace Corps was one such product (an invention for arousing idealism); so were "lite" beer, polarized sun glasses, antibiotics, money-market mutual funds, 800 business telephone numbers, and charter airline flights. Each derived from someone's vision to make something that would fill (or create) a need. Such visions are, of course, the lifeblood of successful entrepreneurs.

The fantasy inventions of young children are the precursors of inventive problem solving ("I need a sword." Picks up long wooden spoon. "This is my sword"). Similarly, children's block play is filled with fantasy inventiveness; they build castles, bridges, and city streets.

By 5 or 6, children's inventive problem solving has become much more adultlike—more complex and thoughtful, manipulating and arranging resources to fulfill envisioned goals. For example, a parent reported that her daughter (5 years, 6 months) had made cut-out figures of characters from the Snow White story, but was stymied over what to use for the glass coffin. Suddenly she ran to the cabinet, pulled out two clear plastic glasses, placed Snow White inside one (on a bed of paper flowers and holding a note that read, "Where is that prince?"), put the cups rim to rim, and Scotch-taped them together. A nice example of inventive problem solving.

Another child (5 years, 2 months), upon overhearing an aunt describe her trepidation about riding public buses between 3 and 4 P.M. because of rowdy school children on their way home, suggested that buses should be made with a sliding door about halfway toward the back. "Then the bus driver could ask the children to ride on one side of the door while the grown-ups ride on the other," she explained. This kind of spontaneous problem solving is not uncommon in children this age.

Some other examples reported include making high-heeled shoes by taping wood blocks under the heels of flats, making a picture frame out of tongue depressors, and fishing out a bead that had fallen in a hole by putting a piece of chewing gum on the end of a chop stick.

Inventing will remain an important part of fantasy play into late childhood.

I've had the pleasure of witnessing two 6-year-old girls spend a thrilling afternoon devising and constructing an intricate "witch-trap," taking into consideration the witch's flying patterns, visual and auditory abilities, hunger drive, strength, and fear of water.

Starting with the recognition of some need or desirable end state the inventive problem solver asks:

1. *What design aspects are essential? What are the minimal functional and structural requirements?*

For instance, for the youngster above, Snow White's coffin had to be see-through, large enough for the cut-out figure and bed, and easy to open and close. For Thomas Edison, a light bulb had to give adequate light, burn for a substantial period of time, and not draw too much energy.

2. *What resources are available? Are there materials or methods that might work even though they aren't ordinarily used for my purposes?*

Many an invention has depended on the inventor realizing that a common object could be used in uncommon ways. One way psychologists have studied this is with Norman Maier's "Hatrack Problem," in which subjects are given two poles of unequal length and a C-clamp, and are asked to make a hatrack with just these items. The solution involves overlapping the poles and clamping them lengthwise so together they are long enough to be wedged between floor and ceiling; the clamp may then be used as a hook for a hat. Because this is not a common use for a clamp the solution is often missed.[3]

In inventive problem solving, the exploration of materials and other resources often involves a lengthy trial and error phase. Edison tried hundreds of materials before finding one that would work as a filament in his light bulb.

But Edison didn't try out materials randomly. Inventors usually have some reason for trying some materials rather than others. For example, in trying to develop a drug to treat AIDS patients, medical researchers are guided by whatever they know about the AIDS virus and the immune cells they infect. For instance, one approach tries to trick the viruses into attaching to a drug designed to "look like" the immune cell receptors that the virus normally attaches to. The guiding assumption is that if the virus attaches itself to the drug, it will ride around harmlessly in the blood-stream, and won't infect any cells. If the drug does fool the virus, the next step is to attach another chemical to it that will kill the virus anchored to it, but not harm the patient.

3. *Are there any principles or procedures I can apply from this or other areas to help overcome obstacles?*

Edison and others who were trying to make a long-lasting light bulb realized they could keep their filaments from burning up too quickly by encasing them in an oxygen-free enclosure, based on the established principle that combustion requires oxygen. The first oxygen-free bulbs were vacuum tubes but the filaments did not hold up well in a vacuum. Irving Langmuir came up with a better way to achieve the same oxygen-free state: he pushed the oxygen out by filling the tubes with nitrogen, an inert gas that did not promote combustion.

The development of three-dimensional images in electron microscopes provides a more recent example of solving a problem by applying principles or procedures from a seemingly remote domain. Robley Cook Williams, an astronomer, aware that the three-dimensional appearance of telescopic images of the moon was due to the shadows cast by sunlight hitting the mountains and craters at oblique angles, surmised correctly that he could create "shadows" behind objects in an electron microscope by blowing vaporized metal dust obliquely across their surfaces. The higher the elevation of an object, the more vapor it blocked and the longer the "shadow" behind it—thus producing a three-dimensional image.

4. *Are there any drawbacks to my solution? And if so, what can I do about them?*

Will my light bulbs explode in people's faces when they burn out? Will my engine give off harmful fumes? Are Peace Corps volunteers likely to contract serious illnesses at their foreign work-sites or might they even be murdered? Will my new medication cause other ailments (produce bad side effects) while curing someone of the disease I'm treating.

A useful way to teach a child about inventive problem solving is to analyze the design of common objects together, and then look for ways to improve the design. A vacuum cleaner or a kitchen sponge will do. Start by specifying its purpose. Then look for *key functional elements* in its design (a suction device on the vacuum cleaner, a dirt beater, a dirt bag (permanent or disposable), a handle, rollers, etc.). Next, consider the *materials* that each element is made of, and whether other materials might have been used (metal vs. plastic body, cloth bags vs. paper bags). Then, evaluate its *form* for efficiency and convenience (Is the vacuum cleaner good for corners, for different pile heights, for short people? Is the sponge effective on pots, on fine glasses?).

Together try to come up with improvements to make the device more efficient, convenient, and versatile. Start by thinking of what an ideal version of the device would do. Then list some frustrations encountered with the current design (one's hands get wet when using a sponge, you have to keep adding soap, it doesn't scour very well). If you come up with improvements, consider possible negative consequences (a wider base in an upright vacuum would make cleaning open areas easier but cause problems between closely spaced pieces of furniture).

It will help if you can show your child different forms of the same device (upright vacuum cleaners, canister types, etc.), particularly if improvements have been made over the years. Discuss which differences appear to be genuine improvements, which were modifications for special purposes (such as vacuuming steps), and which turned out to be drawbacks (perhaps to lower manufacturing costs).

Also try to think of other, possibly better, ways to accomplish the same end. For instance, are there other mechanisms, besides vacuuming, that could remove dirt from carpets? Might something work better than sponges for kitchen cleaning?

Similar methods of analysis can be applied to inventions other than machines. For example, you can evaluate procedures, such as how the supermarket might make finding items easier, or how to speed up the check-out line. List the advantages and disadvantages of the current practice, as well as the goals of an ideal system. You can then put your heads together to try to devise an approach that comes closer to the ideal.

Another way to get your child thinking about inventions is to try to come up with "dream things": devices, procedures, or systems that would make life better. What most of us endure as inconveniences, the inventor sees as challenges. It's a spirit worth fostering in your child.

To inspire the inventor's spirit in your child, make him or her aware of the great inventions and the great inventors. Your library will have many useful books on inventors and inventions and look for museums that have sections on inventions. Also check magazines and newspapers for new inventions and problem areas that inventors are working on. If your newspaper has a section describing new patents, it'll contain lots of interesting ideas to discuss with your child.

In addition, share your own inventions with your child, perhaps innovations you've come up with in your work, or procedures you've developed to handle some household problem. You may have improvised an unusual way to fasten some objects together or to secure something to a wall. These are good things to talk about because they show that inventing can be a part of everyday problem solving.

Tactical Problem Solving

In tactical problem solving one tries to come up with *actions* that accomplish some end more effectively. A tactical problem for a gardener would be, Which plants will grow best here? For a floor tiler it is, How do I cut the tiles to go around molding and other uneven edges? Architects need to figure out, How can I span that distance with these materials? And NASA space-mission controllers must determine which maneuvers will send an errant spaceship back on course.

Here is an example from a parent of a child who had recently turned 6:

It was Halloween, Dina was in costume, and we were off to trick-or-treat in our apartment building (which has 14 floors). Tenants who wanted trick-or-treaters knocking on their doors put their names and apartment numbers on a sign-up sheet in the lobby. We checked which second floor residents had signed up and went there and collected our candy. As I was leading the way back to the lobby to check which of our third floor neighbors were on the list, Dina stopped me and asked, "Couldn't we get a pencil and paper and copy the list so we don't have to go to the lobby after every floor? That'll be very boring."

Tactical problem solving efforts are evident in children's earliest mastery behavior. Here is an example in a child of 8 months:

Danielle had just begun to crawl forward two days earlier, and was now crawling about the living room with determination, doing much better on the carpet than the slippery wooden floor. Her older cousin called her from the corner of the room and Danielle began to crawl toward her with clear purpose. Danielle cut across the carpet and crawled off onto the wooden floor to reach her cousin, but despite serious effort, her progress ended. She managed to get back onto the carpet and crawled along the edge, narrowing the distance between herself and her cousin, though it was not a direct route. Her tactic was clearly to proceed on the carpet as far as she could.

In an example of tactical problem solving with a slightly older child, a father reported that whenever he and his 2½-year-old daughter were dead-locked over some issue and frustration levels were rising precipitously, the little girl would ask for a book. It was an effective tactic for calming both of them down and reestablishing affectionate contact.

In tactical problem solving, the child or adult knows what the outcome is supposed to be, but is faced with an obstacle, which might derive from another person, from a physical barrier, or from one's own inadequacy. We encounter people as obstacles in many settings: in games (chess, football, poker, etc.), business negotiations (How best to sell?), education (How best to teach?), romance (How best to court?), politics (How best to sway votes?), trials (How best to persuade the jury?), and many other situations in which one's goal is to influence or outmaneuver someone.

An example of a child faced with a physical obstacle would be a 9-month-old crawler wanting to come down a staircase. Her tactical options might be, Shall I go head first or behind first? Other examples of children facing tactical problems are a 4-year-old trying to figure out how to get her paper dolls to stand up; a 5-year-old trying to find the hidden word in a complex array of letters; and a 7-year-old trying to figure out which glue is good for which materials.

Sometimes tactics are needed to overcome obstacles that derive from oneself, as when an actor must find a tactic for controlling his stage fright, or when a violence-prone person must learn self-control techniques to stay out of trouble, or when a stroke victim must master new ways of communicating, or when a student must figure out how to keep from forgetting what she reads. For each of these, self-regulation tactics are needed.

Parents and teachers help children master tactical problems, first, by teaching them effective tactics directly and, second, by encouraging them to think through problems thoroughly enough to come up with successful tactics on their own. When a parent says "No, no, turn around" to her 9-month-old (who is about to descend a staircase face first), and then physically turns him around and eases him down backwards, she is teaching him a tactic in a direct way. With a few successful trials his behavior will come under control of the rule, When descending a staircase, turn around and proceed backwards. One will even see him seem to remind himself of the rule (even though he does not yet speak): he'll approach the top step face first, appear to alternate between holding himself back and giving in to the impulse to head straight down, then pivot and make a confident backward descent.

As mentioned before, a good deal of teaching involves the direct passing on of tactics (as in "Keep your eye on the ball," or instructing ballet students to "spot" when doing pirouettes, or science students to take the average of five readings when making measurements, or math students to simplify calculations by converting to logarithms). Obviously, not all passed-on tactics work ("Hold your breath to get rid of hiccups," is a doubtful one).

Various studies show that preschoolers can benefit from direct instruction in tactical strategies. In one, children who were taught to remind themselves to check for similarities and differences (to ask themselves, "How are they the same?" "Why are they different?"), scored higher in a task that required them to decide which of two stimuli best matched a sample. In another study, preschoolers were able to make effective use of a tactic they were taught for solving Missionaries and Cannibals problems (involving moving missionaries and cannibals across a river under certain constraints so that the missionaries don't get eaten).[4]

Children will usually need a number of reminders when learning new tactics. For instance, in reading instruction a parent might teach the tactic, "When sounding out long words, break them down into syllables." As the child encounters longer and less familiar multisyllabic words, and perhaps gets thrown by them, he or she may need some reminders of this tactic. Initially a parent might have to restate the entire rule. Later, it should be sufficient to simply remind the child of the goal of the tactic (such as, "Remember what you're supposed to do when *sounding out long words?*"). As the child shows increased mastery of the task, less explicit, more motivational prompts should work (such as, "Think about it carefully. You know how to do it").

There are many occasions when teaching a tactic will help a child over an obstacle. For instance, a father reported that his daughter (5 years, 9 months) was having trouble with her first try at finding hidden words to match a list of sample words in a workbook exercise. He suggested that she start by picking one sample word, noting its first letter. Then she could check for just that letter among the hidden words. That is all the girl needed to whip through the task, he said.

In another example, a mother reported that her daughter (6 years, 1 month) was working on a workbook decoding problem but was stopped at the fourth symbol in the 10 letter key because it hadn't been printed clearly. The parent came through with a tactic that is useful in many situations: Solve the parts you *can* solve first, and the solution to the other parts may become evident through a process of elimination. In this case, the missing letter was spotted easily once all the other letters were in place.

Obviously, learning new tactics from others doesn't end in childhood. We buy home-repair and auto manuals to acquire a mass of tactics that would take us more than a lifetime to develop on our own. Salesmen and managers take business seminars to acquire new sales and managerial tactics, just as physicians and psychotherapists take "in service" and "continuing education" courses to garner the latest tactics in their respective fields. Serious chess players devote considerable time studying the past games of master players to learn the most effective openings and the best moves for each arrangement of pieces on the board.[5]

In general, games and sports are good vehicles for teaching children about tactics and planning. Such tactics are not revealing what is in one's hand, bluffing, protecting higher ranked pieces (the queen in chess, aces in certain card games), thinking two or more moves ahead, learning the playing styles of opponents to anticipate their moves, keeping track of key events (such as the number of aces thrown) to estimate the probability of future events—all help a child learn to think tactically. Later, parents can use the child's knowledge of game strategies to help him or her understand competitive strategies in other areas, such as business and political negotiations.

When you come across interesting and ingenious examples of tactical problem solving share them with your children. Aspects of a solution may some day be transferable to a problem that your child will encounter. Equally important may be the inspirational impact of your excitement about human ingenuity. The medical news in your newspaper is a fascinating source of tactical problem-solving attempts. New tactics for curing cancer and AIDS are in the news regularly, each based on an area of vulnerability of the disease-causing agent or an area of strength of the body (as an example, treatments have been based on the facts that cancer cells are more vulnerable to heat and need more blood than normal cells). You can find effective tactics in virtually every area of human endeavor from the nonviolent demonstrations for equal rights of Mahatma Gandhi and Martin Luther King to the blitzkrieg assaults of the German army in World War II.

Also share practical tactics for everyday problem solving. One father, whose son had watched him struggle in vain to cut linoleum to fit tightly around molding, learned from a friend that he could get a precise cut by first tracing a pattern on paper with a compass (as the metal point moves along the edge of the molding, the pencil will trace out the exact shape on the paper). The father communicated to his son what a good idea he thought this was and they tried it together—and it worked.

There are a number of ways parents can encourage their children to come up with effective tactics *on their own*. Simply asking a child, "What do you think would be the best way to do this?" will usually start her thinking about tactics, and will also communicate respect for her ability to reason. It should also indicate whether she really understands the problem to be solved and whether the two of you are conceiving of the problem in the same way. If she offers an idea, help her evaluate whether it will work—and if not, why not. You might have her think through the logic of her plan ("If you take the stick out of it, how will it stand up?"), or help her picture its step-by-step execution ("Once you glue those together, do you think you'll be able to cut them?"); or you might have her actually try her idea so she can perceive its outcome—successful or unsuccessful—directly.

If she can't come up with an effective approach, prompt her to think about what she knows about any aspect of the problem that might open the way toward a solution. Also prompt her to examine anything she knows about similar problems that might be applicable to this one. Parents and teachers can find many opportunities for stimulating children to think up tactical solutions. A creative teacher described one such occasion:

My kindergarten class and I were accidently locked on the rooftop playground of our school and our banging on the door did not bring help. I saw that the children were getting nervous and they were not entirely calmed by my assurance that another class was scheduled to come up in 15 minutes and would open the door for us. So I herded them into a huddle to figure out various ways we might get down or signal others of our plight. The children came up with many interesting suggestions, including arranging their jackets to spell out "help" in letters large enough to signal passing helicopters, and tying their jackets into a long chain which could be dangled over the roof above a classroom window in the hopes of catching the attention of the teacher inside.

Persuasion and Other Social Skills

Children have to learn many tactics for dealing effectively with others. These *social skills* include how to initiate interactions with others (such as how to open conversations and join in on group games), how to play and work with others cooperatively, how to get others to find you likable and interesting, how to resolve conflicts in mutually beneficial ways, how to gain trust, how to persuade others to one's positions, and how to evaluate the influence attempts of others. Social intelligence is often neglected in discussions of intellectual abilities, yet we do recognize that not all of us are equally "good with people." We also know that those with superior social skills are not necessarily among the "brightest" in other problem areas. Even within the broad domain of social skills, different people display strengths in some areas but not in others: an inspiring leader might not be a competent negotiator; a successful salesman might not be good at making friends.

Parents can help their children master social situations by teaching them interpersonal tactics, such as greeting others in a friendly way, asking questions that show interest in them, cheering their efforts, applauding their successes, being a good sport (a gracious winner and good loser), and allowing others to "save face," and so on. They also need help in detecting and parrying the manipulative tactics of others, such as attempts to arouse their jealousy or guilt, or to control them through flattery or by playing on their insecurities.

Among the important social skills for children to master are the abilities to construct *persuasive arguments* and evaluate the arguments of others. These are sometimes called "critical thinking" skills. We use persuasive arguments to convince others of the correctness of an action or belief, such as whom to vote for, what products to buy, or what causes to back.

Children start to use persuasive arguments practically as soon as they start to talk; they use them to get parents, siblings, and playmates to do things they want or to stop interfering with them. Two recent studies of 1½- to 3½-year-olds found that even at this early age, children argue for, justify, and negotiate in reasonable ways to promote their positions. The 3-year-olds used more and better arguments than the younger children and, interestingly, parents who were more apt to use reasonable arguments with their children (rather than orders or threats) had children who tended to defend their positions with reasonable arguments.[6]

By the time children turn 5 or 6 many are quite sophisticated spokespersons for their causes. Here is an example from a child of 6 years, 1 month:

> Our cat died and my daughter, Erica, was heartbroken and asked for a new kitten. But my wife and I were hesitant because we thought she might be allergic to cats. Erica had had a cough on and off for the past two years and an allergist had recently suggested it might be a reaction to cat dander. We explained to Erica why we were hesitant to get her a kitten and said we'd vacuum the house thoroughly and see if it had any effect on her cough.
>
> Over the next few weeks her cough subsided but we weren't sure if this was because of the vacuuming since she had periods without coughing even during the time we had a cat. Erica tried hard to convince us that she did not have a cat allergy. When we visited friends who had cats, she would stick her face in their fur to demonstrate that she did not have an allergy. Then we had a visit from an old friend who, after about an hour in our home, began to have a mild allergy attack. She remembered that we had had a cat and told us that she was allergic to cats and suspected that some of the dander was still on our carpets and furniture.
>
> For Erica this was the proof she had been waiting for. She announced that this demonstrated that she was definitely not allergic to cats: "*She* is allergic to cats but I'm not and never was. There must be dander here or her nose wouldn't be running, but look—I am not coughing."

This was good reasoning and persuasive arguing by Erica. But, of course, Erica did not have certain proof to support her position. The friend's allergy attack may have come from something other than cat dander; or perhaps there is more than one type of dander and the vacuuming removed the kind causing Erica's cough but not the kind causing the friend's sniffles. Erica had a strong case, but she was dealing in probabilities, not certainties. In most cases, persuasive arguments are not based on certainties, yet they can still be plausible and logical.

In chapter 4, I cited research showing that preschoolers are able to evaluate the validity of simple arguments stated as basic syllogisms. As their memory and language skills develop they become increasingly adept at evaluating more complex arguments. Still, there are many ploys and tricks that they must learn to watch for. For instance, they need to learn that a critical step in evaluating the validity of arguments is to make sure that terms are used consistently each time they come up, from premise to premise to conclusion. Take the argument, "Children need adventure. Joining a street gang provides adventure. Therefore children need to join street gangs." Certainly the term "adventure" is used differently in the first and second premise. But sometimes it is hard to tell whether a term is being used consistently since many terms in arguments are not clearly defined.

Also, a persuasive argument may be valid in that its conclusion does indeed follow from its premises, but its conclusion may still be false if one or more of its premises is false. Since many persuasive arguments contain premises that are statements of opinion or belief (statements about the best policy, product, candidate, etc.), we frequently find ourselves uncertain about whether or not a position is sound. To overcome this uncertainty, persuaders resort to a variety of tactics which logicians call "fallacies"; these are forms of argument that have persuasive appeal despite the fact that they do not legitimately support the conclusion put forth.

We need to make our children aware of these tactics. Among them are:

Status effects—making it appear that admirable, knowledgeable, or beautiful people support one's claim or use one's product.

Maligning the opposition—associating "bad" people—communists, fascists, nerds, wimps—with those who don't support one's position.

Negative attacks—assailing opponents' positions without demonstrating the value of one's own, as in "Their policies have not succeeded, therefore vote for us."

Emotional appeals—trying to arouse sympathy, guilt, anger or fear to gain support, as when a candidate shows commercials of himself with his children and the flag and juxtaposes images of his opponent with pictures of criminals or atomic bombs exploding.

Testimonial "proof"—citing a few, carefully selected people who claim to have benefited from the position or product.

Circular arguments—supporting one's position with a "reason" that merely propounds the same position in different words, as in, "No country can survive without freedom of speech because any country that does not allow its citizens to speak their minds must inevitably perish."

Concealed premises—as in, "Their team has better players than our team. We can't possibly win. Therefore we should forfeit the game." Unstated is the implicit premise, "It is better to forfeit than to lose," which, if asserted openly, might not gain much agreement.

Omissions or distortions of evidence—as when cigarette manufacturers claim that they should not be held responsible for the ill health of smokers because smoking can't be linked conclusively to any particular individual's ill health. Using misleading (though technically accurate) graphs and statistics would fall into this category.

Overgeneralizations—as when someone argues that because something was so in a similar situation it should be so now, despite the fact that there may be crucial differences between then and now, as in "The antibiotic helped my brother and me when we were sick, so it should help you." In another form of overgeneralization, one rejects a position totally because of an exception to it, as in "I thought you said he was a good player. Well if that's so, how come he lost?"

Irrelevant justifications—as in, "We should vote for Annie for class president because she's one of our closest friends" (ignoring the question of whether she has the qualities needed to make a good class president).

Invisible forces—as when someone claims to have divine backing for his position or attributes causes to forces that only he can perceive because of his special powers.

Most of us have committed one or more of these fallacies when trying to convince others of the correctness of our positions—sometimes because we didn't know better and sometimes because we thought we could get away with it. In order to help a child avoid using illogical or fallacious arguments, teach him the tactic of evaluating his arguments from the perspective of someone who takes an opposite position. Good critical thinkers are always arguing in their heads with their opponents, sharpening (or even abandoning) their own positions by attacking them with the best counterarguments they can imagine. It is a good habit for children to get into.

While most of us commit the fallacies described above inadvertently, some people make their livings by using these and similar techniques to convince the rest of us to embrace some product, person, or idea. Advertisements, political oratory, and marketing and sales pitches provide abundant examples.

Fortunately, children at a young age can learn to recognize and distrust such tactics. Researchers Lizette Peterson and Katherine Lewis of the University of Missouri trained children between the ages of 6 and 10 to distinguish the factual content of television commercials (such as, "It has 10% real fruit juice") from the persuasive techniques or "tricks" used to sell the product.

The researchers spent a half hour going over each of eight persuasive techniques, illustrating each with a sample cereal or toy commercial. The eight persuasive techniques were:

Bribe: You get a "gift" when purchasing the advertised item: "A whistle is in every specially marked box of blank cereal."

Claim: You hear an opinion-based statement regarding the taste or quality of the product: "It is delicious."

Superperson: You are told that the product will endow you with supernatural powers or that someone with supernatural powers advocates the use of the product: "The superpowers supercharge this cereal with good taste."

Person-Like Me: You see happy, popular children using the product and hear: "All the kids will be wanting it."

Familiar Person: The product is pitched or advocated by a popular cartoon character or celebrity (e.g., Fred Flintstone selling cereal).

Music: A catchy tune is used to inject positive affect toward the product.

Humor: A funny story or line is used to induce positive affect toward the product.

Story: An interesting story or plot is used to focus the children's attention on the product.

After the training the researchers showed new commercials to both trained and untrained children, but only those who had received the training were adept at recognizing the "tricks" and distinguishing tricks from factual information. As the researchers put it, "These data clearly suggest that it is possible to teach children to discriminate product information from persuasive advertising techniques at a relatively young age."[7]

Parents can prepare their children—even preschoolers—for these various persuasive "tricks." To start, there are three key concepts that they will need to be clear about: facts, opinions, and beliefs. One way to teach these notions is through the What Is It? game. First give your child examples and definitions of each of these terms:

A *fact* is a statement about the way something really is or about what really happened. For example, "It rained yesterday" states a fact about yesterday's weather. "Giraffes have long necks" states a fact about the bodies of giraffes. A fact may be true or false. "Columbus discovered America in 1592" states a fact, but it isn't true.

An *opinion* states what we think or feel about something. "Giraffes are beautiful" is an opinion about giraffes. Opinions aren't true or false and no one's opinion is better than anyone else's.

A *belief* states something a person thinks is true but cannot prove—at least not yet. "Angels live in heaven" is a belief that some people have, although we have no way of telling if it is true since we can't see angels. "Elephants will become extinct" is a belief about what will happen in the future. With beliefs about the future, we can eventually find out if the belief is true or false (as long as it is not too far in the future).

Start the "game" by stating facts, opinions, and beliefs and asking your child to which category each statement belongs. Here are some examples you might use:

Bats are mammals. (fact, true)

The Amazon river is in the U.S. (fact, false)

Thunder is frightening. (opinion)

Some people are frightened by thunder. (fact, true)

Peter Pan is a great film. (opinion)

There is life on other planets. (belief, testable)

Storms are made by angry gods. (belief, untestable)

It is 28 degrees. (fact)

It is cold. (opinion)

At first you'll have to go over the three categories frequently and explain why particular statements are examples of one or the other. After your child starts to categorize most statements correctly, reverse roles; ask her to give you statements and you say whether they express facts, opinions, or beliefs. You can reinforce these lessons in everyday conversations. Researcher John Flavell and his colleagues have found that in conversations even 3-year-olds respond differently to statements of opinion and statements of fact; they expect people to agree (with them) about things they consider facts but recognize that people hold diverse opinions about matters of taste, such as whether or not they like a candy bar.[8]

Another critical thinking tool that can be taught through the same game format is the difference between a *definition* and an *example*. Definitions list essential facts about the thing being defined. For instance, "Giraffes are animals with long necks" is a definition that states two crucial facts about any giraffe we will ever meet. "Justice is an outcome resulting from procedures that a majority believe offer everyone an equal chance" states three facts about all instances of justice.

Good definitions state enough essential facts to distinguish the thing being defined from anything else (notice that the definition I gave for "giraffe" would certainly not accomplish this). Also, people can disagree over a definition. It is far easier to get people to agree about definitions of concrete objects, such as giraffes, than intangible concepts, such as justice or intelligence.

Examples list instances rather than attributes. Bananas, oranges, and apples are examples of fruit; knowing this doesn't tell us what a fruit is.

For some intangible concepts, such as "beauty," we have a hard time defining the essential attributes, and sometimes the best we can do is point to examples that in our opinion fit the category. For instance, most would agree that the Mona Lisa and the Parthenon are examples of beauty, but we'd find it very difficult to list our criteria for according them that label.

Present statements like the following to your children and ask them to tell you whether they contain examples or definitions:

Carrots, stringbeans, and corn are vegetables. (examples)

Legos, Barbies, and Lincoln Logs are toys. (examples)

Heros are people whom others admire. (definition)

Theaters are places where people see shows. (definition)

You can find exercises like these, and many others, in the *Critical Thinking* workbooks published by the Steck-Vaughn Company of Austin, Texas.

Look for opportunities to discuss arguments with your child. The news will provide many issues that grade-school children can understand and care about. Youngsters overhear many current controversies on the TV news and commonly express interest in at least some of them. Don't be surprised if your 6-year-old perks up and pays attention when hearing stories about the treatment of animals, the plight of the homeless, the abuse of the environment, or massive demonstrations for freedom (as in South Africa and Eastern Europe). Try to present the issues and positions as you understand them. In stating your own positions do not hesitate to acknowledge your own doubts and biases.

Also introduce your child to editorials, columns, op-ed pieces, and other statements by advocates of different sides of an issue. Display your excitement over particularly well-reasoned and well-expressed arguments. Depending on your child's age, you'll probably have to do some rewording and abridging of arguments so she can grasp them. Also make sure she understands why these are important issues. Ask her what she thinks and why, and help her sort through the logic and plausibility of her position.

As your child begins to read stories that take stands on issues, try to make sure she recognizes and evaluates the persuasive messages. The novels of Mark Twain and Charles Dickens, for example, contain forceful messages about social and economic ills and about how people should treat one another.

Your youngster's daily life will provide many opportunities to evaluate persuasive arguments. For example, she might be faced with having to vote for class president and be subject to lobbying from the candidates and her classmates. She might be confused about how one goes about making a wise decision and need help in thinking through what a good class president does, what qualities one needs to do those things well, and which candidates have those qualities.

Also do your best to sensitize your child to the manipulations that are possible with statistics and graphs. John Allen Paulos's book *Innumeracy* covers many of these.

Self-Regulating Tactics

Socrates instructed, "Know thyself." An important reason to know oneself is so that one can act intelligently toward oneself—that is, so that one can regulate one's behavior to better accomplish one's ends. When it comes to learning and problem solving, research confirms that youngsters can indeed improve their intellectual performance through self-regulation tactics; that is, by using what they know about their own learning and problem-solving processes.

Psychologist Barry Zimmerman interviewed students and compiled an extensive list of such self-regulating strategies. They cover a number of metacognitive domains, include metamemory. In his examples, the youngsters were saying, essentially, *I know I do better when I . . . . :*

Review my work: "I check over my work to make sure I did it right."

Organize in advance: "I make an outline before I write my paper."

Provide sufficient preparation time: "I start studying two weeks before exams, and I pace myself."

Do thorough research: "Before beginning to write the paper, I go to the library to get as much information as possible concerning the topic."

Keep written records for study: "I took notes of the class discussions." "I kept a list of the words I got wrong."

Structure my work environment: "I isolate myself from anything that distracts me."

Reward myself: "If I do well on a test, I treat myself to a movie."

Memorize through rehearsal and drill: "In preparing for a math test, I keep writing the formula down until I remember it."

Seek assistance when needed: "If I have problems with math assignments, I ask a friend to help."

Do timely reviews: "When preparing for a test, I review my notes.

Follow instructions: "I just do what the teacher says."

Zimmerman reports that students who used such self-regulation strategies scored higher on both academic achievement tests and teacher ratings.[9]

As children move up through grade school and encounter more and more formalized instruction and examinations, it becomes increasingly important for them to identify the conditions that prompt their best work.

Parents can help by introducing various self-regulating strategies and encouraging their child to try them. They can also provide timely reminders: "Remember how well you memorized that list when you chanted the words out loud?" After a while, reminders can take the form of "Stop and think" signals: "You are going to have to memorize a lot of items so *stop and think* about the best way to do that. What's made memorizing easier for you before?"

Try to tailor strategies to your child's particular learning style and the specific material to be mastered (for instance, there may be times when for a particular youngster, note-taking—usually a useful tactic—becomes more of a hindrance than a help). Discuss in a respectful manner with your child how *she* might prompt her best work, taking her distinctive learning style into consideration.

Recent research on parenting practices affirms the value of a cooperative framework that balances parental supervision with what the researchers call "autonomy support" for the child: Parents who were highly involved in their grade-schooler's educational activities, who set high standards for them, but who also allowed their children to participate in decision making about school and who used reasoning to influence them rather than rewards and punishments, had children who scored higher on measures of self-regulation and competence. Other researchers have found strong positive associations between this kind of parenting and children's school grades and self-confidence.[10]

Within a cooperative framework parents can assert the ideal of *doing one's best,* while communicating their trust that their youngster advocates the same ideal (which most youngsters do). Expressing faith in youngsters by attributing good qualities and intentions to them often stimulates them to try to live up to those good characteristics, presumably because they don't want to tarnish their good reputations. Research shows that attributing good qualities is a powerful motivational technique with children.[11]

There are many self-regulating strategies that a child can try, as Zimmerman's list indicates. Here are a few more that should prove helpful:

- Summarize the main idea in each paragraph as you study.
- Organize what you learn around questions that the teacher is likely to ask.
- Whenever you lose the thread of an argument in a text, read the material again to try to make the connection.
- When frustrated, remind yourself of previous successes.
- When frustrated, remind yourself of your goals, your aspirations that justify the present discomfort.

- Listen to rousing music before an exam (or calming music, or absolutely no music, depending on the individual).

- Place pictures of your intellectual heros in your study area, as well as inspiring passages from their work.

- In a long project (writing a term paper) plan how you will begin the next work session before ending a session (Ernest Hemingway found that this helped him look forward to the next session and avoid the writer's bane of sitting down to a blank page with a blank mind).

- In writing an essay or a story, if you aren't sure how the beginning should go, start in the middle, or start anywhere—just start!

- Get a good night's sleep before an exam.

Memorizing

A number of studies affirm the value of using *mnemonic* aids in memorizing. As an example of a mnemonic aid, a parent reported the following:

Ellen [5 years, 8 months] kept mixing up the meaning of "horizontal" and "vertical," words I had introduced in our discussions of drawing. So I wrote the words for her in capital letters and pointed out the horizontal line in the "H" of horizontal and the up–down orientation of the two lines in the "V" of vertical. She already knew the sounds of the letters *H* and *V* so she could picture the letters whenever she heard or said horizontal or vertical. From then on she had no trouble remembering which was which, although at first she needed a little time to visualize the *H* or *V* to "see" the correct orientation.

Researchers have found a variety of mnemonic procedures to be effective, particularly for learning lists and facts. One such is the "Method of Loci," in which items that need to be memorized in a given sequence (say, historical events) are visualized in specific locations in the home in a logical order (entranceway first, coat closet second).

Another method involves grouping items in some meaningful way; for example, when learning a list of animals, divide them into types, such as "pets," "wild," and "domestics," and note how many there are of each. Some psychologists refer to this process as "chunking," and a number of studies have demonstrated its usefulness.[12] We use chunking when we memorize the 11 numbers needed to dial a long-distance number. Most of us would have trouble remembering a string of 11 random numbers. But the task become manageable by chunking the number into three sections—the initial 1 or 0 to obtain a long distance line, the three-digit area code, and the seven-digit local number.

A third procedure employs visual images (as in the horizontal–vertical example above). In one study students were better able to learn botany concepts through imaginative visualizations. In the researchers' words: "to [help students] represent *dicotyledons* as a subdivision of *angiosperms,* a mnemonic illustration was constructed of an angel (*angiosperm*) holding a dinosaur (the keyword for *dicotyledon*) on a leash."[13]

In helping children study, parents should teach these kinds of memory strategies, and later, when necessary, remind their children to use them. Research shows that even before they are 2, children use memory strategies spontaneously, such as remembering the location of a hidden object by staring at the spot it was last seen and talking about it ("Big Bird hiding") while waiting for the signal to start looking for it.[14]

Parents can help children develop good memories during their earliest years. Researcher Hilary Ratner found that 2- and 3-year-olds who scored highest on various memory tests had parents who made "memory demands" on them—for example, by asking lots of memory questions ("Where did you put your jacket?" "If you touch that again, what is going to happen?" "What do you have that is like this toy?" "Is this the book Grandma gave you?" "What does an airplane do?").[15]

A good way to give your 3- or 4-year-old practice in memorizing is by playing memory games. One type is a concentration game in which picture cards are arranged face down in a grid. Each player turns up two cards on a turn. If the cards match the player earns one point. If not, they are placed face down in the same locations. The next player turns up a card and then tries to earn a point by turning up a matching card. The player who best remembers the pictures and locations of previously turned-up cards has an advantage in finding matches.

In another memory game, you call out items, such as animals or professions, from a list one at a time and your child must perform some behavior that represents the item (roaring for "lion," checking your ears for "doctor"). As you add new items, one at a time, your child must perform an appropriate behavior for each, always starting with the first and running through the entire list.

By 5 or 6, children can benefit from direct instruction in the kinds of mnemonic strategies described above (chunking, visualizing). Parents should be explicit about what they are teaching and why: "These are memory strategies that make it easier to remember things." Once children recognize the helpfulness of a strategy, they are more likely to employ it on their own. Another memory technique that has proved useful is to have children "self-monitor" by checking periodically to see whether they are able to recall the material they have gone over ("Close your eyes and tell me the items you've learned"). Often children believe they have learned something, when in fact they haven't.[16]

Imaginative Problem Solving: Art and Aesthetics

Examples of imaginative problem solving are writing a story, painting a picture, designing a building, decorating a room, and composing a symphony. In imaginative problem solving we create a new entity out of one or another kind of medium, such as paint, words, or musical notes. The entity created is not intended to be directly functional (like a light bulb). It is an "expressive" entity, the creator's reaction to something experienced (to a face, a landscape, the idea of death) and/or his ideas about the medium he is working in (ideas about harmony, light, form, etc). For example, Van Gogh's paintings of peasants reveal his reaction to witnessing their daily struggles for survival. The paintings also convey his ideas about using paint to capture on a two-dimensional surface the dynamics of three-dimensional events.

The notion of art as problem solving was described well by Al Hirschfeld, the famous caricaturist:

> What I do, across all the years of staring at a blank piece of paper, is create a new problem every time, and then solve it to my own satisfaction.[17]

For him, the problem is, "distillation . . . bringing things down to the simplest form."

Pablo Picasso, in an interview, described the formation of artistic problems in his work:

> Do you think it interests me that this picture represents two people? These two people once existed, but they exist no longer. The vision of them gave me an initial emotion, little by little their presence became obscured, they became for me a fiction, then they disappeared, or rather were transformed into problems of all sorts. For me they aren't two people any more, but forms and colors, understand, forms and colors which sum up, however, the idea of the two people and conserve the vibration of their life.[18]

In art, the problems are created by the artist. Sometimes they are relatively circumscribed problems, such as to write a song in a musical play that delineates a character and advances the plot. Sometimes they are monumental problems, as when the composer, Arnold Schoenberg, set out to create music using a new tonal system, or when Pablo Picasso and Georges Braque sought to burst the boundaries of painting through cubism.

A friend, a talented but minor abstract expressionist, once mocked himself by saying, "My failing as an artist has come from the fact that all the important problems in painting have already been discovered." He knew better, but he also knew that the "great" artists were the ones who conceived new artistic goals. Rembrandt, for example, sought a psychological reality that went far beyond other painters of his time; he also used light in more dramatic and realistic ways; and unlike his contemporaries, he explored the expressive impact of the brushstrokes and visible texture of the paint.

Obviously, simply setting up and solving a problem does not make a work of art interesting or significant. To illustrate, a photographer once asked why the photographs on greeting cards were generally not great photographs. "They are usually very skillful," he said, "and, in a superficial sense, even beautiful, with lovely scenes; and many have an emotional quality to them. Yet, there is something missing that makes them, well, greeting cards, and not serious works of art."

I suggested that they were not to be taken seriously because they set up easy problems or offered trivial solutions to difficult problems. For example, it is easy to convey "intimacy" by photographing two pretty people walking arm in arm in a field of flowers. But the solution is trivial; it is intimacy *in general*. Such a photo tells us nothing about these particular people, the obstacles they have had to overcome on their way to "intimacy," what intimacy means *specifically* to them, given the lives they've lived. A photo that conveyed all that, would tell us much more about intimacy— its universal, not its general, aspects—and its beauty would not be based on the prettiness of the surface features. My friend agreed that this would be a much more interesting, and difficult, problem to solve.

There are problems to be solved in every aspect of an imaginative work. In writing, for example, decisions need to be made about plot, characters, point of view, words, and rhythm, among many other aspects. All serious writers are unrelenting in their pursuit of the perfect word or phrase to express the images and sensations they have in mind. Some writers, like Ernest Hemingway and James Joyce, seek to alter or expand our very conceptions of what constitutes good writing.

Artists come upon their problems in many ways. Sometimes they realize that there are truths that have not been expressed by others. For example, a choreographer with whom I have worked felt that other choreographers had not taken sufficient account of the fact that in our daily lives our movements normally derive from interactions with objects. So she began to create dances that incorporated the use of chairs, kitchen utensils, appliances, and other mundane objects.

Sometimes artists discover a problem because of vague feelings of dissatisfaction with something they've produced. Sometimes they can't put the problem into words but they know something crucial has not been achieved— although they obviously don't know what. The novelist Gabriel Garcia Marquez described this dissatisfaction well:

I had an idea of what I always wanted to do, but there was something missing and I was not sure what it was until one day I discovered the right tone—the tone that I eventually used in *One Hundred Years of Solitude*. It was based on the way my grandmother used to tell her stories. She told things that sounded supernatural and fantastic, but she told them with complete naturalness. When I finally discovered the tone I had to use, I sat down for eighteen months and worked every day.

As he wrote, Marquez pictured his grandmother's expression ("with a brick face") as she told her stories.[19]

Sometimes artists discover the problems they are exploring as they work through a piece. The painter Robert Motherwell described it this way:

. . . something in the studio will catch at my attention—maybe a piece of drawing paper or a blank canvas of a certain size. I'll pick it up and make a mark, and the minute I do that, something gets going. I mean, there's no plan working. You don't sit down and say, "I'm going to make a manifesto about the Middle East or paint my lover or the blue sky." You start with some marks and then a kind of dialectic begins among them, and one says to you, "Now, that fourth mark is trying to obliterate me; make me bigger." Or a yellow may tell you it needs a purple to balance it off.[20]

Here is John Fowles on how he discovered the problems to be solved in writing *The French Lieutenant's Woman:*

It started four or five months ago as a visual image. A woman stands at the end of a deserted quay and looks out to sea. That was all. This image rose in my mind one morning when I was still in bed half asleep.

The image haunted him. He tried to ignore it, but it recurred. Then the problem solving began:

I began deliberately to recall it and to try to analyze and hypothesize why it held some sort of imminent power. It was obviously mysterious. It was vaguely romantic. It also seemed, perhaps because of the latter quality, not to belong to today. . . . she was Victorian; and since I always saw her in the same static long shot, with her back turned, she represented a reproach on the Victorian age. An outcast. I didn't know her crime, but I wished to protect her. That is, I began to fall in love with her.[21]

Interestingly, within a work of art, each solution sets up a new problem. A composer writes a musical phrase and must then decide what phrase should follow. With two phrases a more overarching structure begins to form. Now a third phrase must connect not only to the second phrase but must fit with and contribute to the emerging musical structure. Then, as the third phrase defines the larger musical structure more clearly, the composer may revise the first and second phrases to make them more consistent with it. This process of decision, discovery, and revision will continue until the piece is done.

Even when one starts with a definite theme, as Picasso did in his famous anti-war painting, *Guernica,* or Arthur Miller did in his political play, *The Crucible,* a piece will still take unexpected paths for the artist. Arthur Miller has described this process of discovery in his playwriting:

> For myself it has never been possible to generate the energy to write and complete a play if I know in advance everything it signifies and all it will contain. The very impulse to write, I think, springs from an inner chaos crying for order, for meaning, and that meaning must be discovered in the process of writing or the work lies dead as it is finished.[22]

Regardless of the artistic problems being worked on or how they came to mind, the search for an artistic solution is, in essence, a search for perfection: the perfect word, the perfect structure, the perfect balance. Part of the power of great art comes, I believe, from our awareness that we are in the presence of perfection, that nothing must be changed. When listening to a great symphony, we may find ourselves filling with emotion, but realize that it is not over something occurring at that moment in the music; rather, it is the experience of awe over the perfection of the evolving musical structures—that each new development is stunningly correct. Many artists have commented on the agony of this unrelenting search for perfection and the ecstasy that attends moments of success.

Children's imaginative problem solving, like that of adults, originates in many different ways. Some pieces develop in much the same way that Motherwell described. A child playing with blocks will set one down, then decide where another should go, and then another—and, to use Motherwell's phrase, "a kind of dialectic begins among them," and blocks will be placed and replaced in response to an emerging design.

Children's paintings often follow this same path. Their pen and pencil drawings, though, are more likely to depict objects, such as faces, people and animals interacting or in activities, houses, mountains, the sun, dragons, story book characters, and many other entities they've seen or heard about. Some drawings are attempts to reproduce things that interest them; others tell a story; still others are fanciful and combine real and made up elements.

By the time children enter school they ordinarily have explored many art forms. They've drawn and painted; made up stories, rhymes, and even songs; they've sculpted with clay and constructed designs out of blocks and various other materials; and they've created dances and enacted fantasy skits and scenes. Children typically work hard on their creations and take them seriously, often reacting angrily to interruptions.

Child artists often appear to know something that many older artists have to relearn: That art is first of all, an expression of self; it is a communication only secondarily. The artist allows others to witness his passions, his ecstasies, his dredgings for truth and beauty. Yes, artists show their work to others and want to be appreciated, but when the work is done primarily *for* others, to please them, it is likely to be shallow and imitative. Interestingly, even with young children, one can observe that some try to model their art work after other children's (say, by copying the way another child draws flowers), while some strive deliberately to make their creations unique.

If the materials are available children will usually engage in artistic work spontaneously. If your child doesn't show an interest in some materials, you can often spark it by initiating a project, say by starting to make a clay figure or diorama. If no interest emerges, there's nothing to be gained by prodding. Move on to some other activity (unless *you* are enjoying the project and want to complete it). For some activities, parental participation is important. For instance, youngsters are more likely to make up stories and songs if parents get things started ("Let's make up a love song to our cat. 'Oh, beau-ti-ful ca-at, you're cute as can be . . .' Now you make up the next line").

Parents can also help by asking stimulating questions about a child's creations ("So, what did the fox do when he fell in the hole?" or "What about the dog's tail? Is it a happy tail or a frightened tail?"). Carefully timed suggestions are also useful (say, by suggesting a couple of possible rhyming words when the child can't think of any, or by suggesting an unusual angle for a piece in a design project).

During these early years, your enthusiastic responses to your child's creations will encourage her to do more. Treat her work as if a great artist were sharing her masterpieces with you. Delight in them and point out specific things that impress you or that display newly acquired skills ("I like that big red stripe there; it really draws my eye across the entire page"). And ask her to point out aspects that she likes best (but don't make a fuss if she can't). Display some of her work and tell her why ("Because I love to look at them and I want visitors to have the same pleasure"), and put her name and date on them ("Just like grown-up artists"). In other words, treat her art work as *art,* not play.

Criticism of the child's work has no value. She's doing the best she can. It would be as helpful as a Little League coach criticizing his young charges for not having the strength to hit their flyballs to the outfield. Yet *instruction* if handled sensitively can be useful. Unfortunately, art teachers are adamantly against teaching children drawing skills before Junior High School or even High School, based on some unsupported notions of developmental stages. That may be why although virtually all children start out enjoying drawing and painting, and almost all take years of art classes in school, extremely few like to draw or paint when they get older, and even fewer have any sense of personal competency in art.

Grade-school art teachers encourage exploration of the medium (of colors, lines, textures, etc.), which is certainly important. But children often have artistic goals of their own. Most want to be able to make their drawings look like the things they are viewing or imagining—and most would be capable of this with instruction. Unfortunately, by the time they are taught basic representational techniques, most have given up on drawing and think of themselves as having no artistic ability. Their teacher's agenda has not coincided with their own.

Ellen Winner studied the drawings of Chinese children and observed:

> Chinese children do not draw childish drawings. Young children in China make drawings that seem to challenge theories of the developmental course of drawing skill. . . . Instead of the large, messy, semi-expressionist paintings seen in American preschool and elementary schools, in which children reveal their own invented ways of representing, one sees in China small, neat paintings in which children display their precocious ability to master adult ways of representing the world. . . .
>
> Chinese children learn to paint . . . colorful scenes in which the entire space is filled with small figures engaged in a dazzling variety of activities—walking, sitting, jumping, shown from the back and looking up, running with one leg going back and in foreshortening, holding umbrellas, etc. . . . These postures (never seen in drawings by such young children in the West) are no mean feat to depict, and it is quite breathtaking to encounter such a repertoire in children even as young as six.
>
> Such adult-like paintings can be seen in endless supply in any good urban school in China. It is not just the gifted children who draw in this way.[23]

The lesson for American art education is certainly not to emulate the Chinese program, which is based on copying sample drawings provided by the teacher, but to appreciate that children's drawing skills can be developed at a far younger age than present practice allows. The Chinese method of instruction does little to encourage imagination and personal expression, two essential goals in Western art. In contrast, Western modes of representational art instruction *do* encourage personal expression, and they are extremely effective. My complaint is that such instruction comes too late, after most children have given up on art.

Most young children like to paint, make clay sculptures, make music, and make up stories. They lose interest in these activities either when they no longer have any goal that motivates them to continue or when their creations are judged too severely by others. The 3-year-old painter is motivated by the sensory feedback he gets from the emerging patterns of colors and textures. The 4-year-old draftsman is delighted with his growing skill at making faces look more and more like real faces. After a while, though, simply making another pattern is no longer very interesting, and the ability to draw a face to look like a real face reaches a plateau. Without new artistic goals and challenges, their interest soon wanes.

Parents can rouse their children's enthusiasm for creating art by helping them define new goals that are interesting and attainable. A young artist at work may need help recognizing that he or she is exploring problems of composition, perspective, or action. For example, when young children want to draw a boat speeding through the water, they usually place the boat near the center of the paper traveling along a horizontal line where water meets sky. They don't generally consider whether that is the best placement or angle to convey the speed or urgency of the voyage. Perhaps the boat should be seen heading off toward an upper corner of the page. Children don't usually consider such possibilities of composition. Without instruction and without being helped to notice how other artists have worked on similar problems, most will never consider them.

Young children draw from imagination. It is rare to see preschoolers or even young grade schoolers looking at an object to draw it. As they get older they do try to draw what they see, usually trying to reproduce the object's outline. But they soon discover that drawing outlines cannot give them the results they want and most give up. Good instruction can make a difference. It will shift their focus to capturing the object's mass and volume—its three-dimensional impact on a space—and the results will improve.

Similarly, when novices draw a person, they trace an outline to try to depict the body's position, but with training their goal switches to portraying the action the person is engaging in. They learn that drawing a person involves drawing a personality in action and that even sitting still or sleeping is an action. By redefining the problem (volume instead of outline, action instead of position), the artist comes to see his subjects in a new way and his drawings quickly reflect this new perspective.

Most parents aren't going to become expert art teachers, but they can help their children notice aspects of things that they might miss, such as that things far away look smaller than things up close, or that a person's eyes are not at the top of his head but about halfway between his chin and the top of his hairline, or that you can't see a whole object when something is in front of it, or that a person's hair covers the top of the head more like a hat than a rug, or that the rim of the coffee cup on the table looks as if it is oval-shaped, or that a tree is brighter on one side than the other, or that the tree casts a shadow.

If your child's grade-school art teacher tells you that children have to discover these things on their own, take it as seriously as you would if she told you that children have to discover multiplication on their own. On the other hand, don't be troubled if your child doesn't incorporate such information into his or her drawings right away. You are planting seeds and should expect to have to give many reminders and suggestions. Just take care that your suggestions don't come across as commands or criticisms. You want to be careful not to undermine your child's pleasure in expressing his or her own vision. The point is not to prod children to draw things a particular way, but to open up possibilities that they may not discern on their own.

You can use enjoyable drawing projects to enhance your child's awareness of perspective, composition, and other considerations. For example, ask your child to draw a person as seen from a worm's perspective. The feet, of course, should be much larger than other parts of the body. Your child might not do it right, but should be able to understand your explanation of why the feet should be drawn so large:

PARENT: That's a good drawing. But let's check if that's how the worm would see it. What's bigger—my hand or my foot?

CHILD: Your foot.

PARENT: (Placing hand near child's eyes) Now what looks bigger to you, my hand or foot?

CHILD: Your hand, because it's up close.

PARENT: Right. What's the closest part of a person to a worm's eyes? And what's furthest away?

CHILD: The feet are closest so they should look biggest. The head is furthest away so it should look smallest.

A similar lesson can be taught from a bird's-eye-view.

Children recognize the difference between their own drawings and those of older children and adults and usually like the more mature work better.[24]

It is useful to show children more mature art work and to point out one or two elements that the child can appreciate and learn from, such as that all the shadows in the landscape fall in the same direction or that the skin in the portrait has a surprising number of colors in it. To make sure a child isn't discouraged by seeing more mature works, remind him how wonderful his own paintings are and mention some specifics about them; also remind him that young children aren't expected to draw or paint the same as older children and grown-ups.

Also point out the many different ways artists approach their work. Your child's books provide wonderful examples. An illustration by Leo Lionni doesn't look anything like one by Maurice Sendak. See if your child can put the differences in words. Do the same in museums. Portraits by Rembrandt, van Gogh, and Cezanne differ greatly.

In looking at works of art, try to describe what impresses you and ask your child to do the same. For example, the children's author William Steig uses richer and more evocative language than is usually found in children's books. In *Brave Irene,* his story of a little girl trying to deliver an important package in a blizzard, we read "The wind wrestled her for the package" and "In an explosion of fury, she flung her body about." These are marvelous images and the artistry is worth pointing out to a child as you read the story.

And don't hesitate to point out what you don't like, even with works by acknowledged "masters." You want your child to develop a critical eye. I recall having a wonderful discussion with my daughter when she was 5 about the film *The Last Unicorn*—a favorite of ours. She overheard me mention that I thought the movie could have been better and she wanted to know in what way. I explained that all through the film we are told that unicorns are wonderful creatures who should be saved and that life was idyllic when they were around, but we don't ever see a unicorn do anything all that wonderful, and we don't ever learn in what specific ways they made the world better. So (I went on), I don't find myself caring as much about the unicorn as I think I should. She understood and replied, "But they are beautiful—you can see that—and they have real magic," and she felt that that was good enough.

When we have these kinds of discussions there is an important ground rule: Our goal cannot be to try to prove that one of us is right and the other wrong; there is no right or wrong for opinions. We can only explain why we liked or disliked something.

Children reveal aesthetic preferences in their earliest years. Practically from birth (and often to the consternation of their parents), they show very individual partialities for particular colors, tastes, smells, objects, clothes, faces, etc.[25] Before long they begin to express their own preferences in music, art, literature, film, and other art forms. Getting them to enjoy what our culture considers *great* art takes time. Children like things that make sense to them and often they will need guidance before they can recognize and enjoy the structures of great music or the technical skills and psychological insights of great painters and writers. To a 10-year-old a van Gogh landscape may look odd because at first glance it doesn't look like what she's seen in nature. But if it is pointed out that van Gogh worked very hard to capture the movement of the grass and flowers in his painting, she might recognize that van Gogh's rendering really does capture something she's seen on a windy day in the country, perhaps more so than more photographic paintings.

As children's artistic and aesthetic interests develop they can begin to understand the larger, conceptual problems that artists have explored, problems that have led to new insights into how to depict reality (such as pointillism or cubism) and new ways to structure the artistic material (such as new harmonic forms in music, or sculptures that are more about the interplay of textures, colors, light, and space, than the faithful representation of objects).

David Hockney's recent forays into photography is an interesting example of this kind of conceptually based artistic problem solving. In a television interview, Hockney, an eminent contemporary painter, explained how his photographic work developed. He said that in contemplating why paintings had a more powerful impact than photographs, he thought it might be because painters make choices at every point on a canvas while photographers make fewer, more global, choices. Starting from this insight, he devised a new approach to photography in which he takes many pictures of the same subject and then displays them in a carefully composed arrangement. Each photograph, like any photograph, freezes an instant in time and space. But a series of such photographs freezes a *duration* of time in a continually changing space (unlike a motion picture, which doesn't freeze time at all). Each snap of the shutter is a choice, as is the placement of each photograph in the display. The effects he achieves are impressive, as is the reasoning behind his explorations.

Our appreciation of art depends to a large degree on our understanding of the problems being worked on. The impressionists wrote essays and manifestos to educate the public about their work—trying to convince them that they weren't simply being sloppy. As a personal example, a well-known painter once brought slides of her work to a class I was teaching on the psychology of creativity. One painting was a huge canvas that was all orange (somewhat mottled) except for a thin yellow line about two inches in from the sides and across the bottom. My initial response was disinterest, even disdain. Was she kidding? I wondered. As she discussed the picture she referred to the yellow lines as "gravity lines" and as I looked at them I suddenly realized that I wasn't seeing a surface of color but a volume of color. As I looked more carefully, my eye darted about and "into" the surface, and I began to delight in the complexity of this orange universe. The artist had educated me.

Here is a similar episode between a father and daughter:

> When Frances was about six she made two ceramic masks over a span of about four months. She didn't like the second one, which surprised me, because I thought it was the more interesting of the two, particularly because it captured the proportions of a face more closely. Well, its realism was exactly what she didn't like. She explained that she thought it was too ordinary. The realistic nose on the second one was not as interesting, she felt, as the built up, step-like, triangular nose on the first. She had similar objections to her designs on the second: "I put stars on the cheeks" she said with disdain. "That was a lot easier than this," as she pointed to a raised, carefully painted mosaic shape on the cheek of her first mask.

This child's growing sense of artistic and creative purpose was impressive, and not all that rare in children this age—although they may not express it if they don't feel their parents take their creations seriously.

Our own interest in, and appreciation of, art and artistic exploration can help our children develop open, inquiring attitudes toward art. Their aesthetic sensibilities will also be nourished by drawing their attention to the beauty in the world all around them—to the multicolored grandeur of a sunset or the stark intricacies of a lamplit alleyway, to the awesome majesty of a stand of towering trees or the deep mysteries to be found in a puddle on the sidewalk.

We also need to help our children appreciate the significance of art. Sometimes art is taught as a peripheral subject, or at least less important than other areas of human endeavor, like technology, business, or social studies. I know theater artists who are troubled that while the real world has so many unsolved problems they are spending their days creating fantasy lives as if they were children. Musicians sometimes experience similar doubts about a life spent exploring and "playing" sequences of sound. The same holds for painters daubing colors on a canvas. Art can seem like playing—self-indulgent, frivolous. It appears to have no serious function.

When this comes up with my acting students, I remind them that every culture throughout human history has had some form of theater or story telling. I remind them that when archaeologists dig up 30,000-year-old bones they find art in the burial pits. I inform them that within weeks of being released from Nazi concentration camps, Jewish survivors—grieving, ill, in tatters—made their way to make-shift theatres to see plays about their forebears and culture. I instruct them that when autocrats take power the first people imprisoned are usually the poets and artists, and their art is often the inspiration for resistance movements.

Art enriches by reminding us of beauty. It awes and jolts us with startling and ideal patterns. It teaches us who we are and what we might become— the heights and depths to which we may rise or fall. Great works of art tell us eternal truths—what was true for Homer's Greek comrades 3,000 years ago, and for da Vinci's Italian countrymen 500 years ago, and for Shakespeare's English contemporaries 400 years ago. They tell us what will always be true. When your child comes to art, whether as artist or audience, he or she is participating in one of humankind's grandest achievements. That's worth communicating.

Some steps that can be useful in imaginative problem solving are to ask oneself:

1. What am I trying to accomplish? This may be as simple as to make the boat in the picture look like it is going fast. Or, as in the David Hockney example, as complex as increasing the power of photography.

2. How have others worked on this problem? Are there elements I can learn from them without actually copying them? Or perhaps I can see where they failed and learn from their mistakes. (The eminent theater critic Walter Kerr wrote a wonderful manual called *How Not To Write a Play*, describing the traps that young playwrights commonly fall into; in a sense, all artists need to learn from the blunders of their predecessors *how not to* go about their art).

3. Are there more revealing, less superficial, less obvious ways to accomplish what I want? As an example, Edgar Degas was not satisfied with the way other artists painted nudes so he painted them differently:

The nude has always been represented in poses which presupposed an audience, but these women of mine are honest, simple folk, unconcerned by any other interests than those involved in their physical condition. Here is another, she is washing her feet. It is as though you looked through a keyhole.[26]

In essence, he was saying that conventional painting of nudes revealed more about the viewer (the "audience") than the woman, and he was interested in painting the woman—an extraordinary innovation.

4. Am I using the medium to its fullest advantage? For instance, in painting, the medium is usually thought of as the paint, but the canvas is part of the medium too. Ripping the canvas in some way might provide a solution to a problem that paint alone is not solving.

Keep in mind that mastery in an art form is not based on some general ability, but requires intense effort to perfect particular techniques. It is not some general facility with language that makes for a successful writer, but steady labor at one's craft. Few novelists, for example, have written successful plays, though many have tried; and few playwrights have written successful novels. Anton Chekov, considered both a great playwright and a great short story writer, is a rare example. But Chekov worked for years at both forms. Those who attain success in one form and assume they can simply switch to another form because they *know how to write* generally have a rude awakening. Similarly, few great conductors or musicians become outstanding composers. The skills are different, and each requires years to perfect. Having a general facility with music is not sufficient.

Mathematical (and Other Symbolic) Problem Solving

Try this problem:

$$\frac{23 + 23 + 23 + 23 + 23}{5} = ?$$

Now this one:

$$\frac{4}{7} \times \frac{1}{2} = ?$$

Both problems can be solved two ways. For the first problem, most readers will know how to carry out the standard calculations: add the five numbers in the numerator and divide the sum by the 5 in the denominator. Some readers, though, without doing any calculations, will have seen almost immediately that the answer is *23*. They will have noticed that the same quantity (*23*) is added five times, and will know that that is equivalent to multiplying *23* by *5*. They won't bother doing that calculation and then dividing by the 5 in the denominator because they will also know that a quantity doesn't change when it is multiplied and divided by the same number; the two calculations cancel each other out.

For the second problem, too, most readers will know the standard calculation procedure: multiply the two numerators (*4 × 1 = 4*), then multiply the two denominators (*7 × 2 = 14*), then reduce the fraction. Again, some readers will have recognized almost instantly that the correct answer is $2/7$. They will have realized that the question being asked is, What is half of $4/7$? And they will have known that to divide a fraction in half, one simply divides the numerator in half or, alternatively, doubles the denominator.

One needs mathematical knowledge to solve these problems either way, but the second approach in each utilizes deeper insights into mathematical processes, such as that adding a quantity a number of times is equivalent to multiplying that quantity by that number. Mathematicians are ever on the lookout for cues to these kinds of insights. A row of identical numbers is a red flag to a mathematician, signalling "Check this out. You may know something that could be useful here."

As a child develops expertise in mathematics he or she becomes increasingly alert to these "red flags." When faced with a mathematical problem, novice mathematicians start to fiddle with calculations, trying, in a sense, to bully their way to a solution by adding, subtracting, etc., whatever they can, or by feverishly shifting x's and y's around in equations. In contrast, expert mathematicians immediately look for cues to tell them how to proceed.[27] They ask themselves questions like:

- Does this problem fit into a category that can tell me which calculations to use? For instance, the second problem above was solved more easily as a "dividing in half" problem than a "multiplying fractions" problem.
- Can I break off a piece of the problem that is relatively easy to solve, which may then make the larger problem easier? For instance, in an algebra problem with many unknowns, if I can determine that one of the unknowns is equal to or less than zero, it may narrow the possible values of the other unknowns.
- Can I gain some insight by making the problem more concrete? For example, if the problem states, "Train A was traveling at twice the speed of train B . . .", perhaps I can determine how to proceed if I try out 100 miles an hour for train A and 50 miles an hour for train B.

The fostering of mathematical insights can start at a very young age. For example, children's use of the *counting-on* procedure for addition that I described in an earlier chapter reflects a mathematical insight. To use it the child must recognize that a stated number ("5") is invariably the final count word when counting that many things (such as 5 glasses).

Here's an example of a child of 5 years, 8 months acquiring the mathematical insight, *If a whole is divided into two parts, establishing the size of one part absolutely determines the size of the other part:*

Jessy and I were playing the card game Casino, but using a modified scoring system: the winner was the one who took in the most cards. Ordinarily we each counted our own cards at the end of the game, which gave her good practice in counting. But this time I counted mine quickly and said, "I'll bet I know how many you have." She took up the challenge and I gave her the right answer. When her count confirmed my answer she was amazed. "How did you know that?" she asked. I explained that since there were exactly 52 cards in the deck, I merely subtracted my count from 52, and that gave me her count. I clarified by asking her, "If we were playing with a deck of six cards, and I took in four, how many would you have taken in?" She knew immediately and appeared to understand the principle.

The next few times we played Casino, I told her what her count would be and she seemed to enjoy confirming my answer. After awhile, I let her finish counting first (she had 31) and asked her to tell me how many I had. At first she moaned, "That's too hard for me," but then her eyes lit up and she asked, "How much is 52 minus 31?" Since I knew that she could do this kind of subtraction, I said, "You tell me." She ran to her desk, worked out the subtraction with pencil and paper, and proudly announced her answer, which was correct.

Her understanding was apparent the next day when I asked her "If in Casino I had 51 cards at the end of the game, how many would you have?" She said, "One—but that couldn't be. You can't have less than two because you always have to take in a card with another card."

Here is an example of a parent explaining the concept of mathematical sampling to a child of 6 years, 11 months:

We were driving home from summer vacation and Stu said "I'll bet nobody could count how many trees are on that mountain." I agreed, but added, "You know, sometimes people who take care of forests have to know how many trees are on a mountain to tell if the forest is healthy or if too many trees are dying. Do you know how they could tell about how many trees there are without counting them all?" He asked how.

I told him to imagine a giant checker board lying on the mountain, a glass board through which we could still see the trees. He said he could imagine it and I continued: "If you were walking in the forest under that checker board, it wouldn't be that hard to count the trees in one square, would it?" "Not if the square wasn't very big," he said. "Well, if we found that one square had 100 trees, and another square had about 100 trees too, and so did a third square, then it would be a safe guess that all the squares had about 100 trees. Then all we'd have to do is count the number of squares that covered the mountain and that would tell us how many hundred trees were on the mountain. If nine squares covered the mountain, we could figure that there are 900 trees up there. It wouldn't be exact, but it would give us a pretty close estimate.

Then if we did the same thing 10 years later and found that now there were only about 50 trees in a square, what would that tell us?" "That a lot of trees had died or been cut down and new ones hadn't grown in their place," he answered.

This is a somewhat simplified description of sampling procedures. Since the child in this story had never been introduced to the idea of taking an "average"—an important part of sampling—it would have been a mistake to present this complex notion while trying to provide a broad understanding of how sampling works.

Let's look at what's involved in mathematical reasoning (or any form of symbolic reasoning):

1. The reasoning process is initiated by a problem (how to count trees, how to determine the area of a triangle, how to prove that an equation is true).

2. To begin to work on the problem you have to know what all the terms in the problem mean. You can't start solving the problem, "Show that if a function has an inverse, it has only one," unless you know what "function" and "inverse" mean.

3. You also have to know the rules for manipulating the symbols in the problem. Consider the problem:

Prove that there is only one number (not zero) in which $x(x - 1) = 0$.

To solve this you would have to know the rules pertaining to each of the symbols, including the parentheses. For instance, you'd have to know what a minus and an equals sign mean, that x stands for a quantity you must discover, that parentheses indicate that you multiply the quantity inside by the quantity outside, and that to multiply expressions in this form each quantity inside the parentheses must be multiplied by the quantity outside (that is, you must multiply x times x, which equals x^2; and x times -1, which equals $-x$).

4. To really understand the question and proceed systematically you must know the general principles of the domain you are working in. For instance, to solve the above problem, you'd need to know that the only time a multiplication results in a zero is when one of the quantities multiplied is zero; in other words, that any number times zero equals zero. Clearly the only way to get a zero into the left side of the equation is for x to

equal *1*, making the quantity inside the parentheses (*1* − *1*), which of course equals zero. Therefore *x* must equal *1*, and no other number will work.

Step number 4 is the difficult part in symbolic problem solving. Steps 2 and 3 deal with definitions and technical procedures that can usually be mastered with practice, much like learning to follow a recipe. Success with step 4 depends on understanding what the answer has to look like or at least what procedures are likely to be useful (such as that one must come up with a zero on the left side, or that the question calls for a diagram, or that a particular mathematical law applies, or that an orderly trial-and-error approach is required, or that it would be best to convert to logarithms or to a geometric format). To succeed on step 4, one needs to understand what mathematician Alan Schoenfeld has called the "deep structure" of the problem. In other words, using the metaphor employed earlier in this section, one needs to recognize the "red flags" in a problem and know what actions they signify.

There is convincing evidence that this can be taught. Schoenfeld found that mathematics students who were taught problem-solving "heuristics" or strategies along with standard mathematical instruction, performed much better on posttraining problems than similar students who were given only the standard instructions (which consisted of sample problems and worked-out solutions). Similarly, the excellent "Odyssey: A Curriculum for Thinking" program markedly improved the problem-solving and intellectual competency skills of seventh-grade boys and girls.[28]

Let's take a look at a couple of problems in order to illustrate an orderly approach to problem solving. The first problem, shown in Figure 1, is typical of those used in the "Odyssey" program but is actually adapted from a paper by Schoenfeld.[29] The second and third problems, shown in Figures 2 and 3, are from the "Odyssey" program.

Place each of the numbers *1* through *9* in one of the boxes below so that the sum of every column, row, and diagonal is the same.

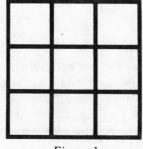

Figure 1

What do we know that can get us started solving the first problem? We know enough to figure out what the sum of each column, row, and diagonal must be. The numbers *1* through *9* add up to *45*. Since the three columns (or three rows) would use all the numbers, then each column (and row) must equal one-third of *45*, or *15*.

Can we break the problem up to determine the placement of at least one number? Yes. Since the center box enters into a sum with every other box (down, across, and the two diagonals), it would help if we could determine its number. Let's try some "extreme cases" to set some limits. A little calculation will quickly show that the center can't be *9* because when it is in a row or column with *8, 7,* or *6,* the sum would exceed *15.* We can't use *8, 7,* and *6* for the same reason. Similarly, we can't put *1, 2, 3,* or *4* in the middle because some of the sums would then fall below *15.* So that leaves *5* for the center.

Are there any constraints on the placement of the other numbers? Yes. If we put *1* in the upper left corner, then *9* has to go at the bottom right (so the diagonal adds to *15*). But then *9* would have to enter into two more sums: the bottom row and the right column. This can't work because if we make the bottom row *9, 4,* and *2* (to equal *15*), then the right column (which must also equal *15*) would have to contain *9, 3,* and *3.* But a number can only be used once. So *1* and *9* have to go into a middle row or column (for convenience, try the middle column, with *1* on top). *Eight* then has to go into a corner, next to *1,* so that *8, 1,* and *6* can form the top row (notice that you can't put *7* with *1* since you'd have to use *7* twice to make *15; 5* is already taken; and smaller numbers added to *1* won't add up to *15*). Once the numbers for the central column and top row are in place, all the other placements follow automatically by making all sums equal *15.*

As Schoenfeld points out, there is another way to solve this problem that uses different information about what the answer has to look like. If you look at the boxes above you'll see we need eight triplets (three rows, three columns, and two diagonals). If we list all the triplets of the numbers *1* through *9* that add up to *15* we come up with the following eight:

1,5,9   1,6,8   2,4,9   2,5,8   2,6,7   3,4,8   3,5,7   4,5,6.

Look again at the boxes in Figure 1 and you'll see that the center square participates in four triplets, the corners participate in three, and the side boxes participate in two. Now, if you look at the list of triplets, you'll see that the number *5* is the only one that appears in four of them, so *5* must go in the center. The even numbers *2, 4, 6, 8* each appear in three triplets, so they must go in the corners. The numbers *1, 3, 7, 9* each appear in two triplets so they must go into the side boxes. A little trial and error will show which even numbers have to go into which corner boxes; going clockwise, *2,4,6,8* won't work since *4* and *6* (and *2* and *8*) have to be on opposite ends of a diagonal, with *5* in between, in order to add to *15*. The clockwise order *2,6,8,4* will solve the problem.

The next problem involves decoding:

Figure out what number each letter represents in the problem below:

$$
\begin{array}{r}
L\ E\ E\ R \\
+\ B\ B\ E\ R \\
\hline
R\ A\ M\ A\ L
\end{array}
$$

What information is given? Two quantities are added together; there are six different numbers represented by the letters *A,B,E,L,M,R;* some numbers are repeated; the two quantities to be added are four-digit numbers so they must be between 1,000 and 9,999, and their sum must equal at least 10,000.

Are there any constraints on what the numbers can be? In other words, are there any "flags?" Yes. We can see that *R*, which occurs three times, must be *1*. This is because the *R* under the plus sign is a carryover from *L* + *B*, and there is no way for a carryover from the sum of two numbers to be more than *1*. *L*, then, must be *2* (*L* = *R* + *R*). We now know that *A* has to be *0* since *L* equals *2* *and* *L* plus *B* produces a carryover. *Two* will produce a carryover only when added to *8* or *9* (*8* + *2* = *10; 9* + *2* = *11*). But the sum of *2* plus *B* can't equal *11* because then *A* would have to equal *1* and we already know that *R* equals *1*. So *B* plus *2* must equal *10*, making *A* equal *0*. Now *E* is easy to get. Since *A* is *0*, *E* plus *E* must be *10*. Therefore, *E* must be *5*.

Because we've established that *L* is *2* and that *B* plus *2* equals *10*, then *B* must be a *7* or *8;* it must be *8* if there is no carryover from the previous column (*8* + *2* = *10*) and it must be *7* if there is a carryover (*7* + *2* + *1* = *10*). Since there is a carryover, *B* must be *7*. We know there is a carryover because we have already learned that *E* equals *5*, and *5* plus *7* or *5* plus *8* both produce a carryover. With *B* set at *7*, *M* must be *3* (since *5* + *7*, plus *1* that was carried over from the previous column, adds to *13*). So now we have decoded the entire sum:

$$
\begin{array}{r}
2\ 5\ 5\ 1 \\
+\ 7\ 7\ 5\ 1 \\
\hline
1\ 0\ 3\ 0\ 2
\end{array}
$$

The next problem involves reasoning about spatial patterns:

In Figure 2 there are 5 squares. Change the position of just 2 lines so that there are only 4 squares of equal size (you can use toothpicks for convenience).

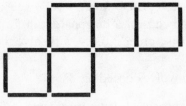

Figure 2

Is there anything we know that can be of help? Any "flags" here? We start out with 16 lines forming 5 squares. We need to end up with 16 lines forming 4 squares.

We can see in the 5-square pattern that 4 of the lines are shared by 2 squares, forming the right side of one and the left side of the adjoining one (or the top and bottom of adjacent squares). But when we divide 16 lines into 4 squares, each line must be part of only one square (since *4 × 4 = 16*). None can be shared (picture 4 squares and count the lines). So our task is to move 2 lines so that no line is shared by 2 squares.

Now that the constraints are clear, some trial and error movements should produce the pattern in Figure 3.

With practice on these kinds of problems youngsters begin to spot the "red flags" when faced with similar problems. What's more, they start to hunt for such "flags" or signals when encountering novel problems. Another way of expressing this is to say that a problem consists of an array of *discriminative stimuli*—stimuli that signal what actions to take and not to take. At the most conspicuous level, stimuli like + and − tell a youngster to add or subtract quantities; their messages are simple and direct. At a "deeper" level, stimuli like the lone *R* in the sum in the decoding problem and the relationship between the number of lines and squares in the spatial-pattern problem specify the boundaries to work within.

Recognizing these deeper cues makes the difference between a helter-skelter exploration and a purposeful and systematic one. For instance, Michelene Chi and her colleagues have shown that physics students who recognize the key signals (or red flags) in motion and force problems are much more likely to solve them than those who have to resort to trial-and-error explorations. One such signal is whether the object is moving or stationary,

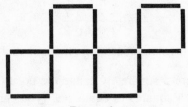

Figure 3

and students who understood that the forces acting on a stationary object always sum to zero (which is why it isn't moving) had a much easier time determining the forces than those who didn't have this knowledge.[30]

When a youngster encounters novel problems he or she may not spot a "red flag" right away, but with instruction and experience the novelty itself becomes a signal, prompting a search for a useful way to organize the information given, including whether there are any constraints that set boundaries on any aspect of the problem. The youngster might, for example, go through a mental checklist of questions, such as the following: "Can I turn anything into a zero?" "Can I ascertain the form the answer must take (such as sets of triplets)?" "Can I plug in numbers to figure out how to proceed?"

Once students start learning to spot the flags in mathematics problems, they need to make sure they read the problems carefully so they aren't fooled by the first flag they see ("Oh, that must be one of those kinds of problems"). Psychologists have used the terms "negative transfer" and "functional fixedness" to describe this tendency to rush into an incorrect solution because a problem appears at first glance to be similar to other problems one has solved.[31] For example, A. S. Luchins gave students a series of "water jug" problems: "You have a water supply and three jugs whose capacities are 21, 127, and 3 quarts, respectively. How can you bring back exactly 100 quarts?" The numbers changed for each problem, but each could be solved the same way: fill the largest jug, pour once into the middle-size jug, and twice into the smallest jug. In the last problem the jugs had the following capacities: 23, 49, and 3—and they had to obtain exactly 20 quarts. Most followed the same procedure they had used before (in other words, they spotted the same flag and went for it), failing to notice the simpler solution of filling the 23 quart jug first and then pouring out 3 quarts into the smallest jug. The moral: Look before you leap.

Reading problems carefully is always important. It is also useful to picture the information given whenever possible. The following problem should illustrate this point:

> A man has 5 pairs of brown socks and 4 pairs of blue socks in his drawer, all mixed together, and he must try to select a pair with his eyes closed. How many socks does he have to remove before he can be sure he has at least one pair of the same color?

This sounds as though it takes some special math procedures to solve, but if you picture the man removing one sock at a time, you'll quickly discover that he only needs to remove three to be sure he has two of the same color.

While parents can find work books that provide lessons in symbolic problem solving, most parents are not going to teach their children mathematical problem solving beyond an elementary level. Still, there are some things they can do. When checking homework make sure your child understands the concepts and has not simply memorized procedures. For instance, if a question asks, "How many 22-seat buses are needed to transport the 50-member chorus to the theater?" and your child's answer is 2.27 buses, you'd have a pretty good idea that he has not understood the question.

Similarly, many basic math notions can be understood in concrete ways. For example, a standard principle in geometry is that in a triangle, the sum of the lengths of any two sides is greater than the length of the third side. A child might memorize this and not really understand it. But by picturing what it says, the truth of the statement becomes obvious. Any child can perceive that a straight line is the shortest distance between two points.

Perhaps the most important thing parents can do is stimulate their child's delight in mathematical problem solving. Solving mathematical problems is akin to solving puzzles and it isn't difficult to get children interested in them. Try to emphasize the game aspects of the problem solving and try to make it a natural part of your interactions. For instance, you might get into the habit of springing a problem on your child at odd times—when driving in the car or going for a walk. Try challenging her with a playful, "Oh, you'll never get this one," and use contexts that will spark her interest ("Here's one about 6 hungry puppies who found 18 hot dogs"). When she finally gets the right answer, regardless of how many hints you had to give, make her feel good about her achievement. If a problem proves too difficult, acknowledge that she hasn't been taught the required skills yet, and that when she learns them, this will be an easy problem for her.

An important skill in mathematical problem solving is being able to recognize and ignore irrelevant information. You can introduce your child to this notion by presenting simple problems with irrelevant information, such as, "A family went on a picnic and took 4 apples, 3 bananas, and 6 hot dogs. How many fruits did they take on the picnic?"

It is unfortunate that mathematics is usually taught as a set of procedures and not as a grand human adventure, beginning thousands of years ago when ancient peoples tried to keep track of stored grain and other valuables. Perhaps more students would be inspired by math, or at least appreciate it as an exciting area of human striving, if they learned more about the lives of mathematicians and the nature of their quests—for instance, that Newton invented the calculus, not to torture undergraduates, but because he was deeply intrigued by the way things in the real world change from moment to moment, and there was no efficient way to describe those changes. The great mathematicians—Pythagoras, Euclid, Archimedes, Pascal, Fermat, Descartes, Newton, Gauss, among others—have influenced our world as much as any other figures in history. Without their contributions almost all modern technology would be impossible.

When youngsters recognize the practical value of mathematics—that it can help you come back from the store with correct change or help you land a rocket on Mars, they are more motivated to master it. When mathematics is taught simply as a set of formulas and operations, rather than as a passionate human adventure and a valuable set of tools, important sources of inspiration are omitted from the instruction. Moreover, unless students are taught about the kinds of problems mathematicians grapple with, what excites them and what they debate about, there is no way they can understand or participate in mathematics as an ongoing creative endeavor.

10

❦

Ordinary and Extraordinary Intelligence

Giftedness and IQ Tests

Individual Differences in Problem Solving: "Gifted" Children

Children will differ considerably in their acquisition of the problem-solving skills described above. Some will become proficient in one or more areas relatively easily, needing minimal instruction; others will have great difficulty and require intensive tutoring. Some, like da Vinci, will do well in many areas; others in only one. No one knows what these differences are based on.

In any case, it is a useful assumption that any normal child can become at least competent in any area of problem solving with proper instruction. It may be that the average child will take longer than the prodigy and may never achieve the same level, but there are many cases of late bloomers who went on to do exceptional work in a field that they seemed at first to have no gift for. And prodigies sometimes "burn out" and lose interest in their special field, and perhaps even lose their special abilities. Educators working with children who have extraordinary "gifts" in an area argue forcefully for a curriculum tailored to these unusual abilities. As an example of such a child, Julian Stanley and Camilla Persson Benbow describe a boy who at the age of 6:

> mastered 2 years of high school algebra. At age 7 he enrolled in a standard high school geometry course but found it too slow-paced and therefore finished the book on his own before Christmas. He also taught himself trigonometry. Before age 7½ he had scored at the 99th percentile

on standardized tests of Algebra I-III, geometry, and trigonometry. His SAT-M score at age 7 was 670, the 91st percentile of college-bound male high school seniors.[1]

Clearly, a child with such extraordinary abilities will be out of place in a standard mathematics class. As Stanley and Benbow put it, he or she will have:

> . . . no really appropriate way to behave. He or she can daydream, be excessively meticulous in order to get perfect grades, harass the teacher, show off knowledge arrogantly in the class, or be truant. There is, however, no *suitable* way to while away the class hours when one already knows much of the material and can learn the rest almost instantaneously as it is first presented. Boredom, frustration, and habits of gross inattention are almost sure to result.

Parents of children who are gifted in math or any other area should look into special programs. But, sometimes parents worry that their gifted child will turn into an oddball or be rejected by other children. Gifted children are certainly unusual, but contrary to myth, they are not inevitably more troubled than other children. Research shows that they are a mixed lot and generally do fine if they find an environment that supports their special abilities. They often prefer older friends and devote much more time to their work than other children, but their work is a great source of pleasure for them.[2]

In grade school, children become increasingly aware of and concerned about individual differences in problem solving ability.[3] It is an issue for most children, but most handle it without noticeable difficulty. Some children, though, become excessively competitive, and some suffer a decline in self-esteem when others appear to be smarter. Still others may become intellectual snobs, flaunting their superior abilities. Parents need to be sensitive to how their children are dealing with such comparisons.

It can be helpful to stress that each person is unique and capable of his or her own special contribution and that many "nongifted" youngsters have gone on to great success by using their particular qualities and abilities to advantage. Precociousness and achievement don't go hand in hand and many who progressed at a slower pace (or through a different route) have achieved the goals they set for themselves. The story of the tortoise and the hare may help a child who is upset because others are progressing at a faster pace.

Competitive children need to be taught lessons in good sportsmanship and that it is truly possible to appreciate and applaud the fine work of others even when envying their success. The love of excellence can go a long way toward offsetting natural feelings of disappointment. Stress that the real competition is with the unknown and the unsolved—not with others who may be working on the same thing. The achievements of others can be useful as a guide to what to strive toward, but not as a sign of one's own inferiority. There is a story that as a young man Beethoven was walking through the park with a friend and upon hearing some brilliant music by Mozart at an open-air concert, lamented that he'd never be able to accomplish anything like that. And he was right. His music was nothing like Mozart's, for which music lovers the world over are grateful. Mozart supposedly wrote effortlessly, with little need of revision—more the hare than the tortoise (although the evidence for this is suspect); Beethoven rewrote laboriously—more the tortoise than the hare.

If your child is gifted, you may also want to try instilling the sense that with special gifts comes a special obligation. Einstein expressed it this way:

> A hundred times a day I remind myself that my inner and outer life are based on the labors of other men, living and dead, and that I must exert myself in order to give in the same measure as I have received and am still receiving.

Actually, with any child, it is worth inspiring a sense of responsibility for using his mind to its fullest capacity. You can do this by making him aware of the long human struggle to improve the quality of life—to cure illness, grow enough food for everyone, and create a more humane and beautiful world—and how each of us, even those who lead ordinary lives in ordinary jobs, can join that struggle and advance those goals by using our abilities fully.

Measuring Problem-Solving Potential: IQ Tests

The key word here is "potential." IQ tests are supposed to do more than measure what people (children and adults) know. And the tests would be of little value if all they measured was one's ability to answer questions like those asked on the tests. IQ tests are supposed to tell us more than that; their purpose is to measure learning or problem solving *potential*—in other words, a person's intellectual capability across a wide range of problem-solving domains.

When the first modern intelligence tests were developed early in this century by Alfred Binet in France, their purpose was to assess which youngsters had sufficient intellectual potential to benefit from education. Binet's test was to serve as a diagnostic tool. His test has gone through many revisions and adaptations, and many other intelligence tests have been developed over the past 80 years, but the main purpose of all remains the same: the evaluation of learning and problem-solving potential. In contrast, when we want to evaluate someone's knowledge or ability in a particular area we use an "Achievement Test" with questions covering only that area.

Well, are IQ test scores useful for predicting children's learning and problem-solving capability? For example, are youngsters who score high on IQ tests likely to do well in the problem-solving domains described in the previous chapter? In some of the domains the answer would certainly be yes. IQ scores correlate highly with mathematical and symbolic problem solving and also with the kind of logical reasoning that goes into diagnostic and inductive problem solving. This is to be expected since IQ questions cover these areas.

But IQ tests don't evaluate imaginative (artistic) problem solving so we shouldn't be surprised if someone with a high IQ turns out not to be very imaginative; nor should it astonish us if someone with an average IQ becomes an exceptional artist. Similarly, since IQ tests don't stress tactical problem solving, a resourceful and street-smart police officer might have only an average IQ, despite uncommon tactical problem-solving abilities. Nor are IQ scores likely to distinguish the brilliant comedian despite his or her genius at spotting unexpected connections between disparate things and a masterful sensitivity to what makes people laugh.

IQ tests are generally *validated* on only certain areas of problem solving—those related to school achievement. The "validity" of a test is of great importance; it tells us what a test can legitimately claim to be measuring. IQ tests are called tests of intelligence but what do the test constructors actually mean by intelligence? How can they (or we) be sure that's what the tests are evaluating?

To say that IQ tests are validated on school achievement is to say that they are a good gauge of the likelihood of doing well in school. In other words, the tests are constructed so that there is a fairly high correlation between IQ scores and school grades—the higher a youngster's IQ score, the more likely he or she will be a high achiever in school. This is referred to as the "predictive" or "criterion" validity of the test. When the tests are made up, the test constructors try out many questions and keep only those that differentiate youngsters in terms of school grades.

So, technically, IQ tests are valid measures of intelligence only with respect to the kinds of intelligence required for success in school, such as verbal and mathematical abilities. Also keep in mind that because the correlation between IQ scores and school performance isn't perfect, the tests don't always provide accurate predictions: there are many children with relatively high IQs who don't do well in school (called "underachievers") and many with relatively low IQs who do. But, on the whole, children's IQ scores, from about the age of five on, are pretty good predictors of school achievement (infant IQ scores don't correlate well with later IQ scores or with school achievement and are primarily useful for diagnosing sensory, motor, and attentional problems).

Although most IQ tests are validated on school achievement, they also have some value for predicting success in life outside of and beyond school, although their accuracy here is considerably less than for school achievement. Obviously, the kinds of skills that are useful in school are also useful in many other domains, and high achievers in school, on average, do better than peers in later pursuits. The value of IQ tests for predicting career success is greatest for extreme cases. Those scoring toward the retarded end of the IQ scale are very unlikely to be successful later in life. In contrast, those scoring extremely high are quite likely to have lives of outstanding achievement. For example, Lewis Terman and his colleagues studied over 1,000 children with IQs of 140 or higher throughout their lives and found them to be unusually successful in virtually all spheres, including occupational achievement, family and community life, and mental and physical health.[4]

For those who score in the more middle range of IQ tests, predictions about their future lives are more uncertain. This may be because there are practical problem-solving skills that are useful in the world beyond school that the tests don't tap, such as social and other tactical skills which are important for success in sales, supervision, and other endeavors that require teamwork and "people management."[5] The tests may also be less accurate because there are many other factors besides problem-solving skills that go into real-world success, factors like motivation, family wealth and connections, and peer influences, as well as the luck of being in the right place at the right time.

There are several different kinds of IQ tests that are given to children. Some are "individual" tests, administered by a psychologist to one child at a time. The two most widely used individual tests are the Stanford-Binet Intelligence Scale (an adaptation of Binet's original test by Louis Terman and his associates at Stanford University) and the Wechsler Intelligence Scale for Children (also called the WISC-R, the "R" standing for Revised Version), developed by David Wechsler and his associates.

There are a number of "group" tests, administered to large numbers of children at the same time, such as the Lorge-Thorndike and Primary Mental Abilities tests. School systems often use group tests for a general evaluation of their student bodies and for placing students in appropriate classes, including accelerated and gifted programs. They will use individual tests when they need a more detailed picture of a child's functioning, such as when evaluating him or her for a special education program.

The predictive validity of IQ tests is as noted above, fairly good, but test constructors also try to give them other kinds of validity, such as *construct* and *content* validity. That is, they try to ask questions on the test that fit their understanding of what the term intelligence means and that include a reasonable sample of possible test items. Whether or not the standard intelligence tests are indeed valid measures of intelligence is hotly debated by psychologists. Some items, like vocabulary words ("Define *ball, hat, stove, dozen*") and fact knowledge ("Who discovered America?" "What is the capital of France?"), appear to have more to do with cultural background than inherent intellectual potential. In addition, as I've mentioned, some areas of intelligence, seem to be largely neglected, such as tactical and imaginative problem solving.

During recent decades a number of intelligence tests have been developed that strive for greater validity in terms of our intuitive ideas about intelligence. These include "culture-free" or "culture-fair" tests, which seek to eliminate any biases in the questions that might favor one ethnic or economic group over another. Howard Gardner and Robert Sternberg are reported to be developing tests of intelligence based on their theories (see chapter 3)— tests that will cover a broader range of abilities than do current tests.

IQ Test Scores

IQ tests are devised so that the average score is 100. A guiding principle behind intelligence test construction is that intelligence is distributed "normally" in the population, meaning that most children should score fairly close to average, while extremely high or low scores should be rare. That is, there should be relatively few children who score 75 or 125, and even fewer who score 65 or 135. On all the major IQ tests, the more extreme the score in either direction, the less often it is found, generating a "bell shaped curve" when the distribution of individual scores is plotted on a graph.

IQ scores were originally computed as a quotient by dividing the child's mental age (MA) by his chronological age (CA) and multiplying by 100 (to avoid decimals). Mental age is based on how well the child answers the questions on the test. If he answers them like the average 10-year-old, then his mental age is ten. If his chronological age is also ten, his score is 100 (10/10 × 100). If his mental age is higher than his chronological age his IQ will be above a hundred (a mental age of 12 for a 10-year-old will give an IQ score of 120). If his mental age is lower than his chronological age, his IQ will be less than 100. The computational methods have been altered somewhat but the basic formulation is the same: children's IQ scores are based on how well they perform compared to age-mates. Obviously, the questions for a 14-year-old are much more difficult than those for a 6-year-old.

Testers sometimes describe scores in terms of "percentiles," which refers to what percentage of the population an individual's scores are above. For instance, a score in the 90th percentile is equal to or higher than the scores of 90 percent of the population. Another frequently used term is the "standard deviation," which can be used to locate a score within a population of scores. This is a statistical concept that refers to the percentage of scores that fall within specified distances from the mean. For instance, when scores on an intelligence test are distributed normally, as theory says they should be, 68.26 percent of individuals fall within one standard deviation from the mean, half above it and half below. So, when an individual's score is said to be one standard deviation above the mean, we know that his score falls within the same range above the mean as 34.14 percent of the population. Describing scores in terms of percentiles and standard deviations are useful because they tell us where an individual's score falls with respect to the scores of other individuals; in other words, how common or uncommon this particular individual's score is.

Following are some of the areas covered by standard IQ tests, along with some sample questions drawn from different tests and covering different age levels. Note that not all of these assess problem solving directly; many questions examine areas, such as memory, vocabulary, and general knowledge, which are presumed to contribute to the child's ability to solve problems. Different tests group items differently. I have organized them in terms of verbal skills, performance skills, general information and concept knowledge, memory, reasoning, and quantitative skills:

Verbal Skills
- Word knowledge (knowing the meaning of "summer," "nonsense," "belfry," etc.);
- Sentence comprehension, including telling sensible from foolish sentences ("Mrs. Smith has no children, and I understand the same was true for her mother");
- Knowledge of rhymes ("What color rhymes with Fred?");
- Decoding (copying symbols from a key to decode a message).

Performance Skills
- Visual-motor skills (copying a simple bridge or a complex pattern constructed out of blocks; copying a drawing of a circle or a square; traversing a maze; copying a knot);

General Information and Concept Knowledge
- Store of information (naming parts of the body, knowing what the stomach does, naming the days of the week, knowing what makes water freeze);
- Recognition of opposites ("In daytime it is light: at night it is ____'');
- Awareness of common concepts (knowing what goes with "Gives milk");
- Ability to discern similarities and differences (similarities between an apple and a peach, an elbow and knee, or an inch and a mile; differences between misery and poverty, or character and reputation);
- Knowledge of functions (knowing what books or houses are for, or in what ways a lamp is better than a candle);
- Ability to apply prior knowledge (naming the missing parts in pictures of familiar objects, such as a car without a steering wheel);

Memory
- Memory for what's been seen, heard, or read (selecting a previously seen picture from an array of pictures, or remembering a series of numbers; or being able to answer questions about a story read to them);

Reasoning
- Recognition of analogical relationships (Birds are to flying as fish are to ____?);
- Logical abilities (such as placing pictures of a sequence of events in a sensible order);
- Ability to analyze a complex stimulus into its parts, and recognize which parts make up a whole (for example, by placing two halves together to form a picture of a rectangle or a common object);
- Ability to make inferences (determining how many holes there will be in a folded piece of paper that the examiner notches);

Quantitative Skills
- Competency with numeration and understanding of mathematical concepts such as "more than," "less than," "add to," and "take away from" (as well as the ability to give the examiner the correct number of blocks when asked, to use subtraction for making change, and to figure out story problems: "At 12 cents each, how much will 4 bars of soap cost?");

The specific questions vary from test to test and are different for different age groups (for instance, copying a square is at the 5-year-old level and the "notched paper" problem is at the 14-year-old level). Along with an overall IQ score, most tests provide a profile of the child's intellectual functioning based on "subtest" scores that give information on strengths and weaknesses in various areas. For example, one child might do better in logical reasoning than visual motor skills; another will do better in math than verbal comprehension.

Can training raise a child's IQ? A number of studies report that it can, but results have varied from substantial to moderate to no significant improvement.[6] Unfortunately, with many intelligence training programs, it is not always clear that the program was actually training for the skills tapped by an IQ test. When one breaks down an IQ test into each of the specific skills covered, it is clear that each can be learned by any normal child with proper instruction. If children improve on these skills their IQs will go up.

But, if we help children improve on just these skills, are we increasing their intellectual "potential," or merely making them better IQ test takers? If IQ tests truly tap essential intellectual skills (such as concept learning, text comprehension, and logic), then we can expect that if we increase a child's abilities in these areas, it will beget improved performance in any domains that are based on these essential skills. I'm not suggesting simply training children to memorize answers to IQ questions, but rather to provide instruction that enables them to perform well on the types of problems that the tests cover.

Put differently, it is best to consider IQ scores a measure of a child's current level of performance in the various areas evaluated by the test, and to use the results to diagnose his or her specific intellectual strengths and weaknesses (and not as a way to pigeonhole the child as smart, average, or dumb). By knowing children's specific intellectual strengths and weaknesses, we are better able to plan educational programs for them, ones that build on their strengths and remediate their weaknesses. We are also in a better position to guide them toward school and career choices that are consistent with their abilities. Unfortunately, because IQ scores are often thought of as measures of children's inherent and immutable mental capabilities, the potentially useful, detailed diagnostic information they provide is rarely used in an effective way.

Are IQ tests racially biased? Black children, *on the average,* don't score as high on IQ tests as white children, and some psychologists, educators, and civil rights leaders say this is because the tests are racially biased. They argue that the tests were originally "standardized" on white, middle-class children—meaning that the questions and scoring system are based on what white, middle-class children know, not on what black children know. There have been attempts to create unbiased or culture-free tests, which attempt to replace culture-bound questions with those that tap more basic intellectual skills. For instance, an inner-city black child is not likely to score well on a question requiring some knowledge of farm life. Clearly, a rural child will have an advantage here, and even an urban middle-class child is more likely than his inner-city schoolmate to have been exposed to farm life through books, museums, or vacation trips.

The jury remains out on whether one can construct a truly culture-free IQ test that still has construct and predictive validity—a test that still appears to measure what we mean by intelligence and continues to make accurate predictions about who will do well in school and career. A culture-free test that isn't valid in these two ways would be of little value. Moreover, even if researchers came up with a truly culture-free test, we would still be faced with the fact that a poor score tells us nothing about what the child might be capable of learning with suitable instruction.

Actually, the cultural bias of IQ tests is only an issue if people (teachers, parents, the children themselves) think of the tests as measuring some immutable entity called intelligence. When one interprets IQ that way, then a poor score by a child becomes a sure sign of future failure, and the child gets treated accordingly. But this kind of problem does not arise and the question of a test's cultural bias becomes less important if, as I've suggested, we think of IQ scores only as indications of current problem-solving strengths and weaknesses in particular areas, and use the data from the scores to teach children the skills and information they haven't yet mastered.

11

☙

Creativity

Creativity is possible in all the problem solving areas described in the last chapter. The creative solution is not just a good solution, it is unique in some way. It gives better answers to old questions or asks significant new questions that no one thought to ask before. But what makes some people more creative than others? Are they simply more intelligent? In one sense, yes. If we are to remain consistent with our definition of intelligence as problem solving ability, creative people are, by definition, the most intelligent since they come up with the best solutions.

But, a number of studies show that the most creative people are not necessarily the highest scorers on standard tests of intelligence—although they do generally score well above average.[1] Moreover, some of the great creative achievers—Einstein, van Gogh, Darwin, the physicist Erwin Schrödinger, among many others—were not recognized as exceptionally brilliant by their teachers, fellow students, or colleagues before their major achievements were published (regrettably, van Gogh's genius was not recognized until after his death). If their contemporaries had taken a vote on who among them was most likely to make the major breakthroughs, none of these would have been chosen.

In addition, while some creative giants, like da Vinci and Michelangelo, made outstanding contributions in more than one area, most have not been especially noted for their brilliance outside their areas of expertise. And even within their areas of expertise, our most eminent creators frequently fell on their eminent faces. Einstein spent much of his later career trying unsuccessfully to disprove quantum theory. The great nineteenth century physicist, Lord Kelvin, refused to accept the electromagnetic theory of light. Isaac Newton, who many consider the greatest scientist of all time, spent years vainly pursuing problems in alchemy. Shakespeare wrote some pretty bad plays and T. S. Eliot some pretty mediocre poems.

In other words, creative people don't necessarily have more raw brain power that sets them inevitably and invariably above others in their field.

Yet they do manage to come up with breathtaking solutions at least some of the time, and some (like Newton and Shakespeare) do it a great many times. A full understanding of creativity should not only account for creative successes, but also for the failures.

In trying to account for creativity, we will look at three key characteristics of creative people: their passion for innovation, extraordinary devotion to their work, and their "catalytic strategies."

A Passion for Innovation

One characteristic of creative people is that they love problems. They are not merely good problem solvers; they are problem *seekers*. They embrace problems. But not any problems. They seek out problems that will allow them to make a personal contribution that advances their field in some way. As Einstein and Infeld described it:

The formulation of a problem is often more essential than its solution, which may be merely a matter of mathematical or experimental skill.

To raise new questions, new possibilities, to regard old problems from a new angle, requires creative imagination and marks real advance in science.[2]

This passion for innovation can occur in any endeavor requiring problem solving—in science, art, industry, sports, crafts, management, law, among others. Some cooks are content following good recipes. Others strive to develop their own dishes and are willing to risk many failures for one exceptional outcome. Some artists are satisfied if they can paint good paintings in the style of Picasso. Whenever Picasso found himself painting in the style of Picasso, he changed his style. Some doctoral and postdoctoral researchers are pleased to work on problems set by their mentors. Others, like James Watson and Francis Crick, who broke the genetic code, are dedicated to pursuing their own vision.

In other words, creativity is, I believe more often than not, the product of a deliberate striving to carve out one's own path. People who distinguish themselves as creative are *motivated* to carve out a distinctive path—a motivation that will find expression in any area that becomes a central pursuit (but not necessarily in their peripheral interests; a creative scientist who enjoys playing the violin may not have any creative aspirations as a musician). Contemporary research with art students supports this position. The problem seekers in the group produced paintings that were judged to be more original and of greater "aesthetic value" than fellow students without this orientation—and they were more likely to have gained recognition as artists five years after graduation.[3]

The importance of problem seeking to creative achievement is also supported by some examples from acting. Laurence Olivier's portrayal of Shakespeare's Richard III is widely regarded as one of the great achievements in acting. But in an interview Olivier related that when he was first offered the opportunity to play Richard he considered turning it down. Another actor had recently done a highly praised version of the part and Olivier felt that because he had nothing new to bring to it, it wasn't worth doing. Most actors don't think this way. They strive mainly to be believable, not necessarily original.

It was only after Olivier discovered an unusual (and insightful) approach to the character that he became excited about doing the role. Marlon Brando expressed a similar motivation in describing his portrayal of an old-West character in the film, *Missouri Breaks*. He said he wanted to play a Western character unlike any he, or any other actor, had ever played before. Again, most actors don't set this as their task.

Many other creative people have expressed this same compulsion for originality—their self-esteem depending, not merely on doing a good job within already established boundaries, but on breaking through those boundaries. The painter Jasper Johns, describing the course he set during his early years as an artist, refers to his commitment *not* to become an abstract expressionist, the dominant style of painting at that time: "I didn't want to do what they did. . . . I decided that if my work contained what I could identify as a likeness to other work, I would remove it." Stephen Sondheim, generally considered the most creative composer in today's musical theater, explained his pursuit of innovation more experientially: "It comes from a feeling of not wanting to cover the same material twice or to bore yourself."[4]

When the motivation for innovation goes unsatisfied, despondency ensues. Picasso expressed his motivation for innovations vividly: "I have a horror of copying myself." Moreover he was highly critical of young artists who did not make innovation a central concern:

> With the exception of some painters who are opening new horizons to painting, the youth of today do not know any more where to go. Instead of taking up our researches in order to react sharply against us, they apply themselves to reanimating the past. Yet the world is open before us, everything is still to be done, and not to be done over again. Why hang on hopelessly to everything that has fulfilled its promise? There are kilometers of painting in the manner of; but it is rare to see a young man working in his own way.[5]

Researcher Donald MacKinnon asked professionals in a number of fields (including scientists, mathematicians, engineers, poets, novelists, and architects) to rate the creativity of their colleagues. He then compared the high and low "creatives" on a number of measures and reported the following about their respective motivations for creativity. Using the architects for illustration, he wrote:

> Above all else he thinks of himself as imaginative; unquestionably committed to creative endeavor; unceasingly striving for creative solutions to the difficult problems he repeatedly sets for himself; satisfied only with solutions that are original and that meet his own high standards of architectural excellence; aesthetically sensitive; an independent spirit free from crippling restraints and impoverishing inhibitions; spontaneous; forthright, and self-accepting. He has a sense of destiny about his career as an architect. . . . and the differences between more and less creative architects are essentially the same as the differences between the more and less creative members of all the groups we have assessed.[6]

This passion for innovation can be found in people engaged in professions that we don't ordinarily associate with creativity. In an interview, the great basketball player Michael Jordan referred to the importance of creativity to his success. He explained that if an opposing team can figure out a way to stop him in a game, he will figure out a way to make sure they can't use the same defense again. "I'm a fan of creativity," he explained with a grin.

Where does this passion for innovation come from? There are many sources. A prominent one is the desire for immortality. History doesn't remember the artists who painted "in the manner of," and Nobel Prizes are not awarded to diligent disciples who follow in their mentors' footsteps; nor will the portals of the Hall of Fame open for athletes who weren't able to outsmart their opponents.

But it is not simply ego I'm referring to, not primarily. It is ideals— the love of splendid achievement more than the love of self. Recall our discussion of the mastery drive. In the child it is expressed in being able to climb the staircase, zip the zipper, open the cabinet, etc. If children could tell us why they want to do these things, their answer would resemble Sir Edmund Hillary's when he was asked why he wanted to climb Mt. Everest: "Because it's there."

But this powerful drive to master what's out there, gets channelled as the child's culture begins to define for him what is worth mastering. He learns from parents, friends, teachers, and the media that mastery means being the smartest, or the richest, or the highest scorer, or the most stylish, or the wittiest, or the nicest, etc. Now, when he begins to pursue any of these goals we call it a drive for excellence—intellectual excellence, athletic excellence, moral excellence, artistic excellence, etc. And if he is also taught that in any of these fields, creative achievement is the highest form of human excellence (and not all cultures teach this), then innovative problem solving becomes the standard for mastery—the ideal toward which to strive.

That ideal (like any ideal) drives one forward, and cries "Courage! Courage!" when one falters. The pantheon of creative heroes inhabit one's thoughts, become one's companions, and one wants to deserve their company. It is *their* approval that counts, *their* watchful eyes that keep one faithful. Einstein said he never felt alone during his years of solitary work on relativity theory; he had Galileo and Newton for company.

The passion for innovation may grow out of boredom and a psychological need for new challenges (as described in the quotation from Stephen Sondheim). More often it derives from a veneration of personal expression and the recognition that since we are all unique, truly personal expression will, of necessity, be innovative. Henry Miller provides an example of this search for one's "own voice." He began this tortuous journey by studying and mimicking the styles of the writers he admired, but this proved worthless:

> Finally I came to a dead end, to a despair and desperation which few men have known. . . . It was at this point . . . that I really began to write. I began from scratch, throwing everything overboard, even those whom I most loved. Immediately I heard my own voice I was enchanted; the fact that it was a separate, distinct, unique voice sustained me. . . . I was whole again.[7]

"Thou shalt find thine own voice!" might be called the First Commandment of Western art. Leonard Bernstein described how, as a young composer, this imperative was impressed upon him by Aaron Copland:

> . . . whenever I came to New York I went to Aaron's. . . . All during those years I would bring him my own music for criticism. . . . I would show Aaron the bits of pieces, and he would say, "All that has to go. . . . This is just pure Scriabin. You've got to get that out of your head and start fresh."[8]

The imperative to find one's own voice is based on the assumption that there is always more to be discovered, new truths, new forms, and that a truly personal perspective will lead to them. Sometimes, though, the imperative, gets misconstrued as a call to be different for its own sake, with results that tend to be bizarre or patternless, and are more likely to appear silly and trivial than startling and imaginative.

Sometimes the drive for innovation comes from a love for the field and a desire to overthrow artificial rules and conventions obstructing the quest for truth. In the following, an angry van Gogh denounces the "academic" approach to art:

> Nothing seems simpler than painting peasants, ragpickers and laborers of all kinds, but—no subjects in painting are so difficult as these commonplace figures! As far as I know there isn't a single academy where one learns to draw and paint a digger, a sower, a woman putting the kettle over the fire or a seamstress. But in every city of some importance there is an academy with a choice of models for historical, Arabic, Louis XV, in short, *all really nonexistent figures*.[9]

Like many a creative thinker, van Gogh saw what others were doing, recoiled, and exclaimed, "No, that's not what it's about! I'll show them." The sense that there is something wrong with what others are doing agitates and ignites the imagination, spurring one to do it better, to do it right. As the choreographer Erick Hawkins put it, "Even with Balanchine, there were places I knew he didn't succeed, where my own awakening heart was seeing that it was not good enough."[10]

This sensitivity to what is wrong is particularly acute in creative scientists and inventors. The discrepancies and inadequacies that most of us disregard or merely grumble about, become sources of irritation and personal challenge to them. The impassioned inventor *must* invent a better mouse-trap. The impassioned scientist *must* make sense of the world.

Scientists who seek creative challenges often fixate on the mismatches between theory and data. When other scientists ignore or try to smooth away theoretical inconsistencies, clinging to the comfort of familiar and neatly wrapped explanations, those who seek creative challenges are drawn to contradictions like magnets, confident that they are the breeding grounds for new theories. Some psychologists have said that creative thinkers can accept more ambiguity than the rest of us. I disagree. They can accept complexity. But ambiguity irks them to the core.

More than once this passion to right wrongs and proclaim a truth has left the creative thinker in a dangerous position, standing alone against powerful authorities. Copernicus and Galileo are the most famous cases, both of whom were accused by the Church of heresy for contradicting Biblical views of the movement of the sun and planets. Galileo sought to defend himself (in vain):

> To command the professors of astronomy to confute their own observations is to enjoin an impossibility, for it is to command them not to see what they do see, and not to understand what they do understand, and to find what they do not discover.[11]

Artists too have had their works banned and burned, and their lives threatened for expressing what those in power didn't want others to hear.

British novelist Salman Rushdie and Czechoslovakian playwright Vaclev Havel are two well-known recent examples. But it is an old story. Shakespeare described it as ''art made tongue-tied by authority'' (in Sonnet 66).

When one reads the ardent outpourings of creative minds, it becomes clear why intelligence tests are of limited value in detecting creative potential in children. IQ-test questions are not designed to assess children's passions for innovation and individual expression, nor their love for a subject; nor their motivation to seek out interesting problems.

So-called tests of creativity have not fared much better.[12] They present various ''original thinking'' problems, such as to think up different ways an object (a steam iron) might be used; or to come up with different titles for short-story plots; or to find associations between apparently unrelated words; or to solve puzzles that require breaking out of customary response patterns. For example, in one puzzle you have to connect all the dots in a grid using a few straight lines; the only way to do this is by extending some of the lines out beyond the boundary of the grid, which few people realize is permissible. In another problem you are given a candle, a book of matches, and a box of tacks, and asked to mount the candle on a wall; the solution requires setting the candle in the box and tacking the box to the wall, but most people don't think to use the box in the solution.

There is no reason to expect that people who manifest real-life creativity will excel on these kinds of problems, which are, essentially, games. In contrast, real-life creativity ordinarily derives from a colossal devotion to the subject matter. On many creativity tests, high scores are obtained by being facile, eccentric, or unconventional (which is why schizophrenics score high on some of them). In the real world, creativity is directed toward meaningful problems, and solutions have to *work*. Novelty is never sufficient.

Extraordinary Devotion to Their Work

Virtually every autobiography and biography of creative men and women refers to the monumental effort that went into their achievements. Creative achievers don't simply work on a problem, they *hound* it—and it hounds them. They have a sense of mission that sustains them through the long stretches of grunt-work and frustration. Einstein, for example, worked doggedly for more than 10 years before coming up with his theory of relativity (starting when he was age 16). In his own words:

> The final results appear almost simple; any intelligent undergraduate
> can understand them without much trouble. But the years of searching

in the dark for a truth that one feels, but cannot express; the intense effort and the alternations of confidence and misgiving, until one breaks through to clarity and understanding, are only known to him who has himself experienced them.[13]

Louis Pasteur expressed the same thought this way:

Let me tell you the secret that has led me to my goal. My strength lies in my tenacity.[14]

Beethoven's notebooks reveal his endless reworking of musical ideas. Contemporaries of Rembrandt wrote that he would spend an excruciating amount of time on every detail, as much time as needed until he got it right—even if he lost a sale. Van Gogh's letters describe him sketching the same subject over and over until he achieved the desired result, achieved what has "already taken form in my mind before I start on it":

If fifty are not enough, I shall draw a hundred, and if that is still not enough, even more, till I have exactly what I want, namely that everything is round and that there is, so to speak, neither beginning nor end to the figure anywhere, but that it makes one harmonious lifelike whole. The only thing to do is to go one's own way, to try one's best, to make the thing live.[15]

These quotations and many others attest to the creative achiever's extraordinary devotion to detail, every detail. They work until it is right. Whether working on a scientific theory or a work of art, they do not gloss over imperfections; one does not hear them say, "Oh, it's good enough."

Thomas Edison's oft quoted, "Genius is one percent inspiration and ninety-nine percent perspiration," sums up the experience that most creative achievers describe. The momentary flash of insight ordinarily follows years of stubborn labor. Even when a discovery is made by chance (as in Alexander Fleming's discovery of penicillin after an experimental mishap), it requires a prepared mind to recognize its significance. As Pasteur expressed it, "In the field of observation, chance favors only the prepared minds." For instance, when Fleming found that the bacteria he was studying had died he quickly realized that whatever killed them might be of use in treating bacterial infections. Fleming's earlier work on bacteria-killing agents "prepared" him to recognize the mishap as a stroke of luck. He traced the cause of death to some moldy bread in the preparation. This now world-famous mold became the basis for the production of penicillin.

Researcher Anne Roe studied a large group of eminent scientists and found one characteristic that was true for all of them:

The one thing that all of these sixty-four scientists have in common is their driving absorption in their work. They have worked long hours for many years, frequently with no vacations to speak of, because they would rather be doing their work than anything else.[16]

One measure of the devotion of the great creators to their work is the astonishing quantity of product they produce. When one contemplates the output of Beethoven, Mozart, Rembrandt, Michelangelo, Shakespeare, Newton, and other greats, it is hard to believe that a single person could have produced so much work.

Catalytic Strategies

When creative people are asked how they got their brilliant ideas, they often cannot say. The ideas just seemed to appear to them, sometimes even when thinking about other things. Some, like the scientist von Kekule and the poet Coleridge, even claimed to have performed exceptional creative acts while dozing (although serious doubts have been raised about the accuracy and veracity of these claims).[17]

Because creative achievers have not been able to describe the immediate antecedents of their insights, some theorists have ascribed the formulation of creative insights to unconscious processes, depicting an inner cauldron of ideas, swirling, colliding and sometimes coupling fortuitously, yielding insightful solutions that then bubble up into consciousness.[18] Once the thinker has gathered and stored lots of ideas, his or her main activity is to wait out the "incubation period," to allow the brew to do its work, and then to emit the requisite "Aha!" when the idea arrives.

No doubt creative insights arrive with an "Aha" (usually after weeks or years of intense contemplation), and no doubt creative thinkers do not have conscious access to the events immediately preceeding their arrival. But our understanding of the creative process isn't at all advanced by the notion of an invisible and unknowable unconscious creative cauldron, a subterranean mind that inhabits us and does all our best thinking. We would still have to explain how that inner mind works and why its stirrings are more productive inside some people than others who presumably also have unconscious ideas bubbling about. Of most importance, a theory based on unconscious processes, doesn't give us a clue as to what to do to increase the flow of insightful precipitates in ourselves or our children.

Actually we shouldn't be surprised that creative people can't tell us what triggered a particular insight. None of us have introspective access to the immediate antecedents of any of our ideas, insightful or not. We simply experience our ideas as they come; we do not experience forming them. We "hear" or "see" them as we think or visualize them, and then we evaluate them ("Hey, that works," or "No, that doesn't fit"). In other words, whether our thoughts are creative or commonplace, we don't know what we think until we think it. Or as writers sometimes say, "I don't know what I have to say until I write it down."

The next time you are in a conversation, arguing some point, pause to ask yourself what led to the choice and arrangement of the words and sentences you just spoke. You will have no idea. They just came out. You may have made some decisions along the way, such as to illustrate your point with an example, but you are not likely to know how the example you decided to use popped into your thoughts; it just arrived. Nor will you have a conscious experience of forming the sentences by which you communicated your example.

Yet the example you chose and the way you expressed yourself were not arbitrary or chaotic. Presumably they served an intended communicative goal, were appropriate to the context, responsive to the other speaker's words and the subject under discussion, consistent with your particular speaking style, reflecting your past experiences, and tailored to the particular person you were speaking to (for example, you would use fewer long words with a child). Moreover, your utterances were, in a sense, creative in that you had never spoken those exact words before, and you may have even surprised yourself with some of what you expressed.

There is a lesson here. Conversation is a part of any creative process. In searching for creative insights to difficult problems we have incessant dialogues—with *ourselves;* we speak our ideas and listen to them. We evaluate them and argue positions back and forth. We pursue the implications of ideas, run into dead ends, and then try other ideas. Sometimes we come up with partial solutions and may realize that the problem itself needs to be redefined (as Newton did in developing his theory of universal gravitation: Aha, it's not about the sun attracting the planets; it's about all the objects in the solar system attracting each other). We also seek out the arguments of others—through books and articles or face-to-face dialogue. And we stimulate our imagery by asking ourselves questions (as Einstein did when he wondered what he would see if he were riding on a light beam); and we make diagrams and models in the hopes of "seeing" patterns that we have not been able to discover through reason (as Watson and Crick did when working out the structure of DNA).

All this self-stimulation appears very rational and methodical, yet the theorists who have tried to explain creativity in terms of unconscious processes assert that creative leaps are basically nonrational events, that there is an unexplained gap between all this purposeful thinking and the appearance of the insightful solution. And they are right—though only partially, I believe. There is a gap, in the sense that creative insights are not automatic, predictable, or deductive outcomes of all this self-stimulation. Still, the discovery process is, I maintain, highly rational, but not in an obvious way. When Einstein started the process of imagining what he'd see while riding on a light beam he had no idea what would come to mind, so one might accuse him of irrationality. But the decision to imagine in this way, to translate a symbolic problem into a sensory one, was, in fact, a supremely rational act. Einstein was using what I call a "catalytic strategy," a strategy that improves one's chances of making creative leaps.

Let me make this clearer with an example from acting. An actress was presenting a scene from *Salome* to Lee Strasberg at The Actors Studio. As her acting partner entered with the freshly severed head of John the Baptist on a tray, the actress's eyes bulged, rasping sounds emerged from her throat, and her body undulated weirdly as she crossed the room and enveloped the bloody head in her arms. In the postscene discussion the actress explained her approach to the character. She believed that Salome must have been insane to order John's head cut off as an act of love, and she wanted to convey this insanity in her performance.

Strasberg asked her if she, in her own life, would behave the same way toward something she loved. She answered no—"But I'm not insane," she added. "Salome didn't think she was insane either," replied Strasberg. "She was in love, as you say. If you make normal love to a bloody head you won't have to work so hard to convince us that you're insane. The only time one sees insanity as you played it is by actors who've never observed insane people. Insane people do normal things, but to abnormal objects."

He then asked her if she had worked out the details of her portrayal in advance, the sounds, the swaying, the grimaces? She acknowledged that she had. "Do the scene again," he said. "But only plan your stimulus in advance, not your behavior." He asked her if she liked puppies, and she nodded yes. "Can you think of a very cute puppy you've known?" She could. "Now, when the head arrives, imagine that you see this puppy sitting on the tray, doing all of its puppy things, and treat the head as if it were the puppy."

The scene began the same way, but this time when the head arrived the actress lit up, caught her breath, and emitted a spontaneous "Ooooh." She giggled and squeaked as she gambolled across the room, beaming at the bloody head. She picked it up tenderly, appearing for a moment as if she might cry over its cuteness. She stroked its hair back and began giving it little kisses on the mouth, laughing as she felt its mouth on hers. Watching these antics directed toward a bloody head, one could not have witnessed a more horrific example of insanity. This was certainly a creative solution to the problem the actress had set: to convey Salome's love and insanity simultaneously.

Now back to the notion of catalytic strategies. Neither Strasberg nor the actress could have known in advance what specific behavior would emerge by using the puppy as a stimulus. Her reactions were not planned (as they had been the first go-round), so here too we have that gap between input and output. But the strategies Strasberg was teaching her were highly rational: reactions must be discovered, not planned; and they must be "organic" responses to credible stimuli. These are basic "method acting" principles, which have been used systematically by actors for a long time. They are also examples of what I am calling, catalytic strategies. They are used precisely because they frequently yield creative solutions to a type of problem that actors must solve.

There are many other well-known examples of catalytic strategies: Michelangelo conceived of sculpture as "the art of taking away," freeing the form from the stone. Einstein relied on visual imagery to solve problems; solutions had to make sense to his senses. This served him well until he was confronted with quantum theory, which conceives of the world in terms that cannot be visualized. In an article on Newton's discovery of gravitation, science historian I. Bernard Cohen attributed Newton's success to his "style," which Cohen says "consists in a repeated give-and-take between a mathematical construct and physical reality. . . . He started with a mathematical construct that represents nature simplified. . . . [and then] compared the consequences of his mathematical construct with the observed principles and laws of the external world.[19] What Cohen calls a style, I am calling a catalytic strategy.

Another example of a catalytic strategy is the set of "ideals" that Robert Motherwell tries to follow in his painting: ". . . 'no nostalgia, no sentimentalism, no propaganda, no discourse, no autobiography, no violation of the canvas as a surface (since it is one), no clichés, no predetermined endings, no seduction, no charm, no relaxation, no mere taste, no obviousness, no coldness.' Oppositely, it must have 'immediacy, passion or tenderness, beingness, as such, detachment, sheer presence as a modulation of the flat picture plane, true invention and search, light, an unexpected end, mainly warm earth colors and black and white, a certain stalwartness.' "[20]

The sculptor Henry Moore described a number of strategies that guide his work, both abstract and representational:

I think the humanist organic element will always be for me of fundamental importance in sculpture, giving sculpture vitality. Each particular carving I make takes on in my mind a human, or occasionally animal, character and personality, and this personality controls its design and formal qualities, and makes me satisfied or dissatisfied with the work as it develops.[21]

For van Gogh an important catalytic strategy (one of many) was his use of color to convey and stir emotion:

I have tried to express the terrible passions of humanity by red and green. . . . You will realize that this combination of red-ochre, green saddened by grey, and the use of heavy black outlines produces something of the sensation of anguish. . . .

I exaggerate the fairness of the hair, I come even to orange tones, chromes, and pale lemon yellow. Beyond the head, instead of painting the banal wall of the mean room, I paint infinity, I make a plain background of the richest, intensest blue that I can contrive, and by this simple combination of the bright head against the rich blue background, I get a mysterious effect, like a star in the depths of an azure sky.[22]

Psychologist Howard Gruber and his students have sought to tease out what I am calling catalytic strategies in the works of Darwin, Benjamin Franklin, and other creative thinkers.[23] For example, Darwin worked on other scientific problems besides evolution, and in each his explanations relied on the notion of "gradualism"—that large changes are brought about through a series of small steps. As Darwin put it, "Nature makes no jumps." This principle played as much of a role in his study of the impact of billions of earthworms on surface geology as it did in his theory of evolution. While his contemporaries were looking for a theory to account for the big differences between species, such as those between elephants and giraffes, Darwin believed that the solution lay in figuring out the small variations, such as why different kinds of finches have very different beaks.

Some catalytic strategies can be applied to many different problem-solving areas. Among these strategies are:

Break it apart. Used, for example, by artists (particularly "minimalists") who seek to isolate and explore a single artistic element in depth.

Stand it on its head. Used by scientists to gain new perspective on a problem. For example, instead of the usual question, Why is there so much street crime? we might gain a new understanding of the forces causing and constraining crime by asking, Why isn't there *more* street crime?[24]

Find an analogy. For instance, farmers in dry climates use drip irrigation to bring scarce water via tubes to individual plants (rather than wasting water by spraying entire fields). Recently, an analogous process, using solar collectors and fiber optic tubes, has been developed to bring scarce sunlight to individual plants in cold climates with little sunshine.

The terms *inspiration* and *insight* usually refer to the discovery of a solution to a specific problem. But discovering how to work on problems, the catalytic strategies, are also important moments of inspiration and insight—perhaps the most important. These discoveries can come in many ways. They come through working through many problems, finding what produces useful and interesting results and what doesn't, and then synthesizing one's discoveries into a formal statement (such as, "Sculpture is the art of taking away"). Here's an example of this kind of trial and error discovery from van Gogh, as described in a letter to his brother:

> What you say of the figure is true, that as figure studies they are not what the heads are. That's why I've thought of trying it in quite a different way, for instance, starting with the torso instead of the head. . . . In these new drawings I have been starting the figures from the torso, and it seems to me that they become fuller and broader this way. (Letter 402)

Catalytic strategies also come from careful thought about what one's true goals are (as in Henry Moore's awareness that "it is the human figure which interests me most deeply." Here is an example from van Gogh, describing with striking clarity his goal in the painting of weavers and their looms:

> If you were to put my study [of a loom] beside the drawing of a mechanic who had designed a weaving loom—mine would express more strongly that the thing is made of oak grimed by sweaty hands; and . . . looking at it, you could not help thinking occasionally of the *workman*. . . . A sort of sigh or lament must issue from that contraption of sticks. (Letter R44)

One may also develop catalytic strategies by analyzing the medium one is working in for elements that might be exploited in new ways. For example, Moore realized that strategically placed holes in a sculpture could enhance the dimensionality of a piece's basic solid form: "The first hole made through a piece of stone is a revelation. The hole connects one side to the other, making it immediately more three-dimensional." Another example was van Gogh's realization that emotional qualities could be conveyed through pure color and the juxtaposition of colors.

Catalytic strategies may also derive from examining what has worked and not worked in the creative attempts of others, and then adapting useful approaches to one's own ends. For instance, van Gogh borrowed Delacroix's strategy of painting from memory rather than from life, thereby enabling the reality he had observed and sketched filter through his own imagination (described in letters 403 and 444).

Not all creative thinkers articulate their strategies for themselves. Some prefer to work intuitively, which does not necessarily mean they aren't approaching their work in regular and reliable ways; it merely means they haven't articulated their work processes or the stimuli they respond to. As an example, imagine a portrait painter who always looks first for the attitude conveyed in his subject's eyes but has not put into words that that's how he begins. I am a strong adherent of analyzing and verbalizing one's intuitive strategies; that is, for developing a conscious craft.

The career of Constantine Stanislavski, the great Russian actor and director, provides an example of an already successful artist searching for and discovering his intuitive strategies—and benefiting from those discoveries. His discoveries formed the foundation of the modern approach to acting and actor training in Europe and America and have inspired many other actors and teachers to continue his explorations. My own research in this area is described in a number of books and articles.[25]

Some creative people resist explicating their creative processes out of fear that their work might then become too formulaic, too obligated to working within their stated strategies—within *yesterday's* strategies—and less responsive to the moment-to-moment flow of impulses, impressions, and feelings. It is a legitimate concern. On the other hand, opting for a strictly intuitive approach, puts one in the position of having to reinvent the wheel with every new problem. As a teacher I strongly recommend the construction of a conscious craft, with the proviso that strategies be continually reevaluated and new ones sought (for instance, I'm sure there are many fruitful ways to approach sculpture besides "the art of taking away").

Fostering Creativity in Your Child

A good way to start is by reading your child Hans Christian Andersen's "The Emperor's New Clothes." Recall that in the story everyone, including the emperor and his smartest ministers, is too intimidated, too afraid to be thought of as stupid, to declare that the emperor is naked—except for one little boy who "tells it like it is." Your child will meet many a naked emperor and will need courage to stand against foolish or shortsighted authorities. So make the moral of Andersen's story clear: *Don't accept what you know is false just because everyone else says it is true.* It is an important lesson if your child engages in creative pursuits. Creative thinkers are invariably dissidents, ever on the lookout for the nakedness of accepted doctrine.

A modern demonstration of the truth contained in "The Emperor's New Clothes" is psychologist Solomon Ashe's classic study of the power of group pressure. Subjects had to make judgments comparing the lengths of lines after hearing others in their group (who actually worked for Asch) make obviously inaccurate judgments. Asch found that a sizable percentage of his subjects went along with the group—some out of fear of ridicule, some because they doubted their own perceptual abilities, and some apparently out of true distortions in their perceptions.[26]

Andersen's "The Ugly Duckling" is another story with an important lesson: Have faith in who you are, your own voice and your own vision. Creative thinkers must, of course, be independent thinkers, searching for truth and beauty in their own way despite what others say is misguided or impossible. Indeed, to the person in pursuit of creative goals, the proclamation, "Impossible!" is likely to be taken up as a gauntlet for the fun of proving otherwise. In an interview, the conductor, John McGlinn, described how the song "Impossible," from Richard Rogers and Oscar Hammerstein's "Cinderella," inspired him as a child and still wafts across his thoughts when others assure him of what he'll never be able to accomplish. Here again, we find a lovely lesson in a common children's narrative.

There are many inspiring stories, poems, and biographies for fostering a growing youngster's commitment to independent thinking. Robert Frost's poem "The Road Not Taken" is surely one. Another are these proud lines from Cyrano de Bergerac's glorious "No, thank you" speech:

> . . . To travel any road
> Under the sun, under the stars, nor doubt
> If fame or fortune lie beyond the bourne—
> Never to make a line I have not heard
> In my own heart; yet, with all modesty
> To say: "My soul, be satisfied with flowers,
> With fruit, with weeds even; but gather them
> In the one garden you may call your own."
>
> (from *Cyrano de Bergerac* by Edmund Rostand)

Stories about creative heroes, their strivings, struggles, and achievements, can be inspiring to children, fostering their belief in the value of creative pursuits. These stories will also make clear that hard work and frustration are a natural part of the creative process—even for the "geniuses."

Teachers and librarians should be able to recommend books at the appropriate reading level for your child that describe the life and work of the great creative heroes of our culture, both past and present. Look for books that highlight the drama of creative striving and the enduring legacy of creative achievements. When parents and children read these together they open up areas for many interesting discussions, and they also share lovely experiences—mutual awe for the best of human achievement.

Point out creativity when you come across it, enthusing over the ingenuity that went into the problem solving. Do this, of course, for the great creative achievements (the wheel, the printing press, Greek theatre, the typewriter, the telephone, the arch, impressionistic painting, the automobile and so many others), but also laud the more modest creations that benefit us in our everyday activities (such as the can opener and other kitchen gadgets, Velcro, spray paint, window screens, dimmer switches, the Sassy Seat, the electric razor, and countless more). In other words, celebrate creativity. If you like, make it a formal celebration. Select some creative heroes and celebrate their birthdays, learning more about them and their achievements, enjoying their creations if possible (looking at their paintings, reading one of their stories, playing their music)—honoring them and feeling honored to be a member of the same species.

Many calendars list the birthdays of famous men and women. On van Gogh's birthday, take your youngster to the museum and look at his paintings, or take out a library book about van Gogh and his work, and spend some time together appreciating his art and commemorating his life. On Galileo's birthday look through a telescope together or go to a planetarium or look him up in an encyclopedia. It's a wonderful way to share an uplifting experience with your child and to introduce her to the best of human culture. If you want your child to strive to use her mind to its fullest, then it is important to provide her with intellectual heroes—both from the past and present. Many major thinkers have talked about the significance of such heroes in their lives, setting a standard to strive toward. It is surprisingly easy to inspire these kinds of ideals in a child.

Children tend to take for granted the things that they've grown up with, like telephones and automobiles. As your child grows, help her appreciate the magnificence of such inventions. The most powerful monarchs of the past could not command what we ordinary citizens command by the flick of a switch. We fly to places in hours that they could only dream about, we summon symphony orchestras by turning a knob, we cure illnesses as a matter of routine that killed off half their populations. Try, too, to help her appreciate the evolution of artistic discoveries, pointing out how different the art work is in different eras.

And share your own creative solutions, even to seemingly small problems. If you can, describe the thinking that led to the solution and try to put your catalytic strategies into words ("I always start by making a diagram"). Discuss the kinds of problems you deal with in your work and hobbies, and ask for her suggestions. You'll be surprised at how thoughtful they will be if you give her enough information to understand the problem.

Of paramount importance, applaud your child's creative solutions—even those that don't ultimately work but reveal interesting thinking ("Daddy, maybe we can stop the leak by putting clay in the faucet; then we can take it out when we want a drink''). Go even further: when she does something creative, don't merely praise the act—let her know you think of her as a creative person. As described in an earlier section, children generally try to live up to the admirable labels we give them.

Children's creativity must be gauged within a framework that is appropriate for them, taking into consideration their limited experience. For example, say a preschooler wants to move all his blocks down a small staircase, and figures out that by placing a game board on the steps he can slide his blocks down and save himself a lot of effort. The child has, thus, reinvented the ramp, and I think most observers would call the solution creative. The same solution by an adult would be less impressive on the assumption that any adult has had considerable experience with ramps and is not really inventing anything new. Even if the child's solution derived from recollections of the slide in the playground, his recognition that the same mechanism could be applied to convey objects purposely from one level to another would be an impressive leap.

Be on the lookout for your child's creative productions in all her activities—in her construction and drawing projects, her social activities (such as original and effective compromise strategies), her academic skills (such as insightful arithmetic strategies, even if they aren't the most efficient), her language skills (a 6-year-old coined the evocative term ''applaudience''), among others. Let her see your delight in her creations. By letting her know that you find her thoughts interesting, you'll help her gain confidence in her own thought processes.

And don't agonize over whether something your child does is *really* an act of creativity. Deciding whether something is creative is always a subjective judgment, and the two criteria we use in judging creativity, innovation and effectiveness, cannot usually be measured precisely. If it seems interesting to you, make a fuss. Here are two examples that I'd put in the creative category: A child of 5 years, 9 months came up with the idea of making baskets in the shape of George Washington's and Abraham Lincoln's faces ''to sell on President's Day.'' Another child (6 years, 2 months) cut out the word-family lists she had been given by her teacher and made a paper house for them, ''because a family should live in a house.'' She made a slit in the house to slide the words through so only one word at a time would be revealed. ''That way I can memorize them,'' she said.

Also, be alert to your child's excessive frustration. Making new things is difficult. The glue doesn't hold, the tooth picks run out, the colors bleed. A helpful hand from you can revive morale and save the project. In addition, a well-timed reminder about the inevitability of frustration can provide some needed perspective.

Another important lesson is that anyone who tries something new has to be willing to put up with some criticism from others. The others might find it silly or think it won't work, or may be jealous that they didn't think of it first. Stories about the criticism and mockery that some of the great creators endured should help here. Many creative achievers have had to learn to persist and maintain their confidence through long periods of neglect and rejection. You may want to teach your child the maxim, "The turtle cannot move forward unless it sticks its neck out." It may help at a time of faltering courage.

It will also help if you teach your child that no one has *the right* to discourage someone else's work. Constructive criticism is encouraging and clarifying, not denigrating and purposefully hurtful. Using the notion of "rights" in this context can fortify a child against the nay sayers and mockers, helping her realize that the problem resides in their attitude, not her striving.

Introduce your child to the notion of catalytic strategies, teaching that there are ways of working that creative problem solvers have found useful. Share whatever you know about these strategies. But also acknowledge that it is often difficult to figure out what strategies have led to a successful solution, that the problem solvers themselves cannot always put their ways of working into words. Make clear that in learning about other people's successful strategies, we may find some that will help in our own work. We will also find strategies that we decide are not for us (we may, for example, decide *not* to employ color the way van Gogh did). But either way, by learning about and evaluating productive ways of working, we are likely to formulate our own goals and strategies more clearly.

Sometimes, even when people are aware of their strategies they won't share them. Mathematicians to this day bemoan the secretiveness of the great eighteenth-century mathematician Carl Friedrich Gauss, who never revealed how he approached problems: "When a fine building is finished, the scaffolding should no longer be visible," he said.[27]

Sometimes we can figure out (or at least formulate a good hypothesis about) a creative person's strategies. As an acting teacher, that is an important part of my job. Whenever I see acting that I admire, my task is to try to define precisely what I am responding to. If I can do that, I can then set up exercises for my students to learn to do what the greats are doing.

Whether you and your child are reading about Einstein or responding to great acting, try to make him or her aware that it is not useful to think of great achievements as simply a matter of luck or talent or some mysterious unconscious forces. These are notions that promote helplessness, the sense that some few are blessed and the rest of us might as well give up. It is much more constructive and heartening to assume that great achievements come from learning effective ways of working, and from learning to look for effective ways of working. I've known many actors and actresses who began their studies with nary a grain of talent, but who, with dedication and good instruction, became exceptionally talented. Talent is a word to *describe* work we like; it does not *explain* how that work was achieved.

As your youngster develops interests in a field, try to sensitize her to its creative aspects. For instance, most youngsters enjoy popular music, some of which is highly creative. Some singers and groups have been very candid and articulate about their creative goals. The Beatles, for example, were continually exploring new musical forms, and, in an earlier era, Frank Sinatra sought to introduce a deeper, more personal level of acting into popular singing than was typical then (or now).

It won't take long before your child knows more than you about some of the fields that interest her. Then let her teach you about the creative aspects. Ask what is new and interesting in the field. It's not important that you like the same things (she may like rock music and you may not, or vice versa); what's important is that you respect each other's interests and can take pleasure in each other's excitement.

Another tactic for fostering children's creativity is to provide them with a good working environment. Their toys, games, and crafts should be organized enough so that they can find things, but not so meticulously that putting things away becomes too painful and time consuming. Giving your child access to crafts drawers, bins, or shelves with lots of interesting odds and ends will extend the possibilities for creative solutions. Most children like to make things ("I'm going to build a bird cage for Tweety"), but if they don't have good supplies that they can rummage through on their own, they soon give up the project.

Creative people, children as well as adults, need time and "space"— psychological space. They need to be allowed to think, to muse, to follow a chain of ideas to completion: they need time for reflection, and time to do their research and finish their projects. A child engaged in feverish, creative thought may not look very different from a child who is moping, but parents need to be sensitive to the distinction. They need to respect their child, as *Thinker*.

Respecting your child is also expressed by letting her projects really be hers. Some parents have a tendency to take over a project, wanting to make it come out "right." This should be avoided. Occasional suggestions and assistance, especially when requested, can be helpful. But the projects must remain the child's, expressing her vision and reflecting her thinking. Parents and teachers must, of course, teach children the requisite skills (how to use glue, how to play a chord, how to solve an equation), but when it comes to creative projects, adults should assume the role of assistant, allowing the child to make her own plans, explore alternatives, go down dead ends, find her way back, revise her plan, and rethink her goal. It is more beneficial for her to experience the creative process than to come out with a lovely product that is really not hers.

When creative thinkers—children included—are not given the time and psychological space they need, they tend to get grumpy. But don't assume that creative people are, by nature, difficult or unfriendly. Writers on creativity love to cite the notorious examples of creative grumps (such as Beethoven), as if grumpiness and creativity went hand in hand. But they fail to mention many other creative greats who were gracious and amiable (Darwin, Ben Franklin, Einstein). Grumpiness may have more to do with not having the time and resources to carry on one's work, than with anything intrinsic to creative people. When one is driven (as Beethoven was), when all one's waking thoughts, and even one's dreams, are a constant whirlwind of problem-solving attempts, it is hard to meet normal social responsibilities. I recall a TV comedy skit in which Beethoven's wife was trying to get him to take out the garbage while he was composing a symphony. He became increasingly grumpy, as did his music.

Whether creative people have more frequent and violent mood swings or more mental illness than the rest of the population, as some researchers have claimed, has not been established. More likely, the emotional ups and downs of creative achievers get a lot more publicity than other people's. Moreover, the many creative achievers who lead stable, quiet lives don't attract media attention.

When you come across studies that report more emotional problems in creative individuals, keep in mind that the methodologies in these studies are usually questionable (for instance, measures of emotional problems are notoriously unreliable) and that research findings may be "statistically significant" yet still trivial. The headline may blare, "Creatives Crazier Than Others," while the data merely show that, while 10 out of 100 noncreative people have mental illness, 14 out of 100 creative people have similar problems. The differences may not be worth making a fuss about.

Creativity Exercises

There are various exercises that parents can do with children to foster the development of one or more aspects of creative problem solving.

1. *Let's Make a Better One.* Select any common item and brainstorm ways to improve it by making it more efficient, convenient, faster, more

versatile, etc. Two useful steps are defining the item's purpose clearly and listing any frustrations encountered in using it. Work out suggested improvements as fully as you can, considering what materials would be needed and what negative effects your new design might produce. For instance, a stronger motor might make more noise, take up more room, produce more heat, and cost more to run. A vacuum cleaner with more suction might pull up carpets and be too difficult to roll.

2. *Dream Things*. This exercise starts with the question, "What would make life better?" Together try to think of an object, a procedure, or an organization that would fill a true need if it existed, and then try to imagine how to bring it about, including what kind of research might be needed and what kinds of materials might have to be developed. Try to cover many different areas, such as transportation (personal rockets), communication (typewriters that understand speech), health, storage, entertainment, among others.

3. *The Remote Associations Game*. Creative problem solving often depends on applying notions from one domain to another. Therefore it should be useful to sensitize a child to look for subtle likenesses between seemingly unrelated objects and concepts. Together pick out any two nouns that the child knows from any kind of written material (a dictionary or any book or magazine). The task is to think of what is similar about or common to both objects regardless of how different they appear on the surface. With some mental exploration and some prompting from you, your child should be able to find something the objects have in common; and even if nothing comes to mind, the search should stimulate thinking about familiar things in new ways.

Is There a Creative Personality?

In their work, creative people share the characteristics that I've discussed, such as a commitment to discovery and innovation. But otherwise, they come in all types and temperaments. Some lead eccentric, Bohemian lives; others are conventional and conservative. Some pursue wealth; others don't. Some are gregarious; some loners. Some require orderly work environments; others prefer clutter. Some describe their motivations in grand, spiritual terms, finding connections through their work to the "universe"; others offer unromantic reasons like, "It's the only thing I could do," or "It gives me more freedom than anything else."

Some, like Mozart and Picasso, were prodigies, showing uncanny ability in childhood; others, like van Gogh and Freud, did not discover their "calling" until adulthood. Novelists and filmmakers focus on the eccentrics, of course, romanticizing their lives beyond any sense of reality. But, in truth, there are no characteristics that apply to creative people across the board.

Nor do creative people come from one type of family background; nor have they had similar educational experiences. Some were encouraged to be independent thinkers by parents or teachers; others had to fight for their independence. Van Gogh's teachers at the Antwerp Academy disliked his personal style so much that they put him back into the beginner's class. So he quit and went to Arles—and the rest is history. Einstein, too, had an unhappy time in school. He wrote caustic letters about the small-mindedness of his teachers:

> The obstacles that these old philistines place in the way of all those who are not their sort are really frightful. It seems to me this type instinctively views every young intelligent mind as a threat to his wormeaten dignity. If he dares to reject my doctoral thesis, then I will publish his letter of refusal, black on white, together with the dissertation, and he will have shamed himself. . . . A pompous group, all of them.[28]

Other eminent creators have also complained of stifling experiences in school, while many others extol supportive teachers and mentors who recognized and nurtured their potential.

An occasional study reports that "creatives" scored "significantly" higher on some personality variable, family characteristic, or educational background than a comparison group. But these differences are usually small, with slightly more creatives than normals scoring higher than average on the characteristic under study. Invariably, though, a fair number of the creatives will have scored average or lower than average on the same characteristic. Ordinarily the researchers ignore these contrary scores when claiming to have discovered a significant cause or correlate of creativity. In general, I am not aware of any studies that have come up with reliable and substantial differences between creative and noncreative people on personality or background characteristics.

Also, be wary of claims that creative people are "right-brained" and that there are special techniques for training the right hemisphere of the brain. This is a flagrant misapplication of findings from patients whose brains were divided surgically for medical reasons. There is no evidence that creative activity resides predominantly in either half of the brain; nor can you train one side of your brain—unless, that is, you are willing to have your brain cut in half. Under normal conditions, both sides of the brain work together and share information. While there is evidence that certain functions are controlled more by one hemisphere than the other (for instance, speech is predominantly controlled by areas in the left hemisphere), brain researchers have absolutely not been able to pin down the cortical locations of creative thinking.

From what I've seen, books that claim to train your "right brain" (such as a popular drawing book), use instructional techniques that are fairly standard in the field, with some common "creativity" exercises added. If the techniques work, it is not because they are especially calibrated to spark the right hemisphere—at least not as far as anyone has ever demonstrated.

In observing and fostering your own child's creative development, try to avoid preconceptions about what a creative child is supposed to be like. Your child may develop a great passion for art and show early signs of creative potential, yet insist on dressing like a little banker. Your child may develop a strong, singular interest early and stay with it for the rest of his or her life, or may go through many changes and ultimately pursue more than one career. Whatever the external form, one of the great gifts of parenthood is having a close-up view of the blossoming of a creative and passionate mind. Enjoy it.

Notes

Chapter 1
Your Child, the Problem Solver

1. Sternberg, R. J. (1982, April). Who's intelligent? *Psychology Today*, pp. 30–39.
2. Macfarlane, A. (1978). What a baby knows. *Human Nature, 1*, 74–81.
3. McGill, D. C. (1986, Dec. 7). Stella elucidates abstract art's link to realism. *New York Times*, p. 102.
   Geist, S. (1968). *Brancusi: A study of the sculpture*. New York: Grossman.
4. Eliot, T. S. (1952). "East Coker." *The complete poems and plays*. New York: Harcourt, Brace and World.

Chapter 2
A Mind Is Born

1. Lamb, M. E. (1981). Developing trust and perceived effectance in infancy. In L. P. Lipsitt (Ed.), *Advances in infancy research* (Vol. 1, pp. 101–127). Norwood, NJ: Ablex.
   Lipsitt, L. P. (1969). Learning capacities of the human infant. In R. J. Robinson (Ed.), *Brain and early behavior: Development in the fetus and infant* (pp. 227–249). New York: Academic Press.
   Gibson, E. J. (1987). Introductory essay: What does infant perception tell us about theories of perception? *Journal of Experimental Psychology: Human Perception and Performance, 13*, 515–523.
   Crook, C. K. (1978). Taste perception in the newborn infant. *Infant Behavior and Development, 1*, 52–69.
   Balogh, R. D., & Porter, R. H. (1986). Olfactory preferences resulting from mere exposure in human neonates. *Infant Behavior and Development, 9*, 395–401.
   Donaldson, M., Grieve, R., & Pratt, C., (Eds.). (1983). *Early childhood development and education: Readings in psychology*. New York: Guilford Press.

White, R. W. (1959). Motivation reconsidered: The concept of competence. *Psychological Review, 66,* 297–323.

Deci, E. L., & Ryan, R. M. (1985). *Intrinsic motivation and self-determination in human behavior.* New York: Plenum Press.

Hunt, J. McV. (1960). Experience and the development of motivation: Some reinterpretations. *Child Development, 31,* 489–504.

2. Fantz, R. L. (1963). Patterns of vision in newborn infants. *Science, 140,* 296–297.

Gorman, J. J., Cogen, D. G., & Gellis, S. S. (1959). A device for testing visual acuity in infants. *Sight-Saving Review, 29,* 80–84.

3. Kagan, J., Lapidus, D. R., & Moore, M. (1978). Infant antecedents of cognitive functioning: A longitudinal study. *Child Development, 49,* 1005–1023.

Kopp, C. B., & Vaughn, B. E. (1982). Sustained attention during exploratory manipulation as a predictor of cognitive competence in preterm infants. *Child Development, 53,* 174–182.

Sigman, M., Kopp, C. B., Parmelee, A. H., & Jeffrey, W. (1973). Visual attention and neurological organization in neonates. *Child Development, 44,* 461–466.

Bornstein, M. H., & Sigman, M. D. (1986). Continuity in mental development from infancy. *Child Development, 57,* 251–274.

Fagan, J. F. (1984). The intellectual infant: Theoretical implications. *Intelligence, 8,* 1–9.

Birns, B., & Golden, M. (1972). Prediction of intellectual performance at 3 years from infant tests and personality measures. *Merrill-Palmer Quarterly, 18,* 553–558.

4. Stevenson, M. B., Ver Hoeve, J. N., Roach, M. A., & Leavitt, L. A. (1986). The beginning of conversation: Early patterns of mother–infant vocal responsiveness. *Infant Behavior & Development, 9,* 423–440.

5. Doman, G. (1985). *How to give your baby encyclopedic knowledge.* Garden City, NY: Doubleday.

Elkind, D. (1987). *Miseducation: Preschoolers at risk.* New York: Knopf.

6. Hall, E. (1970, May). A conversation with Jean Piaget and Barbel Inhelder. *Psychology Today,* pp. 25–32, 54–56.

7. Piaget, J., & Szeminska, A. (1952). *The child's conception of number* (C. Gattegno & F. M. Hodgson, Trans.). New York: Humanities Press. (Original work published 1948).

Piaget, J. (1972). Development and learning. In C. Stendler-Lavatelli & F. Stendler (Eds.), *Readings in child behavior and development* (3rd ed., pp. 38–46). New York: Harcourt Brace Jovanovich.

Kohlberg, L. (1968). Early education: A cognitive–developmental view. *Child Development, 39,* 1013–1062.

8. Stevenson, H. W., & Newman, R. S. (1986). Long-term prediction of achievement and attitudes in mathematics and reading. *Child Development, 57,* 646–659.

9. Elkind, D. (1961). The development of quantitative thinking. *Journal of Genetic Psychology, 98,* 37–46.

   Beard, R. M. (1960). The nature and development of concepts. *Educational Review, 13,* 12–26.

   Dodwell, P. C. (1961). Children's understanding of number and related concept: Characteristics of an individual and of a group test. *Canadian Journal of Psychology, 15,* 29–36.

10. Renninger, K. A., & Wozniak, R. H. (1985). Effect of interest on attentional shift, recognition, and recall in young children. *Developmental Psychology, 21,* 624–632.

Chapter 3
Efforts to Explain Intelligence

1. Gelman, R. (1979). Preschool thought. *American Psychologist, 34,* 900–905.

   Carey, S. (1985). Are children fundamentally different kinds of thinkers and learners than adults? In S. F. Chipman, J. W. Segal, & R. Glaser (Eds.). *Thinking and learning skills* (Vol. 2, pp. 485–517). Hillsdale, NJ: Lawrence Erlbaum.

   Donaldson, M. (1982). Conservation: What is the question? *British Journal of Psychology, 73,* 199–207.

   Schiff, W. (1983). Conservation of length redux: A perceptual–linguistic phenomenon. *Child Development, 54,* 1497–1506.

   Smith, I. D. (1968). The effects of training procedures upon the acquisition of conservation of weight. *Child Development, 39,* 515–526.

2. Piaget, J. (1968). *Six psychological studies.* New York: Vintage.

   Hay, D. F., & Rheingold, H. L. (1984). The early appearance of some valued social behaviors. In D. L. Bridgeman (Ed.), *The nature of prosocial development: Interdisciplinary theories and strategies* (pp. 73–94). New York: Academic Press.

   Borke, H. (1975). Piaget's mountains revisited: Changes in the egocentric landscape. *Developmental Psychology, 11,* 240–243.

3. Dunn, J., & Munn, P. (1985). Becoming a family member: Family conflict and the development of social understanding in the second year. *Child Development, 56,* 480–492.

4. Kates, R. W., & Katz, C. R. (1987). The hydrological cycle and the wisdom of the child. *Children's Environments Quarterly, 4*(2), 3–10.

5. Deutsche, J. M. (1937). The development of children's concepts of causal relations. Minneapolis: University of Minnesota Press.

6. Piaget, J., & Inhelder, B. (1969). *The psychology of the child.* New York: Basic Books.

7. Parsonson, B. S., & Naughton, K. A. (1988). Training generalized conservation in 5-year-old children. *Journal of Experimental Child Psychology, 46,* 372–390.

8. Gardner, H. (1983). *Frames of mind: The theory of multiple intelligences.* New York: Basic Books.

9. Sternberg, R. J. (1986). A triarchic theory of intellectual giftedness. In R. J. Sternberg & J. E. Davidson (Eds.), *Conceptions of giftedness* (pp. 223–243). New York: Cambridge University Press.

Sternberg, R. J. (1988). *The triarchic mind: A new theory of human intelligence.* New York: Viking Penguin.

Sternberg, R. J. (1988). Intelligence. In R. J. Sternberg & E. E. Smith (Eds.), *The psychology of human thought* (pp. 267–308). New York: Cambridge University Press.

Sternberg, R. J. (1982). Reasoning, problem solving, and intelligence. In R. J. Sternberg (Ed.). *Handbook of human intelligence* (pp. 225–351). New York: Cambridge University Press.

10. Coon, H., Fulker, D. W., DeFries, J. C., & Plomin, R. (1990). Home environment and cognitive ability of 7-year-old children in the Colorado Adoption Project: Genetic and environmental etiologies. *Developmental Psychology, 26,* 459–468.

Bouchard, T. J., Jr., Lykken, D. T., McGue, M., Segal, N. L., & Tellegen, A. (1990). Sources of human psychological differences. *Science, 250,* 223–228.

11. Honzik, M. P. (1957). Developmental studies of parent–child resemblance in intelligence. *Child Development, 28,* 215–228.

Scarr, S., & Weinberg, R. A. (1976). IQ test performance of black children adopted by white families. *American Psychologist, 31,* 726–739.

Bronfenbrenner, U. (1975). Is 80% of intelligence genetically determined? In U. Bronfenbrenner & M. A. Mahoney (Eds.), *Influences on human development* (2nd ed., pp. 91–100). Hinsdale, IL: Dryden Press.

Engelmann, S. (1971). The effectiveness of direct verbal instruction on IQ performance and achievement in reading and arithmetic. In W. C. Becker (Ed.), *An empirical basis for change in education* (pp. 461–483). Chicago: Science Research Associates.

Burchinal, M., Lee, M., & Ramey, C. (1986, August). Daycare effects on preschool intellectual development in poverty children. Paper presented at the 94th annual meeting of the American Psychological Association.

Feuerstein, R., Jensen, M., Hoffman, M. B., & Rand, Y. (1985). Instrumental enrichment, an intervention program for structural cognitive modifiability: Theory and practice. In J. W. Segal, S. F. Chipman, & R. Glaser (Eds.), *Thinking and learning skills: Vol. 3: Relating instruction to research* (pp. 43–82). Hillsdale, NJ: Lawrence Erlbaum.

Bretmayer, B. J., & Ramey, C. T. (1986). Biological nonoptimality and quality of postnatal environment as codeterminants of intellectual development. *Child Development, 57,* 1151–1165.

Beckwith, L., & Parmelee, Jr., A. H. (1986). EEG Pattern of preterm infants, home environment, and later IQ. *Child Development, 57,* 777–789.

12. Anastasi, A. (1985). Some emerging trends in psychological measurement: A fifty-year perspective. *Applied Psychological Measurement, 9*, 121–138.

13. Bouchard, Lykken, McGue, Segal, & Tellegen (1990). See note 10.

14. Diamond, A. (Ed.). (1990). *The development and neural bases of higher cognitive functions*. New York: The New York Academy of Sciences.

15. Gibbons, A. (1990). New maps of the human brain. *Science, 249*, 122–123.

16. Rosenzweig, M. R. (1966). Environmental complexity, cerebral change, and behavior. *American Psychologist, 21*, 321–332.

    Diamond, M. C. (1988). *Enriching heredity: The impact of the environment on the anatomy of the brain*. New York: Free Press.

17. Lewis, M., & Goldberg, S. (1969). Perceptual–cognitive development in infancy: A generalized expectancy model as a function of the mother–infant interaction. *Merrill-Palmer Quarterly, 15*, 81–100.

    Lewis, M., & Coates, D. L. (1980). Mother–infant interaction and cognitive development in twelve-week-old infants. *Infant Behavior and Development, 3*, 95–105.

    Bakeman, R., & Adamson, L. (1986). Infant's conventionalized acts: Gestures and words with mothers and peers. *Infant Behavior and Development, 9*, 215–230.

    Gaiter, J. L., Morgan, G. A., Jennings, K. D., Harmon, R. J., & Yarrow, L. J. (1982). Variety of cognitively oriented caregiver activities: Relationships to cognitive and motivational functioning at one and 3½ years of age. *Journal of Genetic Psychology, 141*, 49–56.

    Yarrow, L., MacTurk, P., Vietze, M., McCarthy, M., Klein, R., & McQuiston, S. (1984). The developmental course of parental stimulation and its relationship to mastery motivation during infancy. *Developmental Psychology, 20*, 492–503.

    Wachs, T. D., & Chan, A. (1986). Specificity of environmental action as seen in physical and social environmental correlates of three aspects of twelve month infants' communication performance. *Child Development, 57*, 1464–1474.

    Wachs, T. D. (1987). Specificity of environmental action as manifest in environmental correlates of infants' mastery motivation. *Developmental Psychology, 23*, 782–790.

    Ruddy, M. G., & Bornstein, M. H. (1982). Cognitive correlates of infant attitudes and maternal stimulation over the first year of life. *Child Development, 53*, 183–188.

    Beckwith & Parmelee (1986). See note 11.

    Elardo, R., Bradley, R., & Caldwell, B. (1977). A longitudinal study of the relationship of the infant's home environment to language development at age three. *Child Development, 48*, 593–603.

    Ungerer, J. A., Brody, L. R., & Zelazo, P. R. (1978). Long-term memory for speech in 2- to 4-week-old infants. *Infant Behavior and Development, 1*, 177–186.

Olson, S. L., Bates, J. E., & Bayles, K. (1984). Mother–infant interaction in the development of individual differences in children's cognitive competence. *Developmental Psychology, 20,* 166–179.

Estrada, P., Arsenio, W. F., Hess, R. D., & Holloway, S. D. (1987). Affective quality of the mother–child relationship: Longitudinal consequences for children's school-relevant cognitive functioning. *Developmental Psychology, 23,* 210–215.

Skinner, E. A. (1986). The origins of young children's perceived control: Mother contingent and sensitive behavior. *International Journal of Behavioral Development, 9,* 359–382.

Rubenstein, J. (1967). Maternal attentiveness and subsequent exploratory behavior in the infant. *Child Development, 38,* 1089–1100.

Frodi, A., Bridges, L., & Grolnick, W. (1985). Correlates of mastery-related behavior: A short-term longitudinal study of infants in their second year. *Child Development, 56,* 1291–1298.

Carew, J. V. (1976). *Observing intelligence in young children: Eight case studies.* Englewood Cliffs, NJ: Prentice-Hall.

Bradley, R. H., & Caldwell, B. M. (1984). The relation of infants' home environment to achievement test performance in first grade: A follow-up study. *Child Development, 55,* 803–809.

Gottfried, A. W. (Ed.). (1984). *Home environment and early cognitive development: Longitudinal research.* New York: Academic Press.

Levenstein, P. (1970). Cognitive growth in preschoolers through verbal interaction with mothers. *American Journal of Orthopsychiatry, 40,* 426–432.

Chapter 4
What's Out There?

1. Colette (1966). *Earthly paradise: An autobiography drawn from her lifetime writings* (R. Phelps, Ed.). New York: Farrar, Straus & Giroux, p. 28.

2. Bower, T. G. R. (1971). The object in the world of the infant. *Scientific American, 225,* 30–38.

3. Fantz, R. L. (1961, May). The origin of form perception. *Scientific American, 204,* pp. 66–72.

Salapatek, P. (1968). Visual scanning of geometric pattern by the human newborn. *Journal of Comparative and Physiological Psychology, 66,* 247–258.

Bushnell, I. W. R., Sai, F., & Mullin, J. T. (1989). Neonatal recognition of the mother's face. *British Journal of Developmental Psychology, 7,* 3–15.

Reissland, N. (1988). Neonatal imitation in the first hour of life: Observations in rural Nepal. *Developmental Psychology, 24,* 464–469.

Meltzoff, A., & Moore, M. K. (1977). Imitation of facial and manual gestures by human neonates. *Science, 198,* 75–78.

4. DeCasper, A. J., & Fifer, W. P. (1980). Of human bonding: Newborns prefer their mothers' voices. *Science, 208,* 1174–1176.

5. Brody, L. R., Zelazo, P. R., & Chaika, H. (1984). Habituation-dishabituation to speech in the neonate. *Developmental Psychology, 20,* 114–119.

   Weiss, M. J., Zelazo, P. R., & Swain, I. U. (1988). Newborn response to auditory discrepancy. *Child Development, 59,* 1530–1541.

   Aronson, E., & Rosenbloom, S. (1971). Space perception in early infancy: Perception within a common auditory–visual space. *Science, 172,* 1161–1163.

6. Rochat, P. (1987). Mouthing and grasping in neonates: Evidence for the early detection of what hard or soft substances afford for action. *Infant Behavior and Development, 10,* 435–449.

   Meltzoff, A. N., & Borton, R. W. (1979). Intermodal matching in human neonates. *Nature, 282,* 403–404.

7. Spelke, E. S. (1979). Perceiving bimodally specified events in infancy. *Developmental Psychology, 15,* 626–636.

8. Scaife, M., & Bruner, J. S. (1975). The capacity for joint visual attention in the infant. *Nature, 253,* 265–266.

   Feinman, S., & Lewis, M. (1983). Social referencing at ten months: A second-order effect on infants' responses to strangers. *Child Development, 54,* 878–887.

   Hornile, R., Risenhoover, N., & Gunnar, M. (1987). The effects of maternal positive, neutral, and negative affective communications on infant responses to new toys. *Child Development, 58,* 937–944.

   Lempers, J. D. (1979). Young children's production and comprehension of nonverbal deictic behaviors. *Journal of Genetic Psychology, 135,* 93–102.

   Leung, E. H. L., & Rheingold, H. L. (1981). Development of pointing as a social gesture. *Developmental Psychology, 17,* 215–220.

   Hannan, T. E. (1987). A cross-sequential assessment of the occurrences of pointing in 3- to 12-month-old human infants. *Infant Behavior and Development, 10,* 11–22.

9. Quinn, P. C., & Eimas, P. D. (1986). On categorization in early infancy. *Merrill-Palmer Quarterly, 32,* 331–363.

   Sugarman, S. (1982). Developmental change in early representational intelligence: Evidence from spatial classification strategies and related verbal expressions. *Cognitive Psychology, 14,* 410–449.

   Cohen, L. B., & Younger, B. A. (1983). Perceptual categorization in the infant. In E. Kofsky-Scholnick (Ed.), *New trends in conceptual representation: Challenges to Piaget's theory?* (pp. 197–220). Hillsdale, NJ: Lawrence Erlbaum.

   Colombo, J., O'Brien, M., Mitchell, D. W., Roberts, K., & Horowitz, F. D. (1987). A lower boundary for category formation in preverbal infants. *Journal of Child Language, 14,* 383–385.

Quinn, P. C. (1987). The categorical representation of visual patterns of information by young infants. *Cognition, 27,* 145–179.

Huttenlocher, J., & Smiley, P. (1987). Early word meanings: The case of object names. *Cognitive Psychology, 19,* 63–89.

Sherman, T. (1985). Categorization skills in infants. *Child Development, 56,* 1561–1573.

10. Ross, G. S. (1980). Categorization in 1- and 2-year olds. *Developmental Psychology, 16,* 391–396.

Sugarman, S. (1982). Developmental change in early representational intelligence: Evidence from spatial classification strategies and related verbal expressions. *Cognitive Psychology, 14,* 410–449.

Quinn & Eimas (1986). See note 9.

Hayne, H., Rovee-Collier, C., & Perris, E. E. (1987). Categorization and memory retrieval by three-month-olds. *Child Development, 58,* 750–767.

Roberts, K. (1988). Retrieval of a basic-level category in prelinguistic infants. *Developmental Psychology, 24,* 21–27.

11. Ross (1980). See note 10.

Markman, E. M. (1983). Two different kinds of hierarchical organization. In E. Kofsky-Scholnick (Ed.), *New trends in conceptual representation: Challenges to Piaget's theory?* (pp. 165–184). Hillsdale, NJ: Lawrence Erlbaum.

Brown, R. (1958). How shall a thing be called? *Psychological Review, 65,* 14–21.

12. Gelman, S. (1988). The development of induction within natural kind and artifact categories. *Cognitive Psychology, 20,* 65–95.

Gelman, S. A., & O'Reilly, A. W. (1988). Children's inductive inferences within superordinate categories: The role of language and category structure. *Child Development, 59,* 876–887.

Gelman, S. A., & Markman, E. M. (1987). Young children's inductions from natural kinds: The role of categories and appearances. *Child Development, 58,* 1532–1541.

Sugarman, S. (1983). The development of inductive strategy in children's early thought and language. *The Quarterly Newletter of the Laboratory of Comparative Human Cognition, 5,* 34–40.

13. Bretherton, I., & Beeghly, M. (1982). Talking about internal states: The acquisition of an explicit theory of mind. *Developmental Psychology, 18,* 906–921.

Wellman, H. M., & Estes, D. (1987). Children's early use of mental verbs and what they mean. *Discourse Processes, 10,* 141–156.

Bretherton, I., Fritz, J., Zahn-Waxler, C., & Ridgeway, D. (1986). Learning to talk about emotions: A functionalist perspective. *Child Development, 57,* 529–548.

14. Fabricius, W. V., Sophian, C., & Wellman, H. M. (1987). Young children's sensitivity to logical necessity in their inferential search behavior. *Child Development, 58,* 409–423.

Hawkins, J., Pea, R. D., Glick, J., & Scribner, S. (1984). "Merds that laugh don't like mushrooms": Evidence for deductive reasoning by preschoolers. *Developmental Psychology, 20,* 584–594.

Dias, M. G., & Harris, P. L. (1988). The effect of make-believe play on deductive reasoning. *British Journal of Developmental Psychology, 6,* 207–221.

15. Donaldson, M. (1983). Children's reasoning. In M. Donaldson, R. Grieve, & C. Pratt (Eds.), *Early childhood development and education* (pp. 231–236). New York: Guilford Press.

16. Vosniadou, S. (1987). Children and metaphor. *Child Development, 58,* 870–885.

Gentner, D. (1988). Metaphor as structure mapping: The relational shift. *Child Development, 59,* 47–59.

Alexander, P. A., Willson, V. L., White, C. S., & Fuqua, J. D. (1987). Analogical reasoning in young children. *Journal of Educational Psychology, 79,* 401–408.

Nippold, M., & Sullivan, M. (1987). Verbal and perceptual analogical reasoning and proportional metaphor comprehension in young children. *Journal of Speech and Hearing Research, 30,* 367–376.

17. Price, R. H., & Thorne, K. S. (1988, April). The membrane paradigm for black holes. *Scientific American, 258,* 69–77.

18. Gelman, R., & Gallistel, C. R. (1983). The child's understanding of number. In M. Donaldson, R. Grieve, & C. Pratt (Eds.), *Early childhood development and education: Readings in psychology* (pp. 185–203). New York: Guilford Press.

Hughes, M. (1983). What is difficult about learning arithmetic? In M. Donaldson, R. Grieve, & C. Pratt (Eds.), *Early childhood development and education: Readings in psychology* (pp. 204–221). New York: Guilford Press.

Saxe, G. B., Guberman, S. R., & Gearhart, M. (1988). Social processes in early number development. *Monographs of the Society for Research in Child Development, 52*(2, Serial No. 216).

Bryant, P. E., & Kopytynska, H. (1983). Spontaneous measurement by young children. In M. Donaldson, R. Grieve, & C. Pratt (Eds.), *Early childhood development and education: Readings in psychology* (pp. 222–225). New York: Guilford Press.

19. Antell, S. E., & Keating, D. P. (1983). Perception of numerical invariance in neonates. *Child Development, 54,* 695–701.

20. Papousek, M., Papousek, H., & Bornstein, M. H. (1984). The naturalistic vocal environment of young infants. In T. M. Field & N. Fox. (Eds.), *Social perception in infants.* Norwood, NJ: Ablex.

Belsky, J., Goode, M. K., & Most, R. K. (1980). Maternal stimulation and infant exploratory competence: Cross-sectional, correlational, and experimental analyses. *Child Development, 51,* 1163–1178.

Tamis-LeMonda, C. S., & Bornstein, M. H. (1989). Habituation and maternal encouragement of attention in infancy as predictors of toddler language, play, and representational competence. *Child Development, 60,* 738–751.

Henderson, B. B. (1984). Social support and exploration. *Child Development, 55,* 1246–1251.

21. Palmer, C. F. (1989). The discriminating nature of infants' exploratory actions. *Developmental Psychology, 25,* 885–893.

MacLean, D. J., & Schuler, M. (1989). Conceptual development in infancy: The understanding of containment. *Child Development, 60,* 1126–1137.

22. Korner, A. F., & Grobstein, R. (1966). Visual alertness as related to soothing in neonates: Implications for maternal stimulation and early deprivation. *Child Development, 37,* 867–876.

23. Belsky, Goode, & Most (1980). See note 20.

24. Seifer, R., & Vaughn, B. E. (1987). Family effects on competence during the first four years of life. In B. E. Vaughn (Chair), *Parent-child interactions as sources of competence during childhood.* Symposium presented at Society for Research in Child Development meeting, Baltimore.

25. Hay, D. F. (1979). Cooperative interaction and sharing between very young children and their parents. *Developmental Psychology, 15,* 647–653.

26. Sherman, T. M., & Cormier, W. H. (1974). An investigation of the influence of student behavior on teachers. *Journal of Applied Behavior Analysis, 7,* 11–21.

27. Masur, E. F. (1982). Mothers' responses to infants' object-related gestures: Influences on lexical development. *Journal of Child Language, 9,* 23–30.

Tomasello, M., & Farrar, M. J. (1986). Joint attention and early language. *Child Development, 57,* 1454–1463.

Olson, S. L., Bates, J. E., & Bayles, K. (1984). Mother–infant interaction and the development of individual differences in children's cognitive competence. *Developmental Psychology, 20,* 166–179.

Mervis, C. B., & Mervis, C. A. (1988). Role of adult input in young children's category evolution: I. An observational study. *Journal of Child Language, 15,* 257–272.

Banigan, R. L., & Mervis, C. B. (1988). Role of adult input in children's category evolution: II. An experimental study. *Journal of Child Language, 15,* 493–504.

28. West, M. J., & Rheingold, H. L. (1978). Infant stimulation of maternal instruction. *Infant Behavior and Development, 1,* 205–215.

29. Carew, J. V., Chan, I., & Halfar, C. (1976). *Observing intelligence in young children: Eight case studies.* Englewood Cliffs, NJ: Prentice-Hall.

30. Miller, G. A., & Gildea, P. M. (1987, September). How children learn words. *Scientific American,* pp. 94–99.

Rice, M. L., & Woodsmall, L. (1988). Lessons from television: Children's word learning when viewing. *Child Development, 59,* 420–429.

Heibeck, T. H., & Markman, E. M. (1987). Word learning in children: An examination of fast mapping. *Child Development, 58,* 1021–1034.

Taylor, M., & Gelman, S. A. (1988). Adjectives and nouns: Children's strategies for learning new words. *Child Development, 59,* 411–419.

31. Lucariello, J. (1987). Spinning fantasy: Themes, structures, and the knowledge base. *Child Development, 58,* 434–442.

Howes, C. (1985). Sharing fantasy: Social pretend play in toddlers. *Child Development, 56,* 1253–1258.

32. Dunn, J., Bretherton, I., & Munn, P. (1987). Conversations about feeling states between mothers and their young children. *Developmental Psychology, 23,* 132–139.

33. Taylor, M. (1988). Conceptual perspective taking: Children's ability to distinguish what they know from what they see. *Child Development, 59,* 703–718.

Yaniv, I., & Shatz, M. (1990). Heuristics of reasoning and analogy in children's visual perspective taking. *Child Development, 61,* 1491–1501.

Lewis, C., & Osborne, A. (1990). Three-year-olds' problems with false belief: Conceptual deficit or linguistic artifact? *Child Development, 61,* 1514–1519.

Pratt, C., & Bryant, P. (1990). Young children understand that looking leads to knowing (so long as they are looking into a single barrel). *Child Development, 61,* 973–982.

Piaget, J., & Inhelder, B. (1967). *The child's conception of space.* New York: Norton. (Original work published 1948).

34. Bretherton & Beeghly (1982). See note 13.

Wellman, H. M., & Estes, D. (1987). Children's early use of mental verbs and what they mean. *Discourse Processes, 10,* 141–156.

35. Stevenson, M. B., Ver Hoeve, J. N., Roach, M. A., & Leavitt, L. A. (1986). The beginning of conversation: Early patterns of mother–infant vocal responsiveness. *Infant Behavior and Development, 9,* 423–440.

Keller, H., & Scholmerich, A. (1987). Infant vocalizations and parental reactions during the first 4 months of life. *Developmental Psychology, 23,* 62–67.

Acredolo, L., & Goodwyn, S. (1988). Symbolic gesturing in normal infants. *Child Development, 59,* 450–466.

36. Olson, S. L., Bayles, K., & Bates, J. E. (1986). Mother–child interaction and children's speech progress: A longitudinal study of the first two years. *Merrill-Palmer Quarterly, 32,* 1–20.

37. Nelson, K. (1981). Individual differences in language development: Implications for development and language. *Developmental Psychology, 17,* 170–187.

38. Hart, B., & Risley, T. R. (1974). Using preschool materials to modify the

language of disadvantaged children. *Journal of Applied Behavior Analysis, 7,* 243–256.

39. Uttal, D. H., & Wellman, H. M. (1989). Young children's representation of spatial information acquired from maps. *Developmental Psychology, 25,* 128–138.
   Blades, M. (1989). Children's ability to learn about the environment from direct experience and from spatial representation. *Children's Environments Quarterly, 6*(2,3), 4–14.

40. Prather, P. A., & Bacon, J. (1986). Developmental differences in part/whole identification. *Child Development, 57,* 549–558.
   Tversky, B. (1989). Parts, partonomies, and taxonomies. *Developmental Psychology, 25,* 983–995.

41. Carew, Chan, & Halfar (1976). See note 29.

42. Eimas, P. D. (1985, January). The perception of speech in early infancy. *Scientific American, 252,* pp. 46–52.
   Eimas, P. D., Siqueland, E. R., Jusczyk, P., & Vigorito, J. (1971). Speech perception in early infancy. *Science, 171,* 303–306.
   Jusczyk, P. W., & Derrah, C. (1987). Representation of speech sounds by young infants. *Developmental Psychology, 23,* 648–654.
   Gibson, E. J., & Walker, A. S. (1984). Development of knowledge of visual–tactual affordances of substance. *Child Development, 55,* 453–460.

43. Maurer, D., & Salapatek, P. (1976). Developmental changes in scanning of faces by young infants. *Child Development, 47,* 523–527.

44. Hess, R., & Shipman, V. (1972). Parents as teachers: How lower class and middle class mothers teach. In C. S. Lavatelli & F. Stendler (Eds.), *Readings in child behavior and development.* (3rd ed., pp. 437–446). New York: Harcourt Brace Jovanovich.

45. Hess, R. D., & McDevitt, T. M. (1984). Some cognitive consequences of maternal intervention techniques: A longitudinal study. *Child Development, 55,* 2017–2030.

46. Bauer, P. J., & Mandler, J. M. (1989). Taxonomies and triads: Conceptual organization in one- to two-year-olds. *Cognitive Psychology, 21,* 156–184.
   Fenson, L., & Vella, D., & Kennedy, M. (1989). Children's knowledge of thematic and taxonomic relations at two years of age. *Child Development, 60,* 911–919.
   Scott, M. S., & Greenfield, D. B. (1986). Young children's intensional knowledge of superordinate categories. *Journal of Genetic Psychology, 147,* 219–232.

47. Gelman & Markman (1987). See note 12.

48. Ebeling, K. S., & Gelman, S. A. (1988). Coordination of size standard by young children. *Child Development, 59,* 888–896.

49. Massey, C. M., & Gelman, R. (1988). Preschooler's ability to decide whether

a photographed unfamiliar object can move itself. *Developmental Psychology, 24,* 307–313.

50. Nippold, M. A., & Sullivan, M. P. (1987). Verbal and perceptual analogical reasoning and proportional metaphor comprehension in young children. *Journal of Speech and Hearing Research, 30,* 367–376.

Vosnidadou, S., & Schommer, M. (1988). Explanatory analogies can help children acquire information from expository text. *Journal of Educational Psychology, 80,* 524–536.

51. Eder, R. A. (1989). The emergent personologist: The structure and content of 3½-, 5½-, and 7½-year-olds' concepts of themselves and other persons. *Child Development, 60,* 1218–1228.

52. Brown, R. (1958). How shall a thing be called? *Psychological Review, 65,* 14–21.

53. Piaget, J., & Szeminska, A. (1952). *The child's conception of number* (C. Gattegno & F. M. Hodgson, Trans.). New York: Humanities Press. (Original work published 1941.)

McGarrigle, J. Grieve, R., & Hughes, M. (1978). Interpreting inclusion: A contribution to the study of the child's cognitive and linguistic development. *Journal of Experimental Child Psychology, 25,* 1528–1550.

Markman, E. M., Cox, B., & Machida, S. (1981). The standard object-sorting task as a measure of conceptual organization. *Developmental Psychology, 17,* 115–117.

54. Hoff-Ginsberg, E. (1986). Function and structure in maternal speech: Their relation to the child's development of syntax. *Developmental Psychology, 22,* 155–163.

55. Sheff, D. (1988, January 19). "Izzy, did you ask a good question today?" [Letter to the editor]. *New York Times,* p. A26.

56. Endsley, R. C., & Clarey, S. A. (1975). Answering young children's questions as a determinant of their subsequent question-asking behavior. *Developmental Psychology, 11,* 863.

57. Toner, I. J., Moore, L. P., & Emmons, B. A. (1980). The effect of being labeled on subsequent self-control in children. *Child Development, 51,* 618–621.

Jensen, A. M., & Moore, S. G. (1977). The effect of attribute statements on cooperativeness and competitiveness in school-age boys. *Child Development, 48,* 305–307.

58. Gelman, R., Meck, E., & Merkin, S. (1986). Young children's numerical competence. *Cognitive Development, 1,* 1–29.

59. Gelman, R. & Gallistel, C. R. (1978). *The child's understanding of number.* Cambridge, MA: Harvard University Press.

Saxe, G. B., Guberman, S. R., & Gearhart, M. (1987). Social processes in early number development. *Monographs of the Society for Research in Child Development, 52*(2, Serial No. 216).

60. Piaget, J. (1953). How children form mathematical concepts. *Scientific American, 189,* 74–79.

61. McGarrigle, J., & Donaldson, M. (1974). Conservation accidents. *Cognition, 3*, 341–350.

Gelman, R. (1979). Preschool thought. *American Psychologist, 34*, 900–905.

Donaldson, M. (1982). Conservation: What is the question? *British Journal of Psychology, 73*, 199–207.

Schiff, W. (1983). Conservation of length redux: A perceptual–linguistic phenomenon. *Child Development, 54*, 1497–1506.

Parsonson, B. S., & Naughton, K. A. (1988). Training generalized conservation in 5-year-old children. *Journal of Experimental Child Psychology, 46*, 372–390.

Mehler, J., & Bever, T. C. (1967). Cognitive capacity of very young children. *Science, 158*, 141–142.

62. Hawkins, J., Pea, R. D., Glick, J., & Scribner, S. (1984). "Merds that laugh don't like mushrooms": Evidence for deductive reasoning by preschoolers. *Developmental Psychology, 20*, 584–594.

Harris, P. L., & Bassett, E. (1975). Transitive inference by 4-year-old children? *Developmental Psychology, 11*, 875–876.

Kodroff, J. K., & Roberge, J. J. (1975). Developmental analysis of conditional reasoning abilities of primary-grade children. *Developmental Psychology, 11*, 21–28.

63. Duckworth, E. (1987). *"The having of wonderful ideas" and other essays on teaching and learning.* New York: Teachers College Press.

64. Linn, M. C., deBenedictis, T., & Delucchi, K. (1982). Adolescent reasoning about advertisements: Preliminary investigations. *Child Development, 53*, 1599–1633.

Peterson, L., & Lewis, K. E. (1988). Preventive intervention to improve children's discrimination of the persuasive tactics in televised advertising. *Journal of Pediatric Psychology, 13*, 163–170.

65. Woolley, J. D., & Wellman, H. M. (1990). Young children's understanding of realities, nonrealities, and appearances. *Child Development, 61*, 956–961.

66. Arnold, K. D., Moye, J., & Winer, G. A. (1986). Illusion versus reality: Children's understanding of temperature adaptation. *Journal of Experimental Child Psychology, 42*, 256–272.

Shing, M., & Winer, G. A. (1990). Understanding perceptual processes: Responses to a weight-illusion task. *Developmental Psychology, 26*, 121–127.

Chapter 5
What Leads to What?

1. Marquis, D. P. (1931). Can conditioned responses be established in the newborn infant? *Journal of Genetic Psychology, 39*, 479–492.

Lipsitt, L. P. (1966). Learning processes of newborns. *Merrill-Palmer Quarterly, 12*, 45–71.

Sameroff, A. J. (1971). Can conditioned responses be established in the newborn infant: 1971? *Developmental Psychology, 5,* 1–12.

Moon, C., & Fifer, W. P. (1990). Syllables as signals for 2-day-old infants. *Infant Behavior and Development, 13,* 377–390.

2. Lamb, M. E., & Malkin, C. M. (1986). The development of social expectations in distress–relief sequences: A longitudinal study. *International Journal of Behavioral Development, 9,* 235–249.

Thoman, E. B., Korner, A. F., & Beason-Williams, L. (1977). Modification of responsiveness to maternal vocalization in the neonate. *Child Development, 48,* 563–569.

3. Richie, D. M., & Brickhard, B. H. (1988). The ability to perceive duration: Its relation to the development of the logical concept of time. *Developmental Psychology, 24,* 318–323.

4. Clinton, R. K. (1974). Heart rate conditioning in the newborn infant. *Journal of Experimental Child Psychology, 18,* 9–21.

Donahue, R. L., & Berg, W. K. (1991). Infant heart-rate responses to temporally predictable and unpredictable events. *Developmental Psychology, 27,* 59–66.

5. Mendelson, M. J. (1986). Perception of the temporal pattern of motion in infancy. *Infant Behavior and Development, 9,* 231–243.

Allen, T. W., Walker, K., Symonds, L., & Marcell, M. (1977). Intrasensory and intersensory perception of temporal sequences during infancy. *Developmental Psychology, 13,* 225–229.

Trehub, S. E., Thorp, L. A., & Morrongiello (1987). Organizational processes in infant's perception of auditory patterns. *Child Development, 58,* 741–749.

Haith, M. M., & Hazan, C., & Goodman, G. S. (1988). Expectation and anticipation of dynamic visual events by 3.5-month-old babies. *Child Development, 59,* 467–479.

Canfield, R. L., & Haith, M. M. (1991). Young infants: Visual expectations for symmetric and asymmetric stimulus sequences. *Developmental Psychology, 27,* 188–208.

Smith, P. H., Arehart, D. M., Haaf, R. A., & deSaint Victor, C. M. (1989). Expectancies and memory for spatiotemporal events in 5-month-old infants. *Journal of Experimental Child Psychology, 47,* 210–235.

Smith, P. H., Jankowski, M. B., & Loboschefski, T. (1990). Preverbal infant response to spatiotemporal events: Evidence of differential chunking abilities. *Infant Behavior and Development, 13,* 129–146.

6. Bauer, P. J., & Mandler, J. M. (1989). One thing follows another: Effects of temporal structure on 1- and 2-year-olds' recall of events. *Developmental Psychology, 25,* 197–206.

7. O'Connell, B. G., & Gerard, A. B. (1985). Scripts and scraps: The development of sequential understanding. *Child Development, 56,* 671–681.

Nelson, K., & Gruendel, J. (1981). Generalized event representations: Basic building blocks of cognitive development. In A. Brown & M. Lamb (Eds.), *Advances in developmental psychology* (Vol. 1, pp. 131–150). Hillsdale, NJ: Lawrence Erlbaum.

Carni, E., & French, L. A. (1984). The acquisition of *before* and *after* reconsidered: What develops? *Journal of Experimental Child Psychology, 37,* 394–403.

Pellegrini, A. D., Brody, G. H., & Stoneman, Z. (1987). Children's conversational competence with their parents. *Discourse Processes, 10,* 93–106.

Harner, L. (1975). Yesterday and tomorrow: Development of early understanding of the terms. *Developmental Psychology, 11,* 864–865.

Friedman, W. J., & Brudos, S. L. (1988). On routes and routines: The early development of spatial and temporal representations. *Cognitive Development, 3,* 167–182.

8. Seidel, R. J. (1959). A review of sensory preconditioning. *Psychological Bulletin, 56,* 58–73.

Tolman, E. C. (1949). There is more than one kind of learning. *Psychological Review, 56,* 144–155.

Rescorla, R. A. (1988). Pavlovian conditioning: It's not what you think it is. *American Psychologist, 43,* 151–160.

Estes, W. K. (1964). Probability learning. In. A. W. Melton (Ed.), *Categories of human learning* (pp. 89–128). New York: Academic Press.

Bandura, A. (1965). Vicarious processes: A case of no-trial learning. In L. Berkowitz (Ed.), *Advances in experimental social psychology* (Vol. 2, pp. 1–55). New York: Academic Press.

9. Piaget, J. (1970). Piaget's theory. In P. H. Mussen, (Ed.). *Carmichael's manual of child psychology* (3rd ed., Vol. 1, pp. 703–732). New York: Wiley.

10. Meltzoff, A. N. (1988). Infant imitation and memory: Nine-month-olds in immediate and deferred tests. *Child Development, 59,* 217–225.

11. Lucariello, J., & Nelson, K. (1987). Remembering and planning talk between mothers and children. *Discourse Processes, 10,* 219–235.

Chapter 6
What Makes Things Happen?

1. Hood, L., & Bloom, L. (1979). What, when, and how about why: A longitudinal study of early expressions of causality. *Monographs of the Society for Research in Child Development, 44*(6, Serial No. 181).

Bretherton, I., & Beeghly, M. (1982). Talking about internal states: The acquisition of an explicit theory of mind. *Developmental Psychology, 18,* 906–921.

Byrnes, J. P., & Duff, M. A. (1988). Young children's comprehension and production of causal expressions. *Child Study Journal, 18,* 101–119.

2. Piaget, J. (1974). *Understanding causality* (D. Miles & M. Miles, Trans.). New York: Norton. (Original work published 1971).

Piaget, J. (1930). *The child's conception of physical causality*. London: Kegan Paul.

Siegel, L. S., & Brainerd, C. J. (Eds.). (1978). *Alternatives to Piaget: Critical essays on the theory*. New York: Academic Press.

Borke, H. (1975). Piaget's mountains revisited: Changes in the egocentric landscape. *Developmental Psychology, 11*, 240–243.

Ford, M. E. (1979). The construct validity of egocentrism. *Psychological Bulletin, 86*, 1169–1188.

Taylor, M. (1988). Conceptual perspective taking: Children's ability to distinguish what they know from what they see. *Child Development, 59*, 703–718.

3. Dolgin, K. G., & Behrend, D. A. (1984). Children's knowledge about animates and inanimates. *Child Development, 55*, 1646–1650.

Deutsche, J. M. (1937). The development of children's concepts of causal relations. *University of Minnesota Child Welfare Monograph, No. 13*. Minneapolis: University of Minnesota Press.

4. Peterson, C., & Marrie, C. (1988). Even 4-year-olds can detect inconsistency. *Journal of Genetic Psychology, 149*, 119–126.

5. Bretherton, I., Fritz, J., Zahn-Waxler, C., & Ridgeway, D. (1986). Learning to talk about emotions: A functionalist perspective. *Child Development, 57*, 529–548.

6. Shimony, A. (1988, January). The reality of the quantum world. *Scientific American, 258*, 46–53.

7. Zelazo, P. D., & Shultz, T. (1989). Concepts of potency and resistance in causal prediction. *Child Development, 60*, 1307–1315.

8. Bullock, M., Gelman, R., & Baillargeon, R. (1982). The development of causal reasoning. In W. J. Friedman (Ed.), *The developmental psychology of time* (pp. 209–254). New York: Academic Press.

McCabe, A., & Peterson, C. (1985). A naturalistic study of the production of causal connectives by children. *Journal of Child Language, 12*, 145–159.

Berzonsky, M. (1971). The role of familiarity on children's explanations of physical causality. *Child Development, 42*, 705–712.

Nass, M. L. (1956). The effects of three variables on children's concepts of physical causality. *Journal of Abnormal and Social Psychology, 53*, 191–196.

Golinkoff, R. M., Harding, C. G., Carlson, V., & Sexton, M. E. (1984). The infant's perception of causal events: The distinction between animate and inanimate objects. In L. P. Lipsitt & C. Rovee-Collier (Eds.), *Advances in infancy research* (Vol. 3, pp. 145–151). Norwood, NJ: Ablex.

Sugarman, S. (1984). The development of preverbal communication: Its contribution and limits as promoting the development of language. In R. Schiefelbusch & J. Pickar (Eds.), *The acquisition of communicative competence* (pp. 23–67). Baltimore: University Park Press.

Legerstee, M., Corter, C., & Kienapple, K. (1990). Hand, arm, and facial actions of young infants to a social and nonsocial stimulus. *Child Development, 61,* 774–784.

9. Shultz, T. R. (1982). Rules of causal attribution. *Monographs of the Society for Research in Child Development, 47*(1, Serial No. 194).

Ball, W. A. (1979, March). *The perception of causality in the infant.* Paper presented at the meeting of the Society for Research in Child Development, San Francisco.

10. Kuzmak, S. D., & Gelman, R. (1986). Young children's understanding of random phenomena. *Child Development, 57,* 559–566.

11. Shultz, T. R., & Mendelson, R. (1975). The use of covariation as a principle of causal analysis. *Child Development, 46,* 394–399.

Siegler, R. S. (1976). The effects of simple necessity and sufficiency relationships on children's causal inferences. *Child Development, 47,* 1058–1063.

12. Long, L., & Welch, L. (1941). Reasoning ability in young children. *The Journal of Psychology, 12,* 21–44.

13. Shaklee, H., Holt, P., Elek, S., & Hall, L. (1988). Covariation judgment: Improving rule use among children, adolescents, and adults. *Child Development, 59,* 755–768.

Kuhn, D. (1989). Children and adults as intuitive scientists. *Psychological Review, 96,* 674–689.

14. Piaget, J. (1967, March 21). Unpublished lecture at New York University. Quoted in Phillips, Jr., J. L. (1969). *The origins of intellect: Piaget's theory* (p. 120). San Francisco: W. H. Freeman.

15. White, B. Y., & Horwitz, P. (1987, March). *ThinkerTools: Enabling children to understand physical laws* (Report No. 6470). Cambridge, MA: BBN Laboratories Incorporated.

White, B. (1983). Sources of difficulty in understanding Newtonian dynamics. *Cognitive Science, 7,* 41–65.

16. Koslowski, B., Okagaki, L., Lorenz, C., & Umbach, D. (1989). When covariation in not enough: The role of causal mechanism, sampling method, and sample size in causal reasoning. *Child Development, 60,* 1316–1327.

17. Alloy, L. B., & Tabachnik, N. (1984). Assessment of covariation by humans and animals: The joint influence of prior expectations and current situational information. *Psychological Review, 91,* 112–149.

18. Tinbergen, N. (1951). *The study of instinct.* London, England: Oxford University Press.

Brown, J. L., & Hunsperger, R. W. (1963). Neuroethology and motivation of agonistic behavior. *Animal Behavior, 11,* 439–448.

Funkenstein, D. H. (1955). The physiology of fear and anger *Scientific American, 192*, 74–80.

19. Haviland, J. M., & Lelwica, M. (1987). The induced affect response: 10-week-old infants' responses to three emotion expressions. *Developmental Psychology, 23*, 97–104.

   Ludermann, P. M., & Nelson, C. A. (1988). Categorical representation of facial expressions by 7-month-old infants. *Developmental Psychology, 24*, 492–501.

20. Fabes, R. A., Eisenberg, N., McCormick, S. E., & Wilson, M. S. (1988). Preschoolers' attributions of the situational determinants of others' naturally occurring emotions. *Developmental Psychology, 24*, 376–385.

   Schwartz, R. M., & Trabasso, T. (1984). Children's understanding of emotions. In C. Izard, J. Kagan, & R. Zajonc (Eds.), *Emotions, cognitions, and behavior* (pp. 409–437). Cambridge, England: Cambridge University Press.

   McCoy, C. L., & Masters, J. C. (1985). The development of children's strategies for the social control of emotion. *Child Development, 56*, 1214–1222.

   Russell, J. A. (1990). The preschooler's understanding of the causes and consequences of emotion. *Child Development, 61*, 1872–1881.

21. Ridgeway, D., Waters, E., & Kuczaj II, S. A. (1985). Acquisition of emotion–descriptive language: Receptive and productive vocabulary norms for ages 18 months to 6 years. *Developmental Psychology, 21*, 901–908.

   Weiner, B., & Handel, S. J. (1985). A cognition-emotion-action sequence: Anticipated emotional consequences of causal attributions and reported communication strategy. *Developmental Psychology, 21*, 102–107.

   Gnepp, J., McKee, E., & Domanic, J. A. (1987). Children's use of situational information to infer emotion: Understanding emotionally equivocal situations. *Developmental Psychology, 23*, 114–123.

   Harris, P. L., Donnelly, K., Guz, G. R., & Pitt-Watson, R. (1986). Children's understanding of the distinction between real and apparent emotion. *Child Development, 57*, 895–909.

22. Miller, P., & Sperry, L. L. (1987). The socialization of anger and aggression. *Merrill-Palmer Quarterly, 33*, 1–31.

23. Kelley, H. H. (1972). Attribution in social interaction. In E. E. Jones, D. E. Kanouse, H. H. Kelley, R. E. Nisbett, S. Valins, & B. Weiner (Eds.), *Attribution: Perceiving the causes of behavior* (pp. 1–26). Morristown, NJ: General Learning Press.

   Gnepp, J. (1989). Personalized inferences of emotions and appraisals: Component processes and correlates. *Developmental Psychology, 25*, 277–288.

24. Barber, T. X., Spanos, N. P., Chaves, J. F. (1974). *Hypnosis, imagination, and human potentialities.* New York: Pergamon.

25. Poulin-Dubois, D., & Shultz, T. R. (1990). The infant's concept of agency: The distinction between social and nonsocial objects. *Journal of Genetic Psychology, 151*, 77–90.

Shultz, T. R. (1980). Development of the concept of intention. In W. A. Collins (Ed.), *The Minnesota Symposium on Child Psychology* (Vol. 13, pp. 131–164). Hillsdale, NJ: Lawrence Erlbaum.

Keasey, C. B. (1977). Children's developing awareness and usage of intentionality and motives. In H. E. Howe, Jr. (Ed.). *Nebraska Symposium on Motivation* (Vol. 26, pp. 219–260). Lincoln: University of Nebraska Press.

Hood & Bloom (1979). See note 1.

McCabe & Peterson (1985). See note 8.

Bartsch, K., & Wellman, H. (1989). Young children's attribution of action to beliefs and desires. *Child Development, 60,* 946–964.

26. Nelson-LeGall, S. A. (1985). Motive-outcome matching and outcome foreseeability: Effects on attribution of intentionality and moral judgments. *Developmental Psychology, 21,* 332–337.

    Yuill, N., & Perner, J. (1988). Intentionality and knowledge in children's judgments of actor's responsibility and recipient's emotional reaction. *Developmental Psychology, 24,* 358–365.

    Karniol, R. (1978). Children's use of intentional cues in evaluating behavior. *Psychological Bulletin, 85,* 76–85.

    Piaget, J. (1965). *The moral judgment of the child.* New York: Free Press.

27. Chandler, M., Fritz, A. S., & Hala, S. (1989). Small-scale deceit: Deception as a marker of two-, three-, and four-year-olds' early theories of mind. *Child Development, 60,* 1263–1277.

    Lewis, M., Stanger, C., & Sullivan, M. W. (1989). Deception in 3-year-olds. *Developmental Psychology, 25,* 439–443.

28. Haviland & Lelwica (1987). See note 19.

29. Miller, P. H. (1985). Children's reasoning about the causes of human behavior. *Journal of Experimental Child Psychology, 39,* 343–362.

30. Moran, G., Krupka, A., Tutton, A., & Symons, D. (1987). Patterns of maternal and infant imitation during play. *Infant Behavior and Development, 10,* 477–491.

31. Covell, K., & Abramovitch, R. (1988). Children's understanding of maternal anger: Age and source of anger differences. *Merrill-Palmer Quarterly, 34,* 353–368.

    Weiss, M. G., & Miller, P. H. (1983). Young children's understanding of displaced aggression. *Journal of Experimental Child Psychology, 35,* 529–539.

32. Freud, S. (1947). *Leonardo da Vinci: A study in psychosexuality.* New York: Random House.

33. Gnepp, J., & Gould, M. E. (1985). The development of personalized inferences: Understanding other people's emotional reactions in light of their prior experiences. *Child Development, 56,* 1455–1464.

34. Darley, J. M., & Fazio, R. H. (1980). Expectancy confirmation processes

arising in the social interaction sequence. *American Psychologist, 35,* 867–881.

35. Neuberg, S. L. (1989). The goal of forming accurate impressions during social interactions: Attenuating the impact of negative expectancies. *Journal of Personality and Social Psychology, 56,* 374–386.

36. Bernstein, J. (1975, October 20) I.I. Rabi. *The New Yorker,* p. 47.

Chapter 7
What's Controllable?

1. Schorr, D., & Rodin, J. (1984). Motivation to control one's environment in individuals with obsessive–compulsive, depressive, and normal personality traits. *Journal of Personality and Social Psychology, 46,* 1148–1161.

2. DeCasper, A. J., & Fifer, W. P. (1980). Of human bonding: Newborns prefer their mothers' voices. *Science, 208,* 1174–1176.

3. Lipsitt, L. P. (1979). Learning capacities of the human infant. In R. J. Robinson (Ed.), *Brain and early behavior: Development in the fetus and infant* (pp. 227–249). New York: Academic Press.
   Watson, J. (1972). Smiling, cooing and "The Game." *Merrill–Palmer Quarterly, 18,* 323–339.
   Rovee, C. K., & Rovee, D. (1969). Conjugate reinforcement of infant exploratory behavior. *Journal of Experimental Child Psychology, 8,* 33–39.
   Rovee, C. K., Morrongiello, B. A., Aron, M., & Kupersmidt, J. (1978). Topographical response differentiation and reversal in 3-month-old infants. *Infant Behavior and Development, 1,* 323–333.
   Milewski, A. (1979). Visual discrimination and detection of configural invariance in 3-month infants. *Developmental Psychology, 15,* 357–363.
   Rheingold, H. L., Gewirtz, J. L., & Ross, H. W. (1959). Social conditioning of vocalization. *Journal of Abnormal and Social Psychology, 52,* 68–73.
   Lewis, M., Alessandri, S. M., & Sullivan, M. W. (1990). Violations of expectancy, loss of control, and anger expression in young infants. *Developmental Psychology, 26,* 745–751.

4. Behrend, D. A., Rosengren, K., & Perlmutter, M. (1989). A new look at children's private speech: The effects of age, task difficulty, and parent presence. *International Journal of Behavioral Development, 12,* 305–320.

5. Lipsitt, L. P. (1966). Learning processes of newborns. *Merrill-Palmer Quarterly, 12,* 45–71.
   Piaget, J. (1952). *The origins of intelligence in children.* New York: International Universities Press.

6. Bower, T. G. R. (1974). *Development in infancy.* San Francisco: W. H. Freeman.

Baillargeon, R., & Graber, M. (1988). Evidence of location memory in 8-month-old infants in a nonsearch A-B task. *Developmental Psychology, 24,* 502–511.

Landau, B., & Spelke, E. (1988). Geometric complexity and object search in infancy. *Developmental Psychology, 24,* 512–521.

Haith, M. M., Hazan, C., & Goodman, G. S. (1988). Expectation and anticipation of dynamic visual events by 3.5-month-old babies. *Child Development, 59,* 467–479.

Wellman, H. M., Cross, D., & Bartsch, K. (1986). Infant search and object permanence: A meta-analysis of the A-not-B error. *Monographs of the Society for Research in Child Development, 51*(3, Serial No. 214).

Baillargeon, R. (1987). Object permanence in 3½- and 4½-month-old infants. *Developmental Psychology, 23,* 655–664.

Ruff, H. A., Capozzoli, M., Dubiner, K., & Parrinello, R. (1990). A measure of vigilance in infancy. *Infant Behavior and Development, 13,* 1–20.

7. Caron, R. F., & Caron, A. J. (1978). Effects of ecologically relevant manipulations on infant discrimination learning. *Infant Behavior and Development, 1,* 291–307.

8. DeLoache, J. S., Sugarman, S., & Brown, A. L. (1985). The development of error correcting strategies in young children's manipulative play. *Child Development, 56,* 928–939.

Brownell, C. A. (1988). Combinatorial skills: Converging developments over the second year. *Child Development, 59,* 675–685.

9. Locke, E. A., Shaw, K. N., Saari, L. M., & Latham, G. P. (1981). Goal setting and task performance: 1969–1980. *Psychological Bulletin, 90,* 125–152.

10. Bower, T. G. R. (1989). *The rational infant.* New York: W. H. Freeman.

11. Bates, E., Carlson-Luden, V., & Bretherton, I. (1980). Perceptual aspects of tool using in infancy. *Infant Behavior and Development, 3,* 127–140.

12. Harding, C. G., & Golinkoff, R. M. (1979). The origins of intentional vocalizations in prelinguistic infants. *Child Development, 50,* 33–40.

Sugarman, S. (1984). The development of preverbal communication: Its contribution and limits in promoting the development of language. In R. Schiefelbusch & J. Picker (Eds.), *The acquisition of communicative competence* (pp. 23–67). Baltimore: University Park Press.

Sexton, M. (1983). The development of the understanding of causality in infancy. *Infant Behavior and Development, 6,* 201–210.

Rogoff, B., Mistry, J., Radziszewska, B., & Germond, J. (in press). Infants' instrumental social interaction with adults. In S. Feinman (Ed.), *Social referencing and the social construction of reality in infancy.* New York: Plenum.

Rogoff, B., Malkin, C., & Gilbride, K. (1984). Interaction with babies as guidance in development. In B. Rogoff & J. V. Wertsch (Eds.), *Children's learning in the "zone of proximal development"* (pp. 31–44). New directions for child development, No. 23. San Francisco: Jossey–Bass.

Hay, D. F. (1979). Cooperative interactions and sharing between very young children and their parents. *Developmental Psychology, 15,* 647–657.

13. Rogoff, B. (1991). The joint socialization of development by young children and adults. In M. Lewis & S. Feinman (Eds.), *Social influences and behavior.* New York: Plenum.

14. Cooper, C. R. (1980). Development of collaborative problem solving among preschool children. *Developmental Psychology, 16,* 433–440.

15. Dunn, J., & Munn, P. (1985). Becoming a family member: Family conflict and the development of social understanding in the second year. *Child Development, 56,* 480–492.

16. McCoy, C. L., & Masters, J. C. (1985). The development of children's strategies for the social control of emotion. *Child Development, 56,* 1214–1222.

    Barnett, K., Darcie, G., Holland, C., & Kobasigawa, A. (1982). Children's cognitions about effective helping. *Developmental Psychology, 18,* 267–277.

17. Kaye, K., & Marcus, J. (1981). Infant imitation: The sensory-motor agenda. *Developmental Psychology, 17,* 258–265.

    Abravanel, E., & Gingold, H. (1985). Learning via observation during the second year of life. *Developmental Psychology, 21,* 614–623.

    Meltzoff, A. N. (1985). Immediate and deferred imitation in fourteen- and twenty-four-month-old infants. *Child Development, 56,* 62–72.

    Meltzoff, A. N. (1988). Infant imitation after a 1-week delay: Long-term memory for novel acts and multiple stimuli. *Developmental Psychology, 24,* 470–476.

18. Oshima-Takane, Yuriko (1988). Children learn from speech not addressed to them: The case of personal pronouns. *Journal of Child Language, 15,* 95–108.

19. Dunn & Munn (1985). See note 15.

20. Rogoff (1991). See note 13.

21. Klahr, D. (1985). Solving problems with ambiguous subgoal ordering: Preschoolers' performance. *Child Development, 56,* 940–952.

    Wellman, H. M., Fabricius, W. V., & Sophian, C. (1985). The early development of planning. In H. M. Wellman (Ed.), *Children's searching* (pp. 123–149). Hillsdale, NJ: Lawrence Erlbaum.

22. Schuepfer, T., & Gholson, B. (1983). From response-set to prediction hypotheses: Rule acquisition among preschoolers and second graders. *Journal of Experimental Child Psychology, 36,* 18–31.

23. Flavell, J. (1979). Metacognition and cognitive monitoring—a new area of cognitive–developmental inquiry. *American Psychologist, 34,* 906–911.

    Belmont, J. M., Butterfield, E. C., & Ferretti, R. P. (1982). To secure transfer of training instruct self-management skills. In D. K. Detterman

& R. J. Sternberg (Eds.), *How and how much can intelligence be increased?* (pp. 147–154). Norwood, NJ: Ablex Publishing.

Harlow, H. (1949). The formation of learning sets. *Psychological Review, 56*, 51–65.

24. Judd, C. H. (1908). The relation of special training to general intelligence. *Educational Review, 36*, 28–42.

Ervin, S. M. (1960). Transfer effects of learning a verbal generalization. *Child Development, 31*, 537–554.

25. Crisafi, M. A., & Brown, A. L. (1986). Analogical transfer in very young children: Combining two separately learned solutions to reach a goal. *Child Development, 57*, 953–968.

26. Pratt, M. W., McLaren, J., & Wickens, G. (1984). Rules as tools: Effective generalization of verbal self-regulative communication training by first-grade speakers. *Developmental Psychology, 20*, 893–902.

27. Bentall, R. P., Lowe, C. F., & Beasty, A. (1985). The role of verbal behavior in human learning, II: Developmental differences. *Journal of the Experimental Analysis of Behavior, 43*, 165–181.

28. Brown, A. L., & Kane, M. S. (1988). Preschool children can learn to transfer: Learning to learn and learning from example. *Cognitive Psychology, 20*, 493–523.

Kersh, B. Y. (1962). The motivating effect of learning by directed discovery. *Journal of Educational Psychology, 53*, 65–71.

Haslerud, G. M., & Meyers, S. (1958). The transfer value of given and individually derived principles. *Journal of Educational Psychology, 49*, 293–298.

29. Geppert, U., & Küster, U. (1983). The emergence of "want to do it oneself": A precursor of achievement motivation. *International Journal of Behavior Development, 6*, 355–370.

Heckhausen, J. (1988). Becoming aware of one's competence in the second year: Developmental progression within the mother–child dyad. *International Journal of Behavioral Development, 11*, 305–326.

30. Brehm, J. W. (1966). *A theory of psychological reactance.* New York: Academic Press.

31. White, R. W. (1959). Motivation reconsidered: The concept of competence. *Psychological Review, 66*, 297–333.

White, R. W. (1960). Competence and the psychosexual stages of development. In M. R. Jones (Ed.), *Nebraska symposium on motivation* (Vol. 8, pp. 97–141). Lincoln: University of Nebraska Press.

32. Messer, D. J., & McCarthy, M. E., McQuiston, S., MacTurk, R. H., Yarrow, L. J., & Vietze, P. M. (1986). Relation between mastery behavior in infancy and competence in early childhood. *Developmental Psychology, 22*, 366–372.

Yarrow, L. J., Klein, R. P., Lomonaco, S., & Morgan, G. A. (1975). Cognitive and motivational development in early childhood. In S. Z.

Friedlander (Ed.) *Exceptional infant, No. 3: Assessment and intervention* (pp. 491–502). New York: Brunner/Mazel.

33. Watson, J. S. (1966). The development and generalization of "contingency awareness" in early infancy: Some hypotheses. *Merrill-Palmer Quarterly, 12,* 123–135.

34. Ling, B. C. (1941). Form discrimination as a learning cue in infants. *Comparative Psychology Monographs, 17* (Whole No. 86).

35. Finkelstein, N. E., & Ramey, C. T. (1977). Learning to control the environment in infancy. *Child Development, 48,* 806–819.
    Diener, C., & Dweck, C. D. (1978). Analysis of learned helplessness: Continuous changes in performance, strategy, and achievement cognitions following failure. *Journal of Personality and Social Psychology, 36,* 461–482.
    Abramson, L. Y., Garber, J., & Seligman, M. E. P. (1980). Learned helplessness in humans: An attributional analysis. In J. Garber & M. E. P. Seligman (Eds.), *Human helplessness.* New York: Academic Press.
    Bandura, A. (1977). Self-efficacy: Toward a unifying theory of behavior change. *Psychological Review, 84,* 191–215.
    Rotter, J. B. (1966). Generalized expectancies for internal versus external control of reinforcement. *Psychological Monographs, 80*(1, Whole No. 609).
    Nolen-Hoeksema S., Girgus, J. S., & Seligman, M. E. P. (1986). Learned helplessness in children: A longitudinal study of depression, achievement, and explanatory style. *Journal of Personality and Social Psychology, 51,* 435–442.
    Peterson, C., & Barrett, L. C. (1987). Explanatory style and academic performance among university freshmen. *Journal of Personality and Social Psychology, 53,* 603–607.
    Skinner, E. A. (1986). The origins of young children's perceived control: Mother contingent and sensitive behavior. *International Journal of Behavioral Development, 9,* 359–382.
    Katkovsky, W., Crandall, V. C., & Good, S. (1967). Parental antecedents of children's beliefs in internal–external control of reinforcements in intellectual achievement situations. *Child Development, 38,* 765–776.
    Eisenberger, R., Mitchell, M., & Masterson, F. Q. (1985). Effort training increases generalized self-control. *Journal of Personality and Social Psychology, 49,* 1294–1301.
    Wimmer, H., Wachter, J., & Perner, J. (1982). Cognitive autonomy of the development of moral evaluation of achievement. *Child Development, 53,* 668–676.

36. Bandura, A., & Cervone, D. (1983). Self-evaluative and self-efficacy mechanisms governing the motivational effects of goal systems. *Journal of Personality and Social Psychology, 45,* 1017–1028.
    Emmons, R. A. (1986). Personal strivings: An approach to personality

and subjective well-being. *Journal of Personality and Social Psychology, 51,* 1058–1068.

Elliott, E. S., & Dweck, C. S. (1988). Goals: An approach to motivation and achievement. *Journal of Personality and Social Psychology, 54,* 5–12.

37. Boggiano, A. K., Main, D. S., & Katz, P. A. (1988). Children's preference for challenge: The role of perceived competence and control. *Journal of Personality and Social Psychology, 54,* 134–141.

Gottfried, A. E. (1990). Academic intrinsic motivation in young elementary school children. *Journal of Educational Psychology, 82,* 525–538.

Gottfried, A. E., & Gottfried, A. W. (1989, April). *Home environment and children's academic intrinsic motivation: A longitudinal study.* Paper presented at the biennial meeting of the Society for Research in Child Development, Kansas City, MO.

38. Schulman, M., & Mekler, E. (1985). *Bringing up a moral child: A new approach for teaching your child to be kind, just, and responsible.* Reading, MA: Addison-Wesley.

39. Finkelstein & Ramey (1977). See note 35.

Dunham, P., & Dunham, F. (1990). Effects of mother-infant social interactions on infants' subsequent contingency task performance. *Child Development, 61,* 785–793.

40. Fagen, J. W., Ohr, P. S., Fleckenstein, L. K., & Ribner, D. R. (1985). The effect of crying on long-term memory in infancy. *Child Development, 56,* 1584–1592.

41. Wood, D., & Middleton, D. (1975). A study of assisted problem-solving. *British Journal of Psychology, 66,* 181–191.

Pratt, M. W., & Kerig, P., Cowan, P. A., & Pape-Cowan, C. (1988). Mothers and fathers teaching 3-year-olds: Authoritative parenting and adult scaffolding of young children's learning. *Developmental Psychology, 24,* 832–839.

Freund, L. S. (1990). Maternal regulation of children's problem-solving behavior and its impact on children's performance. *Child Development, 61,* 113–126.

42. Rovee-Collier, C., Earley, L., & Stafford, S. (1989). Ontogeny of early event memory, III: Attentional determinants of retrieval at 2 and 3 months. *Infant Behavior and Development, 12,* 147–161.

43. Sophian, C. (1985). Perseveration and infants' search: A comparison of two- and three-location tasks. *Developmental Psychology, 21,* 187–194.

Wellman, Cross, & Bartsch (1986). See note 6.

Piaget, J. (1954). *The construction of reality in the child.* New York: Basic Books.

Haake, R. J., & Somerville, S. C. (1985). Development of logical search skills in infancy. *Developmental Psychology, 21,* 176–186.

Wellman, H. M., Fabricius, W. V., & Chuan-Wen, W. (1987). Considering every available instance: The early development of a fundamental problem solving skill. *International Journal of Behavioral Development, 10,* 485–500.

Sophian, C. (1986). Developments in infants' search for invisibly displaced objects. *Infant Behavior and Development, 9,* 15–25.

44. Rheingold, H. L., Cook, K. V., & Kolowitz, V. (1987). Commands activate the behavior and pleasure of 2-year-old children. *Developmental Psychology, 23,* 146–151.

45. Acredolo, C., O'Connor, J., Banks, L., & Horobin, K. (1989). Children's ability to make probability estimates: Skills revealed through application of Anderson's functional measurement methodology. *Child Development, 60,* 933–945.

46. Pea, R. D. (1982). What is planning development the development of? In D. Forbes & M. T. Greenberg (Eds.), *Children's planning strategies* (pp. 5–26). San Francisco: Jossey-Bass.

47. Deci, E. L., & Ryan, R. M. (1985). *Intrinsic motivation and self-determination in human behavior.* N.Y.: Plenum Press.

48. Korman, A. K. (1971). Expectancies as determinants of performance. *Journal of Applied Psychology, 55,* 218–222.

49. Meichenbaum, D., & Goodman, J. (1971). Training impulsive children to talk to themselves: A means of developing self-control. *Journal of Abnormal Psychology, 77,* 115–126.

50. Keister, M. E., & Updegraff, R. (1937). A study of children's reactions to failure and an experimental attempt to modify them. *Child Development, 8,* 241–248.

Seifer, R., & Vaughn, B. E. (1987). Family effects on competence during the first four years of life. In B. E. Vaugh (Chair), *Parent-child interactions as sources for competence during childhood.* Symposium conducted at the meeting of the Society for Research in Child Development, Baltimore.

51. Guest, E. A. (1919). It couldn't be done. In *The paths to home.* Chicago: Reilly and Lee Co.

Chapter 8
Core Mastery Skills

1. Durkin, D. (1966). *Children who read early.* New York: Teachers College Press.

Miles, C. C. (1954). Gifted children. In L. Carmichael (Ed.), *Manual of child psychology* (pp. 984–1063). New York: Wiley.

Mills, J. R., & Jackson, N. E. (1990). Predictive significance of early giftedness: The case of precocious reading. *Journal of Educational Psychology, 82,* 410–419.

2. Berninger, V. W. (1987). Global, component, and serial processing of printed

words in beginning reading. *Journal of Experimental Child Psychology, 43*, 387–418.

Byrne, B., & Fielding-Barnsley, R. (1989). Phonemic awareness and letter knowledge in the child's acquisition of the alphabetic principle. *Journal of Educational Psychology, 81*, 313–321.

Siegel, L. S., & Ryan, E. B. (1988). Development of grammatical-sensitivity, phonological, and short-term memory skills in normally achieving and learning disabled children. *Developmental Psychology, 24*, 28–37.

Bialystok, E., & Mitterer, J. (1987). Metalinguistic differences among three kinds of readers. *Journal of Educational Psychology, 79*, 147–153.

Vellutino, F. R., & Scanlon, D. M. (1987). Phonological coding, phonological awareness, and reading ability: Evidence from a longitudinal and experimental study. *Merrill-Palmer Quarterly, 33*, 321–363.

3. Juel, C. (1988). Learning to read and write: A longitudinal study of 54 children from first through fourth grades. *Journal of Educational Psychology, 80*, 437–447.

4. Whitehurst, G. J., Falco, F. L., Lonigan, C. J., Fischel, J. E., DeBaryshe, B. D., Valdez-Menchaca, M. C., & Caulfield, M. (1988). Accelerating language development through picture book reading. *Developmental Psychology, 24*, 552–559.

5. Schmidt, C. R., & Paris, S. G. (1983). Children's use of successive clues to generate and monitor inferences. *Child Development, 54*, 742–759.

Goldman, S. R. (1985). Inferential reasoning in and about narrative texts. In A. C. Graesser & J. B. Black (Eds.), *The psychology of questions* (pp. 247–276). Hillsdale, NJ: Lawrence Erlbaum.

6. Tobias, S. (1987). Mandatory text review and interaction with student characteristics. *Journal of Educational Psychology, 79*, 154–161.

Palincsar, A. S. (1986). Metacognitive strategy instruction. *Exceptional Children, 53*, 118–124.

Stevens, R. J. (1988). Effects of strategy training on the identification of the main idea of expository passages. *Journal of Educational Psychology, 80*, 21–26.

7. Anbar, A. (1986). Reading acquisition of preschool children without systematic instruction. *Early Childhood Research Quarterly, 1*, 69–83.

8. Read, C. (1971). Pre-school children's knowledge of English phonology. *Harvard Educational Review, 41*, 1–34.

9. Perera, K. (1986). Language acquisition and writing. In P. Fletcher & M. Garman (Eds.), *Language acquisition* (pp. 494–518). New York: Cambridge University Press.

10. Stevenson, H. W., Lee, S., Chen, C., Lummis, M., Stigler, J., Fan, L., & Ge, F. (1990). Mathematics achievement of children in China and the United States. *Child Development, 61*, 1053–1066.

11. Hughes, M. (1983). What is difficult about learning arithmetic? In M. Donald-

son, R. Grieve, & C. Pratt (Eds.), *Early childhood and education: Readings in psychology* (pp. 204–221). New York: Guilford Press.

12. Secada, W. G., Fuson, K. C., & Hall, J. W. (1983). The transition from counting-all to counting-on in addition. *Journal for Research in Mathematics Education, 14,* 47–57.

    Fuson, K. C. (1986). Teaching children to subtract by counting up. *Journal for Research in Mathematics Education, 17,* 172–189.

13. Cauley, K. M. (1988). Construction of logical knowledge: Study of borrowing in subtraction. *Journal of Educational Psychology, 80,* 202–205.

14. Dunlap, L. K., & Dunlap, G. (1989). A self-monitoring package for teaching subtraction with regrouping to students with learning disabilities. *Journal of Applied Behavior Analysis, 22,* 309–314.

15. Cummins, D. D., Kintsch, W., Reusser, K., & Weimer, R. (1988). The role of understanding in solving word problems. *Cognitive Psychology, 20,* 405–438.

    Hudson, T. (1983). Correspondences and numerical differences between disjoint sets. *Child Development, 54,* 84–90.

16. Willis, G. B., & Fuson, K. C. (1988). Teaching children to use schematic drawings to solve addition and subtraction word problems. *Journal of Educational Psychology, 80,* 192–201.

17. Kaye, P. (1987). *Games for math.* New York: Pantheon.

18. Hardiman, P. T., & Mestre, J. P. (1989). Understanding multiplicative contexts involving fractions. *Journal of Educational Psychology, 81,* 547–557.

19. Stevenson, H. W., & Shin-ying, L. (1990). Contexts of achievement. *Monographs of the Society for Research in Child Development, 55*(1–2, Serial No. 221).

20. Hyde, J. S., Fennema, E., & Lamon, S. J. (1990). Gender differences in mathematics performance: A meta-analysis. *Psychological Bulletin, 107,* 139–155.

    Paulsen, K., & Johnson, M. (1983). Sex role attitudes and mathematical ability in 4th-, 8th-, and 11th-grade students from a high socioeconomic area. *Developmental Psychology, 19,* 210–214.

    Raymond, C. L., & Benbow, C. P. (1986). Gender differences in mathematics: A function of parental support and student sex typing? *Developmental Psychology, 22,* 808–819.

Chapter 9
Problem-Solving Strategies for Mastery

1. Baron, J. B., & Sternberg, R. J. (Eds.) (1987). *Teaching thinking skills: Theory and practice.* New York: W. H. Freeman.

2. Courage, M. L. (1989). Children's inquiry strategies in referential communication and in the game of Twenty Questions. *Child Development, 60,* 877–886.

3. Maier, N. R. F. (1970). *Problem solving and creativity*. Belmont, CA: Brooks/ Cole.

4. Fjellstrom, G. G., Born, D., & Baer, D. M. (1988). Some effects of telling preschool children to self-question in a matching task. *Journal of Experimental Child Psychology, 46*, 419–437.
   Simon, H. A., & Reed, S. K. (1976). Modeling strategy shifts in a problem-solving task. *Cognitive Psychology, 8*, 86–97.
   Gholson, B., Dattel, A. R., Morgan, D., & Eymard, L. A. (1989). Problem solving, recall, and mapping relations in isomorphic transfer and nonisomorphic transfer among preschool and elementary school children. *Child Development, 60*, 1172–1187.

5. Chase, W. C., & Simon, H. A. (1973). Perception in chess. *Cognitive Psychology, 4*, 55–81.

6. Dunn, J., & Munn, P. (1987). Development of justification in disputes with mother and sibling. *Developmental Psychology, 23*, 791–798.
   Kuczynski, L., Kochanska, G., Radke-Yarrow, M., & Girnius-Brown, O. (1987). A developmental interpretation of young children's noncompliance. *Developmental Psychology, 23*, 799–806.

7. Peterson, L., & Lewis, K. E. (1988). Preventive intervention to improve children's discrimination of the persuasive tactics in televised advertising. *Journal of Pediatric Psychology, 13*, 163–170.

8. Flavell, J. H., Flavell, E. R., Green, F. L., & Moses, L. J. (1990). Young children's understanding of fact beliefs versus value beliefs. *Child Development, 61*, 915–928.

9. Zimmerman, B. J. (1989). A social cognitive view of self-regulated academic learning. *Journal of Educational Psychology, 81*, 329–339.

10. Grolnick, W. S., & Ryan, R. M. (1989). Parent styles associated with children's self-regulation and competence in school. *Journal of Educational Psychology, 81*, 143–154.
    Steinberg, L., Elmen, J. D., & Mounts, N. S. (1989). Authoritative parenting, psychosocial maturity, and academic success among adolescents. *Child Development, 60*, 1424–1436.

11. Grusec, J. E., & Redler, E. (1980). Attribution, reinforcement, and altruism: A developmental analysis. *Developmental Psychology, 16*, 525–534.
    Jensen, A. M., & Moore, S. G. (1977). The effect of attribute statements on cooperativeness and competitiveness in school-age boys. *Child Development, 48*, 305–307.

12. Miller, G. (1956). The magical number seven, plus or minus two: Some limits on our capacity for processing information. *Psychological Review, 63*, 81–97.
    Justice, E. M. (1985). Categorization as a preferred memory strategy: Developmental changes during elementary school. *Developmental Psychology, 21*, 1105–1110.
    Bjorklund, D. F., Ornstein, P. A., & Haig, J. R. (1977). Developmental

differences in organization and recall: Training in the use of organizational techniques. *Developmental Psychology, 13,* 175–183.

13. Rebok, G. W., & Balcerak, L. J. (1989). Memory self-efficacy and performance differences in young and old adults: The effect of mnemonic training. *Developmental Psychology, 25,* 714–721.

Carr, M., Kurtz, B. E., Schneider, W., Turner, L. A., & Borkowski, J. G. (1989). Strategy acquisition and transfer among American and German children: Environmental influences on metacognitive development. *Developmental Psychology, 25,* 765–771.

Cox, B. D., Ornstein, P. A., Naus, M. J., Maxfield, D., & Zimler, J. (1989). Children's concurrent use of rehearsal and organizational strategies. *Developmental Psychology, 25,* 619–627.

Rosenheck, M. B., Levin, M. E., & Levin, J. R. (1989). Learning botany concepts mnemonically: Seeing the forest *and* the trees. *Journal of Educational Psychology, 81,* 196–203.

14. DeLoache, J. S., Cassidy, D. J., & Brown, A. L. (1985). Precursors of mnemonic strategies in very young children. *Child Development, 56,* 125–137.

15. Ratner, H. H. (1984). Memory demands and the development of young children's memory. *Child Development, 55,* 2173–2191.

16. Yussen, S. R., Levin, J. R., Berman, L., & Palm, J. (1979). Developmental changes in the awareness of memory benefits associated with different types of picture organization. *Developmental Psychology, 15,* 447–449.

Barclay, C. R. (1981). On the relation between memory and metamemory. *The Psychological Record, 31,* 153–156.

Fabricius, W. V., & Hagen, J. W. (1984). Use of causal attributions about recall performance to assess metamemory and predict strategic memory behavior in young children. *Developmental Psychology, 20,* 975–987.

Leal, L., Crays, N., & Moely, B. E. (1985). Training children to use self-monitoring study strategy in preparation for recall: Maintenance and generalization effects. *Child Development, 56,* 643–653.

17. Rothstein, M. (1988, June 21). Hirschfeld, the man of 3,000 faces, is honored on his 85th birthday. *New York Times,* p. C15.

18. Zervos, C. (1952). Conversation with Picasso. In B. Ghiselin (Ed. and Trans.), *The creative process* (pp. 55–60). New York: Mentor. (Original work published 1935)

19. Plimpton, G. (Ed.). (1984). *Writers at work: The Paris Review interviews* (sixth series). New York: Viking.

20. Glueck, G. (1984, Dec. 2). The mastery of Robert Motherwell. *New York Times Magazine,* pp. 68–86.

21. Martin, V. (1988, Feb. 7). Waiting for the story to start. *New York Times Book Review,* pp. 1, 37.

22. Miller, A. (1960). Death of a salesman. In T. Cole (Ed.), *Playwrights on playwriting* (p. 275). New York: Hill and Wang.

23. Winner, E. (1989). How can Chinese children draw so well? *Journal of Aesthetic Education, 23,* 41–63.

24. Hart, L. M., & Goldin-Meadow, S. (1984). The child as a nonegocentric art critic. *Child Development, 55,* 2122–2129.

Golomb, C., & Helmund, J. (1987, April). A study of young children's aesthetic sensitivity to drawing and painting. Paper presented in the symposium, *Facets of artistic development,* at the biennial meeting of the Society for Research in Child Development, Baltimore.

25. Langlois, J. H., Roggman, L. A., & Rieser-Danner, L. A. (1990). Infants' differential social responses to attractive and unattractive faces. *Developmental Psychology, 26,* 153–159.

26. Rich, D. C. (undated). *Degas.* New York: Harry N. Abrams.

27. Schoenfeld, A. H. (1985). *Mathematical problem solving.* New York: Academic Press.

28. Schoenfeld, A. H., & Herrmann, D. J. (1982). Problem perception and knowledge structure in expert and novice mathematical problem solvers. *Journal of Experimental Psychology: Learning, Memory, and Cognition, 8,* 484–494.

Schoenfeld, A. H. (1980). Teaching problem-solving skills. *American Mathematical Monthly, 87,* 794–805.

Herrnstein, R. J., Nickerson, R. S., de Sánchez, M., & Swets, J. A. (1986). Teaching thinking skills. *American Psychologist, 41,* 1279–1289.

Adams, M. J. (Coordinator). (1986). *Odyssey: A curriculum for thinking.* Watertown, MA: Mastery Education Corp.

29. Schoenfeld, A. H. (1989). Teaching mathematical thinking and problem solving. In L. B. Resnick & L. E. Klopfer (Eds.), *Cognitive research in subject matter learning.* Yearbook of the ASCD.

30. Chi, M. T. H., Bassok, M., Lewis, M. W., Reimann, P., & Glaser, R. (1989). Self-explanations: How students study and use examples in learning to solve problems. *Cognitive Science, 13,* 145–182.

31. Novick, L. R. (1988). Analogical transfer, problem similarity, and expertise. *Journal of Experimental Psychology: Learning, Memory, and Cognition, 14,* 510–520.

Luchins, A. S. (1942). Mechanization in problem solving. *Psychological Monographs, 54* (Whole No. 248).

Chapter 10
Ordinary and Extraordinary Intelligence

1. Stanley, J. C., & Benbow, C. P. (1986). Youths who reason exceptionally well mathematically. In R. J. Sternberg & J. E. Davidson (Eds.), *Conceptions of giftedness* (pp. 361–387). New York: Cambridge University Press.

2. Janos, P. M., & Robinson, N. M. (1985). Psychosocial development in intellectually gifted children. In F. D. Horowitz & M. O'Brien (Eds.), *The gifted*

and talented: Developmental perspectives (pp. 149–195). Hyattsville, MD: American Psychological Association.

3. Ruble, D. N. (1983). The development of social-comparison processes and their role in achievement-related self-socialization. In E. T. Higgins, D. N. Ruble, & W. W. Hartup (Eds.), *Social cognition and social development: A sociocultural perspective* (pp. 134–157). New York: Cambridge University Press.

4. Oden, M. H. (1968). Fulfillment of promise: 40 year follow-up of the Terman gifted group. *Genetic Psychology Monographs, 77,* 3–93.

5. Sternberg, R., & Wagner, R. K. (Eds.). (1986). *Practical intelligence.* New York: Cambridge University Press.

    Church, A. T., Katigbak, M. S., & Almario-Velazco, G. (1985). Psychometric intelligence and adaptive competence in rural Philippine children. *Intelligence, 9,* 317–340.

    Epstein, S., & Meier, P. (1989). Constructive thinking: A broad coping variable with specific components. *Journal of Personality and Social Psychology, 57,* 332–350.

6. Snow, R. E., & Yalow, E. (1982). Education and intelligence. In R. J. Sternberg (Ed.), *Handbook of human intelligence* (pp. 493–585). New York: Cambridge University Press.

    Zigler, E., & Seitz, V. (1982). Social policy and intelligence. In R. J. Sternberg (Ed.), *Handbook of human intelligence* (pp. 586–641). New York: Cambridge University Press.

Chapter 11
Creativity

1. Mansfield, R. S., & Busse, T. V. (1981). *The psychology of creativity and discovery: Scientists and their work.* Chicago: Nelson-Hall.

    Walberg, H. J. (1988). Creativity and talent as learning. In R. J. Sternberg (Ed.), *The nature of creativity* (pp. 340–361). New York: Cambridge University Press.

2. Einstein, A., & Infeld, L. (1938). *The evolution of physics.* New York: Simon & Schuster.

3. Getzels, J. W., & Csikszentmihalyi, M. (1976). *The creative vision.* New York: John Wiley & Sons.

4. Solomon, D. (1988, June 19). The unflagging artistry of Jasper Johns. *New York Times Magazine,* p. 63.

    Freedman, S. G. (1984, April 1). The words and music of Stephen Sondheim. *New York Times Magazine,* p. 28.

5. Zervos, C. (1952). Conversation with Picasso. In B. Ghiselin (Ed. and Trans.), *The creative process* (pp. 55–60). New York: Mentor. (Original work published 1935)

6. MacKinnon, D. W. (1967). The study of creative persons: A method and

some results. In J. Kagan (Ed.), *Creativity and learning* (pp. 20–35). Boston: Beacon Press.

7. Miller, H. (1952). Reflections on writing. In B. Ghiselin (Ed.), *The creative process* (pp. 178–185). New York: Mentor. (Original published in 1941)

8. Bernstein, L. (1982). *Findings*. New York: Simon and Schuster.

9. van Gogh, V. (1973). Letter 418. *Vincent van Gogh: Paintings and Drawings* (p. 56). Amsterdam: National Museum Vincent van Gogh.

10. Dunning, J. (1990, Jan. 9). The choreographers in man-made festival ponder how to learn. *New York Times,* pp. C13, C16.

11. Galilei, G. (1967). In G. Seldes (Ed.), *The great quotations* (p. 855). New York: Pocket Books.

12. Wallach, M. A. (1985). Creativity testing and giftedness. In F. D. Horowitz & M. O'Brien (Eds.), *The gifted and talented: Developmental perspectives* (pp. 99–123). Washington, DC: American Psychological Association.

13. Einstein, A. (1988). In I. Asimov & J. A. Shulman (Eds.), *Isaac Asimov's book of science and nature quotations* (p. 241). New York: Weidenfeld & Nicolson.

14. Pasteur, L. (1988). In A. Asimov & J. A. Shulman (Eds.), *Isaac Asimov's book of science and nature quotations* (p. 297). New York: Weidenfeld & Nicolson.

15. van Gogh, V. (1973). Letter 408. *Vincent van Gogh: Paintings & drawings* (p. 31). Amsterdam: National Museum Vincent van Gogh.

16. Roe, A. (1952, May). A psychologist examines sixty-four eminent scientists. *Scientific American, 187,* 21–25.

17. Weisberg, R. W. (1986). *Creativity: Genius and other myths.* New York: W. H. Freeman.
Browne, M. W. (1988, Aug. 16). The Benzene Ring: Dream Analysis. *New York Times,* p. C10.

18. Koestler, A. (1964). *The act of creation.* New York: Macmillan.
Ghiselin, B. (Ed.). (1952). *The creative process.* New York: Mentor.

19. Cohen, I. B. (1987). Newton's discovery of gravity. In O. Gingerich (Ed.), *Scientific genius and creativity.* New York: W. H. Freeman. (Reprinted from Scientific American, March 1981.)

20. Glueck, G. (1984, Dec. 2). The mastery of Robert Motherwell. *New York Times,* pp. 68–86.

21. Moore, H. (1952). Notes on sculpture. In B. Ghiselin (Ed.), *The creative process* (pp. 73–78). New York: Mentor.

22. Schapiro, M. (Ed.). (undated). *Vincent van Gogh.* New York: Harry N. Abrams.

23. Gruber, H. E., & Davis, S. N. (1988). Inching our way up Mount Olympus: The evolving-systems approach to creative thinking. In R. J. Sternberg (Ed.), *The nature of creativity* (pp. 243–270). New York: Cambridge University Press.

24. Schulman, M. (1990). The prevention of antisocial behavior through moral

motivation training (or *Why isn't there more street crime?*). In R. Lorion (Ed.), *Protecting the children: Strategies for optimizing emotional and behavioral development* (pp. 255–275). New York: Haworth Press.

25. Schulman, M. (1980). How to approach a scene. In M. Schulman & E. Mekler (Eds.), *Contemporary scenes for student actors*. New York: Penguin.

    Schulman, M. (1984). Overcoming stage fright. In M. Schulman & E. Mekler (Eds.), *The actor's scenebook*. New York: Bantam.

    Schulman, M. (1987). Creating a character. In M. Schulman & E. Mekler (Eds.), *The actor's scenebook*. (Vol. 2). New York: Bantam.

    Schulman, M. (1987). Interview. In E. Mekler (Ed.), *The new generation of acting teachers*. New York: Viking.

26. Asch, S. E. (1965). Effects of group pressure upon the modification and distortion of judgments. In H. Proshansky & B. Seidenberg, (Eds.), *Basic studies in social psychology*, (pp. 393–401). New York: Holt, Rinehart & Winston.

27. Stewart, I. (1987). Gauss. In O. Gingerich (Ed.), *Scientific genius and creativity* (pp. 40–49). New York: W. H. Freeman. (From *Scientific American*, July 1977.)

28. Loewenberg, P. (1988, Jan. 29). Einstein in his youth (Review of *The collected papers of Albert Einstein*). *Science, 239*, 510–512.

Index

MP9W